FACTS IN PUBLIC LAW ADJUDICATION

This book explores critical issues about how courts engage with questions of fact in public law adjudication.

Although the topic of judicial review – the mechanism through which individuals can challenge governmental action – continues to generate sustained interest amongst constitutional and administrative lawyers, there has been little attention given to questions of fact. This is so despite such determinations of fact often being hugely important to the outcomes and impacts of public law adjudication.

The book brings together scholars from across the common law world to identify and explore contested issues, common challenges, and gaps in understanding. The various chapters consider where facts arise in constitutional and administrative law proceedings, the role of the courts, and the types of evidence that might assist courts in determining legal issues that are underpinned by complex and contested social or policy questions. The book also considers whether the existing laws and practices surrounding evidence are sufficient, and how other disciplines might assist the courts.

The book reconnects the key practical issues surrounding evidence and facts with the lively academic debate on judicial review in the common law world; it therefore contributes to an emerging area of scholarly debate and also has practical implications for the conduct of litigation and government policy-making.

Facts in Public Law Adjudication

Edited by
Joe Tomlinson
and
Anne Carter

·HART·
OXFORD · LONDON · NEW YORK · NEW DELHI · SYDNEY

HART PUBLISHING

Bloomsbury Publishing Plc

Kemp House, Chawley Park, Cumnor Hill, Oxford, OX2 9PH, UK

1385 Broadway, New York, NY 10018, USA

29 Earlsfort Terrace, Dublin 2, Ireland

HART PUBLISHING, the Hart/Stag logo, BLOOMSBURY and the Diana logo are trademarks of Bloomsbury Publishing Plc

First published in Great Britain 2023

Copyright © The editors and contributors severally 2023

The editors and contributors have asserted their right under the Copyright, Designs and Patents Act 1988 to be identified as Authors of this work.

All rights reserved. No part of this publication may be reproduced or transmitted in any form or by any means, electronic or mechanical, including photocopying, recording, or any information storage or retrieval system, without prior permission in writing from the publishers.

While every care has been taken to ensure the accuracy of this work, no responsibility for loss or damage occasioned to any person acting or refraining from action as a result of any statement in it can be accepted by the authors, editors or publishers.

All UK Government legislation and other public sector information used in the work is Crown Copyright ©. All House of Lords and House of Commons information used in the work is Parliamentary Copyright ©. This information is reused under the terms of the Open Government Licence v3.0 (http://www.nationalarchives.gov.uk/doc/open-government-licence/version/3) except where otherwise stated.

All Eur-lex material used in the work is © European Union, http://eur-lex.europa.eu/, 1998–2023.

A catalogue record for this book is available from the British Library.

Library of Congress Cataloging-in-Publication data

Names: Tomlinson, Joe (Law teacher), editor. | Carter, Anne, 1980- editor.

Title: Facts in public law adjudication / edited by Joe Tomlinson and Anne Carter.

Description: Oxford [UK] ; New York : Hart Publishing, An Imprint of Bloomsbury Publishing, 2023. | Includes bibliographical references and index. | Summary: "Explores how courts engage with questions of fact in public law adjudication, the role of evidence, and the procedures by which these facts are established"—Provided by publisher.

Identifiers: LCCN 2023025924 | ISBN 9781509957385 (hardback) | ISBN 9781509957422 (paperback) | ISBN 9781509957408 (pdf) | ISBN 9781509957392 (Epub)

Subjects: LCSH: Public law. | Constitutional law. | administrative law. | Judicial review. | Indigenous peoples—Civil rights.

Classification: LCC K3150 .F33 2023 | DDC 342—dc23/eng/20230601

LC record available at https://lccn.loc.gov/2023025924

ISBN: HB: 978-1-50995-738-5
ePDF: 978-1-50995-740-8
ePub: 978-1-50995-739-2

Typeset by Compuscript Ltd, Shannon

To find out more about our authors and books visit www.hartpublishing.co.uk. Here you will find extracts, author information, details of forthcoming events and the option to sign up for our newsletters.

FOREWORD

Facts and evidence play an important role in the judicial determination of public law disputes around the world. Courts now routinely confront a diverse range of materials when they adjudicate claims about the legality of government action. For courts working in a common law tradition, this can be a thorny area. It demands clear thinking about how to approach different types of evidence in particular cases, and how different evidence and facts might inform the application of public law principles more broadly. Courts are required to tread a fine line between going beyond their competencies when assessing evidence and not sufficiently engaging with the context of a case. As the machinery of government grows more complex, not least due to the increasing availability and capacity of digital technologies, the materials that arise in public law disputes are likely to become more complex, and therefore new and difficult questions are on the horizon.

Despite the importance of facts and evidence in public law cases, there has been much less discussion on the challenges – theoretical and practical – that such matters give rise to. This is a significant deficit in our collective understanding of public law. The contributions in this book are written by scholars across the common law world, and, while their analyses are often rooted in their local context, it is plain to see that there are many common themes and questions with which they are grappling. There is also a great benefit, as a number of the chapters in this book demonstrate, to lawyers speaking across disciplines to other experts who deal in complex questions of fact, such as historians and political scientists, and seeking to learn from each other. I, therefore, welcome this book as an important step in developing a greater understanding of the role of facts in public law adjudication across the common law world.

Lord Carnwath
Former Justice of the UK Supreme Court
March 2023

ACKNOWLEDGEMENTS

This project began as a glimmer of an idea over coffee in Melbourne in 2018. As well as the discovery of shared research interests, we both took the view that facts had tended to be overlooked in existing public law scholarship. It seemed to us that questions of fact were necessarily intertwined with public law adjudication, and that many scholars were doing work that could intersect with these important questions in a variety of ways. One of our aims was to bring these scholars together and to provoke a debate across the common law world about the role of facts in public law.

There are many people who have helped to nurture this project from those initial discussions to its final form. First and foremost, we would like to thank Adrienne Stone for her support and encouragement throughout the project. Under Adrienne's guidance, we were fortunate to receive a Workshop Program grant from the Academy of Social Sciences in Australia. This enabled us to convene a workshop at Melbourne Law School in 2019 where we brought together scholars from across Australia. Many of the authors in this edited collection were involved in the original Melbourne workshop, and we were also joined by other speakers and commentators, including Rosalind Dixon, Jeremy Gans, Tanya Josev, Kristen Rundle, Cheryl Saunders, James Stellios, Daniel Stewart, Kristen Walker and Lael Weis. We are grateful to Aftab Hussein and the Centre for Comparative Constitutional Studies at Melbourne Law School for assisting with the organisation of the workshop, and to Hayley Pitcher who provided research assistance on the day.

After a day of fruitful and thought-provoking discussions we decided to embark on an edited collection. We expanded the geographic focus of the book to include other common law jurisdictions, and we invited scholars from Canada, South Africa and New Zealand to submit chapters. We are grateful to Kate Whetter and the Hart team for their support of the book, and to the Hart reviewers who provided important early guidance about the scope of the collection. We have also benefitted from the careful research assistance provided by Rhyse Collins.

Our aim in producing this book was not to offer a comprehensive coverage of facts in public law, but rather to stimulate a discussion about the multifaceted ways facts can and do arise in public law. The chapters in this book, which traverse a variety of jurisdictions and subjects, illuminate the nature of the facts that arise in public law, how such facts can be proved, and the contributions of other institutions and disciplines. We are indebted to our contributing authors for engaging with the topic so thoughtfully, and it has been a pleasure to work with them on this volume. We hope the book is the starting point for many further conversations about facts in public law.

Anne Carter
Joe Tomlinson
February 2023

CONTENTS

Foreword .... *v*
Acknowledgements .... *vii*
List of Contributors .... *xi*

1. *Introduction* *1*
   Anne Carter and Joe Tomlinson

PART I
FACTS IN CONSTITUTIONAL ADJUDICATION

2. *The Rise of Facts in Public Law* *11*
   Paul Daly and Kseniya Kudischeva

3. *Parliaments and Facts: Deepening Deliberation* *29*
   Gabrielle Appleby and Anne Carter

4. *One Important Role of Facts in Constitutional Adjudication* *49*
   Patrick Emerton and Jayani Nadarajalingam

5. *Citizenship Denied – Constitutional Facts, and the Independence
   of Papua New Guinea* *67*
   Rayner Thwaites

PART II
FACTS IN ADMINISTRATIVE LAW

6. *The Interdependence of Process and Substance: Facts, Evidence and
   the Changing Nature of Judicial Review* *87*
   Jason N E Varuhas

7. *Judicial Review of 'Fact Work': Beyond the Law/Fact Distinction* *125*
   Joanna Bell and Elizabeth Fisher

8. *Legality in Fact-finding by Executive Decision-Makers: What Role for
   ultra vires?* *143*
   Emily Hammond

9. *Missing Evidence? The Duty to Acquire Systemic Data in Public Law* *161*
   Joe Tomlinson and Cassandra Somers-Joce

x Contents

10. *The Treatment of Facts in South African Administrative Law* *183*
    Glenn Penfold and Cora Hoexter

11. *Mistake of Fact as a Ground of Review: Distinct and Defensible* *201*
    Hanna Wilberg

PART III
FACTS IN BROADER PERSPECTIVE

12. *Indigenous Oral History in Canadian Courts: The Law of Fact-finding
    and the Wrong Mistake* *225*
    Hilary Evans Cameron

13. *Political Science in the Courtroom: Potential and Pitfalls* *245*
    Zim Nwokora and Jayani Nadarajalingam

14. *History and Historical Facts in Constitutional Law* *263*
    Caitlin Goss

15. *Defactualisation of Justice* *281*
    Shiri Krebs

Index *299*

LIST OF CONTRIBUTORS

Gabrielle Appleby is Professor of Law at the University of New South Wales, Australia.

Joanna Bell is Associate Professor, Jeffery Hackney Fellow, and Tutor in Law at St Edmund Hall, University of Oxford, UK.

Anne Carter is Lecturer in Law at the University of Adelaide, Australia.

Paul Daly is Chair in Administrative Law and Governance at University of Ottawa, Canada.

Patrick Emerton is Associate Professor of Law at Deakin University, Australia.

Hilary Evans Cameron is Assistant Professor of Law at the Toronto Metropolitan University, Canada.

Elizabeth Fisher is Professor of Environmental Law at Corpus Christi College, University of Oxford, UK.

Caitlin Goss is Lecturer in Law at the University of Queensland, Australia.

Emily Hammond is Senior Lecturer in Law at the University of Sydney, Australia.

Cora Hoexter is Professor of Law at the University of the Witwatersrand, South Africa.

Shiri Krebs is Professor of Law at Deakin University, Australia.

Kseniya Kudischeva is Legal Counsel at the Department of Justice, Canada.

Jayani Nadarajalingam is Lecturer in Law at the University of Melbourne, Australia.

Zim Nwokora is Senior Lecturer in Politics and Policy Studies at Deakin University, Australia.

Glenn Penfold is Partner at Webber Wentzel, South Africa.

Cassandra Somers-Joce is an MPhil Candidate at the University of Oxford and a Visiting Lecturer in Law at King's College London, UK.

Rayner Thwaites is Senior Lecturer in Law at the University of Sydney, Australia.

Joe Tomlinson is Professor of Public Law at the University of York, UK.

Jason Varuhas is Professor of Law at the University of Melbourne, Australia.

Hanna Wilberg is Associate Professor of Law at the University of Auckland, New Zealand.

1

Introduction

ANNE CARTER AND JOE TOMLINSON

Across the common law world, the role of facts in public law adjudication has become increasingly significant. Yet, while the topic of judicial review – a key judicial mechanism through which individuals can challenge governmental action – continues to generate sustained interest amongst constitutional and administrative lawyers, there has been little attention given to matters of facts and evidence. For the most part, the focus continues to be on legal principles and their underlying normative foundations, rather than questions of evidence and fact-finding. This is so despite such determinations of fact often being salient to the outcomes and impacts of public law adjudication. A failure to address the role of facts and evidence systematically risks courts making factual assessments in intuitive and inconsistent ways. Equally, it risks important legal protections being misapplied, weakened or even undermined. It also means that public law scholarship is routinely blinkered to a critical part of its subject matter. Against this backdrop, this book explores how courts engage with questions of fact, the role of evidence and the procedures by which these facts are established.

The central objective of this book is to explore critical questions about how courts engage with questions of fact in public law adjudication. This involves considering the relevance of facts to public law disputes, the nature of these facts, the role of the courts and the types of evidence that might assist courts in determining legal issues that are often underpinned by complex and contested social or policy questions. The book also raises questions about whether the existing laws and practices surrounding evidence are sufficient, and how the insights of other disciplines might assist legal thinkers in untangling these knotty issues. More specifically, by inviting a diverse range of scholars from across the common law world to contribute to this objective, we hope to achieve three main goals. First, to provide a substantial original contribution to the emerging area of scholarly debate about the role of facts and evidence in public law adjudication. Second, to reconnect the important questions of evidence that arise in relation to facts in practice with the lively academic debate on judicial review in the common law world.

Third, to speak to practical issues in the conduct of judicial review proceedings and government policy-making that are highly important but subject to limited extended analysis.

The chapters within this book address interrelated themes. Before we turn to set out those themes, we first introduce the chapters themselves across the three broad areas around which we have organised the book: facts in constitutional adjudication; facts in administrative law; and facts in broader perspective.

I. Facts in Constitutional Adjudication

Part I of the book concentrates on the role of facts in constitutional adjudication. The chapters in this part are all concerned, in varying ways, with how facts might inform constitutional interpretation or the resolution of constitutional disputes. Each of the chapters takes a different perspective, ranging from a broad overview of the ways facts arise in different adjudicative contexts (Daly and Kudischeva), to focusing on the discrete issue of citizenship in the Australian setting (Thwaites). Other chapters in this part concern the role of facts about the institutions that underpin constitutional mandates (Emerton and Nadarajalingam) and how courts might evaluate the fact-finding and deliberations of governments (Appleby and Carter). These chapters show that facts can intersect with constitutional law at various stages and in a number of ways, and that decisions as to facts can be critical not only to individual decisions but also to the robustness of constitutional mandates themselves.

Daly and Kudischeva's chapter, which adopts a broad analytical perspective, provides an ideal starting point for this volume. Focusing predominantly on Canadian and English law, Daly and Kudischeva chart the rise of facts in public law across four areas: judicial review of administrative action, judicial review of legislation, systemic challenges to the legality of regulatory regimes, and constitutional causes of action. They illustrate that, despite some historical reluctance to grapple with factual issues, common law courts are increasingly called upon to engage with facts. Daly and Kudischeva identify various reasons that explain this increasing turn towards facts, and they also set out a number of difficulties which arise across the four areas. Their analysis illuminates the range of factual assessments that arise across the public law domain, and also the various judicial techniques and devices that have been adopted by judges in response.

In their chapter, Gabrielle Appleby and Anne Carter look in more detail at the Australian context. They investigate how the adoption by the High Court of an explicit, structured test of proportionality to assess limitations on constitutional freedoms presents fresh challenges for the relationship between courts and parliaments. This development, they show, prompts consideration of whether, and how, the courts can assess and rely upon, or defer to, the fact-finding and deliberations of parliaments. For their analysis, they specifically examine the nature of parliamentary deliberation and what counts as what they term 'fair deliberation' by parliaments. Appleby and Carter propose a series of criteria or standards by which courts might review the robustness of parliamentary enquiries, which have been designed with a view to deepening parliamentary deliberations about constitutional freedoms and their limitations, rather than formalising or judicialising the legislative process.

In contrast to this broad analytic review, Patrick Emerton and Jayani Nadarajalingam focus on a more specific role of facts: facts about the institutions that are referred to by the constitutional text and to which it gives rise. Where a constitution, such as the Australian Constitution, refers to complex social and institutional arrangements, constitutional interpretation depends on courts having knowledge of those arrangements. In this way, the facts with which Emerton and Nadarajalingam are concerned exist prior to exercises of legislative and executive power. Emerton and Nadarajalingam explain the tensions that arise in adjudicating institutional mandates, particularly around the appropriate limits of the judicial role. Drawing on two cases from the High Court of Australia, they illustrate how the Court has (or has not) taken account of the relevant factual conditions. This analysis reveals that if the Court operates in an 'idealised vacuum' it risks eroding the very mandates it is obliged to uphold.

Still focusing on Australia, Rayner Thwaites explores the multiple issues relating to facts and public law arising out of the Australian government's denial of citizenship to an individual, which was grounded in a construal of the citizenship arrangements attending Papua New Guinea's independence. These issues include how the use of historical materials and the legal dispute proceeded from the interpretation and application of provisions of the Papua New Guinea Constitution and transnational arrangements, both of which were treated as questions of fact. Ultimately, it shows how a person's rights and status – in this case, their citizenship – depend upon constitutional facts.

II. Facts in Administrative Law

In Part II of the book, the focus shifts more squarely to administrative law. While some of these issues overlap with those that arise in the judicial review of legislation, there are also some distinct issues and challenges that stem from the nature and history of judicial review of administrative action. Some of these issues were foreshadowed in the chapter by Daly and Kudischeva, but in this part of the collection they assume a more prominent place.

Jason Varuhas surveys the developing role of facts in administrative law adjudication. He begins by introducing the 'standard account' of the treatment of facts and evidence within the English judicial review procedure, whereby judicial review is regarded as an inappropriate forum for testing evidence and resolving disputed questions of fact. Under this standard account, the only evidence generally relevant to a review claim is that which was before the administrative decision-maker, and thus forms part of the historical decision-making record. Varuhas further shows how judicial review procedures reflect this standard approach. The chapter goes on to show how, despite the courts continuing to repeat the standard account, the reality has become increasingly complex. Vaurhas suggests a key driver of complexity in this respect has been changes to substantive law, and he focuses in particular on the UK's Human Rights Act 1998.

Joanna Bell and Elizabeth Fisher consider judicial review of what they call 'fact work'. They start with the observation that, despite the common mantra that judicial review is more centrally concerned with law, judicial review often deals with disputes about facts, the processes used to find them, and the use made of them by decision-makers. They suggest that literature on this aspect of judicial review has been concerned primarily with how the distinction between law and fact is to be drawn in judicial review (and if it is to be drawn at all) and when a court will and should intervene to correct an error of fact. But they encourage lawyers to move beyond the law/fact distinction, and in particular ask the question: what roles do courts play in overseeing the various forms of 'fact work' which is required in public administration? Their chapter seeks to answer this question by mapping three ways in which courts oversee the 'fact work' done in public administration.

Emily Hammond's chapter concentrates on Australian judicial review, and she looks specifically at legality in fact-finding by executive decision-makers. She opens by observing that the executive branch of government routinely engages in the adjudication of individual rights and liabilities, and that the consequences of such determinations might be very similar to a judicial order. Yet, as Hammond notes, the systemic constitutional safeguards could not be more different. Her chapter focuses on whether judicial review imposes meaningful qualitative controls on executive fact-finding, and she charts a shift in the Australian jurisprudence (at least among intermediate appellate authorities) towards reasonableness review of any findings – as a matter of law or fact – that are material. Hammond situates her analysis in the constitutional basis for judicial review of executive action and explains this evolution in the scope of reasonableness review in terms of the inherent incapacity of the executive to unilaterally alter the legal position of subjects. Although focusing on Australia, Hammond's chapter makes some broader observations about the extent to which her approach will increase qualitative control over executive fact-finding, and the pertinence of her analysis in other common law jurisdictions.

Joe Tomlinson and Cassandra Somers-Joce approach the question of facts in public law from a different angle: that of public officials. They look specifically at the duties that public law places on public bodies to collect systemic data on the operation and impact of policies and schemes. By reviewing the existing case law, they argue that the duty of inquiry should have a broader application: it should not be limited to individualised administrative decisions, but can, should and has been applied at the level of systemic administrative decisions. Their argument is that there is an important application gap in practice, and that there is no reason in principle why the duty of inquiry should not operate at a systemic level. Tomlinson and Somers-Joce demonstrate this broader application by reference to the EU Settlement Scheme and suggest there was a deficit in the collection of data by the UK government. This deficit curtailed a comprehensive assessment of the unequal effects of the scheme, which has implications in terms of the ability to scrutinise and improve public policy administration.

In their chapter on the treatment of facts in South African administrative law, Glenn Penfold and Cora Hoexter look closely at two of the most contested areas of fact-finding in judicial review in that jurisdiction. First, when courts are required to scrutinise the impact of an administrative act – its expected benefits and costs – or the administrator's consideration of that impact. Second, when the factual context is relevant to a court's exercise of its discretion to decide upon a just and equitable remedy. Through their close analysis of key cases in each of these domains, they show the importance of facts within South African administrative law, but also that the treatment of relevance and facts in individual cases can vary considerably.

Hanna Wilberg considers the position in New Zealand and England on whether mistakes of fact should give rise to a ground of judicial review. She examines the leading case of *E v Secretary of State for the Home Department*.[1] The status of the case is mixed and, with developments in other areas of judicial review, it may 'seem redundant, and perhaps a little quaint'. However, Wilberg argues that the ground in *E* should be approved, and she questions whether it is redundant as the limits set out in *E* respond to the objections to mistake of fact as a ground. Wilberg concludes that mistake of fact ought to apply in cases that are not clearly covered by the broader move towards greater scrutiny of factual determinations.

III. Facts in Broader Perspective

Part III of the book considers facts from a broader perspective. By looking at facts in different contexts, and from other disciplinary perspectives, the chapters in this part challenge the traditional or 'legal' approaches to facts. While they traverse a range of topics, they each prompt us to see the shortfalls in traditional adjudicative processes and approaches to facts.

Hilary Evans Cameron evaluates the critical question of how the traditional common law approach to evidence law can, or cannot, accommodate Indigenous historical knowledge. Her focus is on Canada's treatment of indigenous people and how the Supreme Court, recognising the injustice of the traditional approach, has responded with changes to the law of evidence designed to ensure that Indigenous

---

[1] [2004] EWCA Civ 49.

oral history evidence receives 'equal and due treatment' in Canadian courts. Evans Cameron uses an error burden framework to evaluate the Supreme Court's changes. She argues that the common law's 'default fact-finding structures' are means to achieve normative outcomes, and courts must be open to modifying them as needed when their effect is normatively misaligned.

Zim Nwokora and Jayani Nadarajalingam tackle the intersection between political science and law. In particular, they investigate the various ways in which political science might be used in the context of the courtroom. Importantly, Nwokora and Nadarajalingam articulate what is meant by 'political science' and some of the challenges that arise when such knowledge is used in the legal domain. They argue that in Australian courts the utilisation of specialist political science knowledge, or expertise, remains low, and such evidence has traditionally featured rarely in constitutional adjudication. They advance a number of reasons for this, such as the tensions between the two disciplines and also the perception that such evidence is not comparable to evidence from the natural or health sciences or from other social sciences such as economics. Nwokora and Nadarajalingam argue that political science evidence should be used more extensively to 'boost the range of facts available to courts'. They demonstrate that such evidence is often germane to the legal questions to be resolved but is rarely used or adequately engaged with. They also address the practical vehicles by which such evidence can be integrated into the legal process, and some of the obstacles that need to be overcome if such evidence is to be more routinely used.

Caitlin Goss also explores how other disciplines, namely history, can inform constitutional law. In her chapter she undertakes a mapping exercise, looking at the various ways history and historical evidence intersect with constitutional texts and adjudication. The first category she identifies is where history is expressly invoked in constitutional texts, such as to bolster a constitution's legitimacy or to endorse or reflect a particular period of history. The second category is where history is used to resolve constitutional disputes. Within this category she identifies several different ways in which courts can and do make reference to history, drawing on examples from a range of jurisdictions. Like Nwokora and Nadarajalingam, Goss identifies a number of challenges that arise when courts rely on expertise from other disciplines, including tensions between the roles of lawyers and historians. Goss's chapter invites us to consider the many ways, both explicit and more subtle, in which history is used in constitutional adjudication. It is clear that the role of history extends far beyond the (occasional) use of historians as expert witnesses and instead that history can permeate constitutional adjudication in multi-faceted ways.

Shiri Krebs also focuses on the contingent nature of legal facts, and she does so by examining Israeli Supreme Court cases on preventive detention. Her chapter draws upon the ontological and epistemological constraints of legal fact-finding in general, combined with specific challenges that arise in the context of counterterrorism cases. Krebs focuses on preventive detention cases, and she contrasts the 'judicial management' model developed in Israel with the 'special advocate' model used in the UK and Canada. As Krebs shows, both models have severe limitations in terms of fact-finding. Krebs illustrates the weaknesses of the 'judicial management' model by reference to two Israeli decisions and demonstrates that – in both 'template'-type and more fully reasoned decisions – the result has been a 'defactualisation' of justice, where a dominant security narrative serves to hamper meaningful fact-finding by courts.

IV. Towards a Public Law of Evidence?

The diverse chapters in this book together point to a range of emerging cross-cutting themes. Five of these are, in our view, particularly worthy of attention.

First, it is a recurring theme in this book that facts and evidence are often somewhat hidden beneath the surface of the legal. This state of affairs can be the product of a lack of attention being directed to facts, including by scholars, but it can also be the result of institutional practices. It is noticeable, for example, that court judgments can present a highly variable record of the treatment of facts and evidence in a particular matter. Much will depend not only on how the matter came to court, how it was argued, and what material was before the court, but also how much of this detail finds its way into the final judgment. For scholars interested in advancing knowledge in this domain, one of the hurdles will be in terms of excavation and data collection, as often the judicial record is incomplete.

Second, and linked to the hidden nature of facts and evidence, is the concern about the inconsistent treatment of facts by courts. While there are some established frameworks and procedures for handling factual disputes in the judicial review of administrative action and constitutional adjudication, they leave a large amount of discretion in the hands of judges and, as a result, scope for inconsistency in how facts play into public law adjudication. There is a principled concern here about equal treatment, but also a concern about what effects such inconsistency might have on the operation of public law itself. This grey area is one that can cover up excesses of judicial power but also acts of judicial avoidance.

Third, the distinction between questions of law and questions of fact is deeply contested in common law jurisdictions. It is clear from the chapters in this book that it remains difficult to define and apply. In addition, as Bell and Fisher suggest, there is a question about whether this distinction is helpful at all. What is clear is that role of evidence and facts in judicial review raises questions which go far beyond this matter. It seems a fundamental doctrinal question ripe for questioning in new ways.

Fourth, it is striking that much of the context for factual determination in public law adjudication is shaped and coloured by the particular policy domain it relates to (e.g. social security, immigration, national security *etc*). The chapters in this book have hinted at the possibility that questions of facts and evidence may well get handled differently in different contexts. Like much of public law, there is much to be gained by revisiting the subject through the prism of public policy functions.

Finally, it is quite clear that, on questions of fact and evidence in judicial review, public lawyers can benefit from other disciplines. Other disciplines, such as history and political science, are capable of providing insights and frameworks for how certain questions might be handled, and also of exposing failures and injustices that may have ossified in traditional public law approaches and procedures.

We hope the chapters in this book provoke further discussion about the role of facts in public law adjudication, and the emerging crosscutting themes to which the authors have pointed. In our view, while some of the issues raised are common to other fields of law, there are some distinct evidential issues that arise when the legality of government action is before the courts. The lack of attention given to such issues means that public law is deficient in this respect, especially when compared to other legal fields such as criminal law. Much of the law of public law evidence still needs to be written.

PART I

Facts in Constitutional Adjudication

2

The Rise of Facts in Public Law

PAUL DALY AND KSENIYA KUDISCHEVA[*]

I. Introduction

As far as facts in public law proceedings are concerned, the Americans got there first. In the early twentieth century, lawyers pioneered the 'Brandeis brief', a lengthy collection of factual evidence collated in support of legal submissions about the constitutionality of legislation.[1] In other common law systems, judges have been much less willing to grapple with factual issues.

In part, this reflects two phenomena of Commonwealth public law. First, judicial review of legislation (especially for conformity with fundamental rights) has a much shorter history than it does in the United States. Second, judicial review of administrative action was performed by way of the prerogative writs, scrutinising the lawfulness of executive decisions on the basis of the paper record before the decision-maker.

Of course, these are general phenomena and, for every generality, there are specific qualifications to make. In Australia and Canada, for instance, there has long been judicial review of legislation on federalism grounds; even there, however, the filing of extensive materials in constitutional litigation is a habit of relatively recent provenance.[2] In administrative law, even if fact-finding on judicial review has always been theoretically possible, common law judges have been reluctant to engage in it.[3]

Since the latter half of the twentieth century, however, courts in Commonwealth jurisdictions have taken on an unmistakably larger role in making factual

---

[*] With thanks to Ittai Bar-Siman-Tov for comments and to the clerks of the Federal Court and Federal Court of Appeal for permitting Professor Daly to present this chapter as a piece of work in progress. The views expressed in this chapter are solely those of the authors in their personal capacity and do not represent the official position of Justice Canada nor the Government of Canada.

[1] See especially *Muller v Oregon* 208 US 412 (1908). So named because of their association with Louis Brandeis, later a justice of the Supreme Court of the United States, although there are examples of Brandeis briefs *avant la lettre*: DE Bernstein, 'Brandeis Brief Myths' (2011) 15 *Green Bag* 2D 9 at 11.

[2] JE Magnet, 'The Presumption of Constitutionality" (1980) 18 *Osgoode Hall LJ* 87.

[3] *R v Fulham, Hammersmith and Kensington Rent Tribunal* [1951] 2 KB 1, 11.

assessments in public law proceedings. Our focus is primarily on Canada and England, but we are confident that our analysis is relevant to similarly situated jurisdictions.

In this chapter, we identify four distinct strands to this larger role: judicial review of administrative action; judicial review of legislation; systemic challenges to the legality of regulatory regimes; and constitutional causes of action. We describe each of these in turn, attempting to explain briefly why each strand has developed, highlighting difficulties that each has given rise to, and the solutions courts have relied upon to alleviate or eliminate these difficulties. Our thesis is that developments in judicial review have caused judges to engage increasingly in factual assessments, causing practical and principled difficulties which, in turn, have provoked judicial responses designed to alleviate or eliminate the difficulties.

As far as section II, Judicial review of administrative action, is concerned, facts are no longer off limits as far as reviewing courts are concerned. Records on judicial review have expanded significantly, and the judicial role has also changed, with a greater willingness to engage in context-sensitive review of the cogency of reasoning and adequacy of evidence. Judges have developed mechanisms of judicial restraint to ward off the dangers of judicial review becoming an appeal on the merits.

Similar phenomena can be glimpsed in the area of section III, Judicial review of legislation. Here, the rise of proportionality as the standard against which legislative infringements of fundamental rights are assessed has required courts to conduct detailed assessments of the justifications for legislators' policy judgements. In response, courts have tried to funnel the consideration of legislative facts through the adjudicative process, emphasised that direct judicial review of legislative decision-making is forbidden, and developed mechanisms for judicial restraint. The upshot is that courts do not second guess legislative value judgements but rather assess the justificatory force of the reasons adduced to support those value judgements, giving appropriate deference especially when the judgements involve sensitive social, cultural, economic or political issues.

Systemic challenges to regulatory regimes, considered in Section IV, raise a separate set of difficulties. Many contemporary regulatory regimes are highly complex. Their multiple moving parts – legislation, regulation, soft law and discretion – may rub up against fundamental rights or the general principles of administrative law: when they do so, individuals or public-interest organisations may bring 'systemic' challenges to the day-to-day operations of a complex field of regulation. Recent decisions indicate a judicial desire to limit the scope for systemic challenges by narrowing the grounds on which they can be made and by insisting that challengers identify a causal link between harm suffered and a breach of law.

Lastly, in section V, the distinctively Canadian phenomenon of using facts as constitutional causes of action places tremendous power in the hands of first-instance judges. In hot-button areas of social policy such as sex work and assisted suicide, first-instance findings of fact about the physical and psychological harms of legal prohibitions have prompted major social change. The scope for trial judges to depart from binding precedent based on findings of fact has recently been reduced, but Canadian courts have not been as anxious to develop additional control mechanisms in this area, perhaps because facts can, realistically, only constitute constitutional causes of action in a limited set of cases where there is a criminal prohibition which causes particular types of personal harm.

In what follows, we deliberately use the broad term 'factual assessments' to denote the judicial treatment of fact-based evidence in public law proceedings. The overriding point of this chapter is to demonstrate that common law judges have, increasingly, been required to make factual assessments from which, in the not-so-distant past, they shied away. As such, we are not inclined to say much more about the ontology of facts in public law proceedings, but rather are happy to provide more grist for the mill of those who are inclined to say more about 'findings' or 'conclusions' of 'fact'.

II. Factual Assessments in Judicial Review of Administrative Action

Common law judges have traditionally been highly reluctant to interfere with factual assessments made by administrative decision-makers. This reluctance flowed in large part from the nature of judicial review of administrative action, devolved from the 'prerogative writs' developed long before the advent of the contemporary administrative state, to permit the King's courts in London to control the activities of inferior tribunals (and to fend off rivals such as the ecclesiastical courts).[4] Certiorari, for example, which facilitated the quashing of legally erroneous inferior tribunal decisions, was entirely a paper proceeding involving the transmittal of the record of the inferior court into one of the King's courts,[5] whereupon the record would be scrutinised for legal error.

Without a trial or viva voce evidence of any type, judicial fact-finding would be very difficult and, indeed, unnecessary, as the facts of the matter would be contained in the record of proceedings. Moreover, too-close scrutiny of factual assessments would cause judicial review of administrative action to resemble an appeal: hence the standard rules that judges may not second guess the weight assigned by administrative decision-makers to relevant factors,[6] that as long as there is sufficient evidence to support them, an administrative decision-maker's factual assessments should stand[7] and that simply making a wrong finding of fact is not, in and of itself, an error of law.[8]

---

[4] The classic telling of the tale is SA De Smith, 'The Prerogative Writs' (1951) 11 *Cambridge Law Journal* 40.
[5] *R v Titchmarsh* (1914) 22 DLR 272, 277–78.
[6] *Tesco Stores v Secretary of State for the Environment* [1995] 1 WLR 759, 780.
[7] *R v Nat Bell Liquors* [1922] 2 AC 128, 151–52.
[8] *Waterford v Commonwealth* (1987) 163 CLR 54, 77. See also *Ryanair Ltd v Flynn* [2000] 3 IR 240, 264; *Wandsworth London Borough Council v A* [2000] 1 WLR 1246, 1255–56.

This is not to say that an administrative decision-maker's factual assessments were off limits as far as the judicial review of administrative action was concerned. So-called 'jurisdictional' facts have always been closely scrutinised by reviewing courts.[9] Where an administrative decision-maker's authority to make a particular decision is contingent on the objective existence of a state of affairs, de novo judicial review is appropriate to ensure that the decision-maker remains within the boundaries of its authority. Judicial review for jurisdictional error of fact helped to ensure – to take a well-known example – that rent tribunals in North London could not declare a 'fair rent' in respect of the Albert Hall.[10] Furthermore, at least *some* factual assessments could be interfered with, where there was no evidence to support them[11] or where conclusions were so unreasonable that no reasonable decision-maker could have come to them;[12] and *egregious* errors in relation to factual matters could give rise to a remedy.[13]

Although many centuries have passed since the prerogative writs were first developed, and the writs have been abolished and/or sidelined since procedural reforms in the mid-twentieth century, the contemporary judicial review procedure still bears their hallmarks.[14] A judicial review is not an appeal;[15] judicial fact-finding is rare;[16] and deference is paid to administrative decision-makers' factual assessments.[17]

Nonetheless, in recent decades, things have changed.[18] In the British Isles, adherence to European Union law and the European Convention on Human Rights has required greater scrutiny of factual matters, to ensure effective remedies and to provide sufficiently robust oversight of decision-making structures lacking high levels of independence and impartiality. Across the common law world, freedom of information legislation, judicial doctrines imposing a 'duty of candour' on governments, statutory reason-giving requirements and access to sophisticated technology have facilitated the creation of extremely detailed records to support reasoned decisions. The walls of non-justiciability have been pushed back

---

[9] See, eg, *R v Shoreditch Assessment Committee, ex parte Morgan* [1910] 2 KB 859, 880.
[10] See, eg, P Daly, *A Theory of Deference in Administrative Law: Basis, Application and Scope* (New York, CUP 2012) 224.
[11] *R v Nat Bell Liquors* [1922] 2 AC 128, 151–52.
[12] *Associated Provincial Picture Houses v Wednesbury Corporation* [1948] 1 KB 223, 228–30.
[13] See, eg, *Secretary of State for Education and Science v Tameside Borough Council* [1977] AC 1014, 1047; *R v Criminal Injuries Compensation Board, ex parte A* [1999] 2 AC 330, 345; *E v Secretary of State for the Home Department* [2004] QB 1044, 1071.
[14] P Daly, *Understanding Administrative Law in the Common Law World* (Oxford, OUP 2021) ch 1.
[15] See, eg, *Michalak v General Medical Council* [2017] UKSC 71, [2017] 1 WLR 4193, [21]–[22].
[16] See the discussion in *Bernard v Canada (Revenue Agency)*, 2015 FCA 263.
[17] See, eg, *Vavilov v Canada (Citizenship and Immigration)* 2019 SCC 65, [125]–[126].
[18] Paul Daly developed the points in this paragraph at length in P Daly, 'Facticity: Judicial Review of Factual Error in Comparative Perspective' in P Cane and others (eds) *Oxford Handbook of Comparative Administrative Law* (Oxford, OUP, 2020); P Daly '*Vavilov* and the Culture of Justification in Contemporary Administrative Law' (2020) 100 *Supreme Court Law Review* (2d) 279. There is also a very valuable discussion in D Knight, *Vigilance and Restraint in the Common Law of Judicial Review* (Cambridge, CUP 2018).

significantly with individuals and interest groups alike capable of demonstrating standing to challenge potentially unlawful decisions. The law of judicial review has evolved away from narrow grounds of review – *Wednesbury* unreasonableness, error of law, error of fact, irrelevant considerations and so on – to a focus on the intensity of review, greater or lesser in any given case depending on the interplay of a variety of contextual factors. In the contemporary judicial review exercise, much depends on whether the administrative decision-maker has provided cogent reasons, based in evidence in the record, to support its decision.

Quite why things have changed in the way they have is a complex matter. Whatever the reason, the result is that judicial review of administrative action has increased in breadth and depth, with more matters subject to increasingly searching judicial oversight. There is no barrier to judicial review of administrative decision-makers' factual assessments. The judicial role is to evaluate the cogency of the reasoned decisions given in support of administrative action, in terms of (depending on the jurisdiction and the issue) reasonableness, rationality or proportionality: performing this role may require judicial scrutiny of an administrative decision-maker's factual assessments, to ensure that these are adequately reasoned and grounded in the evidence placed before the court. Facts are not at all off limits.

These recent developments have created practical and principled difficulties for the law of judicial review of administrative action. In practical terms, there has been pressure to expand the scope of the record in judicial review proceedings[19] and, although the phenomenon has largely escaped academic attention, courts have come to rely more and more on expert evidence to shed light on the reasonableness or proportionality of administrative action.[20] Indeed, the trend in most jurisdictions is towards developing more detailed records of decision, supplemented now by expert evidence tendered by way of affidavit and subjected to cross-examination in the presence of the reviewing judge. However, these procedural developments might well have an effect on the substance of the law: with more detailed records and reasons, it is natural for judges to develop standards of reasonableness, rationality and proportionality which focus attention on the cogency of reasoning and adequacy of evidence.[21]

In terms of principle, the judicial turn to scrutiny of cogency and adequacy pushes judges up against the appeal/review distinction, as there is a risk that courts will end up substituting their judgment for that of administrative decision-makers, transforming review for legality into an appeal on the merits. A variety of doctrinal devices, such as materiality and deference, have been developed to restrain judges from trespassing into the merits. For example, an individual seeking judicial

---

[19] See, eg, B Oliphant and L Wihak, '*Dunsmuir* and the Scope of Admissible Evidence on Judicial Review: Principled Limitations or Path Dependency?' (2019) 69 *U of T LJ* 31.

[20] See, eg, J Tomlinson, K Sheridan and A Harkens, 'Judicial Review Evidence in the Era of the Digital State' [2020] *Public Law* 740.

[21] See, eg, P Daly, 'Updating the Procedural Law of Judicial Review of Administrative Action' (2018) 51 *UBC L Rev* 705.

review of a decision will need to demonstrate, in terms of materiality, that there was a serious error which affected the outcome of the decision-making process[22] and courts have insisted that when it comes to factual assessments, a high degree of deference is due to administrative decision-makers.[23]

In general, the very need to develop such devices reflects the tension between recent developments in judicial review of administrative action and the historical foundations of the courts' jurisdiction to oversee public administration.

III. Factual Assessments in Judicial Review of Legislation

In federal systems, factual assessments can never be entirely off limits in judicial review of legislation. Where the powers of legislative bodies in different levels of government are limited to particular fields, a factual assessment will often be necessary to ensure that the level of government has remained in one of its fields. As has been observed on the High Court of Australia, 'it is the duty of the Court in every constitutional case to be satisfied of every fact the existence of which is necessary in law to provide a constitutional basis for the legislation'.[24]

A straightforward example emerges from the Supreme Court of Canada's decision about the validity of emergency legislation to combat the inflation crisis of the 1970s: extensive evidence was filed to demonstrate (or, from the opponents' perspective, undermine) the factual predicates for federal legislation under Parliament's authority to legislate on matters of national emergency.[25] Indeed, the question there was largely if not entirely factual: was there actually a national emergency to respond to?

In Canadian federalism generally, the effects of a law are relevant to determining its constitutionality, which permits the courts to make factual assessments.[26] This type of factual assessment, however, does not typically present great conceptual or practical difficulties. Much as reference to government policy papers and Hansard has become commonplace in discerning the meaning of statutory provisions, the availability of background material about the passage of legislation and its intended and actual effects can assist judges in determining whether a given law falls within one of the lawmaker's constitutionally accorded fields of responsibility. The judge does not have to *evaluate* the law-maker's factual assessment

---

[22] See, eg, *MZAPC v Minister for Immigration and Border Protection* (2021) 95 ALJR 441.
[23] See, eg, *R (Lord Carlile of Berriew QC) v Secretary of State for the Home Department* [2014] UKSC 60, [2015] 1 AC 945 [32], [58], [99], [112]; *Vavilov v Canada (Citizenship and Immigration)* 2019 SCC 65, [125]–[126]; *Djokovic v Minister for Immigration, Citizenship, Migrant Services and Multicultural Affairs* [2022] FCAFC 3, [104].
[24] *Australian Communist Party v Commonwealth* (1951) 83 CLR 1, 222 (Williams J).
[25] *Re: Anti-Inflation Act* [1976] 2 SCR 373, 79 DLR (3d) 1, 386–91.
[26] *Reference re Firearms Act (Can)* 2000 SCC 31, [16]–[18].

of the situation, testing it for rationality, reasonableness or proportionality but at most only to *determine* whether the factual assessment was accurate. Put another way, federalism questions are black and white, in the sense that a particular matter either will, or will not, be within the constitutional competence of a given level of government, and factual material is helpful in resolving these binary questions.

Judicial review of legislation for compliance with fundamental rights raises very different issues, at least as this practice has developed in common law jurisdictions. The proportionality test typically used to determine whether a legislative provision interferes unduly with a protected right requires a court to evaluate (1) the importance of the objective being furthered; (2) the existence of a rational connection between the means chosen and the achievement of the objective; (3) whether the means chosen were necessary to achieve the objective; and (4) whether the detrimental effects on individual interests caused by the means used outweighed the public interest in achieving the objective.

We acknowledge that it is 'hazardous to talk of proportionality analysis simpliciter, rather than the commitments of particular proportionality theorists, or the doctrines and practices of particular courts'.[27] Nonetheless, it is tolerably clear that the factual assessments required by the various prongs of the proportionality test – especially prongs (3) and (4) – are not comparable to the factual assessments required in federalism cases. The questions are not binary, or black and white, but invariably involve complex value judgements about 'importance', 'rationality', 'necessity', and 'balance'. They are, by definition, evaluative.[28]

The requirement to engage in such factual assessments raises principled and practical difficulties. On the practical side, 'it will sometimes be difficult, if not impossible, for the state to provide reliable and direct evidence of the benefit its measures will achieve',[29] a difficulty which arises especially at prongs (3) and (4). Particularly in areas of social policy where legislation is designed to protect vulnerable groups from inchoate harms – varying from the psychological dangers of exposure to harmful material[30] to pressure felt to avail of assisted suicide[31] – hard evidence which 'can be verified empirically' may be hard to come by. Even if extensive social science evidence is put before the court, and tested by way of cross-examination of expert witnesses, it may be difficult to determine that the legislation must founder on the necessity or fair balance prongs of the proportionality test. Notice that the disadvantages here are not all on the state side: individuals

---

[27] Bradley Miller, 'Proportionality's Blind Spot: "Neutrality" and Political Philosophy'" in G Huscroft, BW Miller and GN Webber (eds), *Proportionality and the Rule of Law: Rights, Justification, Reasoning* (New York, CUP 2014), 371–72.

[28] Professor David Beatty, the leading exponent of the view that judicial review of legislation for proportionality is an exercise in technical, rather than moral reasoning, believes that proportionality involves consideration of 'matters of fact', where there is, in principle, a 'correct resolution' capable of empirical verification: *The Ultimate Rule of Law* (Oxford, OUP 2004) 171. Even here, then, proportionality review requires courts to conduct detailed factual assessments.

[29] *R v KR.J*, 2016 SCC 31, (Brown J dissenting).

[30] See, eg, *Irwin Toy Ltd v Quebec (AG)* [1989] 1 SCR 927, 58 DLR (4th) 577.

[31] See, eg, *R (Nicklinson) v Ministry of Justice* [2014] UKSC 38, [2015] AC 657 [81], [201], [228].

or organisations challenging the constitutionality of legislation must also expend significant resources to mount plausible challenges in the first place (which might not be the best use of the scarce resources of the individuals or organisations concerned).[32]

On the principled side, the factual assessments judges must conduct in proportionality review require them to consider the quality of the legislature's work product and, by extension, the quality of a legislature's deliberation. Ittai Bar-Siman-Tov has argued that there is an emergent species of 'Semiprocedural Judicial Review', based on a series of cases in which 'the quality of the legislature's decision-making process seemed to influence the court's decision about the constitutionality of the law' but 'the quality of that process was not the sole consideration determining the validity of legislation'.[33] This 'rationality check of the policy process' might be attributable to 'the increasing evidence based nature of the policy process'[34] but there can be little doubt that the factual assessments required by proportionality review must involve at least indirect scrutiny of the legislative process.

There have been several responses to these difficulties: a preference for testing social science evidence by the tendering of expert evidence which can be subjected to cross-examination; marking off areas of legislative activity from judicial oversight; and the development of mechanisms for judicial restraint, modulating the application of prongs (3) and (4) in cases involving legislative value judgements.

Some facts relevant to determining the proportionality of legislation will be in the public domain or uncontroversial and, as such, judges may take judicial notice of them.[35] But the social science-type evidence which often underpins legislative interventions (or legislative abstentions) is not generally suitable for judicial notice, as the interpretation of the evidence is often contestable and may be subject to multiple, equally reasonable, interpretations. Accordingly, the Supreme Court of Canada has cautioned against the use of 'Brandeis briefs' in constitutional litigation, instead expressing a preference for the tendering of expert evidence which can be subject to cross-examination.[36] The hope here is that controversial 'legislative' facts can become settled 'adjudicative' facts by the time the court reaches the stage of conducting a proportionality test.[37]

In addition, courts have made clear that there are some areas of legislative activity which are non-justiciable. Direct judicial consideration of the legislative

---

[32] The classic text in this regard remains GN Rosenberg, *The Hollow Hope: Can Courts Bring About Social Change?* (2nd edn, London, University of Chicago Press 2008).

[33] I Bar-Siman-Tov, 'Semiprocedural Judicial Review' (2012) 6 *Legisprudence* 271. See also AD Oliver-Lalana, 'On the (Judicial) Method to Review the (Legislative) Method' (2016) 4(2) *Theory and Practice of Legislation* 135.

[34] A Alemanno, 'The Emergence of the Evidence-Based Judicial Reflex: A Response to Bar-Siman-Tov's Semiprocedural Review' (2013) 1 *Theory and Practice of Legislation* 327.

[35] EM Morgan, 'Judicial Notice' (1944) 57 *Harvard Law Review* 269.

[36] *R v Spence*, 2005 SCC 71 [68]. See also *M v H*, [1999] 2 SCR 3, 58 DLR (4th) 577, [296] (Bastarache J); *Public School Boards' Assn of Alberta v Alberta (AG)* 2000 SCC 2 [4]–[5] (Binnie J); *R v KRJ* 2016 SCC 31 [144] (Brown J).

[37] For the classic distinction, see KC Davis, 'An Approach to Problems of Evidence in the Administrative Process' (1942) 55 *Harvard Law Review* 364, 402–03.

process is, in the common law tradition, strictly forbidden, as it would cause judges to trespass into areas protected by parliamentary privilege.[38] Judges may neither opine on nor grant remedies in respect of areas of legislative activity which are central to the work of the legislature.[39] Semi-procedural review is as far as the courts may go.

Most importantly, courts have developed a variety of mechanisms of restraint. On the one hand, it is clear that where legislation can be characterised as addressing complex social, cultural, economic or other issues on which reasonable people hold a range of differing views, judges will shy away from the conclusion that the legislation unjustifiably infringes fundamental rights. Whether the term 'deference', 'margin of appreciation', or some other equivalent is used, the message is the same: on sensitive matters, judges will be reluctant to second-guess legislatures' factual assessments where legislators are better placed than courts to make such assessments.[40] On the other hand, when reviewing legislation, courts focus less on whether a legislature's factual assessment was right or wrong than they do on whether the government defending the legislation can establish, on a reasoned basis and by reference to evidence in the record, a sufficiently convincing justification for an interference with a fundamental right. There is no need, in this mode of analysis, to directly impugn a legislature's factual assessment or indeed its internal processes.[41]

Once more, however, it is clear that courts find themselves of necessity making factual assessments and having to develop responses to the resulting difficulties.

IV. Systemic Challenges to Regulatory Regimes

In our increasingly complex and fast-changing world, legislatures and executives have erected increasingly complex and fast-changing legislative and regulatory regimes, often supplemented by non-binding soft law instruments.[42] In some areas, like immigration, such regimes push up against fundamental rights. Removing migrants from a jurisdiction may upend their family lives or expose them to physical or psychological harm in their country of origin or a third country. In other areas, the regimes may create tension with the principles of administrative law, for example by authorising the same decision-maker to perform multiple functions (say, investigation and adjudication) thereby potentially prompting a reasonable apprehension of bias, or by failing to require sufficiently robust procedures, or even by contradicting a rule set out in statute or delegated legislation.

---

[38] *R (HS2 Action Alliance) v Secretary of State for Transport* [2014] UKSC 3 [110].
[39] See, eg, *Mikisew Cree First Nation v Canada (Governor General in Council)*, 2018 SCC 40.
[40] See, eg, *Irwin Toy Ltd* (n 30) 993–1000.
[41] See, eg, M Cohen-Eliya and I Porat, 'Proportionality and Justification' (2014) 64 *U of T LJ* 458.
[42] See, eg, R Rawlings, 'Soft Law Never Dies' in M Elliott and D Feldman (eds), *The Cambridge Companion to Public Law* (Cambridge, CUP 2015).

Whether the tension is with fundamental rights or the principles of administrative law, one response is to mount a 'systemic' challenge to the regime. This is facilitated by the liberal contemporary approach to standing in public law matters, so that non-governmental organisations with an interest in the regime in question (the Canadian Association of Refugee Lawyers, say, or the Public Law Project) will be able to bring systemic challenges even though they are not directly affected by the regime.[43] Of course, individuals who have a direct interest, perhaps because their rights were interfered with or they were denied a benefit or status, can also bring a systemic challenge. Regardless of the challenger's identity, the focus of the challenge will be on the way that the system operates, the overall goal being to demonstrate that, in a substantial number of cases, the system generates results which infringe upon fundamental rights or the principles of administrative law. This requires, evidently, a fact-based inquiry: a judge must determine, based on the evidence adduced or the record, whether the threshold for making out a systemic challenge has been reached.

Here, again, difficulties of practice and principle arise.[44] On the practical side, individuals and non-governmental organisations must work extremely hard to build an evidence base or a detailed factual record to permit a court to arrive at the conclusion that there is indeed a systemic problem with the regime. From the courts' perspective, there is the additional problem that the judge necessarily gets only a partial glimpse of the reality of the regime at issue. Judicial review is not an exercise in ethnography or social anthropology in which the judge embeds themselves in day-to-day operations on the front line of public administration. Rather, the judge must make a determination on a balance of probabilities based on incomplete information. Again, there are no binary decisions here, only difficult evaluative judgements.

On the principled side, these regimes have many moving parts. As a consequence, when a fundamental right or a principle of administrative law is breached by the operation of the regime, it may be hard to identify the source of the violation: does it lie in the legislation itself, or in the operation of the legislation by an administrative actor? If there is an agreed statement of facts about how the regulatory regime operates, making these determinations is easier, but where the legislation is operationalised by administrative actors using administrative policies, the picture becomes much less clear.[45] If a violation is established and the source identified, a court must decide on the appropriate remedy: is redress for the individual concerned sufficient, or must the entire edifice of the regime be brought crashing to the ground? Where systemic challenges succeed, difficult questions often also arise about their implications for cases decided and things done under the regulatory regime.[46]

---

[43] See generally, Daly (n 14) ch 6.
[44] See further J Varuhas, 'Evidence, Facts and the Changing Nature of Judicial Review' (*UK Const L Blog*, 15 June 2020). Available at: www.ukconstitutionallaw.org. Last accessed 8 May 2022.
[45] See, eg, *Langlois c Commission municipale du Québec*, 2021 QCCS 2725.
[46] See, eg, House of Commons Library, *Research Briefing: Employment tribunals after R (Unison) v Lord Chancellor*, 5 November 2018, discussing the implications of the decision in *R (UNISON) v Lord Chancellor* [2017] UKSC 51 [2020] AC 869.

Two responses are evident in recent jurisprudence: limiting the scope of systemic challenges; and requiring sufficient proof of a causal link between the operation of the regime and the breach of fundamental rights or principles of administrative law in individual cases.

The most obvious response is to limit the scope of systemic challenges. The recent decision of the United Kingdom Supreme Court in *R (A) v Secretary of State for the Home Department*[47] is instructive. Previously, the English courts had treated as unlawful any policy which 'is in principle capable of being implemented lawfully but which nonetheless *gives rise to an unacceptable risk of unlawful decision-making*'.[48] This 'unacceptable risk' test, Lord Sales and Lord Burnett concluded, is too loose. Instead, a court may intervene 'when a public authority has, by issuing a policy, positively authorised or approved unlawful conduct by others'.[49] Only if the policy 'directs' officials 'to act in a way which contradicts the law' will it be found to be illegal.[50] The difficulty with the lower courts' approach was the emphasis on risk, which amongst other things drew judges into the difficult territory of trying to quantify how often the regime produced problematic results. Lord Sales and Lord Burnett did not evacuate quantitative considerations from the analysis entirely, so 'the significance of the ... restatement ... will depend on how important quantitative considerations turn out to be in practice'.[51] But their Lordships' intention was clearly to limit the scope of systemic challenges by making them turn on qualitative considerations about whether a regulatory regime positively authorises or approves unlawful conduct, not quantitative considerations about how often unlawful conduct occurs, in practice, in a regulatory regime.

Another recent decision, from Canada, exemplifies the insistence on demonstrating a causal link. The applicants in *Canada (Citizenship and Immigration) v Canadian Council for Refugees*[52] challenged the operation of the Safe Third Country Agreement entered into by Canada and the United States. Certain refugee claimants who arrive in Canada via a designated third country are ineligible to seek asylum in Canada.[53] The criteria for designation include adherence to the Refugee Convention and the Convention against Torture, as well as the third country's human rights record.[54] Designations are subject to 'continuing review'.[55] The United States is a designated third country,[56] so certain refugee claimants

---

[47] [2021] UKSC 37.
[48] *R (Suppiah) v Home Secretary* [2011] EWHC 2 (Admin), [137] (emphasis added).
[49] ibid [8].
[50] ibid [41].
[51] P Daly, 'Firming Up Judicial Review of Soft Law' (2022) 72 *Cambridge LJ* 8, 10.
[52] 2021 FCA 72.
[53] *Immigration and Refugee Protection Act*, SC 2001, c 27, s 101(1)(e) [*IRPA*].
[54] ibid s 102(2).
[55] ibid s 102(3). See further, *Directives for Ensuring a Continuing Review of Factors Set Out in Subsection 102(2) of the Immigration and Refugee Protection Act with Respect to Countries Designated Under Paragraph 102(1)(A) of That Act (2015)*, P.C. 2015-0809; Immigration, Refugees and Citizenship Canada, *Monitoring Framework for the U.S. Designation as a Safe Third Country*, June 2015.
[56] IRPA, s 159(3).

arriving in Canada from the United States are turned away at the border and sent back to the United States. The challenge to this regime based on the physical and psychological harm suffered by refugee claimants who had been turned away at the Canadian border succeeded at first instance.[57]

But the Federal Court of Appeal allowed the government's appeal, on the basis that the challenge was misconceived. In essence, the challengers aimed at the wrong target by relying on the evidence of individuals who had suffered harm due to the operation of the regulatory regime. They should, rather, have contested the lawfulness of the continuing review of the designation of the United States, because it would have been the failure of this 'safety valve' which caused the harm suffered.[58] Here, the 'real cause' of the harm complained of was the misfiring of the safety valve:[59] the focus on individual claimants made it impossible to draw 'system-wide inferences' about whether it had been appropriate to designate the United States[60] and directed the court's attention away from the proximate cause of the alleged Charter violations, which was 'how administrators and officials are operating the legislative scheme, not the legislative scheme itself'.[61] Causation, then, is key, with 'systemic' challengers required to demonstrate a link between the harm complained of and the operation of the regulatory regime responsible.[62]

The effect of limiting the scope of systemic challenges and requiring a causal connection is to ensure a properly tailored record for decision. By putting the focus on qualitative rather than quantitative considerations, the UK Supreme Court's new test for the scope of challenges to administrative policies would produce a less sprawling record: if quantitative evidence is less relevant, less of it should be generated. Similarly, one of Stratas JA's concerns about the failure to think seriously about causation was that it would lead to 'the creation of an unduly artificial and narrow evidentiary record'.[63] The plea here, from both sides of the Atlantic, is for systemic challenges to be properly tailored, with an evidentiary record which homes in on the proximate cause of any breach of fundamental rights or the principles of administrative law. This also allows for the provision of appropriate remedies: rather than causing the whole system to grind to a halt or occasioning root-and-branch reform, a declaration or quashing order can be directed at the source of the harm, allowing those responsible to take rapid remedial action.

Again, recent developments have required responsiveness on the part of courts to the practical and principled difficulties thrown up by systemic challenges to the operation of regulatory regimes.

---

[57] *The Canadian Council for Refugees et al v Minister for Immigration and Minister for Public Safety*, 2020 FC 770.
[58] *Canada (Citizenship and Immigration)* (n 52) [70]. Note that this decision has been appealed to the Supreme Court of Canada, which will hear the appeal in late 2022.
[59] ibid [74].
[60] ibid [78].
[61] ibid [89].
[62] See also *R (TN (Vietnam)) v Home Secretary* [2021] UKSC 41 [87].
[63] *Canada (Citizenship and Immigration)* (n 52) [58].

V. Facts as Constitutional Causes of Action

We turn lastly to a distinctly Canadian phenomenon, or at least one we believe to be distinctively Canadian. This is the use of facts to develop constitutional causes of action. In a series of cases in the 2010s, the Supreme Court of Canada struck down regulatory regimes as unconstitutional based on trial-level findings of fact that harm had been caused to individuals in violation of s 7 of the Charter of Rights and Freedoms. In each of these cases, a first-instance court found that the operation of the regulatory regimes in question caused harm to individuals, and on appeal the Supreme Court deferred to these findings of fact.

As s 7 of the Charter is central to these cases, it is necessary to briefly explain the provision and the jurisprudence which has accumulated around it. Section 7 provides: '[e]veryone has the right to life, liberty and security of the person and the right not to be deprived thereof except in accordance with the principles of fundamental justice'. Section 7 is disjunctive and contains three rights: life, liberty, and security of the person. Any infringement must comport with the principles of fundamental justice. That is, if life, liberty, or security of the person is infringed upon without respecting the principles of fundamental justice, s 7 has been violated. The most important principles of fundamental justice are arbitrariness, gross disproportionality, and overbreadth. If an infringement of one of the s 7 rights is arbitrary, grossly disproportionate, or overbroad, this will be a violation. Any such violation can be 'saved' under s 1 of the Charter. Layering the s 1 proportionality test upon the principles of fundamental justice in s 7 creates some complications. The general view is that s 1 will only save a s 7 violation in extraordinary cases. The cases from the 2010s turned out not to be extraordinary. Faced with deprivations of a constitutional right, the Supreme Court gave little weight to moral or political considerations relating to the desirability of regulating sex work or assisted suicide.

Canada (AG) v Bedford involved a challenge to Canada's sex work laws using new social science evidence.[64] Previously, in the so-called *Prostitution Reference*, the Supreme Court had affirmed the constitutionality of federal anti-sex work legislation.[65] But the s 7 challenge in *Bedford* succeeded: the courts struck down the criminal prohibitions on bawdyhouses, living on the avails of prostitution, and communicating in public. Notice that the legislation in question did not criminalise sex work as such. Engaging in sex work was lawful, with these prohibitions designed to reduce the attraction of engaging in sex work and to diminish the risk that third parties – pimps – would profit from the activities of sex workers.

New social science evidence impacted this litigation. The applicants developed a massive record filled with 88 volumes of over 25,000 pages of evidence. The record contained evidence from sex workers and experts in a wide range of

---

[64] 2013 SCC 72.
[65] *Reference re ss. 193 and 195.1(1)(c) of the Criminal Code (Ma.)* [1990] 1 SCR 1123.

social science disciplines.[66] The key findings of fact at trial were that, although violent clients and pimps created the risks to sex workers' safety, the anti-sex-work provisions actively blocked sex workers from taking steps to reduce risk. For example, the living-on-the-avails provision was overbroad. Despite targeting those who exploit sex workers, the provision also captured those who could help increase sex workers' safety and security. The other two provisions, prohibiting bawdyhouses and communicating in public, were grossly disproportionate. Taking sex work out of public view by prohibiting communication cost sex workers their screening ability – speaking with clients in public before relocating. And while the bawdyhouse provision meant to reduce nuisance, this offence criminalised all sex work in fixed indoor locations, even in sex workers' homes, pushing sex workers onto the streets.

Bedford was an extremely important case. For one thing, the Supreme Court admonished the Court of Appeal for 'erroneously substitut[ing] its [own] assessment of the evidence for that of the application judge'[67] rather than deferring to the application judge's fact-finding including on social and legislative facts. For another thing, the Supreme Court held that in situations where the law has evolved or there has been a change in circumstances or evidence 'that fundamentally shifts the parameters of the debate', a trial judge may depart from binding Supreme Court precedent: given the findings of fact of the trial judge, a departure from the *Prostitution Reference* was justified.[68] In combination, these features of *Bedford* meant not only that findings of fact could support a legal conclusion that s 7 of the Charter had been infringed but also that the same findings could justify departure from binding authority.

Bedford thus set the stage for judicial consideration of the hot-button issue of assisted suicide. In *Carter v Canada*, the Supreme Court reconsidered the constitutionality of physician-assisted dying.[69] Grievously ill plaintiffs who were not in a position to end their own lives without medical assistance challenged the former s 241(b) of the Canadian Criminal Code, which criminalised aiding or abetting a person to commit suicide. They developed a significant factual record designed to justify a departure from the Supreme Court's 1993 decision upholding the assisted suicide prohibition against a s 7 challenge.[70] As in *Bedford*, the Supreme Court used the trial judge's findings, 'based on an exhaustive review of the extensive record before her' to uphold the trial decision[71] and rule that the provision violated s 7. The provision violated the right to life by forcing a choice between

---

[66] See D Haak, 'The Good Governance of Empirical Evidence about Prostitution, Sex Work, and Sex Trafficking in Constitutional Litigation Queen's Law Journal' (2021) 46 *Queen's LJ* 187, 192 noting 'expert evidence from a range of social science disciplines including anthropology, criminology, psychology, sociology, history, medical ethics, political science and forensic psychology'.
[67] *Bedford* (n 64) [154].
[68] ibid [42].
[69] 2015 SCC 5.
[70] *Rodriguez v British Columbia (AG)*, [1993] 3 SCR 519, 107 DLR (4th) 342.
[71] *Carter* (n 69) [3].

premature suicide or losing one's ability to control the manner and time of death. The provision violated the right to liberty by removing autonomy over one's body and medical care. And the right to security of the person was violated by subjecting individuals to intolerable suffering.

The violations did not comport with the principles of fundamental justice. While meant to protect the vulnerable from committing suicide in times of weakness, the evidence showed that this prohibition caught individuals outside of the protected class. The apex court relied here on the trial judge's findings[72] to strike down the prohibition as overbroad. The apex court also deferred to the trial judge's fact-finding when deciding that s 1 of the Charter did not justify the prohibition. Could Canada safely replace its blanket ban on physician-assisted suicide with a more permissive regime that respected Canadians' life, liberty, and security of the person? Having heard evidence 'from scientists, medical practitioners, and others who were familiar with end-of-life decision-making in Canada and abroad',[73] the trial judge answered 'yes'. As it was open to the trial judge to find that properly trained physicians could 'reliably assess patient confidence and voluntariness' in assisted suicide,[74] there was a s 7 violation and the Supreme Court's previous decision was no barrier to a finding that the prohibition was unconstitutional.

In *Bedford* and *Carter*, the legal regimes in question, relating to sex work and assisted suicide, had been the subject of passionate public debate (though the extent of serious *parliamentary* consideration of reform is debatable). Nonetheless, despite the democratic imprimatur such regimes bear, they may be challenged in s 7 cases and invalidated where the evidence demonstrates that the regimes cause harm to individuals. In *Bedford* and *Carter*, first instance fact-finding even allowed trial judges to break free of binding precedent.

Practical and principled difficulties again arise. On the practical side, this approach places an important burden on applicants in constitutional cases, who must develop a detailed record. Indeed, there may be a tension between an ever-broader approach to standing – which permits public interest applicants to bring constitutional cases[75] – and the harm-based approach to s 7 – which, in reality, permits only well-funded, high-profile organisations into the arena. And there is an ever-present risk of waste: in *Bedford* and *Carter* the challenges were successful, but there are other high-profile cases where challenges foundered for want of evidence, notwithstanding the significant resources expended by challengers.[76]

On the principled side, in determining such challenges, first-instance judges have enormous power. First, their findings of fact are entitled to deference on appeal, unless the government can demonstrate that the findings were tainted by palpable and overriding error. Second, their findings of fact may justify a departure

---

[72] ibid [68], [86].
[73] ibid [104].
[74] ibid [106].
[75] See generally, *Canada (AG) v Downtown Eastside Sex Workers United Against Violence Society*, 2012 SCC 45.
[76] See, eg *Barbra Schlifer Commemorative Clinic v Canada*, 2014 ONSC 5140.

from binding precedent. Decisions to depart from precedent can be appealed, of course, and an appellate court can substitute its judgment on whether the departure was justified but, nonetheless, these two features place enormous power in the hands of first-instance judges. It is questionable whether first-instance judges are adequately equipped to perform this role. On the one hand, where expert evidence is tendered about the operation of a regulatory regime, judges can make findings of fact as to which body of expert evidence should be preferred. Moreover, in both *Bedford* and *Carter* a causal link between the harm suffered and the legal prohibitions challenged was established: the first-instance judges were not acting as Royal Commissioners. On the other hand, it might be objected that the fact that changes in 'legislative' facts are established through an 'adjudicative' process does not make courts the proper arbiters of whether social change should lead to legal change, especially in circumstances where the necessary change could be achieved by legislative action. Indeed, significant power is also placed in the hands of the social-science researchers who provide the evidence base for such challenges.[77] Perhaps as a matter of constitutional, political or moral theory, there is something to be said for empowering trial courts in this way. But doing so is inconsistent with the ordering of common law legal systems, which funnel questions of principle to apex courts for authoritative resolution.

Soon after *Carter*, the Supreme Court of Canada rowed back from the high water-mark of the 2010s. Faced in *R v Comeau* with a trial judge who had departed from binding precedent based on convincing historical adjudicative facts about the intentions of the framers of the Canadian Constitution, the Court unanimously held that *stare decisis* binds first-instance fact finders in all but the most 'extraordinary circumstances'.[78] Only where 'the underlying social context that framed the original legal debate is profoundly altered' is a departure from precedent warranted[79] – even though here the evidence overwhelmingly favoured the trial judge's preferred interpretation of the constitutional provision at issue, the precedent should have held. More broadly, the message to trial courts was clear: *Bedford* and *Carter* were exceptional cases, the exercises there undertaken by first-instance judges not lightly to be repeated.[80]

Ultimately, given developments in respect of systemic challenges to regulatory regimes, the only areas in which *Bedford* and *Carter*-type challenges are feasible is where there is a distinct criminal law prohibition against a particular type of conduct and the prohibition directly causes serious physical or psychological harm. These limitations were not articulated in terms in *Bedford* and *Carter*, but they are inherent to any challenge using facts as constitutional causes of action. As soon as there is a discretionary element in a regulatory regime, the limitations

---

[77] Haak (n 66).
[78] 2018 SCC 15.
[79] ibid [31].
[80] See, eg, K Froc and M Marin, "The Supreme Court's Strange Brew: History, Federalism and Anti-Originalism in *Comeau*" (2018) 70 *UNB LJ* 298.

developed in the context of systemic challenges to regulatory regimes kick in, reducing the scope for first-instance judges to upset settled precedent based on a detailed factual record, and alleviating the practical difficulties by ensuring an appropriately tailored evidential basis.

In this area, as in the others canvassed in this chapter, greater judicial willingness to countenance factual assessments has created practical and principled difficulties, prompting judicial responses designed to remedy those difficulties.

VI. Conclusion

Our thesis in this chapter has been that with judges playing an increasingly hands-on role in relation to factual assessments in public law cases, a variety of practical and principled difficulties have arisen, prompting judicial responses in turn.

We analysed four areas. First, judges are engaged more and more in factual assessments in judicial review of administrative action. This has led to difficulties of practice (in terms of the content of the record for judicial review) and principle (threatening the appeal/review distinction). In turn, judges have developed practical and principled responses to manage evidence in judicial review cases and to ensure an appropriately restrained role for the courts.

Second, the rise of proportionality has made factual assessments in judicial review of legislation inevitable. Here, on the practical side, judges are drawn into determinations about legislative facts and, on the principled side, to reviewing legislative value judgements about complex matters of policy. In response, judges have attempted to turn legislative facts into adjudicative facts, walled off areas of legislative action from direct judicial interference, and developed mechanisms of judicial restraint.

Third, judges are called upon to make factual assessments in the context of systemic challenges to the legality of regulatory regimes. Again, there are difficult issues of practice and principle, as judges attempt to understand the operations of such regimes on incomplete information and need to determine whether to strike down entire regimes to remedy demonstrated harms. Recent jurisprudence has highlighted two responses, narrowing the scope for systemic challenges on the one hand, imposing hard-and-fast causation requirements on the other.

Lastly, there is the Canadian phenomenon of factual assessments as part of constitutional causes of action. In the 2010s, there were high-profile examples of the Supreme Court of Canada striking down criminal prohibitions, most notably on sex work and assisted suicide, because of factual evidence adduced at trial about the harms these prohibitions caused. This evidence base permitted the first-instance judges to depart from binding precedent. Putting such authority in the hands of trial courts creates practical and principled difficulties relating to the allocation of resources and decision-making authority in common law systems. Indeed, the Supreme Court of Canada signaled a retreat from these high-profile cases later in the decade. Moreover, on closer inspection both sex work and assisted suicide involved distinct legal prohibitions, without any administrative actors exercising discretionary power: wherever discretion exists in a regulatory regime, however (as is much more common), the limitations on systemic challenges will kick in to alleviate practical and principled difficulties.

Our posture in this chapter has been descriptive and analytical, rather than normative. We take no firm view on the seriousness of the practical and principled difficulties we have identified or of the appropriateness of the judicial responses we have noted. There is, however, no doubt that factual assessments now play an increasingly important role in public law adjudication and that with this role comes practical and principled difficulties which call for judicial responses.

3

Parliaments and Facts: Deepening Deliberation

GABRIELLE APPLEBY AND ANNE CARTER

In Australia, the adoption by the High Court of an explicit, structured test of proportionality to assess limitations on constitutional freedoms presents fresh challenges for the relationship between courts and parliaments. In particular, it prompts consideration of whether, and how, the courts can assess and rely upon, or defer to, the fact-finding and deliberations of parliaments. Judicial reliance, or deference, raises the possibility that the judicial-legislative interaction might encourage parliaments to engage in more informed, in-depth and transparent deliberations about highly contested issues involving conflicting constitutional values. In this way, these recent doctrinal developments in proportionality bring with them the possibility of enhancing the institutional strengths of legislatures as constitutional agents, and enhancing the relationship between legislatures and the people. In this chapter we look specifically at the nature of parliamentary deliberation and what counts as what we term 'fair deliberation' by parliaments. We develop a series of criteria or standards by which courts might review the robustness of parliamentary enquiries. These criteria have been developed with a view to deepening parliamentary deliberations about constitutional freedoms and their limitations, rather than formalising or judicialising the legislative process.

The chapter proceeds in three parts. Part I examines the relationship between courts and parliaments in the context of the implied freedom of political communication. It begins by outlining the test of structured proportionality, focusing on the nature of the task to be conducted by courts, and the crucial role of facts in performing that task. We also consider the High Court's position in relation to 'deference' or 'restraint', and how this manifests itself in relation to questions of fact. Building upon our previous work,[1] we adopt a 'spectrum of inter-institutional relations' to analyse the relationship between courts and parliaments. This spectrum

---

[1] G Appleby and A Carter, 'Parliaments, Proportionality and Facts' (2021) 43(3) *Sydney Law Review* 259.

consists of five different positions at which a court *may* engage with parliamentary fact-finding and deliberation. The next question, which we address in Part II, is the need for a robust set of criteria by which courts can assess the nature of parliamentary deliberation. We explain the purpose of such criteria, and also address the risks inherent in articulating criteria in this way. Finally, in Part III we begin the task of sketching out criteria that reflect Australia's unique constitutional setting.

I. Proportionality, Deference and Fact-Finding

In many respects, Australia has come late to the conversation about the relationship between courts and parliaments[2] in the application of proportionality testing, and the appropriateness and level of deference to be accorded to parliamentary fact finding and deliberation in that exercise. This is largely because of a paucity of rights instruments and, indeed, the High Court's forays into this arena have occurred primarily in relation to constitutional limitations on power protecting freedom of political expression and freedom of trade. This late entry has meant the High Court has been able to engage with relatively well-developed jurisprudence from jurisdictions such as the United Kingdom, Europe and Canada. But this has not been a simple legal transplant. Rather, the process of adopting a proportionality test has demonstrated the need to develop an inter-institutional relationship between courts and parliaments that is tailored to Australia's unique constitutional context. Australia's experience has also revealed that, even in more jurisprudentially developed comparator jurisdictions, there remains a lack of clarity as to the role of fact finding in proportionality analysis, and the roles and intersection of courts and parliaments in relation to that exercise.

In this chapter, we look specifically at the High Court of Australia's jurisprudence on the implied freedom of political communication, where the adoption and development of structured proportionality testing has been most developed.[3] Since 2015, a majority of the Court has clarified that a key part of determining the constitutional validity of a particular measure that burdens political communication will be whether it nonetheless is 'proportionate' in its pursuit of a legitimate objective according to a three-part structured proportionality test.[4] Structured

---

[2] We are referring to 'parliament' in the sense of any parliament of the Commonwealth, a State or Territory whose legislation is subject to a constitutional challenge.

[3] We note that, more recently, a majority of the High Court of Australia has adopted a similar structured proportionality test in relation to the freedom of interstate trade and commerce in s 92 of the Australian Constitution: *Palmer v Western Australia* (2021) 95 ALJR 299.

[4] See *McCloy v New South Wales* (2015) 257 CLR 178, where a slim majority of four justices introduced a structured proportionality test that modified the existing 'reasonably appropriate and adapted' test established in *Lange v Australian Broadcasting Corporation* (1997) 189 CLR 520, 567. This structured proportionality test has been endorsed and developed in subsequent cases: see, eg, *Clubb v Edwards; Preston v Avery* (2019) 267 CLR 171, 199–202 [64]–[74] (Kiefel CJ, Bell and Keane JJ), 264–9 [266]–[275] (Nettle J), 329–45 [461]–[500] (Edelman J); *Comcare v Banerji* (2019) 267 CLR 373, 400 [32] (Kiefel CJ, Bell, Keane and Nettle JJ), 451[188] (Edelman J).

proportionality, developed in German administrative law but now commonly used in rights jurisprudence internationally, requires asking questions about whether a law is suitable, that is, whether it has a rational connection to the objective; whether it is reasonably necessary in the sense there is no obvious and compelling alternative means of achieving the same purpose which has a less restrictive effect on the freedom; and whether it is proportionate in the strict sense of balancing the importance of the objective and the extent of the restriction on the freedom.[5]

The application of this proportionality test needs to be informed by facts about the legislative measures and the wider policy setting in which they have been developed.[6] This factual context includes, for instance, information about the intended purpose of the provision, how the law will operate in practice given the policy, social and other factors that exist, the likely consequences or effects, and the availability, efficacy and practicality of alternative measures. The problem of ascertaining facts raises the question that we are concerned with in this chapter: the extent to which courts must alone determine these facts and decisions, or whether parliaments must, or can, produce evidence in support of their own decisions about the proportionality of the particular measure.[7] This, then, raises a further question about procedure: how will courts be satisfied that a parliament itself has not just considered the relevant facts, but has undertaken relevant factual enquiries in such a way that warrants a level of judicial restraint, or deference.

In the more recent Australian implied freedom cases, there are some signs that the High Court is prepared to look at parliamentary fact finding and deliberation to support the Court's reasoning. However, while the recent cases reveal a growing awareness of the fact-sensitive nature of the different stages of the proportionality enquiry, there is no consistent, or at least explicit, framework for when or how to evaluate the fact finding and deliberations undertaken by parliaments. Indeed, the judicial reference to the relevance of parliamentary deliberations has manifested in noticeably different ways. In *Unions NSW v New South Wales [No 2]*, the New South Wales Parliament had failed to make enquiries into how proposed expenditure limits for third-party campaigners would affect the ability of these organisations to campaign.[8] Such an enquiry had been recommended by a parliamentary

---

[5] For an introduction to the literature on the basis and nature of structured proportionality, see A Barak, *Proportionality: Constitutional Rights and their Limitations* (Cambridge, Cambridge University Press, 2012); M Cohen-Eliya and I Porat, *Proportionality and Constitutional Culture* (Cambridge, Cambridge University Press, 2013); G Huscroft, BW Miller and G Webber (eds), *Proportionality and the Rule of Law: Rights, Justification, Reasoning* (New York, Cambridge University Press, 2014); VC Jackson, 'Constitutional Law in an Age of Proportionality' (2015) 124(8) *Yale Law Journal* 3094.

[6] A Carter, *Proportionality and Facts in Constitutional Adjudication* (Oxford, Hart Publishing, 2021) ch 2. See also A Carter, 'Constitutional Convergence? Some Lessons from Proportionality' in M Elliott, JNE Varuhas and SW Stark (eds), *The Unity of Public Law? Doctrinal, Theoretical and Comparative Perspectives* (Oxford, Hart Publishing, 2018) 373, 380–2.

[7] In answering this question, we draw heavily on our previously published work, Appleby and Carter (n 1).

[8] (2019) 264 CLR 595.

committee, but no evidence was presented or considered by the Parliament before the enactment of the measure.[9] In *Clubb v Edwards; Preston v Avery*, decided in the same year, the High Court considered the constitutional validity of safe access zones around abortion clinics.[10] In applying the structured proportionality test, the Court engaged with various evidentiary materials (including statements of compatibility and psychological evidence) that had been before the Victorian and Tasmanian Parliaments in the course of their deliberations before enacting the safe-access zone legislation.

These cases raise, but leave largely unanswered, a number of important questions. First, there is the issue of whether there is a burden of justification on parliaments when passing measures that burden the freedom of political communication. Second, and relatedly, there is the issue of when and how courts should treat material presented to and considered by parliaments during the passage of the impugned law.

The relationship between courts and parliaments in this setting is often approached through the conceptual framework of 'deference' or 'restraint',[11] referring to the weight afforded to the decisions of other constitutional branches of government. In Australia the High Court has, in the past, been reluctant to embrace any general theory of 'deference', claiming that such a concept is at odds with the Court's constitutional role as the final interpreter of the constitutional text.[12] More recently, however, some members of the High Court have indicated that notions of deference might inform the Court's approach to its responsibilities of judicial review in the context of the implied freedom.[13] This accords with the views of commentators who have urged the Court to reconsider its outright rejection of deference[14] and instead take a more nuanced approach that considers the types of enquiries and the nature of the body performing the task.

This more nuanced approach focuses attention on the normative and empirical justifications for deference. The legislature, as the representative constitutional institution, is often considered to be the most appropriate body to investigate and

---

[9] ibid 618 [53] (Kiefel, Bell and Keane JJ); see also 633 [100] (Gageler J), 648–51 [145]–[153] (Gordon J).

[10] *Clubb v Edwards; Preston v Avery* (n 4).

[11] See, eg, C Chan, 'A Preliminary Framework for Measuring Deference in Rights Reasoning' (2016) 14(4) *International Journal of Constitutional Law* 851, 854; JA King, 'Institutional Approaches to Judicial Restraint' (2008) 28(3) *Oxford Journal of Legal Studies* 409; M Hunt, 'Sovereignty's Blight: Why Contemporary Public Law Needs the Concept of "Due Deference"' in N Bamforth and P Leyland (eds), *Public Law in a Multi-Layered Constitution* (Oxford, Hart Publishing, 2003) 337, 340; TRS Allan, 'Human Rights and Judicial Review: A Critique of "Due Deference"' (2006) 65(3) *Cambridge Law Journal* 671; A Kavanagh, *Constitutional Review under the UK Human Rights Act* (Cambridge, Cambridge University Press, 2009) ch 7.

[12] See, eg, *McCloy* (n 4) 220 [90].

[13] See, eg, *Libertyworks v Commonwealth* (2021) 95 ALJR 490, 536 [201] (Edelman J); 552 [288] (Steward J). See also J Stellios, 'The High Court on Constitutional Law: The 2021 Term "Marking out the Limits of Judicial Review"' (ANU College of Law Research Paper No 22.8, February 2022) 63.

[14] M Wesson, '*Unions NSW v New South Wales [No 2]*: Unresolved Issues for the Implied Freedom of Political Communication' (2019) 23(1) *Media and Arts Law Review* 93, 102.

determine contested questions of policy and to reconcile conflicting interests. The legislature also has particular institutional powers, competence and expertise to investigate and determine the necessary factual issues to answer the proportionality questions.[15] To say that the legislature is the most appropriate constitutional institution to engage in these processes of fact-finding and deliberation raises the question of whether it *has* actually engaged in these processes, and whether it has done so *satisfactorily*. Using this more nuanced approach, any deference must be demonstrated or 'earned', and not simply assumed.[16]

This approach to deference and scrutiny is informed by the actual practice of the relevant parliament in a particular case. Cora Chan, writing in the context of the UK's Human Rights Act 1998, has disaggregated first-order reasons (the substance or merit of parliament's deliberations) and second-order reasons (the institutional competence and legitimacy of parliament).[17] In relation to *when* a court should exercise restraint or deference, Chan argues the court should enquire into institutional competence and democratic legitimacy. That is, the court should require evidence of the degree to which the legislature actually has the specific competence or expertise to decide a particular issue.[18] Under Chan's conception of deference, the level of restraint or scrutiny can be scaled to reflect the legislature's specific competence or expertise in a particular case.

When understood in this way, deference can be seen as part of an iterative inter-institutional relationship between courts and parliaments. Judicial responsiveness to the practice of the legislature, for example, is consistent with the idea that the different branches of government should interact and engage with one another in a way in which enhances their institutional strengths as constitutional agents. Liora Lazarus and Natasha Simonsen, also writing in the UK context, have argued that, in applying structured tests of proportionality, the court can develop its doctrine in a way that complements and enhances the institutional strengths of each branch of government.[19] Judicial review of proportionality testing, if done in a careful and responsive way, can enhance the legislature's 'culture of justification',[20] strengthening the constitutional relationship between the legislature and the people.[21]

---

[15] Note, in the US context it has been argued that the legislature's fact finding superiority should not be automatically assumed: see CE Borgmann, 'Rethinking Judicial Deference to Legislative Fact-Finding' (2009) 84 *Indiana Law Journal* 1.

[16] Hunt (n 11) 340.

[17] C Chan, 'Proportionality and Invariable Baseline Intensity of Review' (2013) 33(1) *Legal Studies* 1, 12.

[18] ibid.

[19] L Lazarus and N Simonsen, 'Judicial Review and Parliamentary Debate: Enriching the Doctrine of Due Deference' in M Hunt, HJ Hooper and P Yowell (eds), *Parliaments and Human Rights: Redressing the Democratic Deficit* (Oxford, Hart Publishing, 2015) 386.

[20] E Mureinik, 'A Bridge to Where? Introducing the Interim Bill of Rights' (1994) 10(1) *South African Journal of Human Rights* 31, 32.

[21] ibid; D Dyzenhaus, 'Law as Justification: Etienne Mureinik's Conception of Legal Culture' (1998) 14(1) *South African Journal of Human Rights* 11; M Cohen-Eliya and I Porat, 'Proportionality and the Culture of Justification' (2011) 59(2) *American Journal of Comparative Law* 463.

A. A Spectrum of Institutional Inter-relations

How can one calibrate the correct level of scrutiny, to ensure courts maintain their proper constitutional role in relation to judicial review, while providing inter-institutional respect to, and incentives for, parliaments? To help answer this question, we have developed a 'spectrum of inter-institutional relations'. The spectrum is both relational and iterative, and consists of five different positions at which a court *may* engage with parliamentary fact finding and deliberations. The key points along our spectrum can be described as illustrated below in Figure 1.[22]

Figure 3.1 Proportionality on a spectrum of inter-institutional relations

At one end of the spectrum, Position 1, there is what we term '*full restraint*', where a court accepts or gives conclusive weight to the decisions of a parliament – that is, parliament's fact finding and the deliberations about those facts. This position accepts as superior the institutional competencies of legislatures and provides no independent assessment. In the UK, Aileen Kavanagh has explained this as judicial respect for the views of the legislature as meaning 'the decision embodied in the statute itself'.[23]

At the opposite end of the spectrum, Position 5, is what we term '*no restraint*', where a court places no weight on the views of the relevant parliament and proceeds instead to form its own view on all the relevant factual matters (including conducting its own fact finding). Under this position, the court affords no inter-institutional deference, whether on democratic or empirical grounds, to the superiority of the legislature. There is, thus, no review of the quality of parliamentary fact finding or deliberation.

Between these two extremes there are three potential positions: '*non-evaluative restraint*' (Position 2), '*process evaluation*' (Position 3) and '*process evaluation + unreasonableness review*' (Position 4). Under '*non-evaluative restraint*', if the court can be satisfied that the legislature has engaged with the relevant question, this is sufficient. This might be in the form of:

- explanatory memoranda, second reading speeches and debate in the Parliament;

---

[22] Figure 1 originally published in Appleby and Carter (n 1) 272.
[23] A Kavanagh, 'Proportionality and Parliamentary Debates: Exploring Some Forbidden Territory' (2014) 34(3) *Oxford Journal of Legal Studies* 443, 444.

- the work of parliamentary committees that support the Houses and parliamentarians (including submissions and evidence received by these committees and their reports); and
- other material considered by the Parliament (such as, rights-related statements of compatibility, reports of other bodies such as anti-corruption commissions, law reform bodies or royal commissions).

However, the court still exercises considerable restraint and does not engage in any review beyond the existence of the legislative consideration. The review is, therefore, largely formalistic and might even be described merely as a 'tick-the-box' exercise.

In contrast to *'non-evaluative restraint'*, under *'process evaluation'* a court engages with the substance of the parliamentary fact finding and deliberative processes. This is the first position in which the court is required to undertake a robust procedural review of the legislature's engagement with the relevant enquiries in the proportionality analysis. The court does not take at face value claims parliament is empirically and institutionally superior but will review the evidence of what the legislature has done in a particular case. As explained above, any respect to be accorded to parliament must be 'earned'.[24] If a court adopts *'process evaluation'* review, it will require evidence of two matters:

(a) Evidence of the public deliberations of the Parliament so as to review the scope of the legislative enquiry and deliberation. This is likely to be led by government parties defending the legislation.
(b) Evidence that will allow the court to evaluate the legislative processes, including, for instance, the availability of other information that might have – but did not – inform the Parliament's deliberations. This type of evidence is likely to be led by non-government parties or amicus.

This position is still process driven, but it involves an iterative reflexiveness: the court is responsive to a proactive legislature but, equally, it will step in where the legislature has not adequately engaged. Lazarus and Simonsen have referred to a similar idea in the UK context under the rubric of 'deference', noting its ability to create an iterative relationship that enhances democratic processes:

> [R]igorous and respectful judicial examination of democratic processes enhances constitutional dialogue, increases the opportunities for judicial deference, heightens the transparency with which deference is exercised and therefore makes it more likely that deference will be accorded where it has shown to be justified.[25]

The form of process review that is proposed under this position has many similarities with the review that is evident in some decisions of the European Court

---

[24] Hunt (n 11) 340.
[25] Lazarus and Simonsen (n 19) 385 (emphasis added). See also Kavanagh, 'Proportionality and Parliamentary Debates' (n 23) 479.

of Human Rights (and other European trans-national and domestic courts) and has been referred to as a 'procedural trend', particularly evident in proportionality analysis.[26] In that context, while not abandoning substantive review, the courts appear to be incorporating procedural review into their reasoning.[27] This gives rise to questions about the standard and criteria against which procedural review should be measured, which we address in the final parts of this chapter.

Before moving on from 'process evaluation', it is necessary to note that there are a number of different consequences that might arise from a court finding that the parliamentary fact finding and deliberation have been lacking. The court could simply engage in its own merits review and, based on the material available to it, determine the constitutionality of the challenged measure. Alternatively, it could invalidate a provision without itself undertaking a substantive deliberation of the merits involved. This would create not just an *incentive* for parliament, but a burden to do so.

The next position on our spectrum is 'process evaluation + unreasonableness review', which differs from 'process evaluation' (Position 3) only insofar as it requires a second stage: judicial review of the substantive outcome of the political decision-making process to check for 'unreasonableness'. This is a sort of 'backstop' of judicial review. The court does not end its enquiry after the review and evaluation of the parliamentary processes, but asks whether – based on all the relevant facts and information – the legislature's decision was nonetheless reasonable.[28] There are a number of different consequences that might flow, depending on the court's findings in relation to whether both stage one (process evaluation) and stage two (reasonableness) have been met.

Where the court is satisfied that the parliament did undertake a robust process (ie, conducted relevant enquiries and considered all relevant facts) and, based on that process, did not make an unreasonable decision, the court will not interfere with the parliamentary decision. Where the court is satisfied that the parliament undertook a robust process but nonetheless made an unreasonable decision it will

---

[26] P Popelier, 'The Court as Regulatory Watchdog: The Procedural Approach in the Case Law of the European Court of Human Rights' in P Popelier, A Mazmanyan and W Vandenbruwaene (eds), *The Role of Constitutional Courts in Multilevel Governance* (Cambridge, Intersentia, 2013).

[27] Without reviewing these cases in detail for this chapter, see further *Evans v United Kingdom* [2007] I Eur Court HR 353, 384 [86]; *Hirst v United Kingdom (No 2)* [2005] IX Eur Court HR 187, 215 [79]; *Animal Defenders International v United Kingdom* [2013] II Eur Court HR 203, 236 [114]–[116].

[28] In terms of the concept of 'reasonableness' to be applied, the court may helpfully draw upon the use of the 'unreasonableness' standard in administrative law: a decision that is so unreasonable no reasonable person could arrive at it (*Associated Provincial Picture Houses Ltd v Wednesbury Corporation* [1948] 1 KB 223, 230). Note, however, that the High Court of Australia has more recently developed 'unreasonableness' to include decisions that lack evident and intelligible justification: see, eg, *Minister for Immigration and Citizenship v Li* (2013) 249 CLR 332, 367. These more recent decisions should be approached with caution in the current context as they would likely propel a court into a review of the substantive reasoning process of the Parliament. We have not explored this in further detail here as we are primarily concerned with elaborating the nature of deliberation that is expected of parliaments.

find the legislative provisions invalid. The third option is where the court is not satisfied that the parliament undertook a robust process. In this scenario, the court is left in the same position as it was under in relation to *'process review'* and the same consequences might flow.

B. Locating an Australian Position on the Spectrum

We have previously argued that the Australian position on this spectrum must be informed by the High Court's constitutional role, as well as the Court's understanding of judicial power and its limits.[29] In particular, the Court has repeatedly confirmed that it is the final arbiter of the constitutional text, and that parliaments cannot make conclusive findings of constitutional fact. In other words, parliaments cannot 'recite' themselves into power, and the Court retains responsibility for being satisfied of the existence of constitutional facts.[30] The appropriate position for courts on our proposed spectrum, however, ought also be informed by an appreciation of the constitutional obligations of parliaments within the system given their unique democratic foundations, and the role parliaments play in many spheres because of our system's reliance, particularly in relation to human rights, on political and not legal constitutionalism. In a test of structured proportionality, where there is a need for deliberation around competing interests and values, we argue the High Court should adopt a doctrinal position that provides incentives for more robust inter-institutional constitutional dialogue, drawing on the strengths of each constitutional actor.

For these reasons, it is fairly straightforward to accept that the positions at both extremes are not viable. In addition, Position 2 (*'non-evaluative restraint'*) is also untenable; while this position seems to contemplate *some* review function, in reality, it is likely to be a very weak and formalistic check on parliaments. This leaves *'process evaluation'* and *'process evaluation + unreasonableness review'*. We have argued that the latter is the most desirable and defensible position for the High Court of Australia to adopt. While both positions require courts to undertake a substantive review of parliamentary fact-finding and deliberative processes, and to be informed by appropriate evidence, the added 'backstop' of reasonableness review is most congruent with Australia's constitutional context and the High Court's understanding of its own role. This, then, sets the question that we address in the remainder of the chapter: the types of criteria that the Court might adopt for reviewing the processes of parliaments, and what procedural evidence might be led to satisfy courts of the adequacy of the parliamentary process.

---

[29] Appleby and Carter (n 1) 281–282.
[30] *Australian Communist Party v Commonwealth* (1951) 83 CLR 1, 206. See also KM Hayne, 'Deference: An Australian Perspective' [2011] *Public Law* 75.

II. Criteria and their Limitations

Before commencing to articulate a proposed set of criteria for the Australian context, it is helpful to consider the objective of such criteria. As explained above, our argument is that the adoption of structured proportionality testing presents an opportunity for courts and parliaments to work together to strengthen constitutional deliberation on challenging balancing questions in areas such as freedom of political communication. In the Australian constitutional setting, we have suggested that the courts should evaluate the legislative fact finding and deliberative processes undertaken by parliaments in relation to the three stages of proportionality testing, with an added backstop of '*unreasonableness*' review. This is Position 4 on our proposed spectrum of inter-institutional relations (Figure 3.1).

If such a process-orientated review of parliamentary fact finding and deliberation is to be undertaken, this raises the question *how* are courts to undertake this review? In other words, what standards or criteria should courts use to assess the legislative deliberation?[31] How robust do parliamentary enquiries need to be in any given case? What counts as fair deliberation by parliaments?

A. The Need for Criteria

The overarching aim of the High Court in developing criteria to assess parliamentary engagement must be that such criteria will deepen and strengthen parliamentary deliberation with contested rights issues.[32] As we have observed in our previous scholarship, while the judiciary may be the *ultimate* arbiter of the constitutional text, each branch of government has independent obligations to interpret and apply the Australian Constitution. In developing laws, for instance, often the political branches will have no judicial precedent to guide them.[33]

---

[31] It is worth noting here that there may sometimes be confusion about the terminology to be applied. In the literature, the terms 'method of review' and 'standard of review' are sometimes used interchangeably. In our analysis, structured proportionality testing (of the kind now adopted by the High Court of Australia) is best understood as a 'method of review' as it 'provides the court with a set of questions to be asked': see Kavanagh, *Constitutional Review under the UK Human Rights Act* (n 11) 237. The 'standard of review', on the other hand, refers to the intensity with which the court applies the relevant method of review. For some discussion, see C Henckels, *Proportionality and Deference in Investor-State Arbitration: Balancing Investment Protection and Regulatory Authority* (Cambridge, Cambridge University Press, 2015) 31. The various positions we have set out in Part I, can be understood to import varying levels of deference which alter the standard of review to be applied. The criteria we propose in Part IV help to flesh out how, in practice, the court will carry out this task.

[32] Although Australia lacks an explicit bill of rights, it has a series of express and implied constitutional guarantees. When determining the extent of these guarantees, the Court must make evaluative judgements about whether limitations on these guarantees can be justified. This is particularly evident in the context of the implied freedom of political communication, where structured proportionality reasoning is most developed.

[33] Appleby and Carter (n 1) 269. See also, in the Irish context, C Casey, 'The Constitution Outside the Courts – The Case for Parliamentary Involvement in Constitutional Review' (2019) 61 *Irish Jurist* 36;

In addition, the political and judicial branches have different institutional strengths which bear upon the task of constitutional interpretation.[34] These factors mean that, when setting out criteria for evaluating parliamentary deliberation, we are interested in how the two branches might complement and enhance the institutional strengths of the other.

When it comes to parliamentary engagement, the establishment of clear criteria will provide parliaments with notice of what counts as 'fair deliberation'. That is, the criteria will contain explicit guidance as to the types of enquiries that parliaments ought to undertake to demonstrate that they have properly and substantively engaged with the limitations analysis in question. This will promote transparency in legislative decision-making and will help to ensure that legislative decisions are fully informed and backed by appropriate evidence. Ultimately, it is hoped, developing explicit criteria will encourage parliaments to better engage with their constitutional responsibilities and to better justify to the public, as well as the court, the reasons for their decision-making.

Making more explicit the requirements of parliamentary engagement will, at the same time, strengthen the Court's ability to assess the relevant factual issues. As we set out in Part I, above, the structured proportionality approach now endorsed in Australia by a majority of the High Court is a fact-sensitive test. In applying this test, courts need to be informed by facts about the legislative measures and the wider policy setting in which they have been developed.[35] The development of more explicit criteria for parliamentary deliberation will, it is hoped, increase the evidential record available to courts to inform their own decision-making. In this way, the criteria will work both ways, strengthening the exchange between the judicial and legislative branches.

In order for judicially developed and enforced criteria (such as we propose in Part III, below) to act as an incentive for greater legislative engagement, it is imperative that these criteria are consistently articulated and applied. The Court must be clear not only regarding what it expects of legislative actors, but also how it will respond when the work is done by the parliament. This clear articulation and application of criteria will increase the potential for productive democratic exchange between the courts and the legislature. As Lazarus and Simonsen explain, '[t]he clearer the criteria and the better the reasoning used by the courts when taking a view on the democratic deliberative process, the greater the potential for focused democratic dialogue between the arms of the state'.[36]

---

and, in the Canadian context, V MacDonnell, 'The Constitution as Framework for Governance' (2013) 63 *University of Toronto Law Journal* 624; V MacDonnell, 'The Civil Servant's Role in the Implementation of Constitutional Rights' (2015) 13 *International Journal of Constitutional Law* 383.

[34] Appleby and Carter (n 1) 269. See also M Tushnet, 'Interpretation in Legislatures and Courts: Incentives and Institutional Design' in R Bauman and T Kahana (eds) *The Least Examined Branch: The Role of Legislatures in the Constitutional State* (Cambridge, Cambridge University Press, 2006) 355.

[35] See the discussion at text accompanying n 6.

[36] Lazarus and Simonsen (n 19) 393.

B. Dangers and Limitations

Despite the benefits of the High Court articulating clear criteria for legislative deliberation, there are also risks. First, it is imperative that any criteria are tailored to the distinctive Australian constitutional setting. The criteria developed by other scholars upon which we draw (in Part III below) were developed in the UK context. The UK's Human Rights Act 1998, as well as the overarching role played by the European Court of Human Rights, are obvious points of difference compared to the Australian context. Australia notoriously lacks a bill of rights at the federal level.[37] While there are some express rights contained in the Australian Constitution, more significant in practice has been the advent of implied limitations on legislative power, most notably the implied freedom of political communication.[38] Another distinctive feature of Australian constitutionalism is the separation of judicial power from the executive and legislative power. The strictness with which this separation has been interpreted by the High Court, combined with the dominant influence of formalistic Dixonian legalism as an interpretative approach, means the Court's own role has been tightly confined.[39] Despite these differences in context, the common nature of the task required of judges in applying structured proportionality means some guidance can be sought from other jurisdictions.

Apart from these issues of jurisdictional context, there is also the danger that articulating the criteria might serve to hamper, rather than strengthen, proper parliamentary engagement. In particular, any criteria must be carefully developed so that parliaments are not able to simply adopt the language of proportionality without actually engaging in the substance of the issue. What we are trying to avoid is the potential for a 'tick-a-box' approach where parliaments pay lip service to the test of proportionality but fail to engage in meaningful deliberation. The risk is that any proposed criteria, rather than deepening parliamentary deliberation, may in practice serve to undermine it. As Kavanagh observes, there is a concern that articulating a judicial approach to deference might lead to 'slapdash debate' or 'a rhetorical or superficial nod to … rights'.[40] Yet, as Kavanagh herself acknowledges, we can and should expect more of our democratic institutions. Just as we expect parliaments to engage in a holistic and rigorous fact finding and deliberative

---

[37] B Galligan and FL Morton, 'Australian Exceptionalism: Rights Protection without a Bill of Rights' in T Campbell, J Goldsworthy and A Stone (eds), *Protecting Rights without a Bill of Rights: Institutional Performance and Reform in Australia* (Aldershot, Ashgate, 2006) 18. Note there are a number of state and territory rights instruments, such as the Human Rights Act 2004 (ACT), Charter of Human Rights and Responsibilities Act 2006 (Vic) and the Human Rights Act 2019 (Qld).

[38] A Stone, 'Australia's Constitutional Rights and the Problem of Interpretive Disagreement' (2005) 27 *Sydney Law Review* 29.

[39] For some discussion see M Foster, 'The Separation of Judicial Power' in C Saunders and A Stone (eds), *The Oxford Handbook of the Australian Constitution* (Oxford, Oxford University Press, 2018) 672; A Stone, 'Judicial Reasoning' in C Saunders and A Stone (eds), *The Oxford Handbook of the Australian Constitution* (Oxford, Oxford University Press, 2018) 472.

[40] Kavanagh, 'Proportionality and Parliamentary Debates' (n 23) 472.

processes so, too, we expect courts to be able to distinguish genuine deliberation from rhetorical flourishes.

C. Parliamentary Privilege

The development of criteria by which courts can review the proceedings and deliberations of parliament may also raise questions of parliamentary privilege. In particular, it raises the question of just how far the court can scrutinise or probe the deliberations of the legislative branch. The doctrine of parliamentary privilege, with its roots in the English Westminster tradition, exists to protect the independence and functions of Parliament.[41] One important dimension of parliamentary privilege is the protection it provides to enable individual Members of Parliament to speak freely in the discharge of their constitutional functions and to the internal workings of Parliament itself.[42] This has its origins in Article 9 of the Bill of Rights 1689, which provides that 'the freedom of speech and debates or proceedings in Parliament ought not to be impeached or questioned in any court or place out of Parliament'. In Australia, this finds constitutional and legislative embodiment at both Commonwealth and State level.[43]

The question of when it is permissible for courts to review the proceedings of parliament pivots on the *purpose* for which the parliamentary process is being reviewed. In the UK context, which has historically been more conservative than Australia, Kavanagh has drawn a helpful distinction to resolve this conundrum. She distinguishes between the 'quality of the substantive reasons' offered by MPs during parliamentary debate and the 'quality of the decision-making process in Parliament'.[44] The former are beyond the reach of judicial review, whereas the latter should fall within the court's competency and jurisdiction.[45] We agree with Kavanagh that a focus on the quality of decision-making *process* of a parliament – rather than the substantive merits of Parliament's decision – is appropriate in the Australian context. In particular, it allows courts to avoid parliamentary free-speech issues under Article 9 of the Bill of Rights 1689 and to avoid intruding into matters covered by parliamentary privilege. So, where a court is scrutinising parliamentary processes for the purpose of reviewing whether the parliament meaningfully engaged in the rights analysis, so that the court can apply structured proportionality testing, it seems unlikely to fall foul of parliamentary privilege.

---

[41] E Campbell, *Parliamentary Privilege in Australia* (Sydney, Federation Press, 2003) 1.

[42] Note there is a distinction between the rights and immunities of members of Parliament individually and those of the houses of Parliament collectively, but there is a correlation between the two: see G Griffith, *Parliamentary Privilege: Major Developments and Current Issues* (NSW Parliamentary Library Service, 2007) 3–4.

[43] Campbell (n 41) 10; G Griffith, 'Parliamentary Privilege: First Principles and Recent Applications' (2009) 24(2) *Australasian Parliamentary Review* 71, 72.

[44] Kavanagh, 'Proportionality and Parliamentary Debates' (n 23) 476.

[45] ibid 465.

In addition, of course, courts in Australia, and elsewhere in the Westminster tradition, already frequently refer to parliamentary materials without violating the sanctity of parliamentary privilege. Historically, courts in the common law tradition were prohibited from referring to parliamentary materials (as well as other materials such as commissioners' reports, white papers and explanatory memoranda) for the purposes of statutory interpretation on the basis of parliamentary privilege.[46] In the UK, the 1992 decision of the House of Lords in *Pepper v Hart* heralded a significant shift, and these materials can now be utilised as an aid to interpretation.[47] Australia progressed more quickly in this regard than the UK and, in 1984, the Acts Interpretation Act 1901 (Cth) was amended to allow reference to *Hansard* if certain conditions were satisfied.[48] In Australia, courts are now required to consider the 'context' in which legislation was enacted at the outset (ie, not merely in cases of ambiguity) and context includes parliamentary materials.[49]

With respect to the criteria we develop below – which aim to interrogate the *process* by which parliaments decided to enact particular legislative provisions – while a court will need to look at a range of parliamentary materials to assess the adequacy of the process, this will not be to call into question the proceedings of parliament. Instead, it is the *process* of engagement adopted by parliament that the court is interested in, not the merits or substance of the decision itself. As Kavanagh suggests, this focus on the 'quality of the decision-making process' of parliament should not fall within what is the 'forbidden territory'.[50]

III. Judicial Evaluation of Legislative Fact-finding and Deliberation: A Proposed Approach

In this part, we articulate a proposed set of criteria that the High Court might apply when undertaking structured proportionality testing. These criteria, as explained above, are designed to enable courts to properly scrutinise parliamentary decision-making and to ensure that any deference, or respect, is appropriately justified.

The task of setting criteria has been attempted by others. We build upon these earlier analyses in developing our own, distinctively Australian, criteria. As foreshadowed above, we draw upon the work of Kavanagh, and Lazarus and Simonsen, who have sought to articulate criteria by which parliamentary processes can be evaluated in the UK context. When determining whether courts should interfere with parliamentary decisions, Kavanagh advocates for broad standards that reflect

---

[46] JG Magyar, 'The Slow Death of a Dogma? The Prohibition on Legislative History in the 20th Century' (2021) 50 *Common Law World Review* 120.
[47] [1993] AC 593.
[48] Magyar (n 46) 142; J Dharmananda, 'Using Parliamentary Material in Interpretation: Insights from Parliamentary Process' (2018) 41 *University of New South Wales Law Journal* 4.
[49] Dharmananda (n 48) 9.
[50] Kavanagh, 'Proportionality and Parliamentary Debates' (n 23) 465.

the concepts of focus, deliberation and participation. Lazarus and Simonsen are more prescriptive, setting out a number of distinct criteria that are intended to assess the quality of the legislative process, and thus determine the presumption of judicial deference to parliamentary choice. Given Kavanagh, Lazarus and Simonsen all write from the UK context, and draw upon the same series of European Court of Human Rights cases, it is unsurprising that there are similarities in the criteria that they propose.[51]

Kavanaugh's criteria starts with a relatively straightforward requirement that there is a legislative *focus* on the human rights issue. That is, was the issue 'squarely addressed' by the legislature?[52] This requirement is not expressed, but implicit in Lazarus and Simonsen's criteria.

Lazarus and Simonsen begin their criteria with the question of the 'representative conditions' within which the parliament's democratic debate takes place.[53] Under this criterion, the court would ask 'whether parliament can demonstrate engagement with the otherwise unrepresented voices of the minority'[54] and, more particularly, 'those whose rights would be affected'. This is about 'degree of participation and the quality of the representation involved'.[55] Lazarus and Simonsen postulate that this might even include judicial notice of the 'shape and make-up of the particular democratic legislature', as well as the parliamentary mechanisms directed at human rights deliberation and the representation of minority views in those fora.[56] Kavanagh, similarly, places weight on the representative nature of parliamentary deliberation when formulating her criteria for deference. She describes this in terms of 'participation' or, whether 'the opposing views [were] fully represented in [the] deliberation?'.[57] This enquiry, she adds, contains an evaluative dimension, as the question requires attention be given to whether the relevant views were *'adequately represented'*.[58] This requirement, whether expressed in terms of participation or representation, can be seen as an aspect of parliament's institutional (representative) superiority, one of the traditional reasons for according deference. However, as foreshadowed in Part I above, for both Kavanagh and Lazarus and Simonsen any such superiority is not to be assumed, but must be demonstrated.

In addition to this requirement for participation or representation, the existing criteria developed in the UK also suggest the need to evaluate the quality

---

[51] Lazarus and Simonsen (n 19) include in their criteria the contextual consideration, 'the Courts' democratic mandate, institutional role and place in constitutional culture' (at 398–400). We have incorporated this analysis into our development of the spectrum of review, thus do not include it in our separate consideration of scrutiny criteria in this section.
[52] Kavanagh, 'Proportionality and Parliamentary Debates' (n 23) 464.
[53] Lazarus and Simonson (n 19) 394.
[54] ibid.
[55] ibid 395.
[56] ibid 396.
[57] Kavanagh, 'Proportionality and Parliamentary Debates' (n 23) 463.
[58] ibid 463–4.

and nature of the deliberation by parliament. Kavanagh, for instance, notes that there must be 'active parliamentary deliberation' on the relevant issues.[59] This, Kavanaugh explains, has an 'evaluative dimension' as it requires scrutinising whether the issue was 'fully debated'.[60] Lazarus and Simonsen's criteria are much more detailed with respect to the requirements of fulsome debate. They argue that three matters should be subject to scrutiny. The first is an evaluation of the 'quality of the legislative attention given to the concerns of the affected rights-bearers'.[61] Here, they draw on the concept of 'meaningful engagement', as has been developed in South African constitutional jurisprudence. Meaningful engagement is a process requirement, and is not outcome focused. The second is an assessment of the justifications proffered by the government for the introduction of the measure, and whether alternatives were considered within the context of the broader policy problem.[62] This can be seen as a form of deference on empirical grounds, as it involves assessing whether the parliament was actually empirically better placed to make the assessment. Finally, Lazarus and Simonsen argue the Court must assess the nature of the right being infringed, and accept that, ultimately, some rights should not be infringed regardless of the quality of the legislative debate. This is defending an ultimate judicial backstop, but it also raises an important question as to whether the nature of the right and the nature of the infringement itself formed part of the legislative deliberation.

Expanding and modifying the criteria proposed by Kavanagh, Lazarus and Simonsen, we propose *four criteria*, responsive and tailored to the Australian constitutional positions of the judiciary and the parliament:

1. *Did parliament consider the relevant issues?* This first criterion is a factual enquiry, amounting to a measure of whether the relevant parliament considered matters that pertain to the three steps of structured proportionality testing, regardless of the language that was used in legislative debate.[63] As explained above, we wish to avoid parliaments adopting a formulaic or 'tick-a-box' approach; therefore, it is not the language used by parliament but whether the relevant matters were considered. This criteria can be seen as analogous to Kavanaugh's *'focus'*, or 'squarely addressing' the issue.

2. *Did parliament hear from relevant interests?* This second criterion is a further factual enquiry, about whose interests were heard and considered during the legislative debate. Were all the relevant interests, including those who stand to have their rights affected by the measure, as well as those who stand to

---

[59] ibid 463.
[60] ibid 464.
[61] Lazarus and Simonson (n 19) 396.
[62] ibid 397.
[63] Indeed, Lazarus and Simonsen (n 19) at 398 note that 'moral arguments about rights or their limitations may be present even when the language of rights is not explicit'.

gain by it, heard during the legislative deliberation? These voices may be articulated via different platforms: for instance, through the direct contributions of parliamentarians to legislative debate, or through submissions and evidence provided to parliamentary committees. These platforms themselves will not necessarily be of equal weight. For instance, views presented through a submission to a parliamentary committee may not ultimately be referred to in the final report or in the parliamentary debates. The mere opportunity to make a submission is significantly different to having one's interests and concerns articulated during a second reading speech by the Minister responsible for the Bill.

An assessment of whether parliament heard from relevant interests will, therefore, also require an evaluative exercise. That is, it is not just a matter of whether the relevant interests were *there*, but there must also be a qualitative assessment which examines the nature and breadth of the concerns and whether they were adequately articulated before the legislature. In order to make the necessary evaluation, the court will need to be aware not only of what materials or submissions were presented to the parliament, but also other empirical materials (from third-party sources) about the nature and scope of interests and their concerns regarding the measure. In a matter before the court, this will likely be presented by the party or parties challenging the legislation, or this could be supplemented by submissions and materials provided to the court by interveners or amicus curiae.[64]

3. *Did parliament consider relevant alternatives?* The third criterion asks whether parliament had before it evidence as to the possible alternative measures, and the broader policy context in which those alternatives were considered and rejected by the government. This is directly relevant to the necessity stage of proportionality testing, which is the most heavily fact-dependent stage of the enquiry.[65]

This will be more than an identification of whether there was discussion of policy alternatives, as it will involve an evaluative analysis of whether *all* genuine alternatives were considered and assessed before parliament accepted the necessity of the legislative measure. Where a matter is challenged before the Court, it is likely that the information required to undertake this assessment will be supplied by the party/parties challenging the legislation, and potentially supplemented by submissions and materials provided by interveners or amicus curiae.[66]

---

[64] See, eg, G Appleby, 'Functionalism in Constitutional Interpretation: Factual and Participatory Challenges: Commentary on Dixon' (2015) 43(3) *Federal Law Review* 493; S Kenny, 'Interveners and Amici Curiae in the High Court' (1998) 20 *Adelaide Law Review* 159.

[65] Carter, *Proportionality and Facts in Constitutional Adjudication* (n 6) 34–35.

[66] See references at n 64.

4. *Did parliament deliberate fairly on the material?* The fourth criteria involves the court undertaking an evaluation of the legislative deliberation of the relevant factual material. This is not an evaluation of the *outcome* of the deliberation; that is, it does not involve asking whether the parliament reached the 'right' assessments when balancing different interests. Rather, it involves interrogating the nature of the deliberative process that led to the challenged measure being adopted. So, although it is process orientated, it still requires evaluation. As Mary Scudder writes, in developing her theory of listening in democratic deliberation, 'fair consideration' or 'uptake' (in this case, by a parliament, as assessed by reference to its deliberative record) requires that 'deliberative inputs are duly evaluated in the deliberative process'.[67] It does not, according to Scudder, require that such inputs 'will be reflected in the particular direction of the decision itself'.[68] Our criteria of fair deliberation also draws on the ideas articulated by Lazarus and Simonsen: whether there was engagement with the justifications posited by the government, whether reasonable policy alternatives were not just identified, but evaluated by the parliament in the broader policy context, and whether the parliament engaged in a balancing of the competing interests, particularly those interests that stand to be adversely affected by the policy, and those that stand to benefit from it.[69]

When applying this criterion of fair deliberation, the court will necessarily use proxies for fair deliberation: ultimately, whether the legislature has *genuinely* considered the matters that are part of its public record is a cultural question beyond the review of the courts. However, the court can review the deliberative record, and, in doing so, encourage that record to more accurately reflect the requirements of genuine deliberation. This might include:

- whether the legislative record and debate accurately reflects the concerns of the relevant interests;
- whether the legislative record and debate engages critically with the justification for the policy measure;
- whether the legislative record and debate engages critically with alternatives to the policy measure, given the full policy context in which the measure has been proposed as the most appropriate option; and
- whether the legislative record and debate engages with the relative weight between the seriousness of the constitutional incursions, and the weight of the justification.

---

[67] M Scudder, *Beyond Empathy and Inclusion: The Challenges of Listening in Democratic Deliberation* (New York, Oxford University Press, 2020) 38.
[68] ibid.
[69] Lazarus and Simonsen (n 19).

IV. Conclusion

When applying structured proportionality testing it is the courts, as the ultimate arbiters of the Constitution, which must reach a conclusion about whether a given measure is or is not proportionate. Yet, in applying this test, courts may have regard to the extent to which the relevant parliament itself undertook enquiries. We have suggested that it is appropriate and, indeed, defensible, for courts in Australia to undertake substantive review of parliamentary fact-finding and deliberative processes, informed by appropriate evidence, with the added 'backstop' of reasonableness review. In this chapter we take the project further, developing a set of criteria by which courts can evaluate the robustness of parliamentary deliberation. By articulating and applying these criteria, the High Court will provide concrete guidance to parliaments as to the type and nature of deliberation that is expected. This will, it is hoped, encourage parliaments to better engage with their constitutional responsibilities, and to better justify the reasons for their decision-making. At the same time, the development of more explicit criteria will increase the evidentiary record before the courts, thereby strengthening their ability to assess the relevant factual issues. In this way, the development of criteria works in both directions, ultimately increasing the potential for productive democratic exchange between the judicial and legislative branches.

4

One Important Role of Facts in Constitutional Adjudication

PATRICK EMERTON AND JAYANI NADARAJALINGAM[*]

I. Introduction

This chapter aims to analyse and explain a certain sort of legal reasoning. Its particular focus is adjudication pertaining to certain constitutional implications, and the examples that it uses are Australian ones. We think, however, that the account may be amenable to broader application – though this chapter will not do more than hint at or point towards such possibilities.

Like other constitutions, the Australian Constitution contains various political mandates: it sets out requirements concerning political events that must occur, and political institutions that must exist. These mandates give rise to adjudicative questions which can generate controversy beyond the ordinary controversy that may attend judicial decision-making: they are concerned with central political questions (such as which institutions may or must exist within a political community); and the adjudicative answers given in relation to them have a particular sort of finality, because of the special status of constitutional determinations.[1] In the Australian case, for instance, the Constitution – and the results of constitutional adjudication, which in the Australian legal system are taken to have the force of declarations of constitutional requirements[2] – are binding on all people and institutions within the country.[3]

---

[*] We thank the participants at the 2019 'Facts in Public Law Adjudication' workshop (funded by the Academy of the Social Sciences in Australia) and the 'Legal Theory Online' seminar (29 October 2020) for their comments on earlier versions of this chapter, particularly Anne Carter, Matthew Harding, Nicole Roughan, Dale Smith, James Stellios, David Tan, Joe Tomlinson and Kevin Walton.

[1] For discussion of the 'countermajoritarian difficulty' see, eg, B Friedman, 'The History of the Countermajoritarian Difficulty, Part One' (1998) 73 *New York University Law Review* 333; J Allan, 'A Defence of the Status Quo' in T Campbell, J Goldsworthy and A Stone (eds), *Protecting Human Rights: Instruments and Institutions* (Oxford, OUP 2003); J Allan and G Huscroft, 'Constitutional Rights Coming Home to Roost? Rights Internationalism in American Courts' (2006) 43 *San Diego Law Review* 1; O Bassok and Y Dotan, 'Solving the Countermajoritarian Difficulty?' (2013) 11 *International Journal of Constitutional Law* 13.

[2] See *Amalgamated Society of Engineers v Adelaide Steamship Co Ltd* (1920) 28 CLR 129, 142.

[3] Covering clause 5 makes the Constitution 'binding on the courts, judges, and people of every State and of every part of the Commonwealth'.

These features and consequences of the adjudication of constitutional mandates have produced a range of responses. Some argue that they provide a reason to reject written constitutions altogether, or – if a written constitution is unavoidable for whatever reason[4] – to minimise the mandates it contains, and to try to reduce the scope for adjudicative disagreements that might arise in respect of those that it does contain. For instance, James Allan has repeatedly argued (i) that rights-related constitutional mandates should be eschewed, because the adjudication of such mandates is particularly apt to produce controversy commensurate with its finality, and (ii) that the adjudication of other mandates should be undertaken in accordance with an intentionalist originalist methodology, as this is what will ensure that *adjudication* does not become *value-driven political decision-making*.[5]

A different but in a certain respect similar response is likewise to accept that the adjudication of constitutional mandates will require judicial 'value judgements', but rather than seeking to minimise the role of such judgements via constitutional design and adjudicative methodology, to instead embrace the need to do so.[6]

This chapter sets out a different approach to the adjudication of constitutional mandates, in which the central concern is not 'value judgements' nor facts about original intentions, but rather facts about the institutions with which those mandates are concerned.[7] When the constitutional text refers to complex social and institutional arrangements, constitutional interpretation depends upon having knowledge, including factual knowledge, of those arrangements. This chapter does not set out the approach just described in a hypothetical fashion, as an object of advocacy. Rather, the chapter argues that, at least to a significant extent, such an approach inheres in a particular type of Australian constitutional adjudication, namely, the identification and enforcement of certain constitutional implications. The chapter ends by providing an important example of the approach at work in the leading High Court case of *Lange v Australian Broadcasting Corporation*,[8] and

---

[4] Eg to establish a federation.

[5] J Allan, 'Constitutional Interpretation Wholly Unmoored from Constitutional Text: Can the HCA Fix its Own Mess?' (2019) 48 *Federal Law Review* 30; J Allan and N Aroney, 'An Uncommon Court: How the High Court of Australia has Undermined Australian Federalism' (2008) 30 *Sydney Law Review*, 245. A proponent of (ii) in the US context is Larry Alexander – see L Alexander, 'Constitutional Theories: A Taxonomy and (Implicit) Critique' (2014) 51 *San Diego Law Review*, 623. For a different originalist approach to (i) and (ii), see J Goldsworthy, 'Structural Judicial Review and the Objection from Democracy' (2010) 60 *University of Toronto Law Journal* 137 and 'Originalism in Constitutional Interpretation' (1997) 25 *Federal Law Review* 1 respectively.

[6] One well-known version of this response is R Dworkin's *Law's Empire* (Cambridge MA, Harvard University Press 1988). See also TRS Allan's 'The Moral Unity of Public Law' (2017) 67 *The University of Toronto Law Journal* 1. S Shapiro argues for an alternative to Dworkinian interpretivism: *Legality* (Cambridge MA, Harvard University Press 2011). Shapiro purports to rely on social facts rather than moral values but takes a fundamentally external perspective on what he describes as the 'economy of trust', whereas this chapter is concerned with the inner logic of constitutionally mandated institutions.

[7] This chapter does not deal with the meta-ethical question of the relationship, and difference, between matters of fact and matters of value; nor with the relationship, and difference, between describing and prescribing. Rather, as will emerge in what follows, it approaches the distinction through the methodological and disciplinary contrast between (i) moral and highly normative political philosophy and (ii) political and organisational sociology.

[8] *Lange v Australian Broadcasting Corporation* (1997) 189 CLR 520.

comparing it to an example, the recent case of *Comcare v Banerji*,[9] in which the Court failed to engage properly with the relevant facts about institutions and their workings. In *Lange*, the High Court paid careful attention to developments in the way that Australian electoral politics take place. In *Banerji*, however, and as we will explain, the High Court interpreted and applied the Constitution in a manner quite abstracted from real-world developments, relying instead on an idealised conception of how Australian executive government works.

Recognising that a particular kind of fact plays a central role in the way just foreshadowed neither resolves nor dispels the controversies to which that adjudication gives rise. But it does show that framing such controversies by reference to the role of judicial 'value judgements', or to the legitimacy that is said to flow from an originalist methodology, will tend to obscure rather than reveal what is actually going on in such cases. Although, as noted above, this chapter does not try to generalise from this particular analysis, we suspect that there are other instances where reasoning about facts in the manner described in this chapter may be an important but neglected aspect of adjudication.

II. The Various Roles of Facts in Constitutional Adjudication

There are many roles that facts can play in constitutional adjudication. There are facts about the basic elements of the political system: who are the holders of particular offices, what the constitutional text actually is etc. Generally – at least in Australia – these sorts of facts are uncontroversial. For instance, even during the 1975 constitutional crisis – which culminated in the Governor-General dismissing a prime minister who enjoyed the confidence of the House of Representatives, appointing as prime minister the (hitherto) leader of the opposition who did not enjoy the confidence of that House, and then dissolving both Houses of Parliament on the advice of that newly appointed prime minister – no disagreements of this sort arose. There was debate about whether the Governor-General had acted properly, or lawfully; but it was accepted that the prime ministership did, in fact, change hands, and that the double dissolution and subsequent election were, in reality, what they appeared to be on the surface. Thus, for instance, there were no claims by the former prime minister and former government members to continue as a government or parliament in exile.[10]

More significant in Australian constitutional adjudication are what are called *constitutional facts* – that is to say, facts which must be established as a precondition

---

[9] *Comcare v Banerji* (2019) 267 CLR 373.
[10] For discussions, in the British constitutional tradition, of how to resolve these factual questions when genuine revolutions or coups take place, see HLA Hart, *Concept of Law* (P Bulloch and J Raz eds, 3rd edn, Oxford, OUP 2012), 118–23; J Finnis, 'Revolutions and Continuity of Law' in AWB Simpson (ed), *Oxford Essays in Jurisprudence: Second Series* (Oxford, Clarendon Press 1973).

to determining whether a purported exercise of power is constitutionally valid.[11] The classic example pertains to the Australian parliament's power to legislate in respect of lighthouses: '[a] power to make laws with respect to lighthouses does not authorize the making of a law with respect to anything which is, in the opinion of the law-maker, a lighthouse'.[12] How far this notion extends is a matter of controversy – for instance, in a recent case, Gageler J argued that in many cases a power *to legislate in respect of Xs* does not give rise to questions of constitutional fact, because *X* is to be understood as a 'topic of juristic classification'[13] such that the power is a power to determine, as a matter of law, what shall count as an *X*.[14] Examples of such *X*s, in Gageler J's view, include *alienage, bankruptcy, marriage*, and various categories of intellectual property.[15]

Gageler J's view is contested, at least in respect of some of those *X*s.[16] This chapter does not engage directly with this issue, although it provides at least indirect support for Gageler J's opponents: it is plausible to think that juristic categories are elements of larger institutional schemes, which are themselves facts, hence it is plausible to suppose that juristic categories are constituted by facts rather than legislative choice to a much greater extent than Gageler J appears to allow.[17] Our reason for not engaging directly with this issue is that this chapter does not consider *how facts might directly lend validity to purported*

---

[11] There is extensive literature on the notion of *legislative facts* (of which constitutional facts are a subset) which is typically contrasted with *adjudicative facts*. See KC Davis, 'An Approach to Problems of Evidence in the Administrative Process' (1942) 55 *Harvard Law Review* 364; KC Davis, 'Judicial Notice' (1955) 55 *Columbia Law Review* 945. For a recent detailed discussion of the distinction, including its relevance in the Australian context, see A Carter, *Proportionality and Facts in Constitutional Adjudication* (Oxford, Hart Publishing 2021), ch 3. As Dixon CJ states in *Commonwealth Freighters Pty Ltd v Sneddon*, '[h]ighly inconvenient as it may be, it is true of some legislative powers … that the validity of the exercise of the power must sometimes depend on facts, facts which somehow must be ascertained by the court responsible for deciding the validity of the law' (1959) 102 CLR 280, 292. See also the distinction drawn by Dixon CJ in *Breen v Sneddon* between 'ordinary questions of fact' and 'matters of fact upon which … the constitutional validity of some general law may depend' (1961) 106 CLR 406, 411. As S Gageler notes, the distinction Davis draws between 'adjudicative facts' and 'legislative facts' 'correspond[s] … to what Dixon CJ would later describe in *Breen v Sneddon* as "ordinary questions of fact which arise between the parties" – and "legislative facts" of which constitutional facts were just one example': S Gageler, 'Facts and Law' (2009) 11 *Newcastle Law Review* 1, 17.

[12] *Australian Communist Party v The Commonwealth* (1951) 83 CLR 1, 258. For recent discussion, see *Love v The Commonwealth* (2020) 270 CLR 152, 193–95 [86]–[88] (Gageler J), 271–72 [328]–[330] (Gordon J).

[13] *Love* ibid 328 [86], citing *Attorney-General (Vict) v The Commonwealth* (1962) 107 CLR 529, 578; *The Commonwealth v Australian Capital Territory* (2013) 250 CLR 441, 455 [14].

[14] ibid 193–95 [86]–[88], 196 [90] (Gageler J).

[15] ibid 193 [86].

[16] ibid 271–72 [330] (Gordon J, making reference to both *aliens* and *trademarks*), 288 [394], 305–06 [433] (Edelman J, making reference to *aliens*).

[17] A recent illustration is provided by the majority judgment in *Spence v Queensland* (2019) 268 CLR 355. The case addressed the characterisation of a Commonwealth law whose validity depended upon its subject matter being federal elections, and the majority's identification of that subject matter had regard to relevant facts about how political parties in Australia are organised, and how their participation in federal elections relates to their other electoral and non-electoral activities: 384–85 [2], 397 [36], 410–11 [71]–[73] (Kiefel CJ, Bell, Gageler and Keane JJ).

exercises of legislative or executive power nor *how facts might constitute juristic categories*.[18] Nor is the chapter concerned with the institutional facts that make the Constitution itself possible, either its creation or its endurance. Rather, we are concerned with facts about the institutions that the Constitution refers to and to which it gives rise.[19] Such facts are prior to exercises of legislative and executive power, but they do not bear directly upon validity. Rather, they bear upon the interpretation of the Constitution, and of its mandates, and in this way upon the application of constitutional mandates and associated implications in the context of adjudication.

III. Institutional Mandates and Implications in the Australian Constitution and their Significance

Some political mandates are expressly stated in the text of the Australian Constitution: for instance, sections 7 and 24 of the Constitution require that members of both the Senate and the House of Representatives be 'directly chosen by the people'. There are some political mandates, however, that are taken to arise by implication: for instance, the reference to *State Supreme Courts* found in section 73, which establishes the jurisdiction of the High Court to hear appeals from those courts, generates an implication that such courts must exist.[20]

Some of these mandates have not proven particularly controversial as matters of adjudication. An example is the requirement, found in section 24, that each Original State shall have at least five members of the House of Representatives. Others, however, have proven to be among the most contentious subject matters of litigation in Australia. Perhaps the most pre-eminent example, historically (and prior to the High Court's apparent resolution of the contentions in its decision in *Cole v Whitfield*[21]) was section 92's mandate that *trade and commerce among the States shall be absolutely free*.

As stated above, this chapter is concerned with a particular form of mandate, namely, mandates that figure in a particular mode of constitutional implication.

---

[18] Thus, this chapter does not directly engage with the category of legislative facts.
[19] This chapter does not directly address the dual role of the Constitution as both a speech act *about* institutions and a political act that *establishes* institutions. For an account of the semantics of the constitutional speech act that explains how failures to establish or maintain mandated institutions is unconstitutional, without needing to equate *mandates* with *aspirations* or *norms*, see P Emerton, 'The Integrity of State Courts Under the Australian Constitution' (2019) 47 Federal Law Review 521, and the discussion in the next section.
[20] *Forge v Australian Securities and Investments Commission* (2006) 228 CLR 45; *Kirk v Industrial Relations Commission of New South Wales* (2010) 239 CLR 531. For discussion, see Emerton, 'The Integrity of State Courts' (n 20).
[21] (1988) 165 CLR 360.

In *Theophanous v Herald Weekly Times Ltd*, McHugh J identified three modes of constitutional implication:

> [I]mplications that are embedded in the language of a legal instrument, an implication [that] may ... have to be made in respect of a legal instrument so that it can achieve its apparent purpose or be given a meaning that avoids absurdity or irrationality [and] a necessary implication ... [that] arise[s] from the need to protect the rights or even the existence of a party named in a legal instrument.[22]

The third mode of implication identified by McHugh J is better understood as encompassing two distinct modes. One is, in fact, a special case of the first mode: the naming of a party in the Constitution generates an *existential presupposition* which in turn generates a mandate. The most well-known existential presupposition discussed in the philosophical literature comes from Bertrand Russell's example of the failure of such a presupposition: consider an assertion, here and now, that *the present king of France is bald*. This assertion misfires in a peculiar fashion because, as we all know, there is no present king of France: France is a republic.[23] The misfire results from the contradiction between that fact and the assertion's presentation of the referring term *the present king of France* as talking about something, namely, France's present king.[24]

The Australian Constitution is replete with occurrences of referring terms which are presented as talking about something actually existing: *the Queen, the States, the Supreme Court of any State*, etc. If, in fact, no such things existed, then the constitutional provisions in which those referring terms occur would misfire, just as Russell's example does. However, by virtue of covering clause 5, the Constitution is binding on all people and institutions in Australia, and hence none – including the High Court (and other courts) – is entitled to make its text misfire. Hence none is entitled to render those things referred to non-existent. Hence the use of these referring terms in the Constitution generates a constitutional mandate that they exist.[25]

There is another, different, mode of implication that falls under the third mode identified by McHugh. This sort of implication is that which arises from a mandate

---

[22] (1994) 182 CLR 104, 197–98.
[23] The example is from B Russell, 'On Denoting' (1905) in RC Marsh (ed), *Logic and Knowledge: Essays 1901–1950* (Routledge, 1988), 45–46. See also PF Strawson, 'On Referring' (1950) 59(235) *Mind* 320; B Russell, *My Philosophical Development* (London, Allen and Unwin 1959), 175–80.
[24] For fuller discussion of this example, see Emerton, 'The Integrity of State Courts' (n 20).
[25] ibid. Of course, the High Court, in ensuring that the Constitution's text does not misfire in the way described in the main text, must work within its institutional powers. The Court can, however, interpret what the Constitution requires and adjudicate accordingly, ensuring in its decision-making regarding the legal limits on other constitutional actors that such mandates are not hollowed out (eg, by declaring legislation invalid). In addition, when the Court is declaring the common law, it is not confined to adjudicating limits on the power of other constitutional actors and hence can establish a normative order that gives effect to constitutional mandates. See, for instance, *Lange* (n 9) and *Aid/Watch Inc v Federal Commissioner of Taxation* (2010) 241 CLR 539, discussed in P Emerton, 'Public Reason, Public Benefit, and "Political" Charities' in D Halliday and M Harding (eds), *Charity Law: Exploring the Concept of Public Benefit* (Abingdon, Routledge 2022).

that a particular institution exist, or a particular event occur. The content of such an implication is that nothing which would undermine the existence of the institution, or the occurrence of the event shall be legally permitted.

In the Australian Constitution there are three acknowledged implications that have this character:

(a) the implied limitations on federal (ie, national) legislative power that arise from the constitutional mandate that *there must exist states* (ie, sub-federal entities possessing some degree of independence);[26]
(b) the implied requirement of institutional integrity of state courts, which limits state legislative power, and which arises from the constitutional mandates found in Chapter III of the Constitution that *there must exist State courts apt to perform certain functions within the national system of judicature*;[27] and
(c) the implied political freedoms and entitlements that arise from the constitutional mandate, mentioned above, that *the members of the national Parliament shall be directly chosen by the people*, together with the mandate that *the ministers who make up the national government shall be chosen from among those members of parliament*.[28]

The mandates that underpin the first two of these implications are themselves derived by way of the implication from existential presupposition discussed above.[29] The mandates that underpin the third are stated expressly in the constitutional text. In what follows we will refer to these express mandates as the mandates for representative and responsible government. Henceforth in this chapter we refer to the mandates that generate these implications as institutional mandates, because they pertain to institutions and associated events (such as the choice of members of parliament) that are fundamental elements of the Australian constitutional system.

There is, at least, a fairly banal sense in which all constitutions contain institutional mandates, if only because it is hard to see that an instrument and associated practice that didn't purport to mandate any institutions and associated events could count as a constitution. However, at least within the Australian context, these institutional mandates and the implications that flow from them, have taken on an extremely *thick* character with a highly developed jurisprudence governing them.

---

[26] See, eg, *Melbourne Corporation v Commonwealth* (1947) 74 CLR 31; *Austin v Commonwealth* (2003) 215 CLR 185.
[27] See, eg, *Kable v Director of Public Prosecutions (NSW)* (1996) 189 CLR 51; *Kirk* (n 1). See also Emerton, 'The Integrity of State Courts' (n 20).
[28] See, eg, *Lange* (n 9); *Roach v Electoral Commissioner* (2007) 233 CLR 162; *Rowe v Electoral Commissioner* (2010) 243 CLR 1.
[29] In the case of the second, this is a slight simplification. For a fuller discussion, see Emerton, 'The Integrity of State Courts' (n 20).

In the absence of a general framework of rights guarantees, these institutional guarantees are called upon to do a lot of work. For instance, in the absence of an analogue of the Tenth Amendment to the US Constitution (an express reservation of powers to the states), questions about the burdens that federal (national) law imposes on state (ie, sub-federal) governments are adjudicated by reference to the constitutional mandate that there must exist states and the implication which arises from that mandate. In the absence of any due process or similar guarantee of the right to a fair trial, complaints about unfair legal processes, or about the politicisation of the judiciary, are frequently adjudicated by reference to the constitutional mandate that there must exist state courts apt to perform certain functions within the national system of judicature, and the consequent implication that those courts must possess a certain degree of institutional integrity. In the absence of any guarantee of the franchise, or of free speech, complaints about voting rights, about limitations upon protest and access to public places, about the burden of defamation laws, and the like, are adjudicated by reference to the implied freedoms and entitlements that arise from the constitutional mandates of representative and responsible government.

Compared to rights guarantees, this might seem a circuitous way to provide constitutional protection to these important interests. That may be true, but is not self-evidently true, for at least two reasons:

(i) There are cases where we protect interests not by making those interests themselves the direct locus of the law's operation, but rather by establishing institutional structures whose operation we have reason to think will protect those interests. For instance, we might think that the reason for having a law of taxation is to provide for certain interests in the collective provision of goods within an extremely complex and highly differentiated industrial society; but such interests do not themselves figure within the legal operation of tax law.

(ii) The importance of some interests might be predominantly or even purely instrumental, with such interests depending for their value upon the existence of certain institutions which they presuppose for their existence and salience. The interest in voting in elections is a good candidate for such an interest (eg, it seems hard to argue that people 100,000 years ago, when electoral institutions and the modes of government with which they are associated did not exist and could not conceivably have been brought into existence, had an interest in voting in elections).[30] It is therefore not obvious that it makes more sense to constitutionally protect the interest, rather than the institution that the interest presupposes.

In any event, whether the jurisprudence that has arisen around these mandates ultimately makes sense, or clears some bar of constitutional adequacy,[31] it is

---

[30] Aspects of free speech may be another candidate.
[31] See, eg, PS Karlan's discussion of a different but in a relevant respect similar phenomenon in the American constitutional context, one she describes as 'shoe-horning structural issues into

happening. It plays an important practical role in the Australian system of law and government, and the adjudication of these matters generates the sorts of controversies noted in the introduction. Therefore, just as a constitutional system in which rights play a central role requires (implicitly if not explicitly) some account of what it is to uphold and vindicate the existence of a right, so in Australia the adjudication of these constitutional mandates and the implications to which they give rise must proceed in accordance with a theory of what it is to uphold, and realise, the existence of an institution. Sound adjudication must be (broadly) consistent with a tenable account of institutions.

This is where facts come in. As we will now explain, facts of a certain sort must play a central role in the sort of constitutional adjudication that we are discussing.

IV. The Reality of Institutions, and their Place in Australian Constitutional Adjudication

Institutions and the events associated with them exist and occur in the real world. Furthermore, their existence and occurrence is, in a certain important sense, mind independent. This last claim can be controversial.[32] Institutions are created by the intentional (that is, mind-governed) activities of human beings, and in this respect are not mind independent in the same way that (say) stars are. There are many other things that are not mind-independent in this respect (eg, buildings, moon rockets, and many breeds of domestic animals). What *is* mind-independent about institutions is their actual character and inner logic. Of course, when institutions are systematically designed, they may be *intended* to have a certain character and inner logic.[33] But whether they actually exemplify that character and adhere to that inner logic depends not upon intentions (or what might sometimes be mere wishes); it depends upon the way those institutions actually operate and play out in the real world of unforeseen events and unforeseen challenges. To give one example: when contemporary scholars of democracy express concern about the erosion or decay of democracy in various legal and constitutional systems,[34] they are not (primarily) concerned with what various participants in those systems *believe* to be the case. Those scholars, rather, are trying to understand how those legal and constitutional systems are actually functioning in the real world in which they operate.[35]

---

individual rights claims' and characterises as a 'problem': 'Shoe-Horning, Shell Games, and Enforcing Constitutional Rights in the Twenty-First Century' (2010) 78 *UMKC Law Review* 875, 877.

[32] See, eg, JL Coleman and O Simchen, 'Law' (2003) 9(1) *Legal Theory* 1.

[33] Not all institutions are systematically designed. A common example is the family. See, eg, LA Tilly and JW Scott, *Women, Work and Family* (New York, Holt, Rinehart and Winston 1978). The constitution of the United Kingdom is a more atypical example.

[34] See, eg, S Levitsky and D Ziblatt, *How Democracies Die* (New York, Broadway Books 2019).

[35] K Marx puts the general point thus: '[j]ust as our opinion of an individual is not based on what he thinks of himself, so we cannot judge [a social situation] by its own consciousness': 'Preface',

There are several ways to approach the study of these really extant features of institutions, both generally and in respect of particular institutions: philosophy (especially political and social philosophy); sociology and social theory; political science[36] and political theory; demography; geography; economics; etc. In this chapter we do not intend to prescribe any particular approach as being best-suited or most appropriate to the Australian constitutional context. Rather, we identify one particular approach as being well-suited to that context and broadly consonant with actual practice.

The High Court of Australia is notoriously legalistic in its jurisprudence. For instance, there has been repeated insistence that adjudication in relation to the mandates for representative and responsible government, and their implications, must proceed in accordance with constitutional text and structure.[37] This can be seen as a particular application of the general principle, derived from the foundational *Engineers'* case,[38] that:

> [I]t is not legitimate to construe the Constitution by reference to political principles or theories that find no support in the text of the Constitution. … [T]he Constitution is not to be interpreted by using such theories to control, modify or organize the meaning of the Constitution unless those theories can be deduced from the terms or structure of the Constitution itself. It is the text and the implications to be drawn from the text and structure that contain the meaning of the Constitution.[39]

However, while it is relatively uncontroversial in Australia that interpreting the Constitution requires attributing meaning to the words and phrases used in the constitutional text, this does not settle the relationship between *meaning* and *facts*. The High Court's interpretive methodology has never been literalist or reliant upon a 'thin' conception of what the text means and does not contradict the general proposition that attributing meaning to constitutional text frequently requires identifying and understanding what it is that those words and phrases refer to. Where those referents are complex social and institutional arrangements, constitutional interpretation depends to an important extent upon having knowledge of those arrangements, both practical and theoretical. Reference to *structure* reinforces an understanding of the Constitution as establishing a framework of institutions and not just stating a body of norms abstracted from the world. To sum this up in a slogan, the sort of meaning on which constitutional interpretation frequently depends is the meaning that one finds in an *encyclopedia* rather than a *dictionary*.

Contribution to the Critique of Political Economy (1859) in L S Feuer (ed), *Karl Marx and Friedrich Engels: Basic Writings on Politics and Philosophy* (Fontana, 1984), 85.
   [36] For a discussion of the use of political science in public law adjudication, see Chapter 13 of this book.
   [37] See, eg, *Lange* (n 9); *McCloy v New South Wales* (2015) 257 CLR 178, 215–16 [73] (French CJ with Kiefel, Bell and Keane JJ).
   [38] See n 3.
   [39] *Theophanous* (n 23) 198 (McHugh J).

Australian interpretive methodology thus poses no obstacle to proceeding along the lines suggested above, of having due regard to the factual reality of institutions.[40] The challenge for understanding the role of facts about institutions in Australian constitutional adjudication arises, rather, from conceptions of the proper judicial role. The next section elaborates upon and responds to this point by drawing first upon John Rawls's remarks about legislation in *A Theory of Justice*, and then upon Philip Selznick's work on the sociology of institutions.

V. Adjudicating Institutional Mandates and their Implications

In the work that we draw upon, Rawls is not setting out an account of adjudication or the judicial role. He is setting out a theory of authoritative legislation. But what he says is quite illuminating for our purposes:

> Clearly any feasible political procedure may yield an unjust outcome. ... [Moreover], the question whether legislation is just or unjust, especially in connection with economic and social policies, is commonly subject to reasonable differences of opinion. In these cases judgment frequently depends upon speculative political and economic doctrines and upon social theory generally. Often the best that we can say of a law or policy is that it is at least not clearly unjust.[41]

Rawls' point is that (i) principles of justice typically do not dictate unique solutions to legislative questions, and (ii) that the additional premises that must be combined with principles of justice in order to yield legislative solutions – in particular 'speculative political and economic doctrines and ... social theory generally' are 'commonly subject to differences of opinion'. To use some Rawlsian terminology developed after this passage was written, we might say that such speculative doctrines are not, in themselves, components of public reason.[42] But this is *not* because they are 'value judgements' that belong to some particular, non-universal worldview or 'comprehensive doctrine'.[43] It is because of epistemic limits that exist in relation to certain sorts of facts. None of this renders legislation that relies upon speculative doctrines illegitimate, *provided that* the legislator is aiming at ends that are defensible in public reason and that the legislator's occupying of that office is itself explicable by reference to institutional processes that are defensible

---

[40] P Emerton, 'Political Freedoms and Entitlements in the Australian Constitution – An Example of Referential Intentions Yielding Unintended Legal Consequences' (2010) 38(2) *Federal Law Review* 169; Emerton, 'The Integrity of State Courts' (n 20).

[41] J Rawls, *A Theory of Justice* (Cambridge MA, Harvard University Press 1971), 198–99, 362.

[42] J Rawls, *Political Liberalism* (New York, Columbia University Press 1996), 213, where Rawls describes public reason 'as the reason of citizens as such' and with 'its nature and content ... being given by the ideals and principles expressed by society's conception of political justice'.

[43] For an overview of Rawls's notion of 'comprehensive doctrine', see Rawls *Political Liberalism* (n 42), xxi, xviii–xix, 37–9.

in public reason. This is because, as Rawls points out, 'those who disagree with the [legislative] decision made cannot convincingly establish their point within the framework of the public conception of justice' and hence must accept the legislative outcome – given the other parameters are in place – as if it were an instance of pure procedural justice.[44]

In the context of constitutional interpretation, Rawls' points apply mutatis mutandis: the Constitution itself may not establish one unique answer to the question of whether (for instance) some particular proposal would be impliedly precluded by the mandates for representative and responsible government in virtue of the impairing effect that it might have upon the people's direct choice. To determine such an answer will require relying upon 'speculative political and economic doctrines and upon social theory generally'. And this, being a paradigm of legislative reasoning for the reasons Rawls gives, is not something that – in the Australian constitutional framework – it is appropriate for *judges* to do.

This gives rise to a tension: the High Court (and other courts) are obliged to uphold the Constitution and to ensure that law-making conforms to its requirements, which include the implications that are generated by the institutional mandates we have identified above; but courts are precluded from engaging in legislative-style reasoning which (it seems) may be necessary to fulfil that obligation.

The solution is to identify a form of reasoning about institutions and their realities that does not require judges to do what they are forbidden from doing. We suggest that an appropriate form of reasoning is put forward in the work of the American sociologist of institutions Philip Selznick. This is not the occasion to try and do full justice to Selznick's approach.[45] The essential ideas, however, are as follows.

First, institutions are embedded in society, both (i) drawing from it and (ii) feeding back into it. As Selznick notes:

> When we say that the Standard Oil Company or the Department of Agriculture is to be studied as an institution, we usually mean that we are going to pay some attention to its history and to the way it has been influenced by the social environment. Thus we may be interested in how its organization adapts itself to existing centers of power in the community, often in unconscious ways; from what strata of society its leadership is drawn and how this affects policy; how it justifies its existence ideologically. We may ask what underlying need in the larger community – not necessarily expressed

---

[44] Rawls, *A Theory of Justice* (n 42), 362. For a fuller discussion see P Emerton and K James, 'The Justice of the Tax Base and the Case for Income Tax' in M Bhandari (ed), *The Philosophical Foundations of Tax Law* (Oxford, OUP 2017), 131–34.

[45] P Selznick puts forward his account of institutions primarily in *TVA and the Grass Roots: A Study in the Sociology of Formal Organization* (Berkeley, University of California Press 1949) and *Leadership in Administration: A Sociological Interpretation* (New York, Harper & Row 1957). See also: M Krygier *Philip Selznick: Ideals in the World* (Stanford, Stanford University Press 2012); MS Kraatz (ed), *Institutions and Ideals: Philip Selznick's Legacy for Organizational Studies* (Bingley, Emerald Publishing Limited 2015).

or recognized by the people involved – is filled by the organization or by some of its practices.[46]

Second, and by virtue of the first point, institutions have both a tendency to 'envaluation' – ie, are oriented towards realising some good or goal of social life – but importantly also a liability to be eroded, hollowed out, or otherwise diverted from this orientation. It is not simply given that institutions will survive and flourish, when one considers the various challenges, both old and new, that they will face over time.[47]

Third, and by virtue of the second point, institutions have a certain 'evolutionary' or 'developmental' character, in the sense that institutions, through their actions (and failures to act) shape the social context within which they are located, and thereby also shape the influences upon them.[48]

In the context of the Constitution, the courts have a central role to play in these processes which does not require illegitimately engaging in legislative reasoning. Particularly because Australian courts inherit a common law tradition, and deploy a common law approach to adjudication, can use techniques of legal reasoning both to *identify the particular tendency to envaluation that inheres in a given institution or associated event*, and to *identify and have regard to the interplay between developing institutions and the influences that affect them and to which they must respond*. This also explains why originalist criticisms of this jurisprudence of implications are simply mistaken: if the courts accepted such criticism, they would allow institutional mandates to be hollowed out by failing to take seriously the role the Constitution has assigned to them in respect of those mandates.

A paradigm example of this sort of reasoning about institutions, outside the constitutional context, is the law of trusts. A trust is an arrangement that combines ownership with an other-regarding duty: the trustee owns the property, but is under an obligation to use the incidents of his or her ownership for the benefit of one or more others (whether those be identified or 'abstract' persons).[49] This institutional structure gives rise to challenges – most obviously, the exploitation by the trustee of their property rights in disregard of the other-regarding duty – to which courts have had to respond. A relatively recent example is determining the extent to which provisions of trust instruments that purport to immunise trustees from liability for wrongdoing in the course of their trusteeship should be honoured.[50]

---

[46] Selznick, *Leadership in Administration* (n 46) 6.
[47] For a comprehensive discussion of these points, see Selznick, *Leadership in Administration* (n 46). A pithy summary is found on 142–54.
[48] See also Emerton, 'The Integrity of State Courts' (n 20), 537–38.
[49] '[A] trust exists when the owner of a legal or equitable interest in property is bound by an obligation, recognised by and enforced in equity, to hold that interest for the benefit of others, or for some object or purpose permitted by law': JD Heydon and MJ Leeming, *Jacobs' Law of Trusts in Australia* (Chatswood, 8th edn, LexisNexis Butterworths 2016) 1. The other leading Australian text sets out the same account: Thomson Reuters, *Ford and Lee: The Law of Trusts* (27 February 2021) [1.010].
[50] See, eg, *Armitage v Nurse* [1998] Ch 241; *Wilden v Green* (2009) 38 WAR 429.

This has not involved making externally motivated 'value judgements'. Rather, it has involved drawing upon the understanding of what the trust is, and is for, as an institution, and in light of this determining what is consistent with that and what would rather hollow out or undermine the institution. In simple terms, the conclusion has been reached that such provisions can protect a trustee against negligent but not against fraudulent or dishonest breaches of duty – because for a trustee to act fraudulently or dishonestly in relation to his or her other-regarding duties in respect of ownership of the trust property would be entirely at odds with the core of the trust as an institution.[51] One may or may not agree with this outcome; the present point is that the decisions have been reached by reasoning about what the institution is, and what it demands, if it is to endure and flourish given the challenges that it finds confronting it.

A paradigm within the constitutional context, in which this sort of approach has been most fully developed, is in relation to the requirements of institutional integrity that result from the constitutional mandate that there shall be State courts apt to perform certain functions within the national system of judicature.[52] The existence and (relative) coherence and stability of that jurisprudence, and the broader Chapter III jurisprudence within which it is located, provides a model for the other institutional mandates and resulting implications found in the Constitution. As Gordon J, in her minority judgment in the recent case of *Garlett*, notes, 'the core constitutional values underpinning and protected by Ch III of the Constitution ... must be protected to ensure that State courts are suitable repositories of federal jurisdiction'.[53] Her Honour continues that '[t]he Court must remain vigilant to prevent ... risks from materialising, whether they are "dramatic and obvious" or "small and incremental"'.[54]

VI. Two Examples: One Good, One Bad

We conclude this chapter by making particular reference to the third of the mandates and resulting implications that was set out above, namely, the implied political freedoms and entitlements that arise from the constitutional mandates for representative and responsible government. As mentioned in section 1, we provide one example which shows a sound and appropriate use of facts in the course of interpretation and adjudication (*Lange*); and a second example that illustrates the opposite (*Banerji*).

In *Lange*, the High Court found that the common law of defamation as hitherto declared did not conform to the constitutional mandates for representative and

---

[51] ibid.
[52] Emerton, 'The Integrity of State Courts' (n 20).
[53] *Garlett v Western Australia* (2022) 92 ALJR 888, 932 [199].
[54] ibid 932–33 [199], quoting (in order to compare) *New South Wales v The Commonwealth* (2006) 229 CLR 1, 328 [787].

One Important Role of Facts in Constitutional Adjudication 63

responsible government, *because of* the burden that it would impose on the free political communication that is a necessary incident of the people making their direct choice of members of parliament and thereby holding the government to account. In reaching this conclusion, the Court made the following observations:

> Communications concerning political or government matters ... were central to the system of representative government, as it was understood at federation .... [And] it can hardly be doubted, given the history of representative government and the holding of elections under that system in Australia prior to federation, that the elections for which the Constitution provides were intended to be free elections ...
>
> That being so, ss 7 and 24 and the related sections of the Constitution [including those which mandate responsible government] necessarily protect that freedom of communication between the people concerning political or government matters which enables the people to exercise a free and informed choice as electors. ...
>
> In 1901, when the Constitution of the Commonwealth took effect ... the balance that was struck by the common law between freedom of communication about government and political matters and the protection of personal reputation was thought to be consistent with the freedom ... for which the Constitution provided. Since 1901, the common law ... has had to be developed in response to changing conditions. The expansion of the franchise, the increase in literacy, the growth of modern political structures operating at both federal and State levels and the modern development in mass communications, especially the electronic media, now demand the striking of a different balance from that which was struck in 1901. ...
>
> [T]he content of the freedom to discuss government and political matters must be ascertained according to what is for the common convenience and welfare of society. That requires an examination of changing circumstances and the need to strike a balance in those circumstances between absolute freedom of discussion of government and politics and the reasonable protection of the persons who may be involved, directly or incidentally, in the activities of government or politics.[55]

Here the Court does not rely upon extra-constitutional notions: eg, in saying that the elections were intended to be *free* elections it is identifying the (thick) meaning of the phrase *direct choice*. It does rely upon facts – about the developments that accompany the emergence of mass democracy over the course of the twentieth century – but these are not problematically speculative or conjectural. They are matters of which judicial notice can be taken, and on the basis of which the Court can then identify what the law of defamation must be if it is not to interfere with the constitutional mandate by excessively burdening speech as one necessary incident of that mandate. This is not to say that the Court's approach to the adjudication of the constitutional mandate, which requires paying close attention to facts about the institutions with which the mandate is concerned and how these facts develop and change over time and in light of the new challenges with which they are confronted, is an easy or straightforward undertaking. As Selznick argues, the demands imposed by institutional goals and purposes, including the goals

---

[55] *Lange* (n 9) 560, 565–66 (footnote omitted).

and purposes of constitutional institutions, are not always obvious. He concludes that *institutional leadership* is necessary in order to effectively respond to such demands.[56] By identifying what the law of defamation must be in light of the new demands placed upon the constitutionally mandated democratic order as a result of important changes in social and political life since federation, the Court in *Lange* is demonstrating such leadership. It is ensuring that the constitutional mandate, and the implications to which it gives rise, are not distorted or undermined despite the new challenges they confront.

In *Banerji* the Court upheld the constitutionality of legislation that places significant limitations on political communication by public servants. Our criticism of this case does not, in the context of this chapter, extend to the outcome.[57] Rather, our focus is upon the reasoning. In upholding the legislation, the Court set out a theory of the place of the public service in the Australian system of government, namely, that (as per section 67 of the Constitution) the public servants in each department answer to the minister who heads that department, who in turn (as per section 64) answers to the Parliament, which is in turn elected by the people. As part of this theory the Court articulated the need for ministers to be able to trust and rely upon an impartial public service. What the Court manifestly did not do in its reasoning – in stark contrast with *Lange*[58] – is give any consideration to the extent to which that posited theory of the public service actually fits the contemporary facts.[59] That is not to say that the Court is entitled to depart from the text of the Constitution – of course it is not. But it is not obliged to construct its account of that text's meaning, and its implications, in an idealised vacuum.

The capacity of the High Court to take judicial notice of developments in the role of executive governments in modern states was established by Dixon J when, in the *Communist Party case*, he observed that '[h]istory and not only ancient history, shows that in countries where democratic institutions have been unconstitutionally superseded, it has been done not seldom by those holding the executive power'.[60] In *Banerji*, the Court could and ought to have had regard to commonplace facts about how both electors and parliamentarians, in contemporary Australian political life, come to know what it is that the government and its officials are doing, including the role played by communications by public servants in that respect. These facts are not problematically speculative or conjectural. Having regard to them thus would not have trespassed into the legislative realm and would have upheld the Court's duty to take seriously the constitutional mandate and the

---

[56] Selznick, *Leadership in Administration* (n 46).

[57] For reasons having to do with both how her case was argued (both at first instance and on appeal) and the particular nature of her conduct, having regard to the matters we go on to discuss in the remainder of this section may not have had any bearing on the result for the plaintiff in *Banerji*.

[58] And many of the cases that constitute the Chapter III jurisprudence, as mentioned earlier. See the main text immediately preceding and proceeding n 52.

[59] For one recent account of those facts see especially Y Ng, *Ministerial Advisers in Australia* (Annandale, The Federation Press 2016) ch 2.

[60] *Australian Communist Party* (n 14) 187.

implications to which it gives rise. Instead, by putting forward idealised or largely historical accounts of the political and constitutional institutions in play, rather than paying close attention to the commonplace facts of contemporary social and political life, the Court in *Banerji* arguably facilitated a partial hollowing out and undermining of the constitutional mandate and the implications to which it gives rise. This example thus shows the danger that arises when constitutional adjudication is divorced from a sound appreciation of the facts that are relevant to understanding the full meaning and implications of an institutional mandate: the Court's failure to have regard to them has established a precedent which has the potential to undermine rather than uphold a fundamental mandate found in the Australian Constitution. The example thereby reinforces our contention that, at least in this domain of Australian constitutional jurisprudence, it is a proper reckoning with relevant facts, rather than concern with the making by judges of 'value judgements' or concern with the original intentions of the framers, that is the real site of adjudicative action.

We end this chapter by acknowledging that the approach we argue that the Court should have taken in *Banerji* – and has typically taken in the adjudicative context we are concerned with more generally – is not necessarily an easy or straightforward one. The sorts of facts, outlined earlier in this section, to which the Court in *Banerji* could and ought to have had regard, pose new demands for and challenges to the institutional mandate and the implications to which it gives rise. But if the Court fails to properly acknowledge these challenges and demands and take them seriously, it also fails to take seriously the role the Constitution has assigned to it – by way of covering clause 5 – in respect of this (and other) institutional mandates. The Court has a constitutional duty to have regard to the facts that are at the core of these mandates.

5
Citizenship Denied – Constitutional Facts, and the Independence of Papua New Guinea

RAYNER THWAITES

I. Introduction

In 2016, Mr Troyrone Lee applied to renew his Australian passport. His application was refused. Age 41 at the time of application, he had obtained his first Australian passport weeks before his fourth birthday (having previously been included on his mother's Australian passport) and had renewed his passport without incident since then. The Australian government submitted that its previous issuance of passports to him was in error as he was not an Australian citizen. He was, to quote from the judgment on appeal, 'dumbfounded'.[1] After exhausting internal review, in 2019 he applied to the Australian Federal Court for a declaration that he was an Australian citizen.[2] He was successful, both at first instance and on appeal.[3] The appeal judgment concluded by saying 'it may well be that Mr Lee's case is one which warrants consideration by the Commonwealth of the making of an Act of Grace payment to him'.[4] This chapter is an analysis of that litigation, focusing on the insights and issues it raises with respect to facts in public law adjudication and citizenship.

The Australian government's denial of Mr Lee's citizenship was grounded in its (changed) construal of the citizenship arrangements attending Papua New Guinea's (PNG's) independence ('Independence'). Mr Lee had been born in Papua four months prior to PNG's independence from Australia in 1975. Prior to Independence, persons born in the Territory acquired Australian citizenship. However, the citizenship so acquired was not 'real'.[5] Those whose Australian

---
[1] *Minister for Home Affairs v Lee* [2021] FCAFC 89 [3].
[2] *Lee v Minister for Home Affairs* [2020] FCA 487.
[3] *Lee* (n 1).
[4] ibid [108].
[5] The term 'real' citizenship is taken from the Constitution of Papua New Guinea 1975 s 64, quoted below in n 44.

citizenship relied solely on birth in Papua were not entitled to enter or remain in Australia (outside of PNG). On Independence, those born in Papua who lacked 'real' Australian citizenship acquired the citizenship of PNG.[6] Those who automatically acquired the citizenship of PNG lost their Australian citizenship under Australian law. At issue was the application of those arrangements to Mr Lee's circumstances. His claim to Australian citizenship did not rely solely on his birth in Papua. His parents were naturalised Australian citizens: 'real' Australian citizens. Lee argued that his Australian immigration status as a child should be assimilated to theirs such that he had 'real' Australian citizenship at Independence and had accordingly not acquired PNG citizenship.

The litigation raises the use of facts in public law adjudication at multiple points. The legal dispute proceeded from the interpretation and application of provisions of the PNG Constitution. Foreign law is a question of fact, albeit of a 'peculiar kind'.[7] The peculiarity proceeds from the proposition that 'foreign laws, although formally facts, are nonetheless laws, and are treated as such'.[8] The relevant provisions of the PNG Constitution were construed with reference to transnational arrangements, entering into doctrine as constitutional facts; 'facts which either the Court has, or might reasonably have, regarded as relevant to the determination of a constitutional issue'.[9] In addition, Lee's litigation also turned on the determination of constitutional facts going to validity under the Australian Constitution. The relevant provisions of the PNG Constitution expressly referenced Australian law, where the determinative issue was one of constitutional fact (see sections VI and VII below). In the result, the Australian litigation traversed issues of constitutional fact from both Papua New Guinea and Australia, with the former additionally raising issues going to the treatment of foreign law. The litigation shows how fact and law are not 'hermetically sealed' with law simply being applied to facts.[10] It also shows the dependence of a person's rights and status – here their citizenship – on constitutional facts.

The story ends well, with Mr Lee retaining his Australian citizenship. My analysis centres on the conduct and arguments of the Australian government in the

---

[6] Subject to additional requirements outlined in section III of this chapter, primary among which was the requirement of 'two grandparents who were born in the country or an adjacent area' in s 65(1) of the PNG Constitution.

[7] Lord Collins of Mapesbury et al (eds), *Dicey, Morris & Collins on the Conflict of Laws* (15th edn, London, Sweet & Maxwell, 2019) [9-010].

[8] R Fentiman, *Foreign Law in English Courts: Pleading, Proof and Choice of Law* (Oxford, OUP, 2008) 202. For a succinct account of the main features of this 'peculiarity' see J McComish, 'Pleading and Proving Foreign Law in Australia' (2007) 31 *Melbourne University Law Review* 400, 415–18.

[9] S Kenny, 'Constitutional Fact Ascertainment' (1990) 1 *Public Law Review* 134, 135; B Selway, 'The Use of History and Other Facts in the Reasoning of the High Court of Australia' (2001) 20 *University of Tasmania Law Review* 129. More recently, the High Court has referred to constitutional facts as 'matters of fact upon which … the constitutional validity of some general law may depend': *Mineralogy v Western Australia* (2021) 95 ALRJ 832, 846 [55] (Kiefel CJ, Gageler, Keane, Gordon, Steward and Gleeson JJ), quoting *Breen v Sneddon* (1961) 106 CLR 406, 411–12.

[10] S Gageler, 'Fact and Law' (2008) 11 *Newcastle Law Review* 1, 22.

litigation and the approach they evidence to Australia's neighbours, the historical materials, and its own citizens.

II. The Australian Administration of Papua New Guinea

The legal issues in the *Lee* litigation implicated not one but two processes of national independence: most immediately that of Papua New Guinea from Australia, culminating on Independence Day, 16 September 1975, but also the slow and extended process of Australia's growing independence from Great Britain.[11] Australia came into existence as a legal entity on New Year's Day 1901, through the federation of six British colonies under the Commonwealth of Australia Constitution Act 1900, an Act of the British Parliament. Shortly thereafter, in 1902, British New Guinea was placed under the authority of the Commonwealth of Australia. It was accepted as a Commonwealth territory, Papua, by section 5 of the Papua Act 1905 (Cth).[12] In the wake of the First World War, the other component of what was to become the independent state of Papua New Guinea; the former German possession of New Guinea, was placed under Australian administration by Mandate of the League of Nations in 1920.[13] After 1945, the two Territories were administered jointly under Australian legislation.

It was not until 1949 that citizenship status was introduced into Australian law, by the Nationality and Citizenship Act 1948 (Cth) (see section VI below). Australian citizenship was, and remains, a statutory status. The 1948 Act defined 'Australia' to include 'the Territory of Papua',[14] and section 10 provided that 'a person born in Australia after the commencement of this Act shall be a citizen by birth'.[15] This had the effect of conferring Australian citizenship on those born in Papua. Notwithstanding their formal Australian citizenship, those born in Papua 'had no right to enter or remain in Australia, or even to leave their own country'.[16] Their 'Australian citizenship' was distinct from 'real' Australian citizenship. It was

---

[11] This process had concluded 'at least' by 1986: *Sue v Hill* (1999) 199 CLR 462.
[12] PM McDermott, 'Australian Citizenship and the Independence of Papua New Guinea' (2009) 32 *University of New South Wales Law Journal* 50, 51–52.
[13] For an account of the history and nature of the 'C class' mandate under which Australia administered New Guinea see: C Storr, '"Imperium in Imperio": Sub-Imperialism and the Formation of Australia as a Subject of International Law' (2018) 19 *Melbourne Journal of International Law* 335; M Johnson and C Storr, 'Australia as Empire' in P Cane, L Ford and M McMillan (eds), *The Cambridge Legal History of Australia* (Cambridge, CUP, 2022) 258.
[14] Nationality and Citizenship Act 1948 (Cth) s 5. The relevant portion reads: '"Australia" includes Norfolk Island and the Territory of Papua'.
[15] Residents of (former) German New Guinea became 'Australian protected persons'.
[16] J Goldring, *The Constitution of Papua New Guinea: A Study in Legal Nationalism* (Sydney, Law Book Co, 1978), 204.

a *sui generis* form of Australian citizenship allied, in terms of Australian constitutional law, with Papua's status as an external territory.[17]

Australian constitutional law accommodated this parting of ways between (Papuan) Australian citizenship and the right to enter Australia. The constitutional basis for the exclusion of Australian (Papuan) citizens from Australia was the 'immigration' power. In a 1959 letter, the Australian Minister for Immigration wrote:

> The Migration Act permits the exclusion from Australia of any 'immigrant'. [Decisions and observations by the High Court have suggested] that any person may be regarded as an immigrant who is not a constituent member of the Australian community – whatever his national status may be.
>
> On this basis, legal power exists to prevent the entry to Australia of either natives of Papua, whose national status is that of Australian citizens, or natives of the Trust Territory of New Guinea, who are Australian protected persons.[18]

(The nature and workings of 'immigrant' as a status under Australian constitutional law are detailed in sections VI and VII).

III. The Transfer of Citizenship from Australia to Papua New Guinea

The provisions for acquisition of citizenship in 1975 in the new state of Papua New Guinea responded to the colonial experience of Australian administration[19] and, in particular, the discrimination inherent in an Australian citizenship that did not allow entry into Australia. Acutely conscious of the attenuated form of Australian citizenship that most Papuans held,[20] the citizenship arrangements on

---

[17] *Re Minister for Immigration and Multicultural and Indigenous Affairs; Ex parte Ame* (2005) 222 CLR 439, 454 [22].

[18] D Denoon, A *Trial Separation: Australia and the Decolonisation of Papua New Guinea* (Canberra, ANU Press, 2012) 9, quoting from Australian Archives, Department of Territories, A 452/1, file 60/8329, Minister A.R. Downer to W.C. Wentworth MP, 27 October, 1959. The paraphrase in square brackets is that offered by Denoon.

[19] 'The Constitution was drafted against a background of Australian colonial rule under which discrimination on the grounds of race had pervaded all aspects of the colony's social and economic life and had been given form and substance in the colony's legal regime': G Hassall, 'Citizenship' in AJ Regan, O Jessep and EL Kwa (eds), *Twenty Years of the Papua New Guinea Constitution* (Sydney, Lawbook Co, 2001) 255.

[20] 'Calling Papuan [sic] Australian citizens only makes the Australian government look ridiculous in the eyes of Papuans. We are not, and never will be, Australian citizens until it means the same to us as it does to an Australian and until there is free movement to and from Australia.': AM Kiki et al, submission addressed to the Chairman, the Select Committee on Constitutional Development, The House of Assembly, Port Moresby, 15 April 1966, 3–4, quoted in EP Wolfers, 'Defining a Nation: The Citizenship Debates in the Papua New Guinea Parliament' in FS Stevens and EP Wolfers (eds), *Racism: The Australian Experience – A Study of Race Prejudice in Australia*, vol 3 (2nd edn, Sydney, Australian and New Zealand Book Company, 1977) 303. Sir AM Kiki was the minister assigned responsibility for citizenship matters on Independence.

Independence were intended to be the converse of the Australian pattern of inclusion and exclusion. Only those who had been denied 'real' Australian citizenship automatically became citizens of the newly independent PNG. Those who held 'real' Australian citizenship did not.

There was also a PNG prohibition on dual citizenship, driven in large part by concerns about the economic exploitation of PNG by non-'natives'.[21] Giving effect to the rejection of dual citizenship, provision was made under Australian law for those who automatically acquired PNG citizenship to lose their Australian citizenship.

Section 65 of the PNG Constitution was the primary provision governing the automatic acquisition of citizenship in the new nation, providing in part:

> (1) A person born in the country before Independence Day who has two grandparents who were born in the country or an adjacent area is a citizen.
>
> (2) ...
>
> (4) Subsections (1) and (2) do not apply to a person who –
>
> (a)   has a right (whether revocable or not) to permanent residence in Australia;
>
> ...
>
> unless that person renounces his right to residence in Australia or his status as a citizen of Australia or another country in accordance with subsection (5).

The issues on which the *Lee* litigation came to turn were how the exception contained in section 65(4)(a) should be interpreted (this is addressed in section V) and its application to Mr Lee's circumstances (sections VI and VII).

The PNG Constitution made (and still makes) extensive provision for citizenship. The above provisions fall in Chapter 4, 'Citizenship', comprising 18 sections addressing modes of acquisition and loss.[22] The drafting of these constitutional provisions was informed by extended and sophisticated debate.[23] Citizenship was the topic of the first discussion paper of six produced by the Constitutional Planning Committee charged with developing a draft constitution.[24] The Constituent Assembly that settled the final text of the PNG Constitution devoted a substantial portion of its sitting days to the subject.[25] In short, there are rich

---

[21] Other aspects of the constitutional citizenship arrangements that responded to these concerns included the onerous requirements for naturalisation (requiring eight years residence for eligibility), and the provision that the protection of property granted to citizens shall extend to 'automatic' citizens only (not naturalised citizens) for the first five years after independence.

[22] Key provisions bearing on the legal effect of citizenship are found outside Ch 4, notably ss 50–56 which set out the 'special rights of citizens', including that only citizens can acquire freehold land.

[23] See the selected passages from the citizenship debates in the Papua New Guinea parliament provided in Wolfer's 97-page chapter. Wolfers characterises the debates as 'display[ing] a remarkable mastery of the subject by many members of Papua New Guinea's national parliament, sure not only of the principles they sought to embody in legislation but of even some of the more recondite aspects of legal draftsmanship': Wolfers, 'Defining a Nation' (n 20) 384.

[24] Wolfers 'Defining a Nation' (n 20) 313. The Constitutional Planning Committee, constituted in 1972, was a 15-member, all-party committee of parliamentarians 'to make recommendations for a Constitution for full internal self-government in a united Papua New Guinea with a view to independence'.

[25] Wolfers, 'Defining a Nation' (n 20) 342. The House of Assembly convened as a Constituent Assembly to consider the draft constitution and adopt it on behalf of the people of Papua New Guinea. It sat between 23 May and 26 August 1975.

and extensive legal debates to draw on in an inquiry into citizenship under PNG constitutional law.

The transfer of citizenship from Australia to PNG necessarily required legal mechanisms under the law of both countries.[26] The transfer necessitated tightly interdependent, complementary, citizenship arrangements. The Australian legal mechanism complementing s 65 of the PNG Constitution was a regulation made under the Papua New Guinea Independence Act 1975 (Cth).[27] That Act provided:

> (3) On the expiration of the day preceding Independence Day, Australia ceases to have any sovereignty, sovereign rights or rights of administration in respect of or appertaining to the whole or any part of Papua New Guinea.

Australia gave legal effect to this commitment through regulation 4 of the Papua New Guinea Independence (Australian Citizenship) Regulations 1975 (Cth), which provided in part:[28]

> A person who –
> (a) immediately before Independence Day, was an Australian citizen ... and
> (b) on Independence Day becomes a citizen of [PNG] by virtue of the provisions of the [PNG Constitution],
> ceases on that day to be an Australian citizen.

The key feature of regulation 4 for our purposes is its dependence on the law of PNG.

IV. The Facts and Conduct of the Litigation

Mr Lee was born in Papua on 20 May 1975. The central question in the litigation was whether, though eligible for the automatic acquisition of citizenship on Independence under section 65(1) of the PNG Constitution,[29] he was then removed from that category by the exception in section 65(4)(a), as a person who 'has a right (whether revocable or not) to permanent residence in Australia'. The litigation centred on how this phrase should be interpreted (see section V), and whether its requirements, once the interpretative issue was resolved, were met (sections VI and VII).

---

[26] 'It is for each State to determine under its own law who are its nationals': Convention on Certain Questions Relating to the Conflict of Nationality Laws, opened for signature 12 April 1930, 179 LNTS 89 (entered into force 1 July 1937), s 1.

[27] Section 6 of that Act empowered the making of the relevant regulation.

[28] The validity of reg 4 was upheld by the High Court of Australia in *Ame* (n 16). It was modelled on regulations used by the United Kingdom Parliament in the decolonisation process in the 1960s and 1970s: *Ame* (n 17) 455 [24]. The regulations were repealed on 1 October 2017 under the default sunsetting rules contained in the Legislative Instruments Act 2003 (Cth).

[29] Mr Lee also had two grandparents born in the country (see s 65(1) of the PNG Constitution, quoted in text in section III).

A 2006 decision of the High Court of Australia, *Ame*, had held that Australian citizenship acquired solely by birth in Papua did not confer a right to permanent residence on the Australian mainland.[30] Lee's key ground of distinction was that his parents were Australian citizens by naturalisation at the time of his birth.

The *Lee* litigation centred on the citizenship arrangements attending PNG's independence. The contingency of clarifying these intergovernmental arrangements through private litigation needs to be appreciated, demonstrating an aspect of the Australian government's parochial and limited approach.[31] Among other actions on being denied an Australian passport, Mr Lee had made inquiries of the PNG government as to his citizenship status. As recorded in the judgment on appeal:

> By a letter dated 15 October 2017, [he] was officially advised by Papua New Guinea's Deputy Chief Migration Officer that he was not a citizen of that country. More particularly, the advice stated:
>
> '… you are not a citizen of the Independent State of Papua New Guinea under the PNG Constitution Section 64 and 65 on automatically acquiring PNG citizenship on PNG Independence day on September 16 1975.'[32]

This letter from PNG's Deputy Chief Migration Office was provided to the Australian government.[33] A position adopted by a government official is not determinative of the law. Nonetheless, advice from a senior Papua New Guinean official in these terms might be expected to prompt a response from the Australian government. The letter flags a clear divergence between the two countries with respect to a significant intergovernmental arrangement. The Full Court queried why the Australian government had not sought confirmation and clarification of its position with respect to Mr Lee in the courts of Papua New Guinea, particularly given the centrality of that country's Constitution to the dispute.[34] In the absence of such government action, it fell to a private individual to litigate the apparent breakdown in the complementary citizenship arrangements.

The Australian government's indifference to the foreign relations aspects of the dispute was also evidenced in the way it conducted the Australian litigation. It did not seek particulars of the position of the PNG government through diplomatic channels.[35] Further, it did not seek expert evidence on how to construe the relevant, foreign, constitutional provisions.[36] These are not matters of legal obligation

---

[30] *Ame* (n 16). As a decision on foreign law, a question of fact, the High Court's ruling on ss 64 and 65 of the PNG Constitution in *Ame* may create no precedent: *Neilson v Overseas Projects* (2005) 223 CLR 331, 370 [115]. As an indication of the peculiarities of the fact/law distinction in this area, the Full Court noted that 'the position of this Court relative to the High Court in the judicial hierarchy, might have made any such submission difficult to sustain': *Lee* (n 1) [45].

[31] The points made under this theme were made by the Full Court: *Lee* (n 1) [9]–[10].

[32] ibid [5].

[33] The Australian government was in receipt of the Papua New Guinean advice, at odds with its own interpretation of the PNG Constitution, from May 2018 at the latest: *Lee* (n 1) [9].

[34] ibid.

[35] ibid [10].

[36] Neither did the lawyers for Lee plead foreign law. They nonetheless obtained the remedy sought. The ground for which PNG law was most important was a new ground on appeal (see section V).

but are no less important to foreign relations for that. As a question of fact, foreign law is a matter to be pleaded.[37] If not pleaded by the parties, the default rule is that the court will apply Australian law.[38] In the present case, no one disputed the relevance of the PNG constitutional provisions. The indifference to foreign law went to the interpretation of a foreign constitution. Would an Australian interpretive framework suffice or did recourse need to be had to the law of Papua New Guinea? The lawyers for the Minister expressly argued that the interpretation of the PNG Constitution was, for reasons particular to the relevant provisions, a matter of *Australian* law (see section V).

It was the appeal court that was decisive in ensuring that PNG authorities and legal history received consideration. On appeal, PNG cases were cited and discussed, and secondary legal historical sources, including on the drafting of the PNG Constitution, were quoted and referenced. The Court's ability to introduce this material, with notice to the parties, reflected its character as matters of constitutional fact, going to the interpretation of the relevant constitutional provisions. As regards legal approach, the Court found that PNG's treatment of constitutional facts aligned with the approach taken in Australia,[39] and indeed often drew on Australian authorities.[40]

The bench was well constituted for an analysis of PNG law. Justice Logan was one of two Australian Federal Court judges who also sat on the National and Supreme Courts of Papua New Guinea, hearing civil and commercial appeals.[41] Justice Kerr was a co-author of *The Annotated Constitution of Papua New Guinea* (1984) and a former Dean of the University of Papua New Guinea School of Law.[42]

In addition to matters of interstate relations, the Australian government's conduct raised issues of institutional memory. The Court was clearly of the view that 'Australian officialdom, in contrast it seems with their counterparts in Papua New Guinea' had forgotten the nature and intent of the arrangements with respect to citizenship attending PNG's independence.[43]

In both questions of PNG constitutional law and questions of Australian constitutional law, I argue that the Minister's argument was blinkered; characterised by a partial and acontextual account of the relevant constitutional facts.

---

[37] Fentiman (n 8) 3.
[38] See *Neilson* (n 30) 372 [125]. McComish (n 8) 431–42.
[39] *Lee* (n 1) [50].
[40] See, eg, the extended discussion of Australian, and also American and British authorities, on constitutional facts and judicial notice, including reasons for adjusting their application in the PNG context in *SCR No 2 of 1982 (No 1): Re the Organic Law on National Elections (Amendment) Act 1981* [1982] PNGLR 214, 227–28.
[41] J Logan, 'A Year in the Life of an Australian Member of the PNG Judiciary' (2014) 12 *The Judicial Review* 79, 82.
[42] B Brunton and D Colquhoun-Kerr, *The Annotated Constitution of Papua New Guinea* (Papua New Guinea, University of Papua New Guinea Press, 1984).
[43] *Lee* (n 1) [108].

V. Interpreting the Constitution of Papua New Guinea

On appeal, the Minister introduced a new ground going to the interpretation of the PNG Constitution. He argued that the right to permanent residence in Australia referenced in section 65(4)(a) of the PNG Constitution needed to be acquired by positive 'grant' under the Migration Act 1958 (Cth). The argument began by reading a requirement that the right to permanent residence in Australia be 'granted', contained in another section of the PNG Constitution, section 64(4)(b),[44] into section 65(4)(a) (which makes no reference to 'grant'). Reliance was placed on the commonality between the two provisions noted in the High Court's 2006 decision in *Ame*.[45] The next step in the argument was to read the term implied into section 65(4)(a), namely 'grant', as requiring the issuance of an entry permit under the Migration Act by the Australian authorities. Turning to application, it was argued that, as Mr Lee's parents had never been issued with such an entry permit, they did not fall within the exception in section 65(4)(a). As a result, Mr Lee was argued to have automatically acquired PNG citizenship on Independence, losing his Australian citizenship. Both interpretive steps in the argument were rejected by the Court.

An arresting feature of the Minister's argument was the contention that the interpretation of the relevant provisions of the PNG Constitution was *not* a matter of foreign law. The Minister argued that to characterise the interpretation of these constitutional provisions as foreign law 'ignores the[ir] unique purpose and historical context'.[46] The interpretation of section 65(4)(a) was contended to be a question of Australian immigration law that had been conclusively answered by the Australian High Court in *Ame*.[47]

This contention sought to leverage the true proposition that the constitutional provision asks a question *of* the foreign law (here Australian law), to arrive at the false proposition that foreign (Australian) law determines the scope of the question

---

[44] At Independence, the section read in part:

Section 64 (1) … no person who has a real foreign citizenship may be or become a citizen, and the provisions of this Part shall be read subject to that prohibition …

(4) For the purposes of this section, a person who–

(a) was, immediately before Independence Day, an Australian citizen or an Australian Protected Person by virtue of –

  (i) birth in the former Territory of Papua; or …

(b) was never granted a right (whether revocable or not) to permanent residence in Australia, has no real foreign citizenship.

[45] *Ame* (n 17) 455 [23]: 'The right to permanent residence referred to in s 65(4)(a) is the same as the right referred to in s 64(4)(b), that is to say, the right which a small number of Papuans had received by grant, not a right to which all Papuans had by virtue of birth in the Territory of Papua.' This equivalence was true as applied to the circumstances under consideration in *Ame*, but not in the abstract for all cases, as held in *Lee* (n 1).

[46] Minister of Home Affairs, 'Appellant's Reply Submissions', submission in Minister for Home Affairs v Lee, QUD 137 of 2020, 22 October 2020, [26].

[47] ibid [27].

asked. It was only once the question had been determined by interpreting the PNG Constitution that Australian law could furnish the relevant answer.

The question asked by section 65(4)(a) of the PNG Constitution was whether the person had a right to permanent residence in Australia. From PNG's perspective, it did not matter how that right was arrived at – whether through the grant of an entry permit under the Migration Act 1958 (Cth), or by virtue of being a 'real' Australian citizen. In the latter case, the right to permanent residence could be expressed by saying that the Migration Act did not apply to them. The Full Court supported this broader reading of section 65(4)(a) of the PNG Constitution. It held that the provision encompassed both those with rights to permanent residence under the Migration Act and 'real' Australians to whom the Migration Act did not apply. In adopting this interpretation, it drew on PNG legal materials going to the interpretation of the PNG Constitution.

The Minister's reasoning treated various earlier discussions of PNG citizenship in Australian cases as exhaustive. The decision not to go back to PNG law to situate and contextualise these earlier Australian judgments, which were judgments addressing the law of PNG, led to errors in the Australian government's position, corrected by the courts. The expectation that the government and its lawyers engage with PNG law was not unduly onerous. The relevant material was available through standard research channels, and in English. As noted earlier, expert evidence could have been sought. Engagement with PNG law was what the legal question, dependent on the operation of the PNG Constitution, required.

Having lost the argument on interpretation, the Minister argued that Lee had no right to permanent residence in Australia.[48] The question reduced to whether Lee was an 'immigrant', an issue of constitutional fact under Australian constitutional law.

VI. 'Immigrant' Status[49]

Why was the determinative question for Mr Lee whether he was an 'immigrant'? This is best answered through the history of Australian nationality and its relation to immigration. This history is a matter of Australia's international relations and policy, given doctrinal recognition as constitutional facts informing the interpretation of the relevant head of legislative power: the immigration power in section 51(xxvii) of the Australian Constitution. Reflecting the 'political realities' of the time, there is no 'citizenship' head of legislative power.[50]

One must look elsewhere for authority to legislate with respect to citizenship. The key alternatives are sections 51(xix) 'Naturalization and aliens' and 51(xxvii)

---

[48] This was to reprise the main argument at first instance, though the nature of Minister's argument on this point differed, being reactive to the judgment at first instance.

[49] This section draws on R Thwaites, 'Citizenship and Immigration' in P Cane, L Ford and M McMillan (eds), *The Cambridge Legal History of Australia* (Cambridge, CUP, 2022).

[50] *Re Patterson; ex parte Taylor* (2001) 207 CLR 391, 479–80 [267] (Kirby J).

'Immigration and emigration'. The relevant constitutional membership statuses are thus expressed in negative terms: non-alien and non-immigrant.

Today, we think of nationals as not subject to the core power of immigration, which only applies to non-nationals. This was not the situation for many decades after Australian Federation. Immigration restrictions that cut across the relevant nationality status, that of British subject, were a necessary component of the racially discriminatory 'White Australia' policy that would shape immigration for generations.[51] Many British subjects across the Empire did not satisfy the racial strictures of Australian law and practice and were accordingly denied entry. The common status concealed 'very great discrimination between British subjects by means of immigration regulations'.[52] As the antonym of 'alien' was understood to be 'British subject', British subjects were beyond the scope of the aliens power, leading to reliance on the alternative, the immigration power in s 51(xxvii). The immigration power was held to apply to 'immigrants'.

In defining that term, the High Court simultaneously defined non-immigrants: those who had constitutional membership. In its early decades, the Court came to define 'immigrant' with reference to the concept of 'community': 'the ultimate fact to be reached as a test whether a person is an immigrant or not is whether he is or is not at that time a member of the Australian community'.[53] This concept of 'membership' lacked the legal specificity of connecting factors such as domicile, residence, personal presence or nationality (although the Court drew on these concepts). This lack of specificity was, indeed, part of the concept's appeal. The concept of 'community' relied on certain widespread assumptions concerning the habits, mores, and ethnic composition (assumed to be British or European) of the Australian community.

A final feature of the immigration power was that it was read as subject to an 'absorption' doctrine.[54] A person could become a non-immigrant through absorption into the Australian community, thereby moving beyond the scope of the government's powers of exclusion and removal.[55] The need to identify, weigh and balance connecting factors and assess a person's absorption made the question of whether someone was an immigrant into a multi-factorial, evaluative, issue. These features of the power turned 'many details of the lives of individuals'[56] into constitutional facts, conditioning the validity and application of legislation.

The primary citizenship and immigration statutes continued to be based on the immigration power *after* the introduction of statutory citizenship in 1949.

---

[51] G Tavan, *The Long, Slow Death of White Australia* (Melbourne, Scribe, 2005). The right to enter Australia could also be denied to British subjects on other, non-racial, reasons including requirements as to 'character'.

[52] C Parry, *Nationality and Citizenship Laws of the Commonwealth and Ireland* (London, Steven & Sons, 1957), xv–xvi.

[53] *Potter v Minahan* (1908) 7 CLR 277, 308 (Isaacs J).

[54] The doctrine that later came to be labelled the absorption doctrine was introduced in *Ex Parte Walsh and Johnson; In re Yates* (1925) 37 CLR 36.

[55] It was open to the Commonwealth to establish statutory pre-conditions on such absorption: see, eg, *Kuswardana v Minister for Immigration and Ethnic Affairs* (1981) 54 FLR 334.

[56] *Re Patterson* (n 50), 472–73 [247] (Gummow and Hayne JJ). The quote from *Patterson* was directed to the absorption doctrine.

Australian statutory citizenship did not replace the status of British subject. The two co-existed, as set out in section 7 of the Nationality and Citizenship Act 1948 (Cth): 'A person who, under this Act, is an Australian citizen ... shall by virtue of that citizenship be a British subject.' Under this formulation, the acquisition of national citizenship became primary, and British subjecthood a secondary and derivative status. This co-existence endured until the 1980s, when British subject status was finally expunged from the primary citizenship and immigration statutes.[57]

British subjects who were not Australian citizens (by birth, descent or naturalisation) were still not aliens; indeed, the statute defined 'alien' as a person who was not a British subject.[58] As a consequence, the initial, pre-citizenship, reasons for reliance on the 'immigration' power in preference to the 'aliens' power remained. Insofar as the vast majority of British subjects worldwide were neither 'Australian' nor 'alien', the immigration power was understood to be the only head of power available to the Australian parliament to comprehensively regulate the entry and residence of non-citizens.

Reviewing the above, the constitutional facts attending 'immigrant' status can be seen to operate on two scales. There is a large, slow-moving scale by which historical changes are registered, centred on Australia's gradual independence from Great Britain, the corresponding rise and consolidation of a distinctly Australian nationality, and the long, slow demise of the White Australia policy. This level addresses definitional issues: the factors that are relevant to immigrant status at a given time, and the weight they should be accorded. This historical change calls for careful handling of immigration power precedents from different periods, attentive to whether legal propositions uprooted from one period successfully transplant to the legal and factual matrix of another.

A second, smaller scale addresses the application of the various factors to a person's individual circumstances. At this local level, the weighing of the facts to determine whether someone is or is not part of the 'community' operates to particularise and individualise determinations of 'immigrant' status.

VII. The Relationship between Immigrant Status and Nationality – The Minister's Arguments in the *Lee* Litigation

At both first instance and on appeal, the outcome of the *Lee* litigation turned on whether, as a four-month-old infant at Independence, Troyrone Lee was an

---

[57] See Thwaites (n 49) 566–67.
[58] Nationality and Citizenship Act 1948 (Cth) s 5. In effect, a tripartite regime was established, composed of: (1) Australian citizens (who were simultaneously British subjects); (2) British subjects who were not Australian citizens; and (3) aliens.

'immigrant'. If he was not; if he was a 'non-immigrant', then he had a right to permanent residence in Australia such that he retained his Australian citizenship on Independence. As noted, the question of whether someone is an 'immigrant' converts many details of their life into questions of constitutional fact, and so it was in relation to Lee and his parents. This section focuses on one factor considered in the litigation, namely his parents' naturalisation.

Lee's parents' naturalisation falls to be assessed against large-scale matters of constitutional fact, going to the changing relationship between nationality and immigration powers. For the reasons given in section VI, the authorities that pre-date the introduction of statutory citizenship saw possession of the relevant nationality status, British subject, as but one factor among many in determining immigrant status.

The Minister sought to minimise the significance of the naturalisation of Mr Lee's father and mother as Australian citizens, in 1964 and 1973 respectively, by arguing that their naturalisation was but one factor in 'a multi-factorial, evaluative question' as to whether they were immigrants. Naturalisation was treated as no more than an 'important evidentiary fact'.[59] The proposition that 'naturalised Australian citizens were entitled to reside permanently in Australia' was resisted by the Minister.[60]

The Minister's argument proceeded by abstracting statements and authorities from their historical context; for example, it was submitted that 'an Australian citizen may, depending on his or her circumstances, be an immigrant subject to an exercise of power under s 51(xxvii)'. The authorities of *Walsh*,[61] *Macfarlane*,[62] and *Ex parte Te*,[63] were referenced in support of this proposition.[64]

An evaluation of these authorities shows how the Minister constructed the proposition that an Australian citizen may be an immigrant. The key passage referenced from *Macfarlane* reads:

> Whether any given person is one of the people of Australia is necessarily a question of fact … neither locality of birth nor nationality nor domicile is a decisive test, but simply an evidentiary fact, or more or less weight according to the circumstances of the case.[65]

---

[59] Minister of Home Affairs, 'Appellant's outline of submissions', submission in Minister for Home Affairs v Lee, QUD 137 of 2020, 7 October 2020, [30].

[60] Minister of Home Affairs, 'Appellant's supporting submissions', submission in Minister for Home Affairs v Lee, QUD 137 of 2020, 19 November 2020, [19]. A distinct argument advanced by the Minister, beyond the scope of the current chapter, was that a citizen's right to enter and leave Australia was no more than a general law right, subject to statutory modification: see Minister of Home Affairs, 'Appellant's supplementary submissions on constitutional issues', submission in Minister for Home Affairs v Lee, QUD 137 of 2020, 3 February 2021, [23]. These submissions were contemporaneous with travel restrictions on Australian citizens under the Biosecurity Act 2015 (Cth) in response to Covid-19. This distinct argument goes to the content of the status for *all* Australian citizens.

[61] *Minister for Immigration & Multicultural & Indigenous Affairs v Walsh* (2002) 125 FCR 31.

[62] *R v MacFarlane* (1923) 32 CLR 518.

[63] *Re Minister for Immigration and Multicultural Affairs; Ex parte Te* (2002) 212 CLR 162.

[64] Minister of Home Affairs, 'Minister's Submissions of 3 February 2021' (n 60) [23].

[65] *R v MacFarlane* (n 61) 580.

The application of this passage from 1923 to the situation of Mr Lee's parents is misplaced. It ignores fundamental changes in the legal constitution of the Australian community, registered as matters of constitutional fact. As outlined in section VI, 'nationality' is an umbrella term that has covered different statuses over time. The constitutional role played by 'British subject' in 1923 is radically different from the role played by the statutory status of Australian citizenship in 1975. It will be recalled that the status of British subject did not align with the national community for immigration purposes. It was accordingly relegated to a secondary role in defining that community, and so 'immigrant' status. This is reflected in the 1923 authority. The relationship between statutory citizenship and the Australian community in 1975 was qualitatively different. The proposition that all naturalised Australian citizens are necessarily members of 'the Australian community' was by then arguably a basal assumption of the Australian polity. To use an authority on Australian nationality from 1923 to characterise the position of naturalised Australian citizens in 1975 is to use an umbrella term ('nationality') as a magician's cloak. The same problem attends the reference to *Te* in the Minister's submissions. The passage from *Te* states that status is not determinative of the application of the immigration power, but the examples of status offered are those of 'domicile' and 'British subject', not 'citizen'.[66]

Writing in 1966, two of Australia's most prominent public law academics commented on a possible 'wide' view of the immigration power, whereby a person's immigrant status might remain notwithstanding naturalisation. Enid Campbell and Harry Whitmore stated:

> It is to be hoped that the High Court will take the first opportunity to declare unequivocally that persons who demonstrate their allegiance to Australia by registration or naturalisation are forever beyond the power of deportation possessed by the Commonwealth Government. The aphorism 'once an immigrant, always an immigrant' is offensive to a large proportion of the population of Australia in the mid-twentieth century.[67]

This conveys both that the contrary position had not been foreclosed by High Court authority in 1966, and that pursuing the idea that naturalised Australians remained immigrants would, by 1966, constitute an attack on a shared Australian community united by a common bond of citizenship. Such an argument was no less offensive when applied to events in 1975 by a government in 2016.

An additional consideration is that when, in the 1980s, the government shifted from reliance on the immigration power to reliance on the aliens power,[68] it was

---

[66] *Ex parte Te* (n 63) 191–92 [107].
[67] E Campbell and H Whitmore, *Freedom in Australia* (Sydney, Sydney University Press, 1966) 106. In their 'new and reset' edition of 1973 they register that they were still waiting for 'an unequivocal statement' from the High Court in these terms: E Campbell and H Whitmore, *Freedom in Australia* (2nd edn, Sydney, Sydney University Press, 1973) 196.
[68] A shift given the green light by Gibbs J's statement in 1982 that the assumption that 'a person who is a British subject under the law of the United Kingdom cannot be an alien within s 51(xix)' is 'incorrect': *Pochi v McPhee* (1982) 151 CLR 101, 109 [9].

accepted that a statutory citizen was a constitutional non-alien, thus beyond the reach of statutory immigration powers. The shift to the aliens power did not occasion an abrupt increase in the legal and constitutional significance of statutory citizenship.[69] The emphasis in the authorities on constitutional membership, whether developed in terms of non-immigrant or non-alien status, is on the *gradual* evolution of the key legal relationships.[70] The better view is that statutory citizenship was, at its weakest, the prime factor among equals in determining constitutional membership for some time before the shift to the aliens power in the 1980s, and by 1975.

An authority that featured prominently in the Minister's submissions was the 2002 decision of the Full Court of the Federal Court in *Walsh*.[71] Susan Walsh was born in Papua prior to Independence, to an Australian father and Papuan mother. Her Australian citizenship, acquired by birth in Papua, was held not to have survived Independence. As noted by the Court in *Lee*, in *Walsh* there was limited discussion of any basis on which Ms Walsh might share a right of entry to Australia (outside of Papua) concomitant with that enjoyed by her father. Her parents were not married at the time of her birth, meaning that she acquired the citizenship of her mother, not her father, under the then provisions of the Australian Citizenship Act 1948 (Cth). By way of distinction, the Court in *Lee* emphasised that Troyrone Lee, born to two naturalised Australian citizens, was unequivocally born into the Australian community and for that reason, among others, a non-immigrant. As an Australian non-immigrant at Independence, he was a 'real' Australian citizen, and did not acquire PNG citizenship and lose Australian citizenship. In *Lee*, the Court buttressed this conclusion with reference to domicile. The Lees had purchased a house in Brisbane and all indications were, that having worked for a further period in PNG, they intended to settle permanently in Australia. Should any further evidence of non-immigrant status have been required, this was taken to supply it. Again, in an argument with echoes of arguments rejected a century ago (in *Walsh and Johnson*),[72] it was contended by the Minister's lawyers that as

---

[69] The Minister argued that to focus on citizenship was to conflate the aliens and immigration power: Minister of Home Affairs, 'Minister's Submissions of 3 February 2021' (n 60) [22]. I disagree for the reasons given in the main text. A focus on (here naturalised) citizenship in relation to the immigration power in 1975 is entirely consistent with the constitutional facts attending the immigration power. The shift to the aliens power did make a difference for some *without* Australian statutory citizenship, foreclosing a means of acquiring constitutional membership that had previously been available. Under the immigration power it had been open to argue that those without statutory citizenship had nonetheless been absorbed into the Australian community, holding constitutional membership as non-immigrants. The application of such an absorption doctrine to the aliens power was rejected in *Pochi* (n 68) 111 (Gibbs CJ). cf *Alexander v Minister for Home Affairs* (2022) 96 ALJR 560, 600–01 [184] per Edelman J. A related argument for constitutional membership (as non-aliens), advanced in respect of non-citizen British subjects, was finally foreclosed in *Shaw v Minister for Immigration and Multicultural Affairs* (2003) 218 CLR 28.

[70] See, eg, *Hill* (n 10).

[71] *Walsh* (n 61).

[72] *Walsh and Johnson* (n 54). In dissent, Isaacs J had argued that anyone not born in Australia had immigrated there, and that 'once an immigrant, always an immigrant'. The majority rejected this position.

Troyrone Lee had not lived in Australia pre-Independence, he was an immigrant. As the Court responded, Australian expatriates are born overseas all the time, only coming home later (here, with the added distinction that he was born in what was, pre-Independence, Australian territory).

Repeatedly, the Minister's submissions used propositions from past case law on 'immigrant' status as inert artefacts, transplanting them from the configurations of status, membership and world that had generated them into the qualitatively different world of 1975. The effect was destabilising, undermining the securities afforded by naturalisation in the decade to 1975 by reference to the more tenuous protections afforded by nationality in the 1920s. In this way, the Minister's submissions flagged the potential vulnerability of legal assumptions, and lives, resting on a shared understanding of historical change, as registered in matters of constitutional fact, here the changing factors going to 'immigrant' status and the weight they should be afforded. The corresponding protection against this vulnerability, here provided by the Federal Court, was the careful maintenance of context, both of history and foreign law, as it bore on intergovernmental arrangements.

VIII. Conclusion

Three aspects of the Australian government's actions and legal arguments stand out from the *Lee* litigation. The first is the government's indifference towards Papua New Guinean authorities and law. There is a sense in which this indifference is self-reinforcing. Indifference to the Papua New Guinea legal context, and dismissal of the position of the PNG authorities, enabled the startling proposition that interpretation of a foreign state's constitution was a matter of Australian law. That conclusion in turn obviated the need to engage with foreign law. Again, the decision not to return to the starting point in the PNG Constitution enabled the belief that earlier Australian authorities on the issue were exhaustive in their coverage of PNG law.

A similar indifference to context characterised the Minister's analysis of Australian constitutional developments, most notable in the Minister's resistance to naturalisation's growing legal and constitutional significance over time.

In its analysis of both foreign and Australian constitutional developments the government's approach highlights a vulnerability shared by areas of constitutional law reliant on constitutional facts. Constitutional facts mediate between legal text and the extra-legal context (in the present case comprising inter-state relations: between Australia and PNG, and Australia and the UK). When constitutional facts are forgotten or ignored, they cease to align the law with the fundamental political realities at the relevant critical date.

Which brings us to the third aspect of the litigation. These issues of legal method affect lives. Citizenship status is a fundamental form of security. It gives you a home. In 2016, responding to a routine passport application, the government blithely informed Mr Lee it no longer regarded him as a citizen. What motivated the decision to deny the citizenship of a peaceable, long-term and well-integrated Australian?[73] And then to defend that decision at first instance and on appeal, using legal arguments that minimised the importance of foreign law, Australian naturalisation and the rights attendant on citizenship? The Lee episode raises troubling questions as to motivation on the part of the Australian government.

The Minister's submissions dismissed the contention that Lee would effectively be left stateless if denied Australian citizenship.[74] This was dismissive of the PNG government's position, clearly conveyed in the letter from PNG's Deputy Chief Migration Officer.[75] And it showed indifference to the fate of Mr Lee, someone Australia had accepted as a citizen for over 40 years.[76] Fortunately, this indifference was arrested by the Federal Court. The Court's attention to the full legal context reaffirmed legal assumptions, and a legal status, foundational to Mr Lee's life.

---

[73] I am not suggesting that a person's citizenship should be conditional on any of these matters. That these conditions were met in Mr Lee's case removes a number of possible candidates for government motivation. The judgment also notes that the class of persons to which Mr Lee belonged: 'must surely now have relatively few members': *Lee* (n 1) [11].
[74] Minister of Home Affairs, 'Minister's Submissions of 22 October 2020' (n 46) [12].
[75] See text accompanying n 32.
[76] As recorded by the Court, 'Mr Lee is, quite literally, betwixt and between, in jeopardy of being stateless': *Lee* (n 1) [8].

PART II

Facts in Administrative Law

6

The Interdependence of Process and Substance: Facts, Evidence and the Changing Nature of Judicial Review

JASON N E VARUHAS[*]

I. Public Law Ecosystems

An ecosystem is a geographical area within which animals, plants and other living organisms, and the physical environment, interact and co-exist in complex and dynamic ways. A feature of ecosystems is the interdependence of the component parts: a change in one component can have a knock-on effect on others. Judicial review is not an ecosystem: it is a creature not of the natural world but of the normative order of the law. Yet it shares certain features of an ecosystem. It occupies a discrete normative environment within the legal landscape and is comprised of different component parts, such as substantive norms, remedies, and procedures. Critically, like an ecosystem these components are interdependent: a change in one part of the system can have ripple effects on other parts.

There is perhaps no greater illustration of interdependence within judicial review than the interconnection between procedural norms governing evidence, and substantive norms of judicial review.[1] As this chapter will illustrate, changes in the nature of substantive norms can have significant ramifications for the law and practice of evidence within the judicial review procedure, and vice versa. This includes the possibility of 'feedback loops': a change in a substantive norm may lead to a change in the procedural treatment of evidence, which may in turn feed back into evolution of substantive norms, and so on.

---

[*] My thanks to the editors for comments on this chapter, and to Professors Mark Aronson, Tom Hickman KC, and Richard Rawlings for comments on an early version of this chapter. The origins of this chapter lie in a presentation given at an ASSA Workshop on 'Facts in Public Law Adjudication', Melbourne Law School, August 2019, which was organised by the editors of this collection. I am grateful to the editors for their organisation of the event, and to the participants for a stimulating discussion.

[1] For an excellent illustration of the interconnection between process and substance, within the 'living system' of judicial review, see the models of judicial review presented in C Harlow and R Rawlings, *Law and Administration* (4th edn, Cambridge, CUP, 2022) 812–23.

This chapter begins with an exposition of the 'standard account' of the treatment of facts and evidence within the English judicial review procedure. On this account judicial review is an inappropriate forum for testing evidence and resolving disputed questions of fact. The only evidence generally relevant to a review claim is that which was before the administrative decision-maker, and thus forms part of the historical decision-making record. Unlike in ordinary civil proceedings, formal evidence-gathering techniques, such as disclosure, oral evidence and expert evidence, are rare in judicial review proceedings. It is highly unusual for courts to make formal findings of fact in the face of contested evidence, with any factual disputes generally being resolved in favour of the public defendant. These procedural features follow from the traditional conception of judicial review as a supervisory jurisdiction focused on questions of legality. Factfinding is for the administrative decision-maker. If courts seek to resolve disputed questions of fact they risk entering the 'merits', and thus exceeding their proper supervisory role.

The chapter goes on to show that while courts continue to repeat the standard account as mantra, reality has become increasingly complex. This increased complexity has been driven by a variety of factors. But a central reason – which is the focus here – for changes in the treatment of facts and evidence within review proceedings is that procedural law and practice are adjusting to significant changes in substantive law. The chapter examines the rise of human rights. It explains how the advent of the Human Rights Act 1998 (HRA) has precipitated significant shifts in the treatment of facts and evidence on review and offers critical reflections on these developments. The chapter goes on to chart how the HRA has had knock-on effects on common law judicial review, leading to further procedural shifts. To this end, the chapter considers developments in substantive review, and the novel 'action' for denial of access to justice. Overall, the human rights case study provides a striking illustration of the interdependence of process and substance within the public law system.

II. The Standard Account

A. Facts and Evidence on Judicial Review

In the late 1970s procedural reforms were introduced which established a new procedure, the 'application for judicial review'.[2] Previously each prerogative writ had been associated with its own procedure. The reforms established one unified procedural route for seeking the prerogative remedies. It remains the case that the

---

[2] Senior Courts Act 1981, s 31; CPR Pt 54. On the birth of this procedure see JNE Varuhas, 'The Public Interest Conception of Public Law: Its Procedural Origins and Substantive Implications' in J Bell et al (eds), *Public Law Adjudication in Common Law Systems: Process and Substance* (Oxford, Hart Publishing, 2016).

application for judicial review is the principal procedural route within the court system for claims alleging public law unlawfulness.

The procedure has certain characteristics which distinguish it from ordinary civil procedure. These include a distinctive standing rule, a short three-month limitation period, a permission stage and significant remedial discretion. Proceedings *must* be initiated via this procedure where a claimant seeks an order based on the prerogative writs, such as a quashing order (formerly certiorari) or prohibiting order (formerly prohibition).[3] Outside such cases there are rules governing when claims must or may be streamed via the judicial review procedure, which are discussed below.

Importantly for present purposes the procedure is characterised by a distinctive approach to facts and evidence, which I term 'the standard account'. According to the standard account it is trite law that review procedure is 'not well suited to the determination of disputed questions of fact' or the testing of evidence.[4] These propositions are institutionalised in the Civil Procedure Rules: judicial review is a procedure specifically calibrated to resolution of claims 'unlikely to involve a substantial dispute of fact'.[5] It follows that, while disclosure (formerly, discovery), oral evidence and expert evidence may be permitted in the court's discretion, they shall be very rare, not being part of 'the ordinary stock-in-trade of the prerogative jurisdiction'.[6] The marginal role of evidence and fact-finding within review contrasts with ordinary civil procedure, in which disclosure, cross-examination, expert evidence and judicial resolution of disputed questions of fact are standard. Reflecting the orthodoxy that questions of fact and evidence are of marginal significance in review proceedings, leading judicial review treatises dedicate only a handful of paragraphs to the issue of evidence, while certain topics – such as expert evidence – are never mentioned.[7]

Generally, so the standard account goes, the evidence before the reviewing court shall be limited to witness statements (formerly, affidavits), along with exhibited documents directly related to points raised in the witness statement. These statements and documents are generally produced by parties pursuant to the duty of candour (discussed below), rather than pursuant to formal court orders. On top of court-ordered disclosure being rare, where ordered it is traditionally limited to documents relevant to issues emerging from witness statements.[8]

---

[3] Senior Courts Act 1981, s 31(1); CPR r 54.2.
[4] *R (A) v Croydon LBC* [2009] UKSC 8 [33] (*Croydon*).
[5] CPR rr 8.1(2), 54.1(2)(e).
[6] *Roy v Kensington and Chelsea and Westminster Family Practitioner Committee* [1992] 1 AC 624, 646–47. See CPR 54A PD paras 10.2, 10.3; HMCTS, *Administrative Court Judicial Review Guide* (2022) [7.6.3], [11.2.2], [23.1.8], [23.2.2]. Available at: https://assets.publishing.service.gov.uk/government/uploads/system/uploads/attachment_data/file/1106207/14.130_HMCTS_Administrative_Court_Guide_2022_FINAL_v06_WEB__2_.pdf. The main case authorities concerning the treatment of evidence are considered below.
[7] HWR Wade and CF Forsyth, *Administrative Law* (11th edn, Oxford, OUP, 2014) 547, 554–55, 556–58; H Woolf et al, *De Smith's Judicial Review* (8th edn, London, Sweet and Maxwell, 2018) [16-026]–[16-027], [16-072]–[16-074], [16-080]–[16-081], [17-044]–[17-046]; P Craig, *Administrative Law* (9th edn, London, Sweet and Maxwell, 2021) [17-012], [17-027], [27-056]–[27-058].
[8] *Tweed v Parades Commission for Northern Ireland* [2007] 1 AC 650 [29].

It shall seldom be appropriate or necessary to consider evidence beyond that which was before the decision-maker or which shows the process by which a decision was reached; thus the body of evidence is generally limited to the historical decision-making record, so that consideration of documentary evidence beyond that which was before the decision-maker 'must often be questionable'.[9]

Facts are generally common ground between parties and relevant only to show how the legal issue arises.[10] If there are disputed questions of fact these will ordinarily be resolved in favour of government.[11]

One reason courts are generally unable to resolve disputed questions of fact in the ordinary way is that cross-examination of witnesses is hardly ever permitted.[12] It has even been said that where the challenge is to a decision-maker's finding of fact (permitted on very narrow grounds),[13] 'there should be no question of live witnesses'.[14] Similarly, even in cases where there are questions over what officials knew and thought when they exercised their powers, oral evidence has not been permitted.[15] If a case does squarely raise disputed questions of fact, and would require oral evidence for its proper determination, these may be indicators that the case should not be streamed via review procedure.[16]

B. Rationalising the Standard Account

There are three core rationales for the standard approach: the supervisory nature of judicial review; pragmatic concerns; and the duty of candour.

---

[9] *R (Law Society) v Lord Chancellor* [2018] EWHC 2094 (Admin) [36]; *Bubb v Wandsworth LBC* [2012] PTSR 1011 [25]; *R (Naik) v Secretary of State for the Home Department* [2011] EWCA Civ 1546 [63]; *R (Transport Action Network Ltd) v Secretary of State for Transport* [2021] EWHC 2095 [80]; *Ashbridge Investments Ltd v Minister of Housing and Local Government* [1965] 1 WLR 1320, 1327. And see *Kibiti v Secretary of State for the Home Department* [2000] EWCA Civ 3022 [43]–[44] (in the context of an appeal on a question of law).

[10] *Tweed* (n 8) [2].

[11] *R v Board of Visitors of Hull Prison, ex parte St Germain (No 2)* [1979] 1 WLR 1401, 1410H; *R (Al-Sweady) v Secretary of State for Defence* [2010] HRLR 2 [17]; *R v Fulham, Hammersmith and Kensington Rent Tribunal, ex parte Zerek* [1951] 2 KB 1, 11. This approach in part follows from the allocation of onus in review proceedings: *R (Talpada) v Secretary of State for the Home Department* [2018] EWCA Civ 841 [2].

[12] *St Germain* (n 11) 1410; *R (Safeer) v Secretary of State for the Home Department* [2018] EWCA Civ 2518 [19] (prescribing the very narrow circumstances in which oral evidence may be ordered); *R (Gardner) v Secretary of State for Health and Social Care* [2021] EWHC (Admin) 2946 [9] (regarding conflicting expert evidence). See also *O'Reilly v Mackman* [1983] 2 AC 237, 282; *Talpada* (n 11) [2]; *R (Bancoult) v Secretary of State for Foreign and Commonwealth Affairs* [2012] EWHC 2115 (Admin) [14].

[13] See *Secretary of State for Education and Science v Tameside MBC* [1977] AC 1014, 1030; *Begum v London Borough of Tower Hamlets* [2003] 2 WLR 388 [7]; *E v Secretary of State for the Home Department* [2004] QB 1044. And note *Edwards v Bairstow* [1956] AC 14.

[14] *Bubb* (n 9) [25].

[15] *R (CC) v Commissioner of Police for the Metropolis* [2012] 1 WLR 1913 [28].

[16] *Roy* (n 6) 650, 654; *R v East Berkshire Health Authority, ex parte Walsh* [1985] QB 152, 173; *Sher v Chief Constable of Greater Manchester Police* [2010] EWHC 1859 (Admin) [72], [80]. See also *R (Maiden Outdoor Advertising Ltd) v Lambeth LBC* [2003] EWHC 1224 (Admin) [37].

(i) Judicial Review as a Supervisory Jurisdiction

The principal reason for the restrictive approach to facts and evidence on judicial review, compared to ordinary procedure, is that review – as traditionally conceptualised – is a supervisory jurisdiction.[17]

Where Parliament confers a statutory discretion it is first and foremost for the statutory decision-maker to determine how the discretion should be exercised. The repository is the primary decision-maker. The corollary is that courts are necessarily confined to a secondary, reviewing function. If courts were to substitute their view of the right decision, they would usurp the role of the decision-maker. This is problematic for a range of reasons, including that it would involve the courts undermining parliamentary sovereignty: Parliament has prescribed that it is the statutory decision-maker who is the primary decision-maker, not the court.

As such courts on review are confined to determining questions of legality – such as whether the decision-maker has properly interpreted and abided the terms of the parent statute – and questions of procedural fairness – such as whether the person subject to the decision had the opportunity to put their case.[18] It is legitimate for courts to rule on matters of legality, because within the English constitutional tradition questions of statutory interpretation and compliance with statute are for courts.[19] It is legitimate for courts to scrutinise the process adopted by the decision-maker because matters of process do not pre-empt outcomes, and courts are expert in procedure.

Judicial intervention outside matters of statutory compliance or procedural fairness are necessarily suspect as there is a risk of the court trespassing on the decision-maker's sphere of authority. It follows that the standard for intervention on matters of substance is traditionally set at a very high threshold – denoted by the *Wednesbury* standard – catching only those exercises of power that are patently unreasonable, and thus cannot be considered a genuine exercise of the decision-making mandate. If courts intervened on a lower threshold there would be a serious risk that they would illegitimately trespass upon the decision-maker's territory; the *Wednesbury* formulation is a form of self-denying ordinance.

How is all of this relevant to explaining the restrictive approach to facts and evidence on review?

First, running with the conferral by Parliament of a statutory decision-power, is the 'exclusive jurisdiction to determine facts'.[20] Therefore if the courts re-examined factual conclusions, and substituted their own view of the facts, the court would

---

[17] See the classic statements of principle in *R v Secretary of State for the Home Department, ex parte Brind* [1991] 1 AC 696, 757; *Gillick v West Norfolk and Wisbech Area Health Authority* [1986] AC 112, 192; *R v Chief Constable of North Wales, ex parte Evans* [1982] 1 WLR 1155, 1173; *R v Northumberland Compensation Appeal Tribunal, ex parte Shaw* [1952] 1 KB 338, 346–47.
[18] See, eg, *Talpada* (n 11) [64].
[19] *R (Palestine Solidarity Campaign Ltd) v Secretary of State for Housing, Communities and Local Government* [2020] UKSC 16 [67].
[20] *O'Reilly* (n 12) 282; *R v Hillingdon London Borough Council, ex parte Puhlhofer* [1986] AC 484, 518.

illegitimately usurp the decision-maker's role: the court must not, within a supervisory jurisdiction, place 'itself in the position of the primary decision-maker on a question of fact'.[21] Put another way, factual matters that underpin the decision fall into the 'merits' and are thus for the decision-maker. Cross-examination for example could be used to seek to undermine the decision-maker's findings,[22] while disclosure could similarly be used to seek to question factual findings or dispute the historical record.[23] Expert evidence could be – and has been[24] – relied on to challenge the factual premises of a decision. Put another way, oral evidence, disclosure etc pre-suppose there is some disputed question of fact for the court to resolve. But it is generally inapt for courts to resolve disputed factual questions as in so doing they would bring themselves into competition with the primary decision-maker.[25] Thus courts on review reiterate that they are not concerned with facts, but the legal consequences of those facts found by the statutory decision-maker.[26] This concern not to overstep the mark is reflected in other aspects of review; for example while there are dedicated review grounds for challenging findings of fact, those grounds are very tightly confined.[27]

Second, even putting aside the first point, adjudication of disputed questions of fact could illegitimately draw courts into re-examining the qualities of the decision itself. This follows from the fact that it is difficult to disentangle the normative/qualitative and factual dimensions of a decision, which is the product of a decision-maker applying their judgement to the facts. As the courts have observed, the factual bases of the decision are part of the process of substantive reasoning.[28] If the court makes findings of fact for itself, it risks moving beyond conducting review of another's decision, to making its own decision, based on its own view of the facts.[29]

All of this is summed up in repeated judicial statements that the restrictive approach to facts and evidence follows from the supervisory judicial role on review, that is a role according to which courts are concerned with questions of law and legality, not facts or merits.[30]

---

[21] *R (Begum) v SIAC* [2021] UKSC 7 [125]–[128].
[22] *George v Secretary of State for the Environment* (1979) 38 P&CR 609, 615, approved by *O'Reilly* (n 12) 282.
[23] *Tweed* (n 8) [29].
[24] *Law Society* (n 9).
[25] *R v Secretary of State for the Environment, ex parte Islington LBC* [1991] 7 WLUK 261 (Nolan LJ) (in relation to disclosure).
[26] *O'Reilly* (n 12) 282.
[27] See the cases cited at n 13.
[28] *Law Society* (n 9) [98]. It follows that there is an overlap between rationality review and review for mistake of fact, as acknowledged in *Law Society* ibid.
[29] *Bubb* (n 9) [24]; *Ashbridge* (n 9) 1327. See also *R v Secretary of State for the Home Department, ex parte Momin Ali* [1984] 1 WLR 663, 670 (in the context of an appeal on a question of law).
[30] eg *Bubb* (n 9) [24]–[25]; *O'Reilly* (n 12) 282; *Law Society* (n 9) [36]; *Begum v SIAC* (n 21) [125]–[128]; *DWR Cymru Cyfyngedig v Environment Agency of Wales* [2003] EWHC 336 (Admin) [58]; *R (AB) v Chief Constable of Hampshire Constabulary* [2019] EWHC 3461 (Admin) [117]; HMCTS, *Judicial Review Guide* (n 6) [23.2.2].

The foregoing concerns are reflected in the generally restrictive approach taken to disclosure, oral evidence and expert evidence,[31] and the narrow judicial focus within review proceedings on the historical decision-making record. But the concerns are also evident in more specific principles, such as the principles governing admission of fresh evidence, including expert evidence, as articulated in *R v Secretary of State for the Environment, ex parte Powis*.[32] According to the *Powis* principles fresh evidence is only generally admissible in four categories of case. It is an important feature of each category that admission of fresh evidence would not conflict with the supervisory role of the courts.

First, fresh evidence may be permitted to show what material was before the decision-maker. This category stems from older cases where affidavits had not been put before the court, and where all the court had before it was the Minister's formal order.[33] But today it would be rare to find a case that falls into this category given the contemporary practice, pursuant to the duty of candour (see below), that the decision-maker will put in evidence a witness statement recounting the historical record, with significant documents exhibited.[34] But if fresh evidence were permitted under this category, it would simply go to complete the historical decision-making record; as such, the material is in a sense not truly 'fresh' evidence. It follows that leading such evidence does not raise the spectre of competition between the court and decision-maker in terms of fact-finding: it reveals the historical record, so the court can judge if the decision-maker has gone wrong in law.[35]

Second, fresh evidence may be permitted if relevant to determination of factual questions on which the decision-maker's jurisdiction depends. Such evidence is directed to determining questions of jurisdictional fact, and thus goes to whether the decision-maker had the authority to decide in the first place, rather than going to the factual basis of a decision made within jurisdiction. Importantly, the court, when it determines jurisdictional facts, is not conducting a review as such, but rather adjudicates the matter on 'the merits':[36] the decision is for the court, and no one else.

Third, fresh evidence may be permitted where it goes to determining whether a proper procedure was followed. For example, fresh evidence might demonstrate that in the course of decision-making the claimant was not given notice of

---

[31] Expert evidence is governed by Part 35 of the CPR, and the overarching test governing admission of such evidence is in CPR r 35.1: '[e]xpert evidence shall be restricted to that which is reasonably required to resolve the proceeding'.
[32] *R v Secretary of State for the Environment, ex parte Powis* [1981] 1 WLR 584, 595. See also *Lynch v General Dental Council* [2003] EWHC 2987 (Admin) [19]–[25]; *Law Society* (n 9) [36]–[42]; D Blundell, 'Of Evidence and Experts: Recent Developments in Fact-finding and Expert Evidence in Judicial Review' (2018) 23 *Judicial Review* 243.
[33] *Ashbridge* (n 9) 1327.
[34] ibid.
[35] ibid.
[36] *R v Secretary of State for the Home Department, ex parte Khawaja* [1984] AC 74, 110; *Croydon* (n 4) [26]–[27]; *R (A) v Chief Constable of Kent Constabulary* [2013] EWCA Civ 1706 [58]–[59].

potentially prejudicial material. Such evidence is directed to determining whether a fair process was abided, rather than to scrutinising the outcome of the decision-making process.

Fourth, fresh evidence may be permitted to prove an allegation of bias or other misconduct, such as fraud.[37] Evidence may for example be necessary to determine the decision-maker's intent or motivation, which is not otherwise generally relevant on judicial review. Importantly, such evidence goes to proving the misconduct alleged, as opposed to disputing particular factual findings.

The *Powis* categories continue to govern admission of fresh evidence. However, courts have incrementally added to them over time. For example, reflecting the rise of expert tribunals, and judicial review of such bodies, courts have recognised that fresh expert evidence may be admitted – albeit rarely – to aid the court's understanding of the material under consideration, including so as to explain technical terms.[38] Like the other four categories, evidence in this category does not draw the court into competition with the decision-maker's fact-finding, but is directed to enabling the court to understand the decision under review and issues arising. In this context courts have stressed that expert evidence that goes beyond explanation, and ventures into opinion, will nearly always be inadmissible 'since it will almost invariably involve an attempt to challenge the factual conclusions and judgment of an expert [decision-maker]. That is something which is inappropriate for a reviewing court'.[39] When courts have been invited to mediate competing expert views, they have responded: 'There is no public law argument which would allow the court to prefer any of the opinions of the claimant's experts.'[40]

Thus, the instances in which new evidence may be permitted are those where admission of evidence would be consonant with the supervisory nature of the judicial role. Furthermore, the courts are able to ensure the *Powis* categories are not abused by claimants, as fresh evidence can only be led with the court's permission, albeit at times litigants have disregarded this requirement.[41]

---

[37] Cases involving allegations of *mala fides* or corruption are also cases in which cross-examination may be appropriate: *R (Patel) v Secretary of State for the Home Department* [2015] EWCA Civ 645 [11]; *Jedwell v Denbighshire County Council* [2015] EWCA Civ 1232 [55]. Notably such cases may involve a private law action.

[38] *Lynch* (n 32) [20]–[25]. Expert evidence that goes to explaining technical matters will not typically be required for cases in expert tribunals – which perform a review-like function – as tribunal members have technical expertise: *Tobii Ab (Publ) v Competition and Markets Authority* [2019] CAT 23 [20]–[32].

[39] *Lynch* (n 32) [25]. See also *AB* (n 30) [117], [120]; *Gardner* (n 12) [2]–[17]; *Law Society* (n 9) [36]–[42].

[40] *Transport* (n 9) [150], [152]. See similarly: *Law Society* (n 9) [41], [54], [123]; *DWR* (n 30) [58]–[59]; *R (Bridges) v Chief Constable of South Wales Police* [2020] EWCA Civ 1058 [199]; *R (Mott) v Environment Agency* [2016] 1 WLR 4338 [70]; *R (British American Tobacco UK Ltd) v Secretary of State for Health* [2016] EWCA Civ 1182 [252(ii)].

[41] *Law Society* (n 9) [7], [44]–[49]; *AB* (n 30) [107]–[120]; *R (HK) v Secretary of State for the Home Department* [2016] EWHC 857 (Admin) [10]–[18].

(ii) Pragmatic Concerns

So the principal justification for the cautious judicial approach to facts and evidence on review lies in the supervisory nature of the review jurisdiction. But this reticence is further reinforced by concerns over cost, time, delay and detriment to good administration, which are more general concerns that have permeated the review procedure since its inception, and underpin the multiple judicial discretions on review, including at the permission and remedies stage.[42] These concerns have, over time, been reinforced by an ever-increasing focus within procedural law on proportionate dispute resolution and active judicial case management, encapsulated in the 'overriding objective' of the Civil Procedure Rules.[43]

Thus, regarding oral evidence, Lord Neuberger MR said: 'if judges regularly allow witnesses and cross-examination in judicial review cases, the court time and legal costs involved in such cases will spiral'.[44] Another Master of the Rolls, Lord Denning, had earlier warned that cross-examination must be strictly confined, lest it 'roam unchecked'.[45]

Lord Diplock observed that disclosure can be 'time-consuming'.[46] It can, in combination with the associated need for procedural rulings and directions, contribute to litigation being 'strung out for a very lengthy period'.[47] Such delay can undermine administrative and third-party interests in the speedy determination of validity, and the certainty such determination brings.[48] Put simply, delay can leave administrative processes in an extended state of suspended animation. Disclosure can also be 'costly' and 'oppressive'.[49] There is a risk that disclosure will be used by claimants to conduct a 'fishing expedition' in the hope of turning up some basis for impugning administrative action, which could ultimately be extremely wasteful in terms of time and cost, and lead to the court being 'flood[ed] ... with needless paper'.[50]

Courts have not as often expressed pragmatic concerns in relation to expert evidence.[51] But this is probably because until recently expert evidence was virtually unheard of on review. Yet the same sorts of concerns that arise in connection

---

[42] See generally Varuhas, 'Public Interest Conception' (n 2) eg 54–62, 67–69; Harlow and Rawlings (n 1) 851–52.
[43] CPR rr 1.1–1.4. See, eg, *AB* (n 30) [108]; *Anufrijeva v London Borough of Southwark* [2003] EWCA Civ 1406 [79]–[81].
[44] *Bubb* (n 9) [24].
[45] *O'Reilly* (n 12) 257.
[46] ibid 282. See also *Tweed* (n 8) [56].
[47] ibid 282, 284.
[48] ibid 284.
[49] *Tweed* (n 8) [2].
[50] ibid [2], [31], [56].
[51] But see, eg, *CF v Secretary of State for the Home Department* [2004] EWHC (Fam) [218]; *HK* (n 41) [14]. Expert tribunals, such as the Competition Appeal Tribunal, which perform a function analogous to review, have expressed concerns over wasted time and cost associated with expert evidence. See, eg, *BAA Ltd v Competition Commission* [2012] CAT 3 [80]; *HCA International Limited v Competition and Markets Authority* [2014] CAT 10 [4].

to other formal evidence-gathering processes also arise in relation to expert evidence.

Expert evidence can significantly increase party costs. Allowing admission of expert evidence can draw out proceedings as it can take time for evidence to be garnered – possibly leading to multiple time extensions – and the court will have to manage the process through procedural directions and rulings.[52] More generally admission of expert evidence may increase the complexity of proceedings, leading to cost and delay,[53] and proceedings becoming 'unmanageable'.[54]

The court will be required to scrutinise evidence for admissibility. It is often the case that only some parts of expert witness statements are admissible.[55] The process of evaluating evidence for admissibility can be painstaking as inadmissible statements may be interwoven with admissible statements,[56] and the line between admissible and inadmissible evidence can be difficult to draw.[57] The court will have to identify which evidence is contentious, and which is uncontested; great care is needed as much can depend on these conclusions.[58]

Finally, there is the risk of 'ratcheting up' or escalation.[59] For example a claimant may seek to admit expert evidence, leading the defendant to respond with its own evidence, which in turn prompts a reply from the claimant's expert, so on and so forth. The risk of escalation is real, as it is not difficult to find examples in the case law (and concomitant judicial expressions of exasperation).[60] Escalation exacerbates pragmatic concerns associated with expert evidence, such as concerns over cost and delay.

(iii) Duty of Candour

The final rationale for the differential treatment of facts and evidence within review, compared to ordinary procedure, is that parties to review proceedings are subject to a duty of candour and co-operation.[61] The duty is grounded in the nature of judicial review and its distinctive character compared to 'private' litigation. Courts

---

[52] See, eg, *AB* (n 30) [40]–[43]; *Law Society* (n 9) [45]; *R (Middlebrook Mushrooms Ltd) v Agricultural Wages Board of England and Wales* [2004] EWHC 1447 (Admin) [7]–[15]. For examples of substantial judgments concerning admissibility of expert evidence see *Gardner* (n 12); *R (Good Law Project Ltd) v Minister for the Cabinet Office* [2021] EWHC 2091.

[53] *Law Society* (n 9) [46] (more hearing and pre-reading time required to deal with expert evidence).

[54] *Gardner* (n 12) [22]; *CF* (n 51) [217].

[55] See, eg, *Law Society* (n 9) [50]–[62].

[56] See, eg, *Gardner* (n 12) [10]–[17].

[57] *Lynch* (n 32) [24].

[58] *Law Society* (n 9) [41], [122]–[123]; *Blundell* (n 32) [36].

[59] As noted in *HCA* (n 51) [4].

[60] *Law Society* (n 9) [7]; *Gardner* (n 12) [15]; *Mushrooms* (n 52) [7]–[15].

[61] CPR 54A PD para 10.1; HMCTS, *Judicial Review Guide* (n 6) [7.5]–[7.6], [15.1]–[15.5.3]. See also Treasury Solicitor's Department, Guidance on Discharging the Duty of Candour and Disclosure in Judicial Review Proceedings (*Gov.UK*, January 2010). Available at: https://assets.publishing.service.gov.uk/government/uploads/system/uploads/attachment_data/file/285368/Tsol_discharging_1_.pdf, last accessed 19 December 2022.

emphasise that, whereas in private claims litigants pursue their special interests, in judicial review the courts and public defendants are working together in partnership to uphold the highest standards of public administration.[62]

It seems now to have been confirmed that the duty is owed by all parties to the proceedings.[63] But the duty on government to place its cards face up is 'very high',[64] not least because most of the cards – in terms of evidence – start in the government's hands.[65] As such courts do not 'treat the position of the claimant and respondent ... in the same way'.[66]

The duty arises on government from the point it is aware someone is likely to test a decision.[67] It is a continuing duty which persists through the course of the proceeding.[68]

Pursuant to this duty, the parties, especially government, must assist the court by providing full and accurate explanations of the material facts relevant to the legal issue via written witness statements, and explaining the reasoning behind the decision under challenge.[69] If a particular document is significant, it should ordinarily be exhibited.[70]

The duty requires that neither party mislead the court, intentionally or unintentionally.[71] Parties must not obscure matters of central relevance, fail to identify the significance of a document or fail to disclose material facts.[72] Parties must not be selective in their disclosures, engage in 'spin' or be economical with the truth.[73]

Parties must not simply offload volumes of information, leaving the other party and court to search for a needle in a haystack; rather the parties – typically government – must actively assist the court by drawing attention to matters of particular importance and to documents and specific passages which are significant.[74]

---

[62] *R v Lancashire County Council, ex parte Huddleston* [1986] 2 All ER 941, 945; *Belize Alliance Conservation of Non-governmental Organisations v Department of the Environment* [2004] UKPC 6 [86]; *R (Hoareau) v Secretary of State for Foreign and Commonwealth Affairs* [2018] EWHC 1508 (Admin) [20]; *R (Citizens UK) v Home Secretary* [2018] 1 WLR 123 [106].

[63] *R (Khan) v Secretary of State for the Home Department* [2016] EWCA 416, particularly [71]; *Hoareau* (n 62) [22]–[23]. This includes interested parties: *Belize* (n 62) [87].

[64] *R (Quark) v Secretary of State for Foreign and Commonwealth Affairs* [2002] EWCA Civ 1409, [50]; *Hoareau* (n 62) [18]; *Citizens UK* (n 62) [106].

[65] *Huddleston* (n 62) 945.

[66] *Khan* (n 63) [39].

[67] *R (HM) v Secretary of State for the Home Department* [2022] EWHC 2729 (Admin) [16].

[68] *Khan* (n 63) [48]; *Citizens UK* (n 62) [178].

[69] *Belize* (n 62) [86]; *Khan* (n 63) [35]; *Citizens UK* (n 62) [106]. See also CPR 54A PD paras 4.1–4.2, 6.2. I note in passing there is some ongoing uncertainty concerning the exact demands of the duty, in particular as to whether government must disclose information in regard to potential grounds of challenge that have not been pleaded by the claimant. See the discussion in Lord Faulks et al, *Independent Review of Administrative Law*, CP 407 (March 2021) [4.109]–[4.132] (IRAL).

[70] *Tweed* (n 8) [4]; *Hoareau* (n 62) [24].

[71] *Citizens UK* (n 62) [106].

[72] *Khan* (n 63) [71]; *Citizens UK* (n 62) [106].

[73] *Matter of an Application by Brenda Downes for Judicial Review* [2006] NIQB 77 [31]; *Hoareau* (n 62) [21].

[74] *Hoareau* (n 62) [19]–[20]; *Khan* (n 63) [45]–[46].

It follows from these obligations, that more formal processes, especially court-ordered disclosure, are not generally considered necessary, unless there is a prima face case for suggesting witness statements are inaccurate, incomplete or misleading.[75] In the unusual event that disclosure is ordered it is traditionally confined to issues emerging from witness statements.[76]

III. Taking Stock

In summary, the standard account, repeated as mantra in judgments and textbooks alike, holds that oral evidence, disclosure and expert evidence are rare on review, the evidence before a reviewing court is generally limited to the historical decision-making record, and courts will not generally resolve disputed questions of fact.

The reasons for the standard approach are that it is consonant with the nature of review as a supervisory jurisdiction (and departure from the standard approach would risk courts exceeding their proper role); it facilitates efficient use of court and party resources and avoids delay and detriment to good administration; and more formal evidence-gathering techniques are unnecessary given the duty of candour.

As a general proposition the standard account remains the default setting. However, the treatment of facts and evidence within review proceedings has developed in significant ways so that the law and practice of review are more complex than suggested by the standard account. This chapter cannot provide an account of all changes. Rather it examines a human rights case study. It is in the context of human rights claims that we have seen very significant shifts in the procedural treatment of facts and evidence.

The chapter cannot examine all the factors driving deviation from the standard account. The drivers of change are complex. But one would expect the most obvious driver to be if the reasons supporting the standard account changed in meaningful ways. For example, there has been a spate of recent cases finding parties in breach of the duty of candour.[77] If judges begin to feel they cannot rely on parties to make full and frank disclosure of their own accord then, as the courts have themselves observed,[78] judges may have greater resort to formal techniques such as court-ordered disclosure and cross-examination. There may also be drivers of change unconnected to the reasons underpinning the standard account, such as changes in litigation tactics and practices,[79] the increasingly evidence-based and

---

[75] *Tweed* (n 8) [29]; *Islington* (n 25).
[76] *Tweed* (n 8); *R v Inland Revenue Commissioners, ex parte National Federation of Self-Employed and Small Businesses Ltd* [1982] AC 617, 654.
[77] See, eg, *Khan* (n 63); *Citizens UK* (n 62); *HM* (n 67). See also *Al-Sweady* (n 11).
[78] *Huddleston* (n 62) 947; *Downes* (n 73) [31].
[79] For example, claimants may increasingly see advantages in leading expert evidence, as it may facilitate greater judicial scrutiny of administrative action. This may in turn have knock-on effects for the law governing expert evidence, as courts may be convinced of the advantages of expert evidence in

technical nature of some types of decision subject to review,[80] such as decisions of expert tribunals and complex regulatory decisions,[81] and the rise of technology in public administration.[82]

The chapter seeks to isolate one fundamental driver of change in particular: the interconnection between substance and process. A key reason for selecting the human rights case study is that it provides a prime illustration of how a major change in substantive law can precipitate changes in the procedural treatment of facts and evidence. Of course, this is not to discount that other changes in substantive law have also had ripple effects on the treatment of evidence. For example, it follows from the Court of Appeal's adoption of a novel ground of review for mistake of fact, that 'there may need to be [fresh] evidence to prove it',[83] while the emergence of a systemic dimension in judicial review coincided with significant shifts in the volume and type of evidence considered by courts.[84] However, the HRA represents a paradigm shift within public law, involving introduction of a whole new genus of claim into the public law system, which challenges the fundamental premise of the standard account: that judicial review is a supervisory jurisdiction. Indeed, such is the magnitude of the impact of human rights within public law that other developments in substantive law which have had procedural ramifications, such as emergence of review for factual error and systemic review, have in part been driven,[85] or at least inspired by,[86] human rights law.

---

enabling the court to identify errors which may not otherwise be capable of detection. In *Law Society* (n 9) the claimants flooded the court with expert evidence absent the court's prior permission. Yet the court ultimately ruled much of the evidence admissible and expanded the *Powis* categories to do so. It then relied on the evidence to impugn the challenged decision, as premised on a flawed evidence base.

[80] This may help to explain increasing judicial openness to expert evidence that aids technical understanding and reveals technical error: *Lynch* (n 32); *Law Society* (n 9).

[81] See, eg, the swathes of evidence, including expert evidence, before the court in the following complex regulatory challenge: *R (British American Tobacco (UK) Ltd) v Secretary of State For Health* [2016] EWHC 1169 (Admin); *British American Tobacco* (CA) (n 40).

[82] See, eg, the use of expert evidence and statistics in a challenge to use of facial recognition technology by the police: *Bridges* (n 40) [163]–[202]. See further J Tomlinson, K Sheridan and A Harkens, 'Judicial Review Evidence in the Era of the Digital State' [2020] PL 740; Lord Sales, 'Algorithms, Artificial Intelligence and the Law' (2020) 25 *Judicial Review* 46 [43].

[83] *E* (n 13) [68]; *DWR* (n 30) [52]–[59]. For an earlier example of developments in review for factual error prompting changes in treatment of fresh evidence see: *Hollis v Secretary of State for the Environment* (1984) 47 P & CR 351.

[84] JNE Varuhas, 'Evidence, Facts and the Changing Nature of Judicial Review' (*UK Constitutional Law Association*, 15 June 2020). Available at: https://ukconstitutionallaw.org/2020/06/15/jason-varuhas-evidence-facts-and-the-changing-nature-of-judicial-review/, last accessed 19 December 2022; F Powell, 'Structural Procedural Review: An Emerging Trend in Public Law' [2017] *Judicial Review* 83; A Adams-Prassl and J Adams-Prassl, 'Systemic Unfairness, Access to Justice and Futility: A Framework' (2020) 40 OJLS 561.

[85] Emergence of review for factual error was at least partly driven by a concern to ensure compliance with Convention requirements: *R (Alconbury Developments Ltd) v Secretary of State for the Environment, Transport and the Regions* [2003] 2 AC 295 [53]–[54]; *E* (n 13) [49]. See also *Tower Hamlets* (n 13).

[86] The systemic dimensions of human rights law were arguably one source of inspiration for the emergence of systemic review at common law. See the discussion of these systemic dimensions below: text to nn 153–159 (and see also: text to nn 213–243).

IV. The Rise of Rights

A. The Changes

The HRA entered into force in 2000. The Act created a statutory action for breach of basic individual rights against public authorities. It is in the context of such claims that courts have sanctioned significant deviations from the standard account. Courts have been more open to ordering disclosure and cross-examination and have accepted that they may be required to resolve disputed questions of fact. Indeed the Law Lords have held that, in HRA claims, it may be necessary for courts to reconsider the facts as found by the statutory decision-maker, and to consider facts subsequent to the decision, reaching their own view of the facts, and that necessary procedural adjustments should be made to enable this.[87] This section charts these procedural changes, and the following section examines why the HRA has precipitated these changes.

In *Tweed* the Law Lords considered the traditionally restrictive approach to ordering disclosure within review proceedings had to be revisited in light of the HRA. While the Law Lords envisioned disclosure would remain uncommon, the HRA required 'a more flexible and less prescriptive'[88] approach. Disclosure would no longer be strictly limited to cases where the claimant could point to some prima face inaccuracy in government witness statements. It follows that 'courts may be expected to show a somewhat greater readiness' to order disclosure of material documents in HRA cases, particularly where the court is required to conduct proportionality analysis and where documents are such that they may affect the outcome of the case.[89] Indeed, it has been said that where basic rights are at stake the government's duties of disclosure are heightened, and where the court is involved in fact-finding critical to the outcome of the case, the approach to disclosure 'should be similar to that in an ordinary Queen's Bench action'.[90] It should also be noted that the allocation of onus within HRA claims facilitates voluntary disclosure. Government bears the onus of justifying rights-infringing measures, so that it is liable to lose if it fails to advance evidentiary material in support of a challenged measure.

The courts have also recognised that a more liberal approach to cross-examination may be required in HRA claims. *R (Wilkinson) v Broadmoor Special Hospital Authority* involved a HRA challenge to a medical decision that the claimant be administered drugs against his will.[91] The claimant's and defendant's expert

---

[87] *Manchester City Council v Pinnock* [2011] UKSC 6 [45(b)], [73]–[74]; *Doherty v Birmingham City Council* [2008] UKHL 57 [68], [138]. See also the Supreme Court's differentiation of the approach to issues of fact as between common law review and HRA claims in *Begum v SIAC* (n 21) [125]–[128].
[88] *Tweed* (n 8) [32].
[89] ibid [56]–[57].
[90] *Al-Sweady* (n 11) [25]–[27].
[91] *R (Wilkinson) v Broadmoor Special Hospital Authority* [2002] 1 WLR 419.

witnesses disagreed as to: the nature of the patient's mental illness; whether he had capacity to consent; whether proposed treatments were beneficial; and the risks of administering treatment under restraint. The Court of Appeal considered that to reach a conclusion on the human rights challenge, a court would have to reach its own view on these disputed questions of fact;[92] in turn it ordered that the experts be cross-examined. Indeed, the key question of whether the patient's rights were being violated hinged on which expert view should be preferred.[93] Strikingly, the judges described the proposed adjudicative approach as involving a 'merits review' of the facts.[94] In ordering cross-examination the Court cited its enhanced role in HRA claims[95] – relative to the courts' traditional supervisory role at common law – and the fact the claim could equally have given rise to a battery action, which would have proceeded via ordinary procedure: the procedural treatment of the claim should be no different simply because it was initiated via review procedure.[96]

In a subsequent case, Dyson LJ observed that *Wilkinson* should not be taken as a 'charter for routine applications' for oral evidence.[97] But it is nonetheless clear that oral evidence will more often be required for the fair and rigorous determination of HRA cases, and that courts are more open to ordering cross-examination in the human rights setting.

This changed approach is illustrated by the important decision in *R (Al-Sweady) v Secretary of State for Defence*, which concerned serious allegations of human rights violations by British troops in Iraq.[98] A three-judge panel of the Divisional Court ordered disclosure, and the cross-examination of ten government witnesses. There were significant factual disputes between the parties, which were crucial to the outcome of the case.[99] The Court observed that if the ordinary approach to evidence were adopted – ie, no oral evidence, with factual disputes resolved in favour of government – the government would have succeeded, and there would have been far-reaching consequences, in that government would generally succeed in human rights claims where facts were contested.[100] The Court considered a 'different approach' was needed where 'hard-edged' questions of fact arose and were critical to the outcome of a HRA case.[101] This constituted 'an important exception to the rule precluding the court substituting its own view in judicial review cases'.[102] The Court said that, on this approach, cross-examination might occur with increasing regularity in HRA cases.[103] In addition to these important

---

[92] ibid [26].
[93] ibid [83].
[94] ibid [34], [83].
[95] ibid [25]–[27], [83].
[96] ibid [24], [56], [59], [62], [75].
[97] *R (N) v M* [2003] 1 WLR 562 [39].
[98] *Al-Sweady* (n 11).
[99] ibid [2], [16].
[100] ibid [17]–[18].
[101] ibid [18]–[19].
[102] ibid [18].
[103] ibid [19].

statements of principle, the case also provides a neat demonstration of the interdependence of disclosure and cross-examination. As the Court observed, '[a]n important consequence of the orders for cross-examination was that disclosure was needed to enable effective and proper cross-examination to take place'.[104]

The Court of Appeal has subsequently reiterated that hearing live evidence and resolving disputed questions of fact may be necessary in HRA claims, citing with approval *Wilkinson* and *Al-Sweady*.[105] Similarly, the Supreme Court has cited *Wilkinson* with approval for the proposition that the review procedure can be adapted to enable the court to deal with the evidential demands of the case before it,[106] and Lord Clarke in *Al Rawi v Security Service* cited *Al-Sweady* with approval for the proposition that the same approach to facts and evidence may well be taken on review as in ordinary proceedings.[107] More generally the Supreme Court has spoken of courts forming their own view of the facts in HRA cases, 'by hearing evidence'.[108]

Other cases indicate that because 'contested actions involving a human rights element often require cross-examination' it may be preferable that they be streamed via ordinary procedure, thus avoiding the strictures of the standard approach to evidence on review.[109] In *Wilkinson* Hale LJ observed that in contrast to a case where the lawfulness of delegated legislation is challenged, where the case would have to be initiated via review to access appropriate remedies such as quashing orders,[110] a HRA claim in respect of specific invasions of an individual's rights would more appropriately be streamed via ordinary procedure.[111] In similar vein, the Supreme Court in *Ruddy v Chief Constable of Strathclyde Police* held it was positively inappropriate for a claim seeking damages under the HRA in respect of an isolated act of violence that breached Article 3 to be streamed via judicial review.[112] One may view this decision, and other judicial statements to similar effect, as a manifestation of the more general principle that cases requiring the resolution of disputed factual matters should not ordinarily be streamed via judicial review.[113] Indeed, it is not difficult to find examples of HRA claims being streamed via ordinary procedure, with courts deploying the full range of procedural tools to determine disputed questions of fact, including cross-examination, disclosure and admission of expert evidence.[114]

---

[104] ibid [22].
[105] *Kent* (n 36) [58].
[106] *R (Bourgass) v Secretary of State for Justice* [2015] UKSC 54 [126]; *Croydon* (n 4) [33].
[107] *Al Rawi v Security Service* [2011] UKSC 34 [170].
[108] *Pinnock* (n 87) [74].
[109] *ID v Home Office* [2006] 1 WLR 1003 [104].
[110] Senior Courts Act 1981, s 31(1).
[111] *Wilkinson* (n 91) [61]–[62].
[112] *Ruddy v Chief Constable of Strathclyde Police* [2012] UKSC 57.
[113] *Roy* (n 6) 650, 654; *Walsh* (n 16) 173.
[114] See, eg, *DSD v Commissioner of Police for Metropolis* [2014] EWHC 436 (QB) (liability); [2014] EWHC 2493 (QB) (damages) (upheld: [2018] UKSC 11); *Alseran v Ministry of Defence* [2017] EWHC 3289 (QB).

Considered dicta on the approach to expert evidence in HRA claims streamed via review procedure are scarce. This follows from the limited consideration given to expert evidence within review more generally. But there are strong indications courts are relatively more open to expert evidence in HRA claims versus other review claims which in turn suggests that HRA claims have effectively emerged as a new category in which fresh evidence may be admitted, to be added to the traditional *Powis* categories.

In *Wilkinson* opinion expert evidence was not only admitted, but experts were also cross-examined, such approach being explicitly justified on the basis of the distinctive nature of HRA claims. Other cases similarly suggest courts are more open to expert evidence, given the different nature of the judicial role and greater intensity of judicial scrutiny in human rights claims,[115] while it has been observed in the EU law context that it would be difficult for a court to assess proportionality in the context of technical decision-making, absent expert evidence.[116]

In *R (Nicklinson) v Ministry of Justice*, in which the Supreme Court scrutinised the assisted dying regime for human rights compatibility, Lord Mance considered the complexity of the issues called for the hearing of primary evidence at first instance, including expert evidence, and the opportunity for cross-examination.[117] Earlier, in another HRA challenge to legislation, Lord Hobhouse had observed that '[o]ral witnesses may have important evidence to give' in relation to the 'sociological assessment' required by proportionality.[118] And indeed there are examples of HRA cases involving challenges to legislation where expert evidence has been admitted and relied on.[119]

More generally it is not difficult to find examples where courts in HRA claims consider evidence well beyond that which was before the statutory decision-maker, including where evidence is led by claimants specifically to challenge the robustness or adequacy of the evidence base relied on by the decision-maker.

We see such practice in Article 14 claims challenging general measures on the basis of indirect discrimination. Different types of documentary evidence have been relied on, including statistical and survey evidence, to demonstrate a group with a protected characteristic is disadvantaged in a way others are not, and to establish a causal link between the challenged measure and differential treatment.[120] Statistical evidence, opinion polls, and a variety of other types of

---

[115] *Gardner* (n 12) [18]–[22]; *Mushrooms* (n 52) [84].
[116] *Southampton Port Health Authority v Seahawk Marine Foods Ltd* [2002] EWCA Civ 54 [33]–[34].
[117] *R (Nicklinson) v Ministry of Justice* [2014] UKSC 38 [175]–[182], [224]. His Lordship also observed that it is preferable for the court to hear evidence itself, and reach its own views on that evidence, rather than rely on 'second hand' accounts, for example in official reports.
[118] *Wilson v First County Trust Ltd (No 2)* [2003] UKHL 40 [141]–[142].
[119] *In the matter of an application by the Northern Ireland Human Rights Commission for Judicial Review (Northern Ireland) Reference by the Court of Appeal in Northern Ireland pursuant to Paragraph 33 of Schedule 10 to the Northern Ireland Act 1998 (Abortion) (Northern Ireland)* [2018] UKSC 27 [83]–[84], [232]–[234] (*NIHRC*).
[120] For a good illustrative example see *R (Joint Council for the Welfare of Immigrants) v Secretary of State for the Home Department* [2020] EWCA Civ 542 (*JCWI*).

evidence concerning 'social facts', may be important to proportionality analysis (and in human rights claims more generally), for example so as to understand the broader context in which the challenged measure operates and its impacts.[121]

In an early decision under the Act, Schiemann LJ emphasised that the court should not shut out evidence that is relevant, including evidence beyond the historical decision-making record which was not available at the time of the decision.[122] That case concerned a challenge to a decision to deny leave to remain, where the claimant claimed he suffered a real risk of treatment in breach of Article 3 if he had to return to his home country – a context in which it is important the court have up to date country information.[123]

B. Explaining the Changes

(i) The Nature of Human Rights Adjudication

Traditionally the types of claims streamed via the review procedure were claims for exercise of the High Court's common law supervisory jurisdiction, based on the standard common law grounds of review, namely legality, procedural fairness and rationality. For as long as claims streamed via review procedure were for exercise of the supervisory jurisdiction, the standard procedural approach to facts and evidence could be rationalised. As discussed above, it is a core premise of the standard approach to treatment of evidence within review proceedings that courts are performing a supervisory function.

However, HRA claims are fundamentally different from common law review claims. Specifically, courts in human rights adjudication do not perform a supervisory role. As such a core premise which sustains the standard approach is absent in the HRA setting.

In human rights claims the court is the primary decision-maker.[124] It follows from this that the court itself exercises a primary determinative judgement over the scope, content and meaning of rights, and whether interferences are justified.[125]

---

[121] Many examples could be given. See as illustrative examples: *R (SG) v Secretary of State for Work and Pensions* [2015] UKSC 16 [67]–[77], [188]–[207]; *R (DA) v Secretary of State for Work and Pensions* [2019] UKSC 21 [20]–[34]; *NIHRC* (n 119) [104]–[135].

[122] *R v Secretary of State for the Home Department, ex parte Turgut* [2001] 1 All ER 719, 735.

[123] See also in this regard *HK* (n 41); *E* (n 13).

[124] See, eg, JNE Varuhas, 'Against Unification' in H Wilberg and M Elliott (eds), *The Scope and Intensity of Review* (Oxford, Hart Publishing, 2015); JNE Varuhas, 'Taxonomy and Public Law' in M Elliott, JNE Varuhas and SW Stark (eds), *The Unity of Public Law? Doctrinal, Theoretical, and Comparative Perspectives* (Oxford, Hart Publishing, 2018) 63–78; JNE Varuhas, *Damages and Human Rights* (Oxford, Hart Publishing, 2016) 76–89, ch 4.2.

[125] *Belfast City Council v Miss Behavin' Ltd* [2007] 1 WLR 1420 [12]–[15], [30]–[31], [37], [44]; *R (Begum) v Governors of Denbigh High School* [2007] 1 AC 100 [29]–[31], [68]; *Huang v Secretary of State for the Home Department* [2007] 2 AC 167; *Tweed* (n 8) [53]–[55]; *R (Quila) v Secretary of State for the Home Department* [2012] 1 AC 621 [46], [61], [91]; *E v Chief Constable of the Royal Ulster Constabulary* [2009] 1 AC 536 [13], [52]ff; *Bank Mellat v HM Treasury* [2013] UKSC 39 [124]; *R (Carlile) v Secretary of State for the Home Department* [2014] UKSC 60 [57], [105], [115], [137], [152]; *R (AR) v Chief Constable of Greater Manchester Police* [2018] UKSC 47 [53].

The court must reach its own view on proportionality – the court itself must exercise a value judgement and strike a balance. In doing so it may give weight to the balance struck by government, but the ultimate question of rights-compliance is for the court.[126]

Similarly in private law claims it is for courts alone to determine the scope and content of given rights, such as exclusive possession and liberty, and justifications. As Lord Hoffmann observed, 'the rule of law rightly requires that certain decisions, of which the paradigm examples are findings of breaches of the criminal law and adjudications as to private rights, should be entrusted to the judicial branch of government'.[127] Where a court judges a question such as whether a precaution taken by a defendant was appropriate for the purposes of negligence, it must make its own value judgement as to what would have been a proper precaution, which is determinative. Given these similar features it is no coincidence to find courts in human rights claims analogising to the procedural treatment of private law claims.[128] Similarly, it is no coincidence that when private law claims, such as false imprisonment, happen to be streamed via judicial review procedure, the courts may modify that procedure to mirror ordinary procedure[129] – in the same way they have adapted review procedure in human rights claims, so that it approximates ordinary procedure.

The reason it is legitimate for courts in human rights claims (and private law) to exercise objective judgement over matters of substance is that the juridical basis of the claim is an individual legal right, and within the separation of powers adjudication of legal rights is quintessentially for courts. As Lord Sales said recently of HRA rights, these are free-standing rights, whose protection has been entrusted by Parliament to the courts, and it follows that these rights are enforced by the courts on a substantive basis rather than as a matter of review.[130] Thus, an administrative decision might account for all relevant considerations and be rational in common law terms, so that the exercise of power is valid vis-à-vis the empowering statute. But it might still be impugned on the basis that the court does not consider the balance struck to be fair.[131]

In a common law judicial review claim the court is exercising a supervisory jurisdiction to check whether a primary decision-maker has properly exercised their powers pursuant to a parent statute. The focus is upon the qualities of the exercise of power itself. In contrast in human rights claims the court adjudicates

---

[126] *Huang* (n 125) [16]; *Bank Mellat* (n 125) [129]; *AR* (n 125) [53]; *Carlile* (n 125) [105].

[127] *Tower Hamlets* (n 13) [42].

[128] See, eg, *Wilkinson* (n 91) [24], [56], [59], [62], [75]; *Al-Sweady* (n 11) [27]. See also *A v Essex County Council* [2011] 1 AC 280 [116]; *Rabone v Pennine Care NHS Trust* [2012] UKSC 2 [108].

[129] *R (MH) v Secretary of State for the Home Department* [2009] EWHC 2506 (Admin) [7]. See also the following Court of Appeal decision, criticising the Administrative Court's refusal to allow cross-examination in a false imprisonment claim for damages: *Patel* (n 37) [11], [64].

[130] *DPP v Ziegler* [2021] UKSC 23 [130]–[131] (this statement of principle includes extensive references to relevant authorities, and see the authorities at n 125). See, eg, *Kennedy v Charity Commission* [2014] UKSC 20 [244]–[245] (HRA adjudication involves 'merits review' and is 'not a pure reviewing function', whereas common law review is more 'process than merits').

[131] *Ziegler* (n 130) [130]–[131]; *Carlile* (n 125) [57].

or enforces legal rights in the face of such an exercise of power; the court is not supervising whether a decision-maker has strayed from their statutory mandate, but enforcing free-standing norms in the face of an exercise of that mandate.

As the Supreme Court has emphasised, in order for a court to discharge this function in human rights law, it may have to reach its own views on contested factual issues[132] and consider evidence beyond the historical decision-making record. In doing so it is not competing with the statutory repository's decision-making enterprise. Rather, the court is engaged in its own, distinct decision-making enterprise, determining whether legal rights have been violated – and within that enterprise the court *is* the primary decision-maker. As Lord Sumption has observed, the HRA altered 'traditional notions of the constitutional distribution of powers', and according to the responsibility bestowed upon the courts to uphold rights, 'there can be no absolute constitutional bar to any inquiry which is both relevant and necessary to enable the court to adjudicate'.[133] Other courts have linked the necessity of the court interrogating factual matters to the fundamental importance of the rights that form the juridical basis of the claim.[134] There is also the practical point that domestic courts may be required to interrogate the facts for themselves so as to fulfil the UK's obligations under the Convention, so that a failure to engage with factual matters may lead to breach of the Convention.[135]

If the court in a HRA claim simply deferred to the decision-maker's account of the facts, or refused to resolve a disputed question of fact that was critical to determining whether an interference occurred and/or was justified, it would risk abdicating its constitutional responsibility for adjudicating and protecting basic legal rights.[136] Given this constitutional function the courts should actively scrutinise with care human rights claims to assess whether there are disputed factual matters to be determined, so that appropriate procedural directions can be given.[137]

Thus, human rights claims are conceptually distinct from common law review claims, and it follows that approaches to evidence that might be considered impermissible in the context of the latter are legitimate and necessary in the context of the former. In turn the shifts in the procedural treatment of facts and evidence in human rights claims provide a stark illustration of the interdependence of process and substance within the public law system.

---

[132] *Pinnock* (n 87) [45(b)], [73]–[74]; *Doherty* (n 87) [68], [138]; *Al-Sweady* (n 11) [18].
[133] *Carlile* (n 125) [29]–[30].
[134] *Wilkinson* (n 91) [25]; *Al-Sweady* (n 11) [25]–[26].
[135] *Wilkinson* (n 91) [26]–[27]; *Pinnock* (n 87) [45(b), [73]–[74]; *Bourgass* (n 106) [104]–[126]. Note in this regard the Article 6 requirement of a tribunal with 'full jurisdiction': European Court of Human Rights, Guide on Article 6 of the European Convention on Human Rights – Right to a Fair Trial (Civil Limb) (31 August 2022) [187]–[203]. Available at: www.echr.coe.int/documents/guide_art_6_eng.pdf, last accessed 19 December 2022.
[136] *Al-Sweady* (n 11) [18].
[137] ibid [29].

(ii) Features of Human Rights Claims

There are four particular features of human rights claims which mean that courts may be required to determine disputed matters of fact, and roam beyond the historical decision-making record, which in turn have driven greater judicial openness to oral evidence, disclosure, and fresh evidence.

First, human rights claims are individualistic. They involve specific individuals claiming that their rights – which protect their personal interests – have been interfered with in a way that is unjustifiable in the circumstances of their case.[138] This distinguishes human rights claims from review claims, which are grounded in general legal standards, such as rationality or legality, and focused squarely on the qualities of an exercise of power and thus how a decision-maker went about their task.

In human rights claims, courts may need to determine the treatment that was actually suffered by the individual and how it affected them, as for example in a claim of inhuman or degrading treatment.[139] Difficult causal questions may arise, such as whether there is a causal link between disadvantage suffered by the claimants and an allegedly discriminatory measure[140] or whether there is a causal link between the police's failure to take operational steps required by Articles 2 or 3, and the victim's loss of life or ill-treatment.[141] Questions such as whether a claimant faced a real and immediate risk to life, and what precautions might have been reasonable for an authority to take in response, can only be answered with close understanding of what actually happened.[142]

Moreover, questions of justification depend on a judicial balancing of factors *on the facts of the individual's case*, and as such the court will need to determine the specific circumstances of the individual case before it is able to undertake the balancing calculus, including the degree of prejudice or harm suffered by the claimant (as one factor to be balanced). As Lord Bingham observed in *Tweed*, human rights claims 'tend to be very fact-specific' with judgments as to proportionality calling for 'careful and accurate evaluation of the facts'.[143]

Second, as the courts observe, proportionality involves an inquiry of a different character to the traditional common law head of rationality.[144] With proportionality the court is not reviewing a primary decision-maker, checking whether a decision is within a range of reasonable decisions, but must itself determine the

---

[138] *Quila* (n 125) [59], [80]. See, as a straightforward illustrative example, the focus on the prejudice suffered by the particular claimant in the circumstances in: *R (Elan-Cane) v Secretary of State for the Home Department* [2021] UKSC 56 [42].
[139] *Al-Sweady* (n 11) [15]–[16]; *Ruddy* (n 112) [33]; *Alseran* (n 114).
[140] *JCWI* (n 120) [50]–[80], [158]–[166].
[141] *DSD* (liability) (n 114) [225(v)], [226], [285]–[313]; *Van Colle v Chief Constable of Hertfordshire* [2009] 1 AC 225 [138]; *Savage v South Essex Partnership NHS Foundation Trust* [2010] EWHC 865 (QB) [82], [89]; *Daniel v St George's Healthcare NHS Trust* [2016] 4 WLR 32 [30]–[33], [140]–[144].
[142] *Rabone* (n 128); *Van Colle v Chief Constable of Hertfordshire* [2006] 3 All ER 963 (QB); [2007] 1 WLR 1821 (CA).
[143] *Tweed* (n 8) [3].
[144] See n 125. For a detailed comparative treatment of the role of facts in proportionality analysis see A Carter, *Proportionality and Facts in Constitutional Adjudication* (Oxford, Hart Publishing, 2022).

balance between competing concerns. In doing so it may give weight to considered views of the decision-maker, but the decision is ultimately for the court. To properly carry out this task the court must apply a 'closer factual analysis of the justification for restrictions imposed … than used to be undertaken on judicial review challenges'.[145]

Specifically the court must engage in an 'exacting analysis of the factual case advanced in defence of the measure'.[146] This need to closely scrutinise justifications has driven liberalisation of disclosure, as the court needs to have before it the body of evidence on which the government grounded its rights-infringing acts, so it can judge for itself whether that evidence, including the government's policy advice and analysis,[147] provides a convincing case for limiting rights, and what other alternative – and potentially less restrictive measures – might have been open. As in *Tweed*, this might require government to disclose original documentation, rather than simply providing summaries or narrative accounts in witness statements.[148] This evidence may also be critical to determining to what degree the court should, in conducting its own evaluation, place weight on the government's decision; for example, if the government's decision-making processes lacked rigour, this may suggest little deference is due.

Thus, government might seek to defend a rights-infringing measure on the basis it will have beneficial consequential effects, such as deterring unlawful or antisocial conduct. Whether that purported justification is convincing may depend on whether the government undertook reliable studies *ex ante* of how the measure would affect behaviour, or whether it can produce *ex post* evidence demonstrating the measure's effectiveness. Similarly, government may argue that a rights-infringing measure is justified as it avoids costly burdens; whether this justification is convincing may depend on whether the government can produce evidence to substantiate its claim.

Because the court must reach its own view of whether an interference is justified, it 'is not restricted to the matters before the decision-maker' and may consider material beyond the historical decision-making record.[149] This can include competing evidence introduced by the claimant, which may post-date the government's decision, and be designed to challenge the factual premises of the government's case.[150] Again, this is permissible in principle because the court is not reviewing the decision made, but rather forming its own objective judgement of whether an infringement is justifiable.

Where primary legislation is subject to a HRA challenge, it has been accepted that courts may look at parliamentary materials to an extent that is not permissible

---

[145] *Tweed* (n 8) [54].
[146] *Bank Mellat* (n 125) [20].
[147] See, eg, the comprehensive policy background to the challenged measure set out in *R (Carmichael) v Secretary of State for Work and Pensions* [2016] UKSC 58, app 2.
[148] *Tweed* (n 8) [39]–[42].
[149] *Mushrooms* (n 52) [84].
[150] See text at nn 114–123.

The Interdependence of Process and Substance 109

outside HRA cases, so as to provide relevant background for the proportionality analysis; this background includes understanding the broader context of the legislation, including the social ill the legislation sought to address, and what was considered to be the likely effect of the legislation.[151] To the extent this practice impinges upon Article 9 of the Bill of Rights 1689 and parliamentary privilege, it is considered necessary to allow the court to perform its constitutional function of assessing compliance with Convention rights.[152] However, as the Supreme Court had recently emphasised there are limits to the use that can be made of such material; in particular the proportionality of a legislative measure is not to be judged by the quality of the parliamentary debate.[153]

Third, human rights claims can have systemic dimensions, which in turn require the court to understand how systems operate. For example, the general Convention requirement that rights be practical and effective, not theoretical or illusory, may require the court to scrutinise not only whether rights are protected 'on paper', but also whether they are protected in reality. This may demand consideration of the operation of legal or administrative systems. Thus, compliance with Article 6 depends on whether it is practically possible for people to access court, which may depend on consideration of evidence of the practical effects of impediments within the justice system such as court fees or limits on legal aid.[154] A remedy might be available in principle but evidence might show that in practice it is never granted, raising questions over whether it is an effective remedy for the purposes of Article 13.[155] There are obligations under Article 3 to establish and maintain systems which effectively protect against ill-treatment,[156] and to avoid systems that create significant risks of ill-treatment.[157] Evaluation of the legality of particular systems may depend on evidence of how the system is being operated, including evidence of practices within the system.[158]

Another example of the systemic dimensions of human rights law is the jurisprudence on indirect discrimination under Article 14. Proving that a measure or system is discriminatory often depends on availability of statistical and survey evidence which demonstrates that the measure or system in operation systematically disadvantages a given group.[159] Studies by government and the claimants

---

[151] *Wilson* (n 118) [51]–[67]; *R (Project for the Registration of Children as British Citizens) v Secretary of State for the Home Department* [2021] EWCA Civ 193 [92]–[101].
[152] ibid.
[153] *R (SC) v Secretary of State for Work and Pensions* [2021] UKSC 26 [7(iii)], [163]–[186].
[154] *R (Unison) v Lord Chancellor* [2017] UKSC 51 [108]–[117]. See further ECtHR, *Guide on Article 6 of the European Convention on Human Rights* (n 135) [113]–[133].
[155] *McFarlane v Ireland* (2011) 52 EHRR 20 [107]–[129].
[156] See, eg, *MC v Bulgaria* (2005) 40 EHRR 20 [148]–[166].
[157] See,eg, *R (Munjaz) v Ashworth Hospital Authority* [2005] UKHL 58.
[158] See, eg, *MC* (n 156) [172]–[174]; *Munjaz* (n 157) [81]; *BK v Secretary of State for Justice* [2015] EWCA Civ 1259 [64]–[67].
[159] *Essop v Home Office* [2017] UKSC 27 [28]; *JCWI* (n 120). See also the very helpful analysis of the use of statistics in discrimination cases in: Lady Rose, 'A Numbers Game? Statistics in Public Law Cases' (2022) 27 *Judicial Review* 39.

may conflict, so that the court may be required to determine which evidence is to be preferred.

Fourth, HRA claims may include a claim for damages under section 8 of the Act, determination of loss requiring a fact-sensitive inquiry into the specific effects of the violation on the individual, as well as resolution of other fact-sensitive issues such as causation.[160] As such the Supreme Court has held that in HRA damages claims 'courts should resolve disputed issues of fact in the usual way', according to 'ordinary rules of evidence and procedure'.[161] This may involve admission of expert evidence including medical reports, for example detailing the psychological and/or physical effects of the violation, as well as cross-examination.[162]

Indeed, the fact-sensitive nature of damages claims in general makes them inappropriate for resolution via the review procedure, given the default restrictive approach to fact-finding and evidence. As such many HRA damages claims have been streamed via ordinary procedure, including where pleaded alongside parallel tort claims.[163] Alternatively the lawfulness of government action may be determined via review procedure, with the damages claim then transferred to the County Court or a division of the High Court to be determined via ordinary procedure.[164] It is notable that the Civil Procedure Rules bar a claim solely seeking damages from proceeding via review procedure – this being an institutional recognition of the inaptness of the procedure for testing evidence and determining factual questions.[165]

The foregoing principles are reinforced by the Supreme Court's decision in *Ruddy*, holding that it was positively inappropriate for a damages claim for a past act of physical violence in breach of Article 3 to be streamed via review procedure, the Court distinguishing such a rights-based claim for damages from a claim seeking exercise of the court's traditional supervisory review jurisdiction.[166]

C. Two Reflections: Experts and the Limits of Evidence

Thus, the advent of human rights law – a fundamental change in substantive public law – has resulted in significant shifts away from the standard account of the procedural treatment of facts and evidence.

Let me offer two critical reflections in light of the HRA jurisprudence.

---

[160] Varuhas, *Damages and Human Rights* (n 124) 212–18. On causation see: J Edelman, S Colton and JNE Varuhas, *McGregor on Damages* (21st edn, London, Sweet & Maxwell, 2021) [50-158]–[50-174].
[161] *R (Sturnham) v Parole Board* [2013] 2 AC 254 [13(5)], [37], [39].
[162] See, eg, *DSD* (liability and damages) (n 114); *Alseran* (n 114).
[163] ibid. For further examples see Edelman, Colton, and Varuhas (n 160) [50-049]. And for a full treatment of the law governing the appropriate forum for HRA damages claims see Edelman, Colton and Varuhas (n 160) [50-040]–[50-052].
[164] HMCTS, *Judicial Review Guide* (n 6) [12.8.4].
[165] CPR r 54.3(2).
[166] *Ruddy* (n 112) [15]. See also *ID* (n 109) [104].

(i) Statistics, Expert Evidence and Cross-examination

First, though there has been a significant procedural shift, procedure has not fully caught up with substance. We arguably see a hangover of the standard account in relation to expert evidence specifically. Because HRA claims are often brought via review procedure, the default setting is that expert evidence – and proper testing of expert evidence, including via cross-examination – is rare. This practice persists even in cases where courts would significantly benefit from expert input, specifically where courts are dealing with contested and complex statistical or survey evidence.[167] Also militating against a greater role for expert evidence is that domestic courts appear to have been influenced by the ECtHR's broad-brush treatment of evidence, including statistical evidence and surveys.[168] But the ECtHR's approach follows from its role as a supranational court that performs a supervisory function. It is not institutionally equipped to conduct full trials. In contrast, within the supranational human rights framework it is domestic courts that have primary responsibility for upholding rights, and these courts do have the procedural tools to rigorously test evidence. The different institutional positions of domestic courts and the ECtHR has been recognised by the Supreme Court in the context of HRA damages claims, the Court prescribing that courts 'should resolve disputed issues of fact in the usual way even if the European court, in similar circumstances, would not do so'.[169]

Consider the illustrative example of indirect discrimination claims. As discussed above, such claims rely heavily on statistics, surveys and social-science-style experiments. Some courts have taken a more robust approach to evaluating such evidence than others, but even where analysis is more detailed[170] it remains 'relatively light touch'.[171] In most cases such evaluation has occurred absent expert evidence and oral testimony, including where studies conflict or are disputed. This is striking and raises serious questions about the rigour of the judicial approach and conclusions reached. The proper evaluation of such evidence ought to include systematic scrutiny of sample size, selection bias, statistical significance, repeatability, independence of the study authors, whether the study in fact supports the author's claimed conclusions, and other methodological questions. In turn proper scrutiny requires the aid of experts, given that – as the Supreme Court acknowledges[172] – evaluation of statistical evidence is far removed from judicial expertise and experience; judges are experts in legal doctrine, not social science

---

[167] See especially *JCWI* (n 120).
[168] ibid [75], citing *DH v Czech Republic* (2008) 47 EHRR 3 [178]–[179].
[169] *Sturnham* (n 161) [13(5)], [37], [39].
[170] See, eg, *JCWI* (n 120) [50]–[80], [167].
[171] *Rose* (n 159) [29]–[30].
[172] *R (A) v Secretary of State for the Home Department* [2021] UKSC 37 [65].

methodologies. Some courts in HRA discrimination challenges have recognised the limits of judicial expertise and experience in relation to statistics, saying that if the court is to rely on statistical analysis, it requires 'properly prepared expert reports',[173] especially where statistics are contested and give rise to difficult issues of interpretation.[174] Other decisions acknowledge the difficulty of the issues raised by competing and contested surveys and studies.[175]

Given the rather jejune judicial approach to evaluation of survey and statistical evidence, Lady Rose, speaking extra-judicially, has suggested that courts in public law cases could benefit from considering the more rigorous approaches to such evidence developed in other legal contexts, including intellectual property and competition law.[176] In those contexts dedicated guidelines, which include built-in disclosure requirements, have been developed to facilitate rigorous judicial scrutiny of statistical and survey evidence and to guide decisions over admissibility of, and the weight to be given to, such evidence. This guidance also ensures a consistent approach; in contrast the approach on judicial review has been ad hoc. Significantly, in these settings survey results are usually presented to the court by an expert, who can be cross-examined in relation to method and conclusions.

Courts in commercial settings have also developed case management techniques, including a staged approach to admission and evaluation of survey evidence, to ensure evidence adds value, and to guard against wasted cost and delay. Such a set, structured approach which is well-known to litigants would be valuable in judicial review as there have been examples of parties flooding the court with expert evidence absent permission, much of this evidence subsequently being ruled inadmissible.[177]

It is notable that in the *British American Tobacco* litigation, which involved a highly complex regulatory review and EU and HRA proportionality challenges, the trial judge – faced with a large body of evidence including expert reports – sought to fashion a framework, and structured case management approach, to govern admission and assessment of social science evidence such as econometric studies.[178] The judge acknowledged evaluation of such evidence pushes the bounds of judicial expertise, and it followed that engagement of experts – possibly including independent assessors – as well as cross-examination were important

---

[173] *R (Roberts) v Commissioner of the Metropolitan Police* [2012] EWHC 1977 (Admin) [48]–[51] (in relation to the question of whether stop and search powers were being used in a racially discriminatory manner).

[174] *R (Roberts) v Commissioner of the Metropolitan Police* [2014] EWCA Civ 69 [32] (on appeal from *Roberts* (n 173)). The case was appealed to the Supreme Court, but on other grounds: [2015] UKSC 79.

[175] *JCWI* (n 120) [60], [167].

[176] Rose (n 159) [28]–[49].

[177] *Law Society* (n 9) [7], [44]–[49]; *AB* (n 30) [107]–[120]; see also *HK* (n 41) [10]–[18]. A more structured, disciplined approach would be consonant with the increasing judicial calls for 'procedural rigour' on judicial review: HMCTS, *Judicial Review Guide* (n 6) [2.1].

[178] *British American Tobacco* (HC) (n 81) [633]–[649].

features of the proposed framework. The judge observed that if courts did not put in place measures to facilitate judicial understanding and scrutiny of complex social science evidence the result could often be that claimants would lose notwithstanding the merits of their claim.

The trial judge's innovation was met with a frosty reception in the Court of Appeal,[179] which rejected the need for such a framework, preferring a case-by-case approach to treatment of evidence. The Court's reasoning is underpinned by the standard account: it is not the court's role to resolve technical disputes between experts, which would require cross-examination. The Court's reticence may be understandable in relation to claims for exercise of the common law supervisory jurisdiction. But the Court's analysis, in relying on a rote incantation of the standard account, fails to get to grips with the changed nature of judicial review *at least in certain settings*, specifically HRA claims. The brute fact is that up-to-date procedural machinery is needed. As indirect discrimination cases demonstrate, statistical and survey evidence are critical to the resolution of key legal questions in human rights law, and courts need to be able to rigorously scrutinise such evidence so as to properly discharge their enhanced constitutional role under the HRA. This is not to say an unmodified procedural transplant from commercial contexts is necessarily appropriate but institutional learning from other legal fields might 'provide a useful starting point'.[180]

(ii) The Limits of Evidence

Second, it is important for courts to be attentive to the limits of evidence within proportionality analysis, and the pragmatic limits on government's capacity to gather evidence.

Consider *R (Quila) v Secretary of State for the Home Department*, which involved a HRA challenge to a new immigration rule, which prohibited the grant of leave to remain to a spouse where the applicant or sponsor was aged under 21.[181] The prescribed age had previously been 18. The government's stated goal in uplifting the age was to deter forced marriage. A Supreme Court majority held the rule constituted a disproportionate interference with the Article 8 rights of those applicants who would be prevented from entering unforced marriages. The principal reason for the majority conclusion was that the government was unable to put forward conclusive evidence of the number or extent of forced marriages that would be prevented by the rule change, so that the harm prevented by deterring forced marriages could be weighed against the harm due to disruption of unforced marriages.

---

[179] *British American Tobacco* (CA) (n 40) [251]–[253].
[180] Rose (n 159) [50].
[181] *Quila* (n 125).

One concern raised by the majority reasoning is that it is far from clear whether it would be possible to produce 'robust' or 'conclusive'[182] evidence of the precise number of forced marriages that would be prevented by the rule, or the extent of any deterrence effect. Indeed, there was seemingly no evidence before the court to indicate how this could be done from a methodological perspective.[183] Nor is it clear what the Justices would consider conclusive or robust evidence. These points reinforce the need for expert evidence when dealing with what are essentially questions of social science methodology, removed from judicial competence.

As Lord Brown observed in dissent, a principal reason why the quest for a perfectly accurate evidence base might be illusory is that very many forced marriages are 'hidden', in that they are never brought to government's attention, so official data is necessarily incomplete.[184] Moreover, it was not as if there was no relevant evidence before the court. For example, evidence showed around 30 per cent of forced marriages in the UK are in the 18–20 age range, that seeking entry into the UK was one motivation for forced marriage, that the vast majority of forced marriages occur within immigrant communities, and that the older a spouse the greater their capacity to resist forced marriage.[185] What was striking was that the majority at times[186] became rather fixated with the need to identify the exact number of forced marriages that the rule would prevent, without ever asking whether a reliable figure could feasibly be produced, and passing over other salient evidence before the court. This brings to mind Lord Reed's observation in *Bank Mellat v HM Treasury* that courts should be careful not to be 'over-particular about the reasoning or evidence relied on by the decision-maker'.[187]

It must be recalled that proportionality demands an ultimate value judgement, which may be heavily informed by evidence but which transcends the evidence base, requiring normative judgement including consideration of variables beyond facts. The *Quila* majority, while acknowledging the evaluative character of proportionality,[188] nonetheless at times seemed to view the question of justification as being solely or largely dictated by evidence (and specifically the lack of a precise set of statistics). In contrast Lord Brown emphasised that questions of justification require a judgement call.[189] For Lord Brown it followed that weight should be accorded to a range of other factors. These included that other EU countries had set a similar age requirement, that

---

[182] ibid [50], [77].
[183] Similarly, Lord Wilson set out ten questions that needed to be answered, but with respect it was not obvious that they could all be answered. As his Lordship himself observed, the questions 'are not easily answered': *Quila* (n 125) [48]–[50].
[184] ibid [87].
[185] ibid [10]–[11], [48].
[186] ibid [47], [53]–[55], [58], [75], [77].
[187] *Bank Mellat* (n 125) [94].
[188] *Quila* (n 125) [44].
[189] ibid [91].

a small majority of those who responded to a consultation on the rule change supported it, and that there was some *ex post* anecdotal evidence the rule had been effective.[190] Recognition that statistical information is only one aspect of proportionality and that a judgement call is ultimately required also brings into focus that the judgements of others, such as the statutory decision-maker, may warrant weight.[191]

What was clear in *Quila* was that the rule would prevent some forced marriages – no one argued the rule was completely ineffective – but that a far greater number of unforced marriages would be disrupted. So as a matter of principle the case comes down to a value judgement, taking into account available evidence, and apportioning relative normative weight to the risk of allowing forced marriages if the age is not raised to 21, versus the risk of temporarily disrupting a far larger number of unforced marriages. It is not obvious that apportioning heavy weight to the harm that might be caused by even a few forced marriages is unjustifiable. Of course, one reading of the majority judgments is that they took a different view, not least as they demanded evidence of 'substantial'[192] deterrence effects. But it was not explained why *some* deterrence effect was insufficient to justify the rule. In turn this omission reflects that the normative dimensions of balancing were lost sight of.

More broadly, the foregoing discussion raises interesting questions over how far government can be expected to go in terms of evidence gathering before adopting policies. *Quila* might be taken to suggest that, before a measure is adopted, a commissioned empirical study is required which 'conclusively' supports the measure. There are obvious benefits of such approach. But on the other hand, such a pre-requisite could have negative effects, including cost, delay, ossification of public administration, lack of experimentation, and administrative unresponsiveness. Government may fail to adopt measures which might have ultimately served the common good, because the exact behavioural effects of the measure could not reliably be predicted ex ante.

This is not to argue against evidence-based policymaking, but to adopt a realistic approach[193] to public administration which acknowledges other important considerations – including the irreversible harm that might be done if no policy action is taken – the limits of evidence, and that some variables are simply unknowable. As the US Supreme Court has recognised in unanimously ruling that the Administrative Procedure Act does not require empirical studies to be undertaken before rules are adopted, it 'is not unusual in day-to-day agency decisionmaking' for administrative action to be underpinned by imperfect data.[194]

---

[190] ibid [88], [90].
[191] ibid [91]. See also *Bank Mellat* (n 125) [93]. More deference may be owed where assessments are predictive in nature: *Mott* (n 40) [69] (albeit in a different context).
[192] *Quila* (n 125) [50].
[193] *Huddleston* (n 61) 945J.
[194] *Federal Communications Commission v Prometheus Radio Project* 592 US __ (2021).

V. Wider Ripple Effects

Introduction of a new legal phenomenon, such as the HRA, into the public law system can, much like introduction of a new species into a natural environment, have far-reaching ripple effects, which destabilise the established order in complex and unpredictable ways. We have seen how the advent of human rights law has led to significant changes in the procedural treatment of facts and evidence on review, specifically in HRA claims. But the emergence of human rights law has also had ripple effects on other areas of *substantive* law, being the catalyst for changes in the common law of judicial review, which in turn have precipitated further changes in the *procedural* law of review. While it is only possible here to give a brief account of some of the most important ripple effects, it is important that they be addressed as they form an important part of the story of the impact of the HRA on treatment of facts and evidence within review procedure.[195] The analysis illustrates two further points. First, it reiterates the interdependence of process and substance. Second, it illustrates that the path of legal change in relation to facts and evidence is not necessarily linear: deviations from the standard account may be followed by its reassertion.

A. Substantive Review

Ideas of rights and proportionality have been floating around in common law review for some time.[196] But the period since 2014 has been a significant phase of activity. During 2014–2015 the Supreme Court decided *Kennedy v Charity Commission* and *Pham v Secretary of State for the Home Department*,[197] which both suggested that, at least where basic interests are at stake, proportionality might supplant rationality as the common law head of substantive review.[198] The Court envisioned a 'synthesis' of human rights law and common law review.[199] Subsequently, in *R (Bourgass) v Secretary of State for Justice* the Court, invoking these developments in substantive review, which require courts to carefully examine treatment experienced by specific individuals and justifications for that treatment, signalled greater openness to judicial resolution of disputed questions of fact and cross-examination, citing the HRA case of *Wilkinson*.[200]

---

[195] There are other ripple effects which are not considered here, such as the role of human rights law in driving the adoption of a mistake of fact ground, as noted at n 85.

[196] For an overview of the developments see: JNE Varuhas, 'Administrative Law and Rights in the UK House of Lords and Supreme Court' in P Daly (ed), *Apex Courts and the Common Law* (Toronto, University of Toronto Press, 2019).

[197] *Kennedy* (n 130); *Pham v Secretary of State for the Home Department* [2015] UKSC 19.

[198] Note that there are further examples of proportionality entering common law review, specifically in the context of substantive legitimate expectations. See, eg, *R (Patel) v General Medical Council* [2013] EWCA Civ 327.

[199] *Kennedy* (n 130) [46].

[200] *Bourgass* (n 106) [124]–[126]. See *Wilkinson* (n 91).

At the same time we have seen examples of courts applying reasonableness review with greater intensity,[201] including under the more intensive 'anxious scrutiny' variant of *Wednesbury*, adoption of which was originally driven by a concern to protect human rights.[202] Invoking this anxious scrutiny variant, Lord Carnwath in *R (Kairie) v Secretary of State for the Home Department*, while observing that the approach to evidence should not mirror that in HRA claims, nonetheless observed that the power to determine facts and hear oral evidence on review 'needs to be recognised'.[203] Earlier, in *R v Secretary of State for the Home Department, ex parte Launder* the Law Lords had held, in applying anxious scrutiny, that they could take into account material beyond the decision-making record, regarding events subsequent to the administrative decision under challenge.[204]

More recently, in *R (Law Society) v Lord Chancellor* the Divisional Court recognised rationality challenges as a new category of case in which fresh evidence may be admitted beyond the decision-making record, adding to the longstanding *Powis* categories – the Court observing that the categories may need to develop given the way public law has evolved since *Powis* was decided, no doubt alluding to the growing intensity of substantive review.[205] Whereas there had previously been a modest extension of the *Powis* principles to allow admission of expert evidence where needed to clarify technical terms,[206] *Law Society* effected a further extension, allowing expert evidence where it is alleged there is a serious technical error in the decision-maker's reasoning. This is a significant expansion of the circumstances in which fresh evidence may be permitted, and – unlike the established *Powis* categories – opens up the possibility of expert evidence being admitted for the sole purpose of challenging the factual bases of the decision under review. It is unsurprising therefore that admission of such evidence in *Law Society* led the Court deep into the factual premises that underpinned the challenged decision, the Court ultimately impugning the decision because it was based on economic modelling which adopted flawed methodologies, so that the decision proceeded from unsafe factual foundations.[207] It should be noted that the errors identified were held to be incontrovertible, and were demonstrated by uncontested evidence from the claimant's expert. Nonetheless, the case starkly illustrates the 'snowball' effect. The more intense the degree of judicial scrutiny becomes under substantive

---

[201] *R (Litvinenko) v Secretary of State for the Home Department* [2014] EWHC 194 (for comment see JNE Varuhas, 'Ministerial Refusals to Initiate Public Inquiries: Review or Appeal?' [2014] CLJ 238); *R (Bradley) v Secretary of State for Work and Pensions* [2008] 3 All ER 1116 (for comment see JNE Varuhas, 'Governmental Rejections of Ombudsman Findings: What Role for the Courts?' (2009) 72 MLR 102).
[202] *R v Secretary of State for the Home Department, ex parte Bugdaycay* [1987] AC 514; *Brind* (n 17); *R v Ministry of Defence, ex parte Smith* [1996] QB 517.
[203] *R (Kiarie) v Secretary of State for the Home Department* [2017] UKSC 42 [46]–[47].
[204] *R v Secretary of State for the Home Department, ex parte Launder* [1997] 1 WLR 839, 860–863.
[205] *Law Society* (n 9) [36]–[41].
[206] *Lynch* (n 32).
[207] *Law Society* (n 9) [118]–[124].

review, the more evidence the court will need to properly discharge its function,[208] and with more evidence, the court shall be drawn ever further into the substance of decisions including scrutiny of their factual premises – so on and so forth.

Of course, these developments, occurring within common law review, raise concerns over compatibility with the orthodox conception of judicial review as a supervisory jurisdiction. First, the proportionality doctrine derived from human rights law requires courts to strike a balance for themselves,[209] which is difficult to reconcile with the basic premise of review as a supervisory jurisdiction, according to which it is the statutory repository that is the primary decision-maker. Second, if courts determine disputed questions of fact for themselves, and/or are drawn into scrutinising the factual underpinnings of the decision-maker's determination, the more difficult it shall be to maintain they are not entering 'the merits', on the traditional understanding of that concept.

Perhaps because of these concerns *Kennedy* and *Pham* have fallen by the wayside in the Supreme Court's jurisprudence. The cases have hardly been cited in recent years. Where cited, the Court has 're-interpreted' the judgments as not involving a departure from reasonableness as the common law head of substantive review, and emphasised that the decisions do not sanction a court placing itself in the shoes of the decision-maker.[210] The Court has also signalled a change of tone, no longer postulating fusion of common law review and human rights law, instead warning of the 'profound constitutional implications' of replacing the 'traditional *Wednesbury* tests'.[211] Further, in a stream of recent decisions the Court has invoked *Wednesbury*-simpliciter without question and with no mention of proportionality.[212] In turn, this seeming course correction in the development of substantive review is liable to precipitate reassertion of the standard approach to evidence and facts.

B. Principle of Legality, Systemic Review and *Unison*

Just as developments in substantive review started to cool off, the Supreme Court began to show renewed interest in the common law principle of legality, specifically the 'augmented' legality principle which incorporates a proportionality dimension.[213] On this approach, where a statutory power affects a basic common law interest or value, the power will be read as subject to an implied proportionality

---

[208] ibid [36]–[41]; *Lynch* (n 32) [22] (without expert evidence 'the Court might well be unable to consider properly any irrationality argument').
[209] See, eg, *Pham* (n 197) [108]. See also *Kennedy* (n 130) [51].
[210] *Begum v SIAC* (n 21) [81]; *Elgizouli v Secretary of State for the Home Department* [2020] UKSC 10 [178] (contrast Lord Kerr's views in dissent: [107]). See also *R (Keyu) v Secretary of State for Foreign and Commonwealth Affairs* [2016] AC 13.
[211] *Poshteh v Royal Borough of Kensington and Chelsea* [2017] UKSC 36 [42].
[212] See, eg, *Begum v SIAC* (n 21) [124]; *Ziegler* (n 130); *R (Friends of the Earth Ltd) v Heathrow Airport Ltd* [2020] UKSC 52 [119]. See also *SC* (n 153) [146].
[213] JNE Varuhas, 'The Principle of Legality' (2020) 79 CLJ 578.

limit (unless the provision provides otherwise), supplying a powerful basis for judicial intervention at common law.[214]

The high point of these developments was the Supreme Court's 2017 decision in *R (Unison) v Lord Chancellor* which struck down an order which imposed fees on employment tribunal users, on the basis that the order unjustifiably interfered with access to justice.[215]

The case marked the culmination of two parallel lines of jurisprudence: the augmented principle of legality case law and developments in structural or systemic review. Importantly both the proportionality and systemic dimensions have significant ramifications for treatment of facts and evidence.

In terms of the legality principle the Court held that the principle involved proportionality analysis analogous to that applied in HRA cases.[216] In turn, this opens up the possibility of arguing that procedural adjustments made in HRA claims should apply to legality claims with a proportionality dimension, as the nature of the judicial inquiry is more or less the same. The fact the augmented principle places at least an evidential onus on government to justify its acts, and involves the court rigorously scrutinising the evidential foundation of the challenged measure and its impacts according to proportionality,[217] means that an array of information, including policy studies, statistics, and so on, will be put before a court – and the court will need this information to discharge its function.[218]

In terms of systemic review, the *Unison* case involved an abstract challenge based not on a claim that a specific individual had been prevented access to the tribunal, but rather that the fees system presented a systemic risk that people would be prevented from accessing justice.[219] This systemic dimension owes much to a line of judicial review cases involving challenges to administrative systems on the basis they posed unacceptable risks of procedural unfairness, the best example being *R (Howard League) v Lord Chancellor*.[220] Indeed, later judgments have analysed *Unison* and the *Howard League* structural unfairness doctrine as adopting common approaches,[221] these developments in turn carrying echoes of the systemic dimensions of HRA law.[222] Systemic review has

---

[214] ibid 592–600.
[215] *Unison* (n 154).
[216] ibid [88]–[89].
[217] ibid [99]–[101]. See also *R (Cherry) v Prime Minister* [2019] UKSC 41 [51], [61].
[218] *Unison* (n 154) [6]–[59]. For an earlier example of a court considering information beyond the decision-making record in applying the augmented principle see: *R v Secretary of State for the Home Department, ex parte Simms* [2000] 2 AC 115, 127–28.
[219] *Unison* (n 154) [87], [90]–[98].
[220] *R (Howard League) v Lord Chancellor* [2017] EWCA Civ 244. See also *R (Detention Action) v First-Tier Tribunal (Immigration and Asylum Chamber)* [2015] 1 WLR 5341. See further Varuhas, 'Changing Nature of Judicial Review' (n 84).
[221] See, eg, *Law Society* (n 9) [129]–[130].
[222] See text at nn 153–159, and note that these systemic dimensions of HRA law featured in *Unison* itself: (n 154) [108]–[117].

significant implications for evidence because (i) within such challenges it seems government bears an evidential onus;[223] and (ii) these challenges require a judicial inquiry into how systems operate in reality, including the incentive effects they create.[224] Such inquiry may depend on evidence which extends well beyond the decision-making record including official reports, multiple witness statements from those with knowledge of the system, hypotheticals, and statistical and survey evidence.[225]

Both of these dimensions of *Unison* raise serious legitimacy concerns. First, proportionality involves the court striking a balance for itself, which is difficult to reconcile with the supervisory nature of review. In *Unison* the Court applied no deference.[226]

Second, systemic review raises legitimacy concerns because it involves courts evaluating entire administrative systems – applying no or very little deference[227] – when judges are not expert in design of large administrative systems. This task would be more suited to an ombudsman or public inquiry.

Third, because both dimensions draw the courts deep into facts and evidence, they raise concerns that the court is seriously trespassing upon the decision-maker's role. In *Unison* the factual premises of the government's decision-making were subject to direct challenge and criticism by the Court.[228] Indeed the Court's decision can be said to proceed from the Court's own evidence base,[229] including its own microeconomic analysis,[230] much of this evidence post-dating the making of the fees order.

These concerns having been raised by scholars[231] and the Independent Review of Administrative Law,[232] the Supreme Court's jurisprudence has taken a striking turn. Over the last year the Supreme Court has seemingly begun to sideline and water down the principle of legality.[233] It has also kyboshed the structural unfairness doctrine, principally on the basis that it took courts beyond their legitimate

---

[223] *Howard League* (n 220) [52], [75], [78], [80], [84], [92], [108], [122].
[224] *Unison* (n 154) [38]–[59], [90]–[98]; *Howard League* (n 220) [51]–[147].
[225] *Unison* (n 154) [6]–[59]; *Howard League* (n 220) [12].
[226] *Unison* (n 154) [90]–[102]; See also Varuhas, 'The Principle of Legality' (n 213) 611–13.
[227] ibid; *Howard League* (n 220) [38], [55].
[228] See, eg, *Unison* (n 154) [46], [56], [58]–[59], [93], [99]–[100].
[229] ibid [6]–[59], [90]–[102], and see in particular [97].
[230] ibid [100].
[231] Varuhas, 'The Principle of Legality' (n 213) especially 611–13; Varuhas, 'Changing Nature of Judicial Review' (n 84); JNE Varuhas, 'Submission to the Independent Review of Administrative Law' (*SSRN*, 26 October 2020) [34]–[38], [54]–[58]. Available at: https://papers.ssrn.com/sol3/papers.cfm?abstract_id=3884673, last accessed 19 December 2022.
[232] IRAL (n 69) [2.50], [3.29]–[3,34], Conclusion [7]. Following on from the IRAL process, the government also critiqued the legality principle in particular: Lord Chancellor, 'Keynote Address on Judicial Review' (*Gov.UK*, 21 July 2021). Available at: www.gov.uk/government/speeches/lord-chancellors-keynote-speech-on-judicial-review, last accessed 19 December 2022.
[233] The Court has become increasingly reluctant to recognise new triggers for the legality principle and has re-emphasised ordinary techniques of interpretation. See in particular: *R (O) v Secretary of State for the Home Department* [2022] UKSC 3; *R (Coughlan) v Minister for the Cabinet Office* [2022] UKSC 11. See also *Elgizouli* (n 210).

role within a supervisory jurisdiction.[234] The Court in these cases has also sought to limit judicial reliance on extrinsic materials such as legislative reports, Hansard and statistical evidence.[235]

However, notably the Court has exempted *Unison* from these developments.[236] This is curious because *Unison* was a product, indeed the culmination, of these two strands of doctrinal development, and the legitimacy concerns raised in respect of those strands of jurisprudence in principle apply equally to *Unison*.

How does one rationalise all of this? It is difficult to say for sure but on one view the Supreme Court has begun to adopt a revisionist understanding of *Unison*, according to which *Unison* involved recognition of a new 'public law action' for breach of the fundamental individual right of access to justice. In the Supreme Court's important decision in *R (A) v Secretary of State for the Home Department* the Court did not explain *Unison* as a manifestation of the legality principle, and explicitly distinguished it from the structural unfairness cases. *Unison* is instead said to have recognised a fundamental right which imposes a 'legal obligation' on the executive not to introduce impediments to access to court.[237] This characterisation may suggest *Unison* – on a revised understanding – did not involve a claim based in judicial review but rather that the case established a novel public law action, the juridical basis of which is a free-standing legal right or obligation. On this view the action would be a common law analogue of the statutory action created by the HRA. That is, it may be that HRA claims and the *Unison* action are of the same genus, and conceptually distinct from common law review.

This rationalisation is supported by the fact courts have emphasised that in such claims their role is the same as in HRA adjudication: the court is the ultimate arbiter of whether the right has been breached, and justifications.[238] That the adjudicative approach is the same in each context follows from the fact the court is performing the same role: the approach 'follows from the constitutional role of the judiciary whereby questions of legal right are the province of the courts'.[239]

If this is correct, questions will undoubtedly arise as to whether the creation of such a novel public law action is appropriate, especially as it involves the court bestowing upon itself the role of primary decision-maker. But the doctrine is not going anywhere as the Supreme Court has very deliberately preserved *Unison*.

Returning to the issue of evidence, it seems that the likely knock-on effect of these developments will be a closer alignment of the procedural treatment of the *Unison* action and HRA claims. In other words, one would expect greater

---

[234] *A* (n 172) (see [65] in particular); *R (BF (Eritrea)) v Secretary of State for the Home Department* [2021] UKSC 38.
[235] *O* (n 233) [30]–[33]; *Coughlan* (n 233) [13]–[14]; *A* (n 172) [41], [65].
[236] *A* (n 172) [66], [80]; *BF* (n 234) [68]–[69]; *O* (n 233) [33]–[36].
[237] *A* (n 172) [80]. But note that the analysis in *O* (n 233), may be said to adopt the more natural reading of *Unison* as applying the principle of legality.
[238] *R (DSD) v Parole Board* [2019] QB 285 [190]; *Law Society* (n 9) [132]. See also *Unison* (n 154) [88]–[89].
[239] *Law Society* (n 9) [132]–[133].

openness to disclosure, oral evidence, resolution of disputed questions of fact, and fresh evidence including expert evidence.[240] In regard to the last, it is notable that despite the decision in *Unison* relying heavily on an array of statistical and survey evidence, and microeconomic analysis, it appears no expert evidence was before the Court.[241] It is not surprising, therefore, that senior judges describe the Court's evaluation of survey and statistical evidence as 'relatively light touch'.[242] If courts are to base their decisions on such evidence, they need to adopt a rigorous approach, which will often require expert assistance, given – as the Supreme Court has itself observed[243] – statistical analysis is removed from judicial experience.

VI. Conclusion

The chapter has examined the law and practice of facts and evidence within the judicial review procedure. The analysis commenced with the standard account, according to which review procedure is not generally an appropriate forum for resolution of factual controversies. Disclosure, oral evidence and expert evidence shall be rare. However, the chapter demonstrated that over time the treatment of facts and evidence within review proceedings has become more complex than suggested by the standard account. Specifically, in the context of HRA claims, courts have developed a more flexible approach to facts and evidence, which can bring review procedure closer to ordinary procedure, while there have been ripple effects for procedural treatment of some types of common law claims.

Key to understanding these developments is a recognition of the close interdependence of substance and process. The core reason for development of the standard, restrictive approach to facts and evidence within review proceedings is that historically the principal type of claims streamed via the procedure were common law judicial review claims for exercise of the High Court's supervisory jurisdiction. However, HRA claims are fundamentally different in nature. The court does not exercise a supervisory jurisdiction, but rather a primary jurisdiction, determining matters of substance – including facts – for itself. It follows from the nature of human rights law, that procedural adjustments were necessary to allow courts to properly perform their constitutional function of determining claims of right. To the extent the common law has developed in ways that bring it closer in nature to HRA law, further procedural realignments have occurred.

Ultimately this chapter has demonstrated the importance of understanding public law as a system, comprised of component parts which each occupy their own discrete space within the normative environment but are intrinsically

---

[240] In *A* the Court envisioned statistics would continue to play a role in *Unison* claims: (n 172) [80].
[241] But note that in subsequent lower court decisions it has been accepted that expert evidence may be required to properly determine access to justice claims: *Law Society* (n 9) [43].
[242] Rose (n 159) [29]. See also the critique in Varuhas, 'Changing Nature of Judicial Review' (n 84).
[243] *A* (n 172) [65].

interconnected in complex ways. A change in one part of the system is liable to have ripple effects on other parts of the system. Importantly, one cannot fully understand each component without understanding how it interrelates with other components. Thus, one cannot claim full understanding of the judicial review procedure without understanding the substantive nature of claims streamed via that procedure. By the same token, one cannot fully understand substantive law, absent an understanding of procedure.

7

Judicial Review of 'Fact Work': Beyond the Law/Fact Distinction

JOANNA BELL AND ELIZABETH FISHER

We have, jointly[1] and separately,[2] undertaken several projects which have involved reading substantial bodies of judicial review case law, at both appellate and first instance levels. One thing which struck us both is that judicial review challenges, in routine and low-profile ways, often deal with disputes about facts: the processes used to find them and the use made of them by decision-makers.[3] In one sense, this is entirely unsurprising: facts are crucial to the statutory tasks many public authorities perform, can be deeply contentious and therefore seem likely to give rise to disputes. It does, however, run counter to the common mantra, often repeated in the academic literature, that judicial review is centrally concerned with law, as opposed to fact[4] and is, as a legal process, inherently unsuited to the resolution of disputes about facts.[5]

What scholars see in case law is fundamentally shaped by the questions scholars ask of it.[6] Asking the wrong questions can cause us to miss crucial elements or otherwise gain a distorted view. When it comes to the extent to which judicial review is concerned with facts, two issues have dominated the academic literature. First, how the distinction between law and fact is to be drawn in judicial review,[7] if it is to be drawn at all.[8] Secondly, when a court will, and should, intervene to correct

---

[1] See, eg, J Bell and E Fisher, 'Exploring a Year of Administrative Law Adjudication in the Administrative Court' [2021] PL 505.
[2] See, eg, E Fisher, 'Law and Energy Transitions: Wind Turbines and Planning Law in the UK' (2018) 38(3) OJLS 528; J Bell, 'Remedies in Judicial Review: Confronting an Intellectual Blindspot' [2022] PL 200.
[3] See also discussion of review for 'mistakes' in S Nason, *Reconstructing Judicial Review* (Oxford, Hart Publishing, 2017) ch 6.
[4] See, eg, T Endicott, *Administrative Law* (4th edn, OUP, 2021) ch 9.
[5] See, eg, D Blundell, 'Of Evidence and Experts: Recent Developments in Fact-Finding and Expert Evidence in Judicial Review' (2018) 23(4) *Judicial Review* 243.
[6] Bell and Fisher (n 1).
[7] See, eg, T Endicott, 'Questions of Law' (1998) 114 LQR 292.
[8] See, eg, R Williams, 'When is an Error Not an Error? Reform of Jurisdictional Review of Error of Law and Fact' [2007] PL 793.

an error of fact.[9] Our aim in this chapter is to encourage scholars to move away from these questions, which we do not think help to illuminate the case law, and instead to take up a different one. Namely, what roles do courts play in overseeing the various forms of 'fact work' which is required in public administration?

We develop our argument over three sections. Section 1 introduces the notion of 'fact work.' In addition to explaining what we mean by the term, we distinguish two kinds – fact assembly and fact deployment – and begin to highlight the variety of ways in which legislation requires public authorities to engage in fact work. Section 2 then turns to the case law. In it, we map three ways in which courts oversee the 'fact work' done in public administration. Finally, Section 3 explains why, in our view, focusing on the law/fact distinction and the extent to which courts will correct factual errors has led to a distorted and incomplete view of the case law.

Three caveats should be noted before we begin. Firstly, we focus on the case law of England and Wales. Our arguments, however, are relevant in other common law jurisdictions.[10] Secondly, our focus is on judicial review undertaken pursuant to domestic administrative law grounds. We recognise that courts often adjudicate on other issues, such as claims under the Human Rights Act 1998, in judicial review and that courts engage with facts in these contexts.[11] This issue, however, falls outside of the scope of our analysis. Thirdly, our analysis is far from exhaustive. Our overarching aim is to encourage scholars to think in greater depth about the different kinds of 'fact work' carried out by public authorities and the roles courts play in overseeing it. What we offer here is a starting point.

I. From Thinking about 'Facts' to Thinking about 'Fact Work'

It is a trite but important point that the majority of functions exercised by public authorities in England and Wales are set out in statutory frameworks.[12] Legislation requires and empowers public authorities to do a great many things.[13] To name but a few examples (which have particular prominence in judicial review challenges)[14] public authorities have statutory discretions or duties to give individuals leave to enter and remain in the UK,[15] to grant permission for the development of land,[16]

---

[9] See, eg, TH Jones, 'Mistake of Fact in Administrative Law' [1990] PL 507; M Kent, 'Widening the Scope of Review for Error of Fact' [1999] *Judicial Review* 239.
[10] Although note the significance of legal culture, eg *Sydney Water Corporation v Marrickville Council* [2014] NSWCA 438 [43].
[11] A Carter, *Proportionality and Facts in Constitutional Adjudication* (Oxford, Hart Publishing, 2021).
[12] T Poole, 'The Executive in Public Law' in J Jowell and C O'Cinneide (eds), *The Changing Constitution* (9th edn, Oxford, OUP, 2019).
[13] J Bell, *The Anatomy of Administrative Law* (Oxford, Hart Publishing, 2020) ch 3.
[14] Nason (n 3) ch 4; Bell and Fisher (n 1); Bell, 'Remedies in Judicial Review' (n 2) 208; R Thomas, 'Mapping Immigration Judicial Review Litigation: An Empirical Legal Analysis' [2015] PL 652.
[15] Immigration Act 1971 pt I.
[16] Town and Country Planning Act 1990, s 70.

to recommend an individual's release, transfer or recall to prison[17] and to provide support for vulnerable children.[18]

To do these things, public authorities work with facts: that is, they work with information that is understood to be an accurate statement about an aspect of the physical or social world. Working with facts is a common feature of administrative practice,[19] but the type of facts that administrative decision-makers work with vary significantly along different dimensions.

Some decision-makers are working with individualised facts. For example, legislation requires them to determine whether person X has Y characteristics which leads to Z legal consequences.[20] Such decision-making, and thus facts, tend to be context bound to a point in time and space. Working with such facts has parallels with the role of facts in the triadic relationship of a court trial, although the rules of evidence are unlikely to apply.[21] Facts are asserted by one party, other parties have a chance to rebut them, and a decision-maker decides in light of the information generated. Determining a planning application is a case in point.[22] In contrast, other decision-makers are working with more 'universal' or 'systematic' facts,[23] for example, about the natural environment or the economy.[24] Working with the latter type of facts is seen as the hallmark of modern administrative bureaucracy.

However, that is not the only way in which the facts that decision-makers work with vary. Facts may be about the past,[25] present,[26] or future.[27] Some facts require specific expertise to work with, others not so much. There is also considerable variety across the administrative processes in which facts are worked with. Case workers work with facts.[28] So do tribunals.[29] And there are many institutional and legislative variations.[30]

---

[17] Criminal Justice Act 2003, s 239.
[18] Children Act 1989, Pt III.
[19] E Fisher, 'The Open Road?: Navigating Public Administration and the Failed Promise of Administrative Law' in E Fisher, J King, and A Young (eds), *The Foundations and Future of Public Law* (Oxford, OUP, 2020) 212–15.
[20] See, eg, *R (Kaur) & Ors v The Secretary of State for the Home Department* [2018] EWCA Civ 411.
[21] On the nature of that triadic relationship, see, eg, M Shapiro, *Courts: A Comparative and Political Analysis* (Chicago, The University of Chicago Press, 1981) 1.
[22] *R (Connolly) & Ors v Secretary of State for Communities and Local Government* [2009] EWCA Civ 1059.
[23] On the distinction between more contextual and more universal facts, see, eg, M Poovey, *A History of the Modern Fact: Problems of Knowledge in the Sciences of Wealth and Society* (Chicago, The University of Chicago Press, 1998) 1–2.
[24] See, eg, *Secretary of State for Environment, Food & Rural Affairs v Downs* [2009] EWCA Civ 664.
[25] See, eg, *R (Jones) v First-tier Tribunal* [2013] UKSC 18, [2013] 2 AC 48.
[26] See, eg, *R (Richards) v The Environment Agency* [2022] EWCA Civ 26 (17 January 2022).
[27] See, eg, *R (ClientEarth) (No 2) v Secretary of State for the Environment, Food and Rural Affairs* [2016] EWHC 2740 [27]–[36].
[28] R Thomas, *Administrative Law in Action: Immigration Administration* (Oxford, Hart Publishing, 2022) ch 5.
[29] ibid ch 6.
[30] Cf Special Educational Needs and Disability Regulations 2014, SI 2014/1530 with Pt 4 and sch 4, Town and Country Planning (Environmental Impact Assessment) Regulations 2017, SI 2017/571.

Facts are also often 'travelling' between different contexts. Work with facts in one context has legal relevance in another.[31] And there are many overlaps and interrelationships between all the examples provided above. Given all this, it is not surprising that facts give rise to many different types of legal questions in judicial review cases.[32] Nor is it surprising that scholars have noted how difficult it is to identify what a 'fact' is.[33]

All this is a reality of public administration. As noted in our introduction, our interest in this chapter is the questions scholars ask of the case law. The identification of a 'fact' is usually done in the context of the fact/law distinction.[34] Questions of law are understood as the province of the courts, while questions of fact (with a few exceptions) are not. Besides the complexities outlined above, there is a further problem – many of the questions in judicial review involve how a decision-maker applies the law to the facts – a situation which is neither solely a question of law nor a question of fact but a mixture of the two. The problem is that answer doesn't yield an answer to what the appropriate role of the court is if a question pertaining to a fact is put before it.[35]

Our basic aim in this chapter is to question the utility of focusing on the fact/law distinction and in the last section we will return to reflect on that distinction. But that reflection cannot occur without illuminating features of the case law which are often overlooked. We do that by focusing in on two points that were made in the above, which are easily overlooked.

First, the work that administrative decision-makers do with facts is nearly always governed by legislation. That legislation will determine whether any specific fact is relevant. Second, what is governed is not so much 'facts' but the 'work' that administrative decision-makers do with 'facts'. In other words, what has legal significance is 'fact work' not facts. By 'work' we mean 'action or activity involving physical or mental effort and undertaken in order to achieve a result'.[36]

A broad distinction can be drawn between two types of 'fact work' that administrative decision-makers are required to do pursuant to legislative regimes. First, 'fact work' is done to 'assemble' facts. That is, to establish how the state of things is, and/or what has happened, is to be understood. We use the term 'assemble' rather than, for instance, 'establish' or 'find' to reflect the variety of facts and processes public authorities engage with and in.[37] Some facts may be relatively

---

[31] This is particularly in relation to a problem such as climate change where decision-makers are often drawing on facts about climate change from other institutions. See, eg, *Friends of the Earth Ltd & Ors, R (on the application of) v Heathrow Airport Ltd* [2020] UKSC 52 [79]. On the concept of travelling facts, see, eg, P Howlett and M Morgan (eds), *How Well Do Facts Travel?: The Dissemination of Reliable Knowledge* (Cambridge, CUP, 2011).

[32] For analysis of different type of legal arguments about facts, see, eg, P Craig, 'Judicial Review, Appeal and Factual Error' [2004] PL 788.

[33] Endicott, 'Questions of Law' (n 7).

[34] ibid.

[35] ibid.

[36] *Oxford English Dictionary*.

[37] See helpful discussion in Carter (n 11) ch 3.

ubiquitous,[38] but they need to be collated in one place. Other facts may relate to a particular person at one point of time. As seen above, facts may relate to the past, present, or future. Fact assembly may involve different forms of evaluative judgement or predictive analysis.[39]

The second type of 'fact work' that legislation often required occurs once facts are assembled. This type of 'fact work' concerns how a public authority 'deploys' facts in decision-making. That is, how they determine which set of facts relates to the question (or questions) a decision-maker is tasked with addressing. Again, there are different ways facts are deployed in decision-making processes. A fact may trigger a particular consequence. If Fact A exists, then X will happen. More commonly, facts will be relevant to the exercise of discretion.

The statutory functions of the Parole Board provide a neat example of these two types of fact work. The Board's essential task is to assess the degree of risk a prisoner poses to make a recommendation as to whether they should be released, transferred or recalled to prison.[40] In order to do that the Board will need to assemble the facts. In a case, for instance, in which a prisoner claims to have experienced a mindset shift,[41] the Board will need to undertake the task of assessing the accuracy of these claims. This is the first type of fact work. Having established the facts, the Board will also need to form a view on what their relevance is for the questions it is tasked for resolving. What, for instance, do the Board's findings concerning the prisoner's mindset shift show about the degree of risk to the public they would pose on release? This is the second type of fact work.

The difference between fact assembling and fact deploying is the former looks backward from a fact to the conditions of how a fact is produced,[42] whereas the latter moves forward and is concerned with the work that a fact does in a decision-making process. These stages may not always be neatly delineated from one another under a decision-making framework and there will be arguments about the virtues and vices of such delineation.[43] Both types of fact work also overlap and interrelate. How facts are deployed will affect what facts are assembled and vice versa. A classic example is that if emphasis is placed on the value of objective or quantitative knowledge in decision-making, that will then shape the type of facts assembled.[44]

---

[38] On the idea of what is 'ubiquitous', see, eg, H Collins and R Evans, *Rethinking Expertise* (Chicago, The University of Chicago Press, 2007) 15–23.

[39] E Fisher, P Pascual and W Wagner 'Understanding Environmental Models in Their Legal and Regulatory Context' (2010) 22 *Journal of Environmental Law* 251.

[40] *R (Browne) v Parole Board* [2018] EWCA Civ 2024 [45]–[53].

[41] See, eg, *R (DSD) v Parole Board* [2018] EWHC 694 (Admin), [2019] QB 285.

[42] This distinction and the language of 'forward' and 'backward' looking is inspired by the discussion of positive and negative modalities in B Latour, *Science in Action: How to Follow Scientists and Engineers Through Society* (Cambridge MA, Harvard University Press, 1987) 23.

[43] See, eg, the debate about separating risk assessment from risk management in public health decision-making: E Fisher, 'Framing Risk Regulation: A Critical Reflection' (2013) 4 *European Journal of Risk Regulation* 125.

[44] E Fisher, *Risk Regulation and Administrative Constitutionalism* (Oxford, Hart Publishing, 2007) ch 1.

All that being said, these two types of fact work are distinct. Identifying both, underscores that decision-makers are doing two different types of reasoning about facts. They are reasoning *about* facts and reasoning *with* facts.

Statutory frameworks provide in different ways, and in differing degrees of detail, for the various forms of 'fact work' a public authority may be required to undertake. Consider, first, fact assembly. In some areas, legislation may prescribe a detailed procedure to be followed. For instance, fact assembly within the Parole Board[45] and Special Immigration Appeals Commission[46] is subject to detailed rules on, for instance, evidence and cross-examination. In other cases, legislation may direct a public authority to assemble the relevant facts, without prescribing a process for doing so. Section 184 of the Housing Act 1996, for instance, simply requires local housing authorities to conduct 'inquiries' into whether individuals are homeless or threatened with homelessness. Where no statutory procedure for fact assembly is provided for, the public authority may itself adopt, or be the subject of, guidance[47] with which they are obliged to comply with in the absence of good reason.[48]

Legislation may also mandate fact assembly in more indirect ways. Consider the Children Act 1989, the central aim of which is to consolidate and expand a series of protections for child welfare, including by placing local authorities under a duty to provide assistance.[49] The Act does not specify how local authorities (and other institutions) are, in cases of disputed facts, to determine whether a person is a child. But the Act does offer a definition of 'child' as a person under the age of 18.[50] In performing its functions under the Act, however, a local authority must necessarily engage in the 'fact work' of forming an initial view on a person's likely date of birth.

Similar points can be made in relation to the second form of fact work: fact deploying. On the one hand, legislation may provide that, once assembled, a fact has very specific consequences. The Children Act 1989 is again a pertinent example. Once it is established that a person is a 'child' they are treated as a beneficiary of a series of specific statutory rights. Statute may provide, however, that a fact is one relevant factor among many of which the decision-maker is required to take account.[51] The facts as set out in an environmental impact assessment (EIA) are an example. Regulation 26 of the Town and Country Planning (Environmental Impact Assessment) Regulations 2017 requires a decision-maker to examine an

---

[45] Parole Board Rules 2019 (SI 2019/1038) Pt 3.
[46] Special Immigration Appeals Commission (Procedure) Rules 2003 (SI 2003/1034) Pt 2.
[47] See, eg, Home Office, *Assessing Age* (14 January 2022). Available at: https://assets.publishing.service.gov.uk/government/uploads/system/uploads/attachment_data/file/1119545/Assessing_age.pdf>, last accessed 14 April 2023.
[48] *R (Mandalia) v Secretary of State for the Home Department* [2015] UKSC 59, [2015] 1 WLR 4546 [29]–[31].
[49] Children Act 1989, Pt III.
[50] ibid s 105(1).
[51] See, eg, Town and Country Planning Act 1990, s 70(2) and Planning and Compulsory Purchase Act 2004, s 38 which require that 'material considerations' be taken into account.

EIA, 'reach a reasoned conclusion' in relation to it, and 'integrate that conclusion into the decision as to whether planning permission or subsequent consent is to be granted'. The scheme does not mandate a particular outcome, rather it directs planning authorities to exercise judgement in deploying the facts set out in the EIA.

The analysis in this section is brief and far from exhaustive. What it begins to show, however, is that the functions of public authorities are governed by a broad variety of legislative frameworks, and those frameworks require decision-makers to engage in a range of different kinds of 'fact work'. Sometimes that fact work will be subject to detailed statutory provision. Often it will not.

II. Court Oversight of Fact Work

Given the broad variety of circumstances in which public authorities are required to engage in 'fact work' it is unsurprising that reviewing courts are called on from time to time to review the *lawfulness* of how it is carried out. In this section we highlight three ways in which courts perform this oversight role. Before turning to them, some more general points are in order.

There is no settled account of judicial review of what we term 'fact work'. Textbooks deal with the relevant case law in different ways. Some texts have a separate chapter dealing with 'error of fact'.[52] Others consider the case law as part of a discussion of errors of law,[53] jurisdiction[54] or substantive review.[55] The case law is also categorised under different headings: mistake or error of fact;[56] about control/supervision of the fact-finding process;[57] or about facts, findings and/or evidence.[58] Our aim here is to provide a different schema and one which we think better illuminates the case law than available accounts.

Some of the case law discussed below will be familiar to public law academics: *R (A) v Croydon LBC*[59] and *E v Secretary of State for the Home Department*[60] are well-known as the leading authorities on review of 'precedent' facts and for material mistake of fact respectively. Both have been the subject of extensive

---

[52] P Craig, *Administrative Law* (9th edn, London, Sweet & Maxwell, 2021) ch 17.
[53] Endicott, *Administrative Law* (n 4) 356–73. See also Endicott, 'Questions of Law' (n 7), Williams (n 8).
[54] CF Forsyth and IJ Ghosh, *Wade & Forsyth's Administrative Law* (12th edn, Oxford, OUP, 2022) ch 8; M Elliott and J Varuhas, *Administrative Law: Text, Cases and Materials* (5th edn, Oxford, OUP, 2017) 65–76.
[55] H Woolf et al, *De Smith's Principles of Judicial Review* (2nd edn, London, Sweet & Maxwell, 2020) [11-037]–[11-052]; P Cane, *Administrative Law* (4th edn, Oxford, OUP, 2004) ch 9.
[56] See, eg, Craig, *Administrative Law* (n 52) ch 17; M Fordham, *The Judicial Review Handbook* (7th edn, Oxford, Hart Publishing, 2021) 49.
[57] See, eg, Endicott, *Administrative Law* (n 4) 356–73; Elliott and Varuhas (n 38) 65–76.
[58] Wade and Forsyth (n 38) 202–12.
[59] *R (A) v Croydon LBC* [2009] UKSC 8, [2009] 1 WLR 2557 (*Croydon*).
[60] *R (E) v Secretary of State for the Home Department* [2004] EWCA Civ 49, [2004] 2 WLR 1351.

analysis.[61] By approaching the case law through a different lens, however, we hope to shed new light on these cases. For instance, our discussion below very clearly highlights that while these cases are both concerned with facts in public administration, they involve courts overseeing 'fact work' of very different kinds and in very different ways.

Our discussion also highlights that court oversight of fact work is far from exhausted by grounds (such as precedent fact and material mistake of fact) which are explicitly concerned with 'facts'. Scholars have sometimes sought to encourage courts to move away from, what has been termed, an 'absorption' approach (in which factual disputes are 'absorbed' by general grounds of review) and instead to develop grounds of review explicitly concerned with factual errors.[62] Our discussion in this section highlights, however, that the grounds of review as they relate to legislative frameworks continue to be important in facilitating court oversight of fact work. These grounds ought not to be left out of the picture.

Finally, and most fundamentally, the difficulties of drawing a neat line between law and fact in judicial review have sometimes led commentators to the 'cynical'[63] view that, when it comes to alleged factual errors, courts will intervene when they feel they ought.[64] In contrast, our analysis highlights how court oversight of fact work is structured by legislation and established bodies of legal doctrine. The picture is not neat. Nor is it uniform.[65] The law is also continuing to develop. However, fundamentally, court oversight of fact work involves, not the exercise of unstructured discretion, but the development and application of legal doctrine in relation to different legislative frameworks.

A. Review of Fact Assembly

The first judicial role we draw attention to is review of a decision-maker's approach to fact assembly. As we explained above, legislation often requires public authorities to assemble facts. Legislation may stipulate a detailed process for doing so. Or it may make no specification at all. In carrying out the 'work' of assembling facts, public authorities are required to comply with the grounds of judicial review. They must, therefore, act in a manner which is procedurally fair, give consideration to all mandatory relevant, and ignore all irrelevant, considerations, and more generally approach the issue rationally which, pertinently, includes a requirement to take

---

[61] In addition to other references, see, eg, E Lui, '"Fairness" for Mistake of Fact: A Mistake in Fact' [2020] PL 428.

[62] C Forsyth, 'Error of Fact Revisited: Waiting for the *Anisminic* Moment' (2018) 23(1) *Judicial Review* 1 [9].

[63] M Aronson, M Groves and G Weeks, *Judicial Review of Administrative Action and Governmental Liability* (7th edn, London, Thomson Reuters, 2022) [5.30]; Woolf et al (n 39) [11-038].

[64] See, eg, Williams (n 8).

[65] A point which can be made about administrative law more broadly: see especially Bell, *Anatomy of Administrative Law* (n 13) chs 3, 7.

reasonable steps to gather the relevant information.[66] Courts play an important role in determining what these standards require in different statutory contexts and ensuring these standards are complied with.

As with judicial review more generally, legislative context is crucial:[67] what constitutes a fair and rational approach to fact assembly depends on the nature of the statutory function the decision-maker is performing. Consider, for instance, the compilation of an environmental report for the purposes of the EIA regime. A report is an important step in the assembly of facts. Crucially, however, it is only one part of a broader process which also involves various forms of subsequent mandatory consultation. This is reflected in the approach courts take when called upon to determine whether the content of a report is rational. Sullivan J (as he was then) in the leading case *Blewett, R (on the application of) v Derbyshire County Council* explained the proper approach as follows:

> The Regulations should be interpreted as a whole and in a common-sense way. ... [The Regulations] recognise that an environmental statement may well be deficient, and make provision through the publicity and consultation processes for any deficiencies to be identified so that the resulting 'environmental information' provides the local planning authority with as full a picture as possible. There will be cases where the document purporting to be an environmental statement is so deficient that it could not reasonably be described as an environmental statement as defined by the Regulations ... but they are likely to be few and far between.[68]

Because, in other words, an environmental report serves merely as a *starting point* for assembling the facts with later opportunities to address defects or omissions, a report should not be deemed irrational merely because it does not address all possible environmental impacts.

Review of the lawfulness of fact assembly can sometimes involve addressing relatively narrow questions. In *Basma v Manchester University Hospitals NHS Foundation Trust*, for instance, the question was whether the health authority had acted irrationally in giving no weight to informal evidence that the applicant had been able to take five steps unassisted in the prior year.[69] Similarly, in *DSD*, the High Court gave careful consideration to the question of whether, in the circumstances, the Parole Board's failure to make further inquiries into the extent of the applicant's potential offending rendered its decision irrational and therefore unlawful.[70]

In many areas of public administration, however, the assembly of a particular kind of fact is a routine aspect of the public authority's role in discharging their obligations under legislation. Where this is the case, courts have played an

---

[66] Sometimes known as the '*Tameside* duty of inquiry'. For discussion see especially *R (Plantagenet Alliance Ltd) v Secretary of State for Justice* [2014] EWHC 1662 (QB) [99]–[110]; *R (Balajigari) v Secretary of State for the Home Department* [2019] EWCA Civ 673, [2019] 1 WLR 4647 [70].
[67] Bell, *Anatomy of Administrative Law* (n 13) ch 3.
[68] *R (Blewett) v Derbyshire County Council* [2003] EWHC 2775 (Admin) [41].
[69] *R (Basma) v Manchester University Hospitals NHS Foundation Trust* [2021] EWCA Civ 278.
[70] *DSD* (n 41).

important role in articulating guidelines for ensuring the legality of that fact work in light of that legislation and the grounds of review. These guidelines are often 'cross-cutting' in the sense that they do not focus on one ground of review: their aim is to offer a concise and amalgamated summary of how a public authority is expected to approach the assembly of facts to act lawfully.

Probably the most developed example is the so-called '*Merton* principles'[71] which apply in age assessment cases. The High Court in *R (AS) v Croydon* in 2011 offered a useful summary of ten key principles, which include the following:

(1) An appropriate adult should accompany the child and should be present during the interview.

...

(4) The assessors should pay attention to the level of tiredness, trauma, bewilderment and anxiety of the child and his or her ethnicity, culture and customs should be a key focus throughout the assessment.

...

(9) The conclusions reached by the assessors should be explained with reasons which, although they may be brief, should explain the basis of the assessment and any significant adverse credibility or factual findings.

(10) The reasons should be internally consistent and should not exhibit any obvious error of inadequate explanation for not accepting any apparently credible and consistent answers.[72]

These principles are a striking illustration of what we mean by judicial guidance often being 'cross-cutting'.[73] Principles (1) and (9), for instance, deal with representation[74] and the duty to give reasons and therefore relate primarily to procedural fairness. Principle 4, in contrast, is most naturally seen as a direction on relevancy. Meanwhile principle 10 seems concerned primarily with the rationality of decisions.

Local authorities have long had to perform the 'fact work' of making age assessments, and the *Merton* principles have been developed over many years. Public administration, however, does not stand still[75] and public authorities are sometimes required to engage in new forms of 'fact work'. A flurry of case law has, for instance, recently emerged on the processes used within the National Referral Mechanism[76]

---

[71] *R (B) v Merton LBC* [2003] EWHC 1689 (Admin) (*Merton*).
[72] *R (AS) v Croydon* [2011] EWHC 2091 (Admin), [19]. Other significant case law includes *R (FZ) v London Borough of Croydon* [2011] EWCA Civ 59, [2011] PTSR 748 (*FZ*); *R (A) v Croydon LBC* [2009] EWHC 939 (Admin) (on the role of paediatrician reports); *R (M) v London Borough of Waltham Forest* [2021] EWHC 2241 (Admin) (on the role of evidence relating to height and the development of teeth).
[73] See *Merton* (n 71) [49].
[74] See also *FZ* (n 72).
[75] J Bell, 'Sources of Dynamism in Modern Administrative Law' (2021) 41(3) OJLS 833.
[76] An administrative measure introduced to incorporate the Council of Europe Convention on Action against Trafficking in Human Beings, CETS No 197, Warsaw, 16 May 2005 (ECAT). See also Home Office, National Referral Mechanism Guidance: Adult (England and Wales) (*Gov. UK*, 19 May 2022).

and tribunals[77] for determining whether there are 'reasonable' and 'conclusive' grounds[78] for believing a person is a victim of human trafficking. These cases are illustrations of courts beginning to craft judicial guidance on fact assembly in a new context. In 2020, the Court of Appeal in *R (MN) v Secretary of State for the Home Department*[79] helpfully distilled the principles developed so far on credibility assessments. The following is enough to give a flavour of its content:

> (1) The decision whether the account given by an applicant is in the essential respects truthful has to be taken by the tribunal or competent authority caseworker on the totality of the evidence, viewed holistically.
>
> ....
>
> (3) ... it is open to a doctor to express an opinion to the effect that his or her findings are positively supportive of the truthfulness of an applicant's account and where they do so that opinion should be taken into account.
>
> ...
>
> (5) The weight to be given to any such expression of opinion will depend on the circumstances of the case. It can never be determinative, and the decision-maker will have to decide in each case to what extent its value has to be discounted.[80]

Much like the *Merton* guidance, these principles provide amalgamated guidance on how fact finders may comply with the grounds of review in a highly specific decision-making context.

B. Precedent Fact: *Judicial* Fact Assembly

In the cases considered in the previous section, courts deployed the general grounds of review to review the lawfulness of a decision-maker's approach to fact assembly. Occasionally, however, courts have gone further. Namely, by *undertaking for itself* the fact work of fact assembly. The leading case is *Croydon*.[81] The case turned on a

---

Available at: www.gov.uk/government/publications/human-trafficking-victims-referral-and-assessment-forms/guidance-on-the-national-referral-mechanism-for-potential-adult-victims-of-modern-slavery-england-and-wales#:~:text=The%20National%20Referral%20Mechanism%20(%20NRM,involve%20 multiple%20forms%20of%20exploitation, last accessed 14 April 2023; Home Office, National Referral Mechanism Guidance: Adult (England and Wales) (*Gov.UK*, 1 May 2022). Available at: www.gov.uk/government/publications/human-trafficking-victims-referral-and-assessment-forms/guidance-on-the-national-referral-mechanism-for-potential-adult-victims-of-modern-slavery-england-and-wales#:~:text=The%20National%20Referral%20Mechanism%20(%20NRM,involve%20multiple%20 forms%20of%20exploitation, last accessed 14 April 2023.

[77] *MS (Pakistan) v Secretary of State for the Home Department* [2020] UKSC 9, [2020] 1 WLR 1373; M Grundler, 'Expanding the Right to Remain as a Trafficked Person under Article 4 ECHR and ECAT' (2021) 84 MLR 1093.
[78] ECAT (n 76) art 10.
[79] *R (MN) v Secretary of State for the Home Department* [2020] EWCA Civ 1746, [2021] 1 WLR 1956.
[80] ibid [113].
[81] *Croydon* (n 59).

question of construction[82] concerning the term 'child' within the Children Act.[83] The Supreme Court considered that, properly construed, whether a person is or is not a child is a 'precedent' or 'jurisdictional' fact.[84] In consequence, the appropriate role of a court in judicial review of an age assessment is to re-examine the relevant evidence to make 'its own determination as to the actual age or date of birth'.[85] That is, the court undertakes the work of assembling the facts for itself.

The precedent fact doctrine is not confined to local authority age assessments: other legislative provisions have been deemed to create precedent facts necessitating courts to undertake fact assembly. The House of Lords in *R v Secretary of State for the Home Department, ex parte Khawaja* famously concluded that the question of whether a person is an 'illegal entrant' is an issue of precedent fact, necessitating a fresh judicial finding as to whether the applicant had obtained entry to the UK through fraudulent means.[86] Another common example is where the applicant is 'seeking a declaration ... that she is a British citizen',[87] usually for the purpose of applying for a passport: whether a person meets the requirements of citizenship are 'precedent fact[s] for the court to determine'.[88] The courts are also invited from time to time to apply the precedent fact doctrine in new legal contexts.[89] In *R (Bluefin Insurance Services Ltd) v Financial Ombudsman Service Ltd*,[90] for instance, the Administrative Court treated the question of whether a complainant was a 'consumer' for the purposes of the Financial Services and Markets Act 2000[91] as a precedent fact.

The effect of treating an issue as a precedent fact is to fundamentally change the nature of judicial review for a particular category of challenges. Re-hearing the primary evidence to assemble facts is not the 'habitual'[92] work of an Administrative Court judge. It requires a deviation from the normal principles of evidence. Oral evidence and cross-examination are, for instance, more routinely admitted and permitted.[93] Undertaking fact assembly also requires a very different type of legal expertise to be brought to bear.[94]

---

[82] ibid [54].

[83] Children Act 1989, s 17.

[84] For a discussion of this in the Australian context, see E Fisher, '"Jurisdictional" Facts and "Hot" Facts: Legal Formalism, Legal Pluralism, and the Nature of Australian Administrative Law' (2015) 38 *Melbourne University Law Review* 968.

[85] *R (F) v Lewisham LBC* [2009] EWHC 3542 (Admin), [2010] PTSR 13 [9].

[86] *R v Secretary of State for the Home Department, ex parte Khawaja* [1984] AC 74, [1983] 2 WLR 321 (HL).

[87] *R (Orire-Banjo) v Secretary of State for the Home Department* [2020] EWHC 3516 (Admin) [8].

[88] ibid [8]. See also *R (Harrison) v Secretary of State for the Home Department* [2003] EWCA Civ 432 [34]; *R (Din) v Secretary of State for the Home Department* [2018] EWHC 1046 (Admin) [2].

[89] See, eg, *R (Datamatics UK Ltd) v Secretary of State for the Home Department* [2016] EWHC 1780 (Admin).

[90] *R (Bluefin Insurance Services Ltd) v Financial Ombudsman Service Ltd* [2014] EWHC 3413 (Admin).

[91] Financial Services and Markets Act 2000, s 226(6); *Financial Services Handbook*, DISP rule 2.7.3 (discussed at *Bluefin* (n 90) [18]).

[92] *FZ* (n 72) [31].

[93] ibid [5]: 'most of these cases are now likely to require the court to receive evidence to make its factual determination.'

[94] ibid [31] (on transfer of age assessment challenges to the Upper Tribunal).

Recognition of a precedent fact can also give rise to legal questions about how a reviewing court is to approach its task. This is evident in the case law which has followed *Croydon*. In *FZ*, for instance, the Court of Appeal grappled with the question of what must be shown at the permission stage to be granted leave for judicial review.[95] In *R (CJ) v Cardiff CC*,[96] the Court of Appeal clarified that the burden of proof has no relevance in age assessment challenges:[97] 'neither party is required to prove the precedent fact. The court, in its inquisitorial role, must ask whether the precedent fact existed on the balance of probability'.[98] The lower courts have also been required to work out the legal implications of the *Croydon* decision for adjournments,[99] admissibility of evidence,[100] costs,[101] transfer of cases to the Upper Tribunal[102] and interim[103] and final relief.[104]

The Court's fact assembly role flows from a statute.[105] In so doing, the precedent fact doctrine has limited scope. Specifically, it applies where the fact work involved is necessary and is capable of being adjudicated upon by a court. As Lord Hope noted in *Croydon*:

> The initial decision taker must appreciate that no margin of discretion is enjoyed by the local authority on this issue [whether someone is a child]. But the issue is not to be determined by a consideration of issues of policy or by a view as to whether resort to a decision by the court in such cases is inappropriate. It depends entirely on the meaning of the statute. We must construe the Act as we find it. As I have said, when the subsection is properly construed in the light of what section 105(1) provides, the question admits of only one answer.[106]

The court thus takes on that limited fact work itself on the basis that the fact is legally required to be determined properly and there is not another means for it to legally occur.[107]

C. Review of Fact Deployment

A third and final role played by courts in overseeing 'fact work' entails a review of a decision-maker's approach to *deploying* facts. As explained above, once a fact

---

[95] ibid [9], [26], concluding that the proper question is whether 'the material before the court raises a factual case which, taken at its highest, could not properly succeed in a factual hearing'.
[96] *R (CJ) v Cardiff CC* [2011] EWCA Civ 1590, [2012] PTSR 1235.
[97] cf *Din* (n 88) [2] (in a citizenship challenge, the applicant bears the burden of proof).
[98] *CJ* (n 96) [22].
[99] *R (SH (Afghanistan)) v Secretary of State for the Home Department* [2011] EWCA Civ 1284.
[100] *R (S) v London Borough of Croydon* [2011] EWHC 2091 (Admin).
[101] *R (M) v Croydon LBC* [2012] EWCA Civ 595.
[102] *FZ* (n 72).
[103] *R (AXA) v Hackney LBC* [2021] EWHC 1345 (Admin).
[104] *S* (n 100).
[105] *Croydon* (n 59) [54].
[106] ibid [54].
[107] Fisher, '"Jurisdictional" Facts and "Hot" Facts' (n 84) for an extended discussion of this.

has been assembled, a public authority must then determine its implications for the questions it is tasked with addressing. Sometimes legislation stipulates these implications specifically. Often it requires the public authority to form a judgment. As with fact assembly, reviewing courts play an important role in ensuring that facts are deployed in accordance with the legislative framework and the general grounds of judicial review.

Consider a recent cluster of cases concerned with the legal (ir)relevance of unproven allegations against a prisoner. In both *R (Morris) v Parole Board*[108] and *R (Pearce) v Parole Board*,[109] the Parole Board had placed emphasis on allegations made against the prisoner which had not resulted in conviction in recommending against release. The High Court and Court of Appeal respectively held that the Parole Board was permitted to make its own factual findings relating to such allegations. In *deploying* those facts, however, the Parole Board was required to act fairly. In particular, where the Parole Board was unable to make a factual finding on the balance of probabilities, it was contrary to common law principles of fairness to nonetheless place weight on the existence of 'concerns'.[110]

Morris and *Pearce* are illustrations of reviewing courts assessing the lawfulness of fact deployment against the general grounds of review of fairness, relevancy and rationality. It is also pertinent to draw attention to a ground of review explicitly concerned with 'facts', namely the material mistake of fact (MMOF) ground. This ground was concretised in the landmark case *E* and enables judicial intervention where four conditions are met:

> First, there must have been a mistake as to an existing fact, including a mistake as to the availability of evidence on a particular matter. Secondly, the fact or evidence must have been 'established', in the sense that it was uncontentious and objectively verifiable. Thirdly, the appellant (or his advisers) must not been have been responsible for the mistake. Fourthly, the mistake must have played a material (not necessarily decisive) part in the Tribunal's reasoning.[111]

At first glance, this ground of review may appear to concern the assembly of facts. Analysis of the post-*E* case law, however, suggests differently. To explain why, it is important to emphasise the second criterion of *E*: the relevant error must be 'uncontentious and objectively verifiable'. Post-*E*, the courts have adopted a narrow understanding of this criterion, effectively confining the doctrine to cases in which a factual error is *conceded*. As such, where there continues to be a dispute between the parties about whether the public authority made a factual error, the courts have found the second *E* criterion to be absent.[112] As Thornton J put it in *Johnson v Royal*

---

[108] *R (Morris) v Parole Board* [2020] EWHC 711 (Admin), [2020] ACD 119.
[109] *R (Pearce) v Parole Board* [2022] EWCA Civ 4, [2022] 1 WLR 2216.
[110] ibid [37], [47].
[111] *E* (n 60) [66]. While *E* itself concerned a statutory appeal, the Court of Appeal explicitly extended the ground to judicial review, remarking on the 'gradual assimilation' of the two procedures: [41].
[112] See, especially, *R (Chalfront St Peter Parish Council) v Chiltern DC* [2014] EWCA Civ 1393 [99]–[108]; *MT (Algeria) v Secretary of State for the Home Department* [2007] EWCA Civ 808 [69].

Borough of Windsor and Maidenhead, in applying the MMOF ground the courts have not seen it as their role as being to:

> [D]ecide between competing recollections of events. It is not, however, necessary for the court to attempt to resolve the actual dispute between the parties because the doctrine of mistake of fact requires that the 'mistake' fact be 'established' in the sense of being uncontentious and objectively verifiable.[113]

This narrow approach means it is very difficult, perhaps impossible, to find successful MMOF challenges other than those in which the mistake is abundantly clear on the evidence (for instance, because it is clearly stated in a consultation document,[114] a decision letter,[115] report[116] or judgment[117]) and where the public authority therefore concedes that it fell into factual error.[118]

In consequence, when courts review under the MMOF ground, they are not concerned with flaws in assembling facts (those flaws have been conceded) but rather with whether flawed factual premises have been *deployed* unlawfully. The case law highlights two broad instances where this will be the case.

The first is where the public authority does not correct the mistake because it believes, rightly or wrongly, that it lacks the legal power to reopen its decision. Public authorities' powers and functions are mostly defined by statutes. Sometimes statutes explicitly or implicitly confer on public authorities a power to reopen earlier decisions. In other contexts, however, public authorities become *functus officio* post-decision and therefore lack the power to correct a decision based on a clear factual error on their own initiative. In these circumstances, appeal or judicial review may be the only way to undo the error and the MMOF ground has proven a useful way of facilitating intervention.

E itself is an example of a case of this kind.[119] A more recent and straightforward illustration is *R (DPP) v Sunderland Magistrates's Court*.[120] A District Judge refused an application to adjourn a trial based on a (concededly) mistaken belief that the appellant had not attended court. However, 'when the truth was discovered ... the District Judge was functus officio and so there was nothing he could do about it'.[121] The appellant appealed by way of case stated. The High Court accepted that MMOF was a permissible ground of intervention and allowed the appeal on the basis that each of the *E* criteria was met.

See also *R (Patel) v Secretary of State for Communities and Local Government* [2016] EWHC 3354 (Admin) [23]; *R (Robinson) v Secretary of State for Communities and Local Government* [2016] EWHC 634 (Admin), [39]; *R (Onwuama) v Ealing LBC* [2017] EWHC 847 (Admin) [17].

[113] *Johnson v Royal Borough of Windsor and Maidenhead* [2019] EWHC 160 (Admin). [68].

[114] Eg *R (Police Superintendents' Association) v HM Treasury* [2021] EWHC 3389 (Admin).

[115] Eg *R (Hiam) v Secretary of State for Communities and Local Government* [2014] EWHC 4112 (Admin); *R (Gopikrishna) v Office of the Independent Adjudicator for Higher Education* [2015] EWHC 207 (Admin); *R (Wallpott) v Welsh Health Specialised Services Committee* [2021] EWHC 3291 (Admin).

[116] Eg *R (Watt) v London Borough of Hackney* [2016] EWHC 1978 (Admin).

[117] Eg *R (Ground Rents Ltd) v Upper Tribunal* [2013] EWHC 2638 (Admin).

[118] As noted by Beatson LJ in *Chalfront* (n 112) [106]: 'there was no suggestion in any of these cases that the evaluation was controversial.'

[119] *E* (n 60).

[120] *R (DPP) v Sunderland Magistrates' Court* [2018] EWHC 229 (Admin), [2018] 1 WLR 2195.

[121] ibid [38].

A second and more common scenario in which the MMOF ground plays a role occurs where a public authority concedes a factual error but maintains that the decision should nonetheless stand because the error did not affect the decision-making process and/or outcome.[122] In cases of this kind, the fourth criterion articulated in *E* – that the mistake 'must have played a material part in the tribunal's reasoning'[123] – often comes to the foreground as the major source of contention: many challenges stand or fall depending on whether the reviewing court finds that the materiality threshold is met.

III. Beyond the Law/Fact Distinction

As promised, we now return to the fact/law distinction. Our argument in this chapter has a positive and a negative element. We have focused primarily on the positive: encouraging scholars to more thoroughly probe the various forms of 'fact work' undertaken in public administration and the various roles courts play in overseeing it. As Lady Hale noted in *Croydon*, '[c]ases are not concerned with how to improve fact-finding, but with what is legally required'.[124] The issue of what is legally required results in a court needing to assess how legal and administrative frameworks govern the deployment and assembling of facts. That will be different in different circumstances. In particular, the legal question for the court may be about how a fact is deployed (*E*) or to how facts are assembled (*Merton*). Different legislative and administrative frameworks govern fact work in different ways. In carrying out judicial review, courts are reviewing the processes by which facts are deployed and assembled rather than facts alone. This is because those processes are constituted, limited, and held to account by law.

That is the positive element of our argument, The negative element is that two commonly posed questions – Where is the line between law and fact to be drawn in judicial review? When do courts intervene to correct factual errors? – do not help to illuminate the case law. The way in which the law/fact distinction came to be deployed in analysis of judicial review case law is a topic worthy of detailed historical study. Here, we limit ourselves to making two key points.

First, despite its prevalence in textbooks and academic commentary, the law/fact distinction is not an inherent feature of the legislative architecture of judicial review. Judicial review is defined in the Civil Procedure Rules as follows:

a 'claim for judicial review' means a claim to review the lawfulness of –

(a) an enactment; or
(b) a decision, action or failure to act in relation to the exercise of a public function.[125]

---

[122] In addition to examples cited below, see also *R (Ecotricity Next Generation Ltd) v Secretary of State for Communities and Local Government* [2015] EWHC 189 (Admin).
[123] *E* (n 60) [66].
[124] *Croydon* (n 59) [8].
[125] CPR Pt 54, r 1(2).

Nothing in this definition requires courts to delimit law from fact, or indeed to categorise other types of error.[126] It is true that judicial review is limited to review of the 'lawfulness' of a decision. But that alone tells one nothing about whether, when and how facts are relevant in assessing lawfulness.

The law/fact distinction is, and has long been, used in a variety of contexts across the English and Welsh legal system. It has long played a role in delineating the functions of actors and institutions within the court and tribunal system. In the criminal law context, for instance, issues of fact broadly rest with the jury and issues of law with the trial judge. In civil litigation, appellate courts overturn a trial judge's decision only on legal, as opposed to factual, matters.[127] Similarly, the relationship between the First-tier tribunals, the Upper Tribunal and Court of Appeal continues to be shaped by the distinction between law and fact.[128] In light of this, it is perhaps unsurprising that commentators have looked to the law/fact distinction as a means of distinguishing between the roles of the public authority and court in judicial (and statutory) review.

The law/fact distinction, however, is not the right intellectual device for helping to make sense of the modern judicial review case law. Not only is the line between law and fact notoriously difficult to draw[129] and acutely context sensitive,[130] to seek to explain case law by reference to it can obscure the way in which case law is reasoned. The law/fact distinction presents us with pre-labelled categories of error. It suggests the starting point in judicial review is for the court to identify the box into which an alleged error falls and to shape its approach to review accordingly. This is not, however, how reviewing courts reason. As the analysis above illustrates, legal reasoning in judicial review proceeds in a different way. A reviewing court's first task is always to understand the nature of the, usually statutory, task a public authority is required to discharge. The central question in determining a challenge is then whether, in performing that function, the public authority has erred in a way which constitutes a recognisable legal error. To analyse judicial review case law through the lens of the law/fact distinction is to force it to fit into a structure which is external to it.

Secondly, it is also unhelpful to approach the case law by asking in what circumstances a reviewing court will intervene to correct a 'mistake' or 'error' of fact. None of the roles courts play in overseeing fact work highlighted is well described in this way. Consider an obvious candidate: review of a precedent fact. As we explained above, where legislation creates a precedent fact the judicial review exercise changes fundamentally, and the courts performs the 'fact work' of fact assembly for itself. Certainly, there will be cases when a court will disagree with the conclusion reached by a local authority. The basis of intervention in these

---

[126] See also Senior Courts Act 1981, s 31.
[127] See, eg, *Jackson v Murray* [2015] UKSC 5, [2015] 2 All ER 805.
[128] See especially *Jones* (n 25).
[129] Williams (n 8); *Lawson v Serco Ltd* [2006] ICR 250 (HL) [34].
[130] *Jones* (n 25) [43]–[46]; Lord Carnwath, 'Tribunal Justice – A New Start' [2009] PL 48, 63–64.

cases, however, is not that the public authority made an *incorrect* factual finding per se. Consider the following judicial observation on the role of the reviewing court in age assessment cases:

> A court ... is not in truth considering whether it has been shown on the balance of probabilities that a particular date is the true date of birth. The likelihood will be that, if there is a range of birth dates, which ever one is selected will, on the balance of probability, not be the correct one. In other words ... it will be more likely that the date selected is wrong. What in fact the court is doing is making an assessment of what is the most likely date of birth. It is comparing the likelihood of a wide potential range of dates and picking the one which the evidence suggests is more likely than the rest to be accurate.[131]

As this passage highlights, by their very nature, it will be impossible to know with certainty in an age assessment case what the 'correct' date of birth is, and therefore whether the local authority erred. A court is therefore replacing one probably wrong answer with another probably wrong answer. Rather, the essence of these cases is that legislation is thought to necessitate that the court undertakes the 'fact work' of assembling contentious facts for itself.

Consider another obvious candidate: review for MMOF. As highlighted above, in practice this ground operates in cases where a public authority has *conceded* a factual error. The central question in a case is not, therefore, whether a public authority has erred in fact. The focus of review is usually whether the mistaken factual premise influenced decision-making in a manner which was 'material' and therefore unlawful.

IV. Conclusion

Einstein is quoted as having said that if he had an hour to solve a problem and his life depended on it, he would spend 55 minutes working out what question to ask and five minutes solving it. Thorough analysis of case law cannot be done quickly. The quote does, however, emphasise the importance of ensuring that questions are framed in a way which serves to illuminate and not obscure or distract.

Our argument in this chapter has been that to focus on the law/fact distinction in analysing judicial review case law is to ask the wrong questions of it. If we want to understand the various ways in which courts interact with facts in judicial review, we should pose a different question: namely, what role(s) courts play in overseeing 'fact work'. We have not here offered a conclusive answer to that question, but a starting point. We hope to encourage readers to think more deeply about the fact work done in public administration and the legal doctrines which structure its oversight.

---

[131] *R (N) v Croydon LBC* [2011] EWHC 862 (Admin) [9].

8

Legality in Fact-finding by Executive Decision-Makers: What Role for ultra vires?

EMILY HAMMOND

In the contemporary regulatory landscape, the executive routinely engages in adjudication of individual rights or liabilities. The exercise often involves the application of general rules that are not inherently non-justiciable, to facts which are not inherently inapt for judicial determination. In a practical sense, the consequences of an executive determination of individual rights or liabilities may be very similar to a judicial order. Both kinds of decision can manifest a polity's distinctive public powers to unilaterally affect the legal position of subjects – whether by conferring or terminating licences and permits, or imposing new liabilities which range in severity and include civil control orders and detention. Yet despite the functional similarities, the systemic constitutional safeguards against arbitrariness in an exercise of judicial power (on the one hand) and executive power (on the other hand) could not be more different. This is particularly notable in Australia where the Constitution makes the exercise of judicial power in identified subject matters exclusive to courts,[1] and provides safeguards for the essential characteristics of courts as institutions for the administration of justice.[2] This constitutional scheme is rightly emphasised as a strong protection for individuals in relation to governing power, because it delivers significant qualitative constitutional safeguards for adjudication in exercise of judicial power by courts. Yet its existence points to a

---

[1] That is, only courts can exercise judicial power in the nine categories of subject-matter identified in ss 75 and 76 of the Constitution as falling within federal jurisdiction. This constitutional rule emerged first for Commonwealth judicial power (see *Waterside Workers' Federation of Australia v JW Alexander Ltd* (1918) 25 CLR 434) and 100 years later for State judicial power (see *Burns v Corbett* (2018) 265 CLR 304).

[2] That is, Australian parliaments cannot validly confer jurisdiction on courts in terms that substantially impair their essential or defining characteristics as courts, which include institutional and decisional independence, procedural fairness, adherence to open court principles and reason giving. Leading authorities are *Lim v Minister for Immigration* (1992) 176 CLR 1, 36–37 (for Commonwealth legislation) and *Kable v New South Wales* (1996) 189 CLR 51 (for State legislation).

stark contrast: when it comes to adjudication by the executive, the sole recognised constitutional safeguard in Australia is a mandated measure of judicial review to detect and remedy invalid or unauthorised (or 'ultra vires') purported decisions.[3]

In this context there is a natural interest in how judicial review functions as a safeguard against arbitrariness in executive decision-making. One particularly thorny issue of relevance to this collection is whether judicial review imposes meaningful qualitative controls on executive fact-finding. Across a range of regulatory contexts, the quality of fact-finding has a significant bearing on the intelligibility of decisions. The factual issues for resolution in executive decision-making may include issues such as whether an individual has engaged in the conduct elements of a criminal offence, or whether there is a real risk an individual will engage in future conduct identified in statute. It would be naive to think that executive fact-finding is necessarily simple, or that there can be no justiciable criteria for determining relevance or the probative value of materials relied on in executive decision-making. Yet it remains a point of fundamental importance to judicial review, to distinguish the legal and factual merits of a decision.

While this is a large topic, one area of concern for Australian administrative law is the effect of the ultra vires doctrine on review of fact-finding for legal unreasonableness. Leading Australian authorities appear to require an identifiable statutory anchor before standards of reasonable fact-finding can be applied as conditions on executive decisional authority. The requirement for a statutory anchor was applied strictly in High Court decisions to 2010 (discussed below), which tethered reasonableness norms to findings specified by statute as a necessary precondition to decision-making power. The concern raised by judgments in such terms is that, by requiring statutory provisions as markers for the application of reasonableness norms, the ultra vires doctrine drastically limits the normative effect of judicial review on executive fact-finding. Using this statute-contingent approach, legal reasonableness does not condition all material findings, only those which are required by statute as a precondition to power.

In this chapter, I consider the implications of the ultra vires principle for the scope of legal reasonableness in executive fact-finding. I do so from the perspective of Australian law, but the account concerns the constitutional characteristics of executive power at common law and so may be relevant to other jurisdictions represented in this volume. My overarching contention is that the ultra vires doctrine associated with entrenched review in Australia is, at least on one reading of Australian authorities, central to judicial review of executive action because it gives effect to executive inherent incapacity to affect rights or obligations. So understood, I argue, the ultra vires principle is compatible with reasonableness

---

[3] Australian usage favours 'jurisdiction' instead of 'vires' to refer to an executive decision-maker's authority to decide; and in Australian case law an 'ultra vires' decision would more conventionally be described as a purported decision affected by 'jurisdictional error'. These are conclusory terms, indicating that the decision is 'invalid', because it is affected by material breach of a legal condition on power. I use 'ultra vires' here as it may be more recognisable to readers who are not immersed in Australian law.

requirements applying to any finding that is material – in point of law or fact – to a decision in purported exercise of statutory or prerogative power to affect individual rights or obligations. As such, ultra vires doctrine does not require the stricter statute-contingent approach to reasonableness review epitomised in High Court authorities through to as recently as 2010.

Part I addresses Australian authorities on the incidence of reasonableness norms for executive fact finding. I show that there has been a decisive shift, in intermediate appellate authorities, to favour judicial application of reasonableness to findings that are material – in point of law or fact – to executive decisions. By contrast, in earlier Australian authorities, it was clear that reasonableness conditioned findings that are made material by the express or implied terms of legislation. It was doubtful whether reasonableness conditioned findings that are material to an exercise of unstructured executive discretion. Part II reflects on the interplay between this shift in the incidence of reasonableness norms and judicial thinking about the constitutional basis for judicial review of executive action. Finally, Part III provides some comments and observations on the potential future development of Australian law; and how this episode in Australian public law might relate to developments in other jurisdictions represented in this volume.

I. Judicial Review and Reasonableness in Executive Fact-finding

Before turning to the main discussion, it may be helpful to provide some introductory observations about the Australian approach to judicial review of executive action, and to review fact-finding in particular.

Australia's written Constitution provides a minimum measure of judicial review which cannot be removed or frustrated by ordinary legislation.[4] This entrenches review to remedy ultra vires state action – action impaired by 'invalidating' or 'jurisdictional' legal error. Relatedly, Australian law retains a distinction between invalidating ('jurisdictional') and non-invalidating ('non-jurisdictional') legal error. To establish that executive adjudication is ultra vires, an applicant for review must demonstrate that the executive decision is affected by breach of a legal duty that is a condition on the valid exercise of a decision-making power.[5]

---

[4] That is, the minimum provisions for judicial review that cannot be denied by ordinary legislation: *Plaintiff S157/2002 v Commonwealth* (2003) 211 CLR 476 (for review of Commonwealth powers); *Kirk v Industrial Court of New South Wales* (2010) 239 CLR 531 (for review of state powers). This minimum provision is not exhaustive of review opportunities at general law. Subject to legislation, intra vires decisions may be subject to certiorari (for error of law on the face of the record), declaratory or injunctive relief, or remedies under enacted schemes for review of, or appeal from, administrative decisions.

[5] On the method of making this distinction see, eg, *Wei v Minister for Immigration and Border Protection* (2015) 257 CLR 22, 32–34 [23]–[28] (Gageler and Keane JJ).

While there is an entrenched measure of review in Australia, Australian authorities hold that courts have a limited mandate to evolve the legal duties imposed on executive decision-making. Most straightforwardly, it is said that the courts' role in review must not go beyond enforcing the *legal* duties of executive decision-makers: '[t]he merits of administrative action, to the extent that they can be distinguished from legality, are for the repository of the relevant power and, subject to political control, for the repository alone'.[6] More subtly, Australia's senior judges urge a legalistic method for identifying and applying legal duties of executive decision-makers:

'[T]he scope of judicial review must be defined not in terms of the protection of individual interests but in terms of the extent of power and the legality of its exercise. In Australia, the modern development and expansion of the law of judicial review of administrative action have been achieved by an increasingly sophisticated exposition of implied limitations on the extent or the exercise of statutory power, but those limitations are not calculated to secure judicial scrutiny of the merits of a particular case.'[7]

This orthodox message is brought to the foreground when review touches on issues that go directly to 'the merits' of a decision – issues of fact, policy or discretionary balancing.

When it comes to fact finding, the default[8] legal norms evolved in the context of judicial review[9] are notoriously 'thin'. Australian law recognises just two. The first and most well-established is that a finding must be based on some probative material.[10] The adjective 'probative' exerts *some* qualitative control on fact-finding, as it requires material that is logically capable of informing assessment of the likelihood of a fact.[11] However, the qualitative control is minimal. The requirement is satisfied if even a skerrick of probative material is available to the decision-maker. Judicial application of this norm does *not* entail any scrutiny of whether the reasoning process by which the finding is reached is rational or logical.

---

[6] *Attorney-General (NSW) v Quin* (1990) 170 CLR 1, 35 (Brennan J).
[7] ibid.
[8] The common law standards are default in the sense that they apply generally (to powers that satisfy common law threshold principles) but can be excluded or modified by sufficiently clear legislation: *Saeed v Minister for Immigration and Citizenship* (2010) 241 CLR 252, 258–59 [11]–[15].
[9] The norms refer to the legal standards for decision-making, breach of which may establish grounds for a remedy in judicial review.
[10] *Australian Broadcasting Tribunal v Bond* (1990) 170 CLR 321, 355–56 (Mason CJ). The reference is to probative material rather than 'evidence' because the rules of evidence do not typically apply to executive decision-making. A more comprehensive statement of the norm distinguishes between findings and inferences of fact: a decision-maker errs in law if they draw an inference that is 'not open' on the primary facts, in the sense that there are *no* primary facts found or admitted that can logically support the inference: *Bond* 355–56, 359–60 (Mason CJ).
[11] The point is illustrated by the ruling in *R v Australian Stevedoring Industry Board; Ex parte Melbourne Stevedoring Co Pty Ltd* (1953) 88 CLR 100 that some instances of workers' unexplained absences were not probative of the stevedoring companies' fitness to hold a licence. See also rulings that information about a visa-holders past offending is not probative of an unacceptable risk due to a likelihood that a person would commit offences of a similar nature and in a similar fashion, eg *Assistant Minister for Immigration and Border Protection v Splendido* (2019) 271 FCR 595.

Nor does it entail any scrutiny of what a reasonable decision-maker might make of the material. It does not, for instance, support scrutiny of whether a fact finder has unreasonably relied on a skerrick of material that is manifestly outweighed by material to the contrary.[12]

Australian law also recognises some scope for review of executive fact-finding against a (slightly) more expansive standard of reasonableness. This norm requires that findings or inferences are reasonably open on a rational and logical evaluation of the material before the decision-maker.[13] This arguably requires that the deliberative pathway in fact followed by a decision-maker be logical and rational.[14] Whether that is so or not, it applies a slightly more intensive scrutiny to findings than *simply* to require the existence of a skerrick of probative material. On the other hand, a court exercising supervisory jurisdiction will not intervene for any lapse in logic or because the court strongly disagrees with the finding a decision-maker has made.[15] The court's task is to evaluate the character of the finding, to identify whether it falls within the range of findings that can be reached by a reasonable person adopting a logical and rational approach to the material.[16] A finding might be impugned on review if:

> [O]nly one conclusion is open on the evidence, and the decision-maker does not come to the conclusion, or if the decision to which the decision-maker came was simply not open on the evidence or if there is no logical connection between the evidence and the inferences or conclusions drawn.[17]

Put another way, the finding fails to meet the required standard if the decision-maker's reasons are 'unintelligible'.[18] This evaluative standard can apply contextually and with reference to accepted notions of reasoning beyond strict logic. Thus, it is possible for substantive principles recognised in the legal system to inform the standard of reasonableness.[19]

---

[12] *Bond* (n 10) 358–59 (Mason CJ).

[13] *Minister for Immigration and Citizenship v SZMDS* (2010) 240 CLR 611, 625 [40]–[42] (Gummow ACJ and Kiefel J), 638 [102]–[103] (Crennan and Bell JJ).

[14] See, eg, *Plaintiff S183/2021 v Minister for Home Affairs* [2022] HCA 15 [42]–[43] (Gordon J). The alternative is an 'objective' requirement that the ultimate determination viewed objectively is one which *could* have been reached on the material through a rational and logical reasoning-process. The uncertainty on this point arises from ambiguous passages in the joint reasons of Crennan and Bell JJ in *SZMDS* (n 13), 647–48 [130]. For commentary and critique of a purely 'objective' rationality standard see: R Derrington, 'Migrating to a Principled Approach Towards Reviewing Jurisdictional Facts' (2020) 27 *Australian Journal of Administrative Law* 70, 79–81; J Hutton, 'Satisfaction as a Jurisdictional Fact – A Consideration of the Implications of SZMDS' in N Williams SC (ed), *Key Issues in Judicial Review* (Annandale, The Federation Press 2014) 60–61; M Smith, 'According to Law, and Not Humour: Illogicality and Administrative Decision Making after SZMDS' (2011) 19 *Australian Journal of Administrative Law* 33, 50–51.

[15] The low *intensity* of scrutiny of fact finding is widely recognised in cases and comment, including the sources cited (n 14).

[16] *SZMDS* (n 13) 648 [131], 649–50 [135] (Crennan and Bell JJ).

[17] ibid 649–50 [135] (Crennan and Bell JJ).

[18] ibid 650 [135] (Crennan and Bell JJ).

[19] In *Plaintiff S111A/2018 v Minister for Home Affairs (No 4)* [2022] FCA 329 [340]–[41] Mortimer J held that any rational decision-maker would discard as wholly unreliable information obtained directly as a result of torture.

II. The Incidence of Reasonableness Standards for Fact-finding in Australian Law

A notable – and some might say surprising – point of contention in Australian authorities has been whether a standard of reasonableness applies to executive fact-finding that is *not* specifically required by statute as the basis for an authorised exercise of statutory power. The uncertainty stems from two significant High Court judgments on judicial review of executive fact-finding: *Bond*[20] and *SZMDS*.[21] In both cases, the High Court confined unreasonableness challenges to executive findings of fact required by statute as a precondition to power.

A. Australian Law to 2010: A Confined Site for Reasonableness Review of Factual Findings

Bond and *SZMDS* support two points of doctrine that, when combined, strictly limit the scope for judicial scrutiny of factual findings for legal unreasonableness:

(i) unreasonableness in fact finding is not recognised as an 'error of law'; and
(ii) unreasonableness review is available for factual findings required by statute as the basis for an operative decision, or an essential preliminary to an operative decision.

The significance of the first of these two points is substantial. Both at common law and under legislatively created avenues of review, administrative decisions that involve an error of law may be set aside by a court exercising supervisory jurisdiction. This ground allows challenges to findings that contribute to, or provide the basis for, a reviewable decision in a factual sense.[22] However, the traditional doctrine, applied in *Bond*, is that an administrative finding of fact goes wrong in law only if it is made without *any* probative material.[23]

The second point from *Bond* and *SZMDS* is that unreasonableness in fact-finding can only establish grounds for review if it affects findings required by statute as a precondition to power. This was the position articulated in *Bond* for review under the Administrative Decisions (Judicial Review) Act 1977 (Cth) ('ADJR Act').[24] The constraint was subsequently reiterated as an aspect of the common law ultra vires doctrine in *SZMDS*. In that much-discussed decision, four members

---

[20] [1990] HCA 33, (1990) 170 CLR 321.
[21] *SZMDS* (n 13).
[22] *Bond* (n 10) 353 (Mason CJ), 367–68 (Deane J), 384 (Toohey and Gaudron JJ). Mason CJ notes that the materiality criterion can be applied more or less strictly but at the very least requires that the decision may have been different if the error had not occurred.
[23] ibid 355–56, 359–60 (Mason CJ).
[24] ibid 359 (Mason CJ).

of the Court[25] expressly endorsed a reasonableness norm for fact-finding but confined its reach to findings material to a determination required by statute as a precondition to power.[26]

The intended narrow scope for reasonableness review of fact-finding is laid out clearly in the joint reasons of Gummow ACJ and Kiefel J in *SZMDS*.[27] Their Honours recognise that reasonableness review of fact finding carries a risk of inviting intrusive review of decisions on their merits, but explain that the concern is mitigated if 'the distinction between jurisdictional fact and other facts then taken into account in discretionary decision-making is kept in view'.[28] Their Honours explain that a reasonableness requirement applies to findings of jurisdictional fact only[29] and does not extend to 'alleged deficiencies in what might be called "intra mural" fact-finding by the decision-maker in the course of exercising jurisdiction to make a decision'.[30] The joint reasons of Crennan and Bell JJ in *SZMDS* similarly confine their endorsement of reasonableness review to findings affecting a determination required by statute[31] and emphasise that serious irrationality in fact-finding generally does not in itself give rise to legal error.[32]

SZMDS approved, from the Australian side, the divergence in Australian and English public law after the House of Lords extended reasonableness review from findings of jurisdictional fact to findings taken into account in discretionary decision-making.[33] Gummow ACJ and Kiefel J considered that a statutory requirement that an administrator decide a factual issue remains 'the appropriate marker for enforcement of legality'.[34] The whole tenor of their Honours' reasons makes clear that a reasonableness criterion strictly tethered to fact finding required by statute is deemed acceptable precisely because it does not otherwise disturb the scope of review for error of law in fact finding as a very confined site of supervisory jurisdiction.[35]

---

[25] *SZMDS* (n 13) 625 [40]-[42] (Gummow ACJ and Kiefel J), 638 [102]-[103] (Crennan and Bell JJ). The fifth judge sitting on this appeal, Heydon J, specifically refrained from any decision on the availability of a rationality criterion for challenging findings of fact in judicial review.

[26] In *SZMDS*, the Court refers to the subjective determination specifically required by the statute as a 'jurisdictional fact'. The 'fact' being the existence of the subjective state of mind required by the statute, which is 'jurisdictional' because it is an essential precondition to enliven the statutory authority. This language was first adopted in *Minister for Immigration and Multicultural Affairs v Eshetu* (1999) 197 CLR 611, 651 [130] (Gummow J).

[27] While their Honours dissented in the result, their account of the legal principles is taken as authoritative.

[28] *SZMDS* (n 13) 624 at [39].

[29] ibid 625 at [42].

[30] ibid 624 at [38].

[31] ibid 643-44 at [119], 648 at [132].

[32] ibid 636 at [94]-[95], 643-44 at [119].

[33] ibid 621 at [26], 622 at [31] (Gummow ACJ and Kiefel J), referring to *Television Capricornia Pty Ltd v Australian Broadcasting Tribunal* (1986) 13 FCR 511, 514, 519-520 where Wilcox J emphasised that the novelty of *Secretary of State for Education and Science v Tameside Metropolitan Borough Council* [1977] AC 1014, as understood by Australian law-makers at the time, was that it extended a recognised ground for review of jurisdictional fact to review of any facts taken into account in an exercise of discretionary power.

[34] ibid 619 at [18].

[35] ibid 616 at [5]-[6].

The logic of the *Bond-SZMDS* position would seem to be that it is inappropriate for judicial review to scrutinise the quality of fact-finding outside of enacted criteria that must be applied as essential preliminaries to authorised decisions. Precisely *why* this should be so is not explained. In *Bond*, Mason CJ observed that review of fact finding generally would expose the steps in administrative decision-making to comprehensive review by the courts, and 'bring in its train difficult questions concerning the extent to which the courts should take account of policy considerations when reviewing the making of findings of fact and the drawing of inferences of fact'.[36] The judicial policy connecting *Bond* and *SZMDS* would therefore seem to have two aspects. Most straightforwardly, confining review to findings required by statute as a precondition to power avoids opening 'the floodgates' for challenges to fact finding on review for error of law. Relatedly, confining reasonableness review as *Bond* and *SZMDS* does avoid certain (albeit largely unstated) risks that judges perceive may arise if courts were to be called on to determine what is rational and reasonable by reference to non-enacted executive policies.[37] It would seem that these two factors in combination support the *Bond-SZMDS* position, confining reasonableness review to findings required by statute as the mandated basis for decision-making.

B. Australian Law Since 2010: A More Expansive Site for Reasonableness Review Emerges

The High Court has not formally overruled *Bond-SZMDS* on the incidence of reasonableness review of executive fact-finding. Yet in the interval since *SZMDS*, intermediate appellate authorities have overcome the narrow approach *SZMDS* endorsed. The emergent position supports reasonableness review of findings that are material – in point of fact – to a reviewable administrative decision. This includes findings that are required by statute as a basis for the decision but goes further. It also reaches findings made pursuant to non-enacted policies for the exercise of unstructured statutory discretions if they contribute to the decision in a causal sense. Three key staging points in these doctrinal developments can be outlined as follows.

(i) High Court Initiates a Rethink of the Standard of Reasonableness for Discretionary Decision-making

Recall that *Bond* and *SZMDS* drew a categorical distinction between findings required by statute as a precondition to power and findings made in the course

---

[36] *Bond* (n 10) 341.
[37] Suggesting a conceptual link to Australian law's insistence that executive statements and policies do not have legal effects on the decision-making process, discussed in eg, Weeks, 'The Use and Enforcement of Soft Law by Australian Public Authorities' (2014) *Federal Law Review* 6; A Sapienza, *Judicial Review of Non-Statutory Executive Action* (Alexandria, The Federation Press 2020) 148–60.

of exercising discretionary power. Just three years after *SZMDS*, the strictures imposed on reasonableness review of fact-finding were put in doubt when the High Court handed down a judgment – *Minister for Immigration v Li*[38] – which effectively erases any substantive distinction between these types of findings, by endorsing reasonableness review of a discretionary decision-maker's reasoning process.

In *Li*, the High Court intervened to set aside an administrative decision on the ground of legal unreasonableness for the first time in over 50 years. In doing so, the Court gave reasons which were widely read as implementing a significant rethink of this 'safety net' ground. As one aspect of this, the Court appeared to recognise that reasonableness requires following a reasoning process that not only avoids legal error but is also logical and rational.[39] As Gageler J pointed out, once this is recognised there is no substantive distinction between the standard of reasonableness applicable to statutory discretions and the standard of reasonableness applicable to a determination required by statute as a precondition to power.[40] While the Court did not specifically address the implications for fact-finding as such, *Li* seems to imply that the legal unreasonableness can arise from the material decision-making process, and so can arise if a discretionary decision is based on unreasonable findings or inferences of fact.

(ii) Reasonableness Review of Factual Findings Material to Discretionary Decisions Post-Li

Since *Li*, the Federal Court has accepted that a standard of reasonableness equivalent to that applied in *SZMDS* can also be applied to the findings on which a discretionary decision is based. For example, the Court has adopted this approach in review of visa cancellation decisions made by the minister personally pursuant to unstructured statutory discretions.[41] Australian migration law contains multiple visa cancellation powers which are interrelated in complex ways. Some of these are unstructured statutory discretions vested in the minister, enlivened by a preliminary finding that the visa holder does not satisfy the statutory character test due to their past criminal offending. Where discretion is enlivened, the governing statute does not provide any criteria, nor does it give force of law to any criteria the minister may choose to adopt, as a matter of general policy to guide the exercise of discretion in individual cases. As the Federal Court recognises, the exercise of such an unstructured statutory discretion does not involve the formation of a state of mind required by statute and so did not attract the reasonableness standard

---

[38] (2013) 249 CLR 332.
[39] ibid 365 [72] (Hayne and Bell JJ), 375 [105] (Gageler J). See also *Minister for Immigration and Border Protection v SZVFW* (2018) 264 CLR 541, 573 [82] (Nettle and Gordon JJ).
[40] *Li* (n 38) 370, [90].
[41] See, eg, *Muggeridge v Minister for Immigration and Border Protection* (2017) 255 FCR 81. The Migration Act 1958 (Cth), s 501(2) provides that the Minister *may* cancel a visa if the Minister is satisfied that the visa holder does not satisfy the statutory character test.

from *SZMDS*. Yet the Court has relied on the principle in *Li* to support an inquiry into whether the discretionary decision itself is affected by legal unreasonableness because it is based on an illogical or irrational finding. In this way, the Court seamlessly extended reasonableness review to findings that are material in point of fact to a discretionary decision.[42] Taking their cue from the High Court's judgment in *Li*, intermediate appellate courts have extended reasonableness review to findings material to discretionary decisions in point of fact, by reference to the discretionary decision-maker's own policy criteria.[43]

(iii) Reasonableness of Material Findings as a Question of Law

The final break with the *Bond-SZMDS* approach is seen in *Haritos v Commissioner of Taxation*.[44] In this judgment, a specially-convened five-member Bench of the Federal Court held that the reasonableness of a finding of fact material to an administrative decision is a question of law.[45] The Court did so on the express basis that unreasonable material fact-finding *gives rise to an error of law*.[46] On the face of it, this flatly contradicts the careful demarcation made, in *Bond* and *SZMDS*, between unreasonableness in fact-finding and legal error.[47]

The 'question of law' identified by the Federal Court in *Haritos* was whether a tribunal decision on a taxpayer's objection to an income tax assessment involved legal error because the Tribunal had drawn a conclusion about the nature or character of certain evidence that did not satisfy the *SZMDS* reasonableness standard.[48] The Federal Court appears to have reasoned that, if it can be a jurisdictional error to make a jurisdictional finding which is 'irrational or illogical' in the *SZMDS* sense, it must also be an error of law to make a material finding which is 'irrational or illogical' in the *SZMDS* sense.[49]

Haritos demonstrates just how far the law travelled in the five-year period since *SZMDS*, with the emergence of substantially similar standards for scrutiny of

---

[42] *Muggeridge* (n 41), 89–91 [35].

[43] It may not be mere coincidence that the Federal Court also now recognises departure from non-enacted policy can give rise to a ground for judicial review: A decision-making process may be judged illogical or perverse by the decision-maker's own criteria irrespective that they are not legally binding: see *Jabbour v Secretary, Department of Home Affairs* (2019) 269 FCR 438, 457 [89] (Robertson J).

[44] (2015) 233 FCR 315. This is not an isolated case. For instance, in *Wesiak v D & R Constructions (Aust) Pty Ltd* [2016] NSWCA 353, [73]; and *D'Amore v Independent Commission Against Corruption* [2013] NSWCA 187, [76]–[83] state that there is an error of law where a finding of fact is not reasonably open on the whole of the evidence.

[45] Thus, engaging the statutory avenue of appeal in the Administrative Appeals Tribunal Act 1977 (Cth), s 44. Leave to appeal to the High Court on the scope of 'question of law' in s 44 was refused: *Commissioner of Taxation of the Commonwealth of Australia v Haritos* [2015] HCATrans 337. *Haritos* is considered authoritative for similarly worded statutory appeals: D Kerr, 'What is a Question of Law Following Haritos v Federal Commissioner of Taxation?' [2016] *Fed J Schol* 18.

[46] *Haritos* (44) 387–88 [217].

[47] For more about the departure from *SZMDS*, see E Hammond 'A Negotiation Concluded? The Normative Structure of Error of Law Review of Fact-Finding' (2020) 98 *AIAL Forum* 70.

[48] *Haritos* (44) 386–391 [209]–[228].

[49] ibid 386 [212].

statutory preconditions and discretions. While the Court in *Haritos* does not rely on this directly, it would seem that the emergent standard for reasonableness in discretionary decision-making has erased any substantive distinction between the legal standards for deliberation on issues specified by statute as preconditions to power and issues adopted by discretionary decision-makers as a matter of (non-statutory) policy. This supports recognition that unreasonableness in findings *material* to an exercise of statutory power gives rise to legal error – whether the materiality is established by enactment that a finding must be made as a precondition to power *or* by the reasoning in fact followed at the discretion of the decision-maker.

III. Inherent Executive Incapacity as the Constitutional Rationale for ultra vires

Australian law's recent adoption of a materiality criterion for reasonable fact-finding marks a fundamental change from the earlier position, put forcefully in *SZMDS*, that a statutory requirement to determine a factual issue marks the limits of legality. This also, I suggest, can be related to a significant shift in thinking about the constitutional rationale for review of ultra vires executive action. In this part, I provide an hypothesis that ultra vires can be understood to reflect a fundamental constitutional characteristic of executive power –namely inherent executive incapacity to unilaterally affect subjects' rights or obligations. So understood, ultra vires supports legality operating on any elements of executive action that are material – as a matter of law or fact – to an executive decision.

A. The Traditional Parliamentary Supremacy Premise for ultra vires

In orthodox accounts, ultra vires serves a principle of parliamentary supremacy. That is, review for ultra vires ensures executive decision-makers stay within the legal parameters laid down by parliament. As is well known, this understanding does not dictate just one necessary view on acceptable judicial methods for discerning statutory conditions on power. To mention just two well-known variations, Professor Wade considered that judges must be able to demonstrate that they are carrying out 'the will of Parliament as expressed in the statute conferring power' and that this limits legality to express statutory provisions and provisions implied by orthodox methods of statutory interpretation.[50] Professors Forsyth and Elliott proposed that acceptable judicial methods extend to applying common law presumptions that common law legality requirements apply unless their

---

[50] W Wade, *Administrative Law* (6th edn, Oxford, OUP 1988) 42.

application is clearly excluded by the statute. Meanwhile, critics of the ultra vires doctrine have sought to show that it rests on flawed assumptions about the implications of parliamentary supremacy.[51]

B. An Inherent Incapacity Premise for ultra vires?

Understanding ultra vires as a reflection of parliamentary supremacy makes perfect sense in the context of an English flexible constitutional system predicated on the sovereign legislative power of parliament. However, parliamentary supremacy is not the only relevant constitutional principle bearing on judicial review in Australia. Another constitutional principle with a strong bearing is the separation of judicial and executive power. This principle can, in turn, cast new light on the premise for judicial review of ultra vires executive action. In Australia, I suggest, recent High Court authorities implicitly recognise that a constitutional premise for ultra vires lies in the inherent incapacity of the executive to unilaterally alter the legal position of subjects. This recognition is, I suggest, discernible in recent High Court statements explaining the legal consequences of a finding of ultra vires, when read in context of contemporary judicial statements on the nature of executive power.[52]

As recent High Court judgments emphasise, judicial review for ultra vires involves a judicial determination whether an executive decision attracts the operation of a statutory power, so that rights or obligations are as specified in the executive decision by force of statute. To understand ultra vires in this way highlights that the judicial purpose of identifying whether a decision is 'authorised' is not *simply* to give effect to statutory conditions on decision-making. Rather, it is to determine whether the decision has the legal consequences and effects that statute would confer on an authorised decision.[53] More precisely, in review of executive decision-making that purports to affect rights or liabilities, the issue is 'whether the rights and liabilities of the individual to whom the decision relates are as specified in that decision'.[54] If the objective of the ultra vires inquiry is understood in this way, it can apply with equal force to decisions in purported exercise of prerogative powers capable of producing legal effects.[55]

---

[51] Different perspectives are collected in CF Forsyth (ed), *Judicial Review and the Constitution* (Oxford, Hart Publishing 2000). Australian commentary has also emphasised a parliamentary supremacy rationale for ultra vires/jurisdictional error, see, eg, LB Crawford and J Boughey, 'The Centrality of Jurisdictional Error: Rationale and Consequences' (2019) 30(1) *Public Law Review* 18.

[52] The discussion in this part draws on more detailed discussion in E Hammond, 'The Duality of Jurisdictional Error' (2021) 32(2) *Public Law Review* 132.

[53] *Hossain v Minister for Immigration and Border Protection* (2018) 264 CLR 123, 132 [23] (Kiefel CJ, Gageler and Keane JJ).

[54] *Minister for Immigration and Multicultural Affairs v Bhardwaj* (2002) 209 CLR 597, 613 [46]. This point is repeated in *Hossain* (n 53) and *Oakey Coal Action Alliance Inc v New Acland Coal Pty Ltd* (2021) 272 CLR 33, 48–49 [48] (Kiefel CJ, Bell, Gageler, Keane JJ).

[55] On the distinction between prerogatives that are and are not capable of producing legal effects see Sapienza (n 37) 24–30.

This judicial account of ultra vires may be – at least on one reading of Australian authorities – driven by underlying constitutional characteristics of executive power. That is, ultra vires can plausibly be read as giving effect to a constitutional premise that the executive does not possess any power over the rights or liabilities of subjects *except* for power given by statute or common law prerogatives. The absence of any inherent executive power over the legal position of subjects apart from what is given by statute or common law prerogatives has been given strong emphasis in recent Australian judicial and scholarly accounts of executive power. The narrow point made in Australian authorities is that there is no prerogative to dispense with the operation of the general law.[56] The deeper significance of this point becomes clear when read in context of Australian law's categorisation of executive action as involving: (i) a statutory power or capacity; (ii) a prerogative power or capacity; or (iii) a capacity derived from the polity's legal personality.[57] The capacities derived from legal personality cannot be exercised unilaterally to establish legal authority over the rights or obligations of others.[58] Accordingly, legal powers to unilaterally affect rights and obligations can only be derived from statute or prerogative. To say that there is no prerogative power to dispense with the operation of general law is to emphasise the executive's inherent incapacity to unilaterally alter rights or obligations. Executive action can only unilaterally alter or affect rights and liabilities to the extent that it engages the operation of statute or a common law prerogative power to directly alter rights or obligations.

An inherent incapacity premise for ultra vires is also, I suggest, reflected in the notable tendency in Australian authorities to approach judicial review of executive action authorised by statute as an exercise to determine the action's statutory effect. This way of speaking about review of statutory executive action registers the basal proposition that executive action authorised by statute can have no effect on the general law apart from what it draws from statute. As one significant aspect of this, an executive decision under statutory authority has no legal power over the rights or liabilities of subjects apart from what it acquires as a *factum* by which legislation operates.[59]

---

[56] *Plaintiff M68/2015 v Minister for Immigration and Border Protection* (2016) 257 CLR 42, 99 [136] (Gageler J), noting this has long been recognised as a fundamental principle of the legal system, see, eg, *A v Hayden* (1984) 156 CLR 532, 580 (Brennan J).

[57] Note the Australian categorisation of executive powers makes a distinction between the non-statutory powers and functions unique to a polity and those that have their source in the legal personality attributed to a polity. It follows the categorisation in Bl Comm 232: see *Plaintiff M68/2015* (n 56) 96-99 [129]-[136] (Gageler J). See also Sapienza (n 37) 8-9, ch 2.

[58] This is not to deny that legal persons can, by mutual exercise of legal capacities, establish legal relationships within which the parties' possess and exercise powers over rights and liabilities.

[59] *Federal Commissioner of Taxation v Munro* (1926) 38 CLR 153, 176 (Isaacs J). The decision made in exercise of statutory authority is viewed as 'adjunct to legislation', 'the factum by reference to which the Act operates to alter the law in relation to the particular case': *R v Trade Practices Tribunal; Ex parte Tasmanian Breweries Pty Ltd* (1970) 123 CLR 361, 371 (McTiernan J), 378 (Kitto J).

Judicial recognition of an inherent executive incapacity premise for ultra vires may also, I suggest, explain why Australian judges have expressed concerns about the notion that unauthorised executive decisions may be valid and effective unless and until set aside by a court on judicial review.[60] The High Court has warned that this concept should be used with caution as it does not provide the necessary 'more elaborate description' of the legal effects of invalidity in decisions *other than* the judicial orders of superior courts.[61] More recently, there are indications that the Court considers the concept of a 'voidable' decision inapplicable to unauthorised executive decisions.[62] While the Court has not laid out its concerns in precisely these terms, it seems plausible that this move might draw on the constitutional logic of an inherent incapacity premise for ultra vires: for the reasons given, an unauthorised executive decision simply cannot manifest the polity's legal powers to unilaterally alter the operation of general law.[63]

C. An Inherent Incapacity Premise Supports a Materiality Marker for Legality

When we centre our understanding of ultra vires on inherent executive incapacity, a clear constitutional purpose for the doctrine is revealed: that purpose is to ensure that legal authority over rights and obligations is not misattributed to executive decisions in purported but invalid exercise of statutory or prerogative powers. So understood, it is appropriate that the focus of review under this doctrine will fall on aspects of the decision-making process that have a material effect on a decision made in fact, in purported exercise of a statutory or prerogative power. As noted, the doctrine conceptualises an executive decision as a factum by which legislation or prerogative operates. Viewed in these terms, the executive action associated with the decision is relevant in judicial review only when it affects the decision through which public power over the law operates. This, in turn, makes materiality an appropriate marker for legality in the executive decision-making process. Put simply, executive conduct in a decision-making process becomes relevant in law as and when it affects the decision through which statute or prerogative operates.

It might be objected that, strictly speaking, an inherent incapacity premise establishes materiality as a *necessary* element of jurisdictional error. It explains why *im*material errors do not invalidate a purported exercise of statutory or prerogative power: an error that does not affect the decision should not render it ineffective as a factum for the operation of statute or prerogative. Logically, denying that

---

[60] On the concept generally, see C Forsyth, '"The Metaphysics of Nullity" Invalidity, Conceptual Reasoning and the Rule of Law' in C Forsyth and I Hare (eds), The Golden Metwand and the Crooked Cord: Essays in Honour of Sir William Wade QC (Oxford, Clarendon Press 1998).
[61] *Kable* (n 2) 129–130 [20]–[22] (French CJ, Hayne, Crennan, Kiefel, Bell and Keane JJ).
[62] *Oakey Coal* (n 54).
[63] The legal efficacy of *judicial* orders of *inferior courts* is a different and more difficult topic.

*im*material errors invalidate is not the same thing as recognising that all material errors invalidate.[64]

Yet the point remains that an inherent incapacity premise for ultra vires is conducive to adopting materiality as a marker for legal reasonableness. A materiality marker would seem appropriate for those default or generic standards for official decision-making implied from the common law as conditions on statutory powers. To see that this is the case, we need only recognise that judicial application of these standards is based on a qualitative evaluation that they are appropriate to regulate a polity's assertion of public powers over subjects.[65] Such common law standards are applied to executive decisions as *facta* for statutory or prerogative effects on subjects. If that is so, it would stand to reason that the common law standards would by default apply to elements of the decision-making process material to the decision through which the statutory or prerogative effect is realised.

The implied condition of reasonableness can, I suggest, be viewed as a case in point. A condition of reasonableness is implied (subject to contrary legislation) on the strength of a common law assessment that decisions concerning individuals made in exercise of public powers should be made according to reason.[66] This justification supports review if the decision is affected by legal unreasonableness. Or, in other words, it supports judicial scrutiny for legal unreasonableness in material steps in the decision-making process. The logic of this position is clear: if a step displaying unreasonableness is critical to the decision made, it imparts legal unreasonableness to that decision. The quality inheres in the decision, and so to the statutory or prerogative effect on the individual that arises on the fact of that decision. And the logic serves a more substantive normative principle: since the concern of the common law is to regulate the exercise of public powers over individuals, then the common law should in principle reach those elements of the executive decision-making process that affect a decision through which statutory or prerogative power flows.

IV. Prospects, and Pertinence Outside Australia

Executive adjudication plays an important role in contemporary regulation and is not infrequently relied on to similar practical effect as adjudication by courts exercising judicial power. Yet there are significant structural, institutional safeguards against arbitrariness in judicial adjudication that do not operate on executive adjudication. In Australia, for example, judicial review to remedy ultra vires action is

---

[64] The former proposition is now well established in Australia, see *MZAPC v Minister for Immigration and Border Protection* (2021) ALJR 441, 452–53 [31]–[34] (Kiefel CJ, Gageler, Keane and Gleeson JJ). However, a material error may yet be non-jurisdictional, see, eg, *Project Blue Sky Inc v Australian Broadcasting Authority* (1998) 194 CLR 355.
[65] Compare *Hossain* (n 53).
[66] *Li* (n 38) 351 [29] (French CJ), 369–70 [88]–[89] (Gageler J).

the singular constitutional safeguard for individuals whose rights or liabilities are subject to executive decision-making. But can judicial review offer a meaningful safeguard against arbitrariness in the executive resolution of factual issues?

This chapter has considered, from an Australian perspective, the effects of ultra vires doctrine on the incidence of reasonableness standards for executive fact-finding. I have suggested that Australian authorities implicitly recognise an inherent incapacity premise for ultra vires doctrine; and that this, in turn, supports judicial application of a legal reasonableness standard to findings that are material in point of law or fact to executive decision-making.

It is important to be realistic about what this reconfiguration of review doctrine offers as a qualitative control on executive fact-finding. Recognising a materiality criterion for legality is unlikely to radically transform established parameters for judicial scrutiny of executive fact-finding. The incidence of reasonableness review is only one part of a wider edifice of judicial restraint in reviewing executive fact-finding. As noted, the test for legal unreasonableness is very stringent. A causal test for materiality may impose a significant threshold, for instance if it requires the applicant to show that the decision would not have been made but for the finding.[67] Additionally, the onus of demonstrating materiality falls on the applicant for review,[68] executive decision-makers may not be required to provide written reasons, and any written reasons that are provided must be read with a 'benign' eye.[69]

There is nevertheless value in demonstrating that a materiality criterion is a suitable fit with the ultra vires doctrine. This is an important point in any jurisdiction which uses the ultra vires concept to explain the constitutional scope of judicial review.[70] As many commentators have noted, the courts' application of ultra vires doctrine tends to emphasise the statutory source of executive authority. The reasons for this have been much debated and analysed. Recognising an inherent incapacity for ultra vires offers a new perspective on its operation. It frames the courts' emphasis on the statutory source of authority for executive action *not* as a claim that the statute is the sole source for legal conditions on authorised decision but *rather* as a claim that the statute is the sole source of a decision's legal effects. This provides a new way of understanding the specific demands that ultra vires doctrine imposes on judicial review. In essence, the doctrine requires a focus on executive decisions *as facta through which statute (or prerogatives) operate*. Importantly, this is a demand that can be met by adopting materiality

---

[67] The issue here is the precise test of materiality. *MZAPC* (n 64) and *Bond* (n 22) adopt a default test that the outcome *may* have been different had the error not been made. However, the ADJR Act's 'mistake of fact' ground has been construed to require applicants to prove that the decision *would* have been different: *Minister for Immigration and Multicultural Affairs v Rajamanikkam* (2002) 210 CLR 222.
[68] As held by 4:3 majority in *MZAPC* (n 64).
[69] For example, *Plaintiff M64/2015 v Minister for Immigration and Border Protection* (2015) 258 CLR 173, 185–86 [25], 196 [59]–[60] (French CJ, Bell, Keane and Gordon JJ), 199–200 [72]–[73] (Gageler J).
[70] Noting that in Australia, it describes an entrenched minimum measure of judicial review, see (n 4).

as the criterion for the reach of conditions on decision-making implied from the common law.

It might be thought that an inherent incapacity premise for ultra vires is a more obvious fit for a legal system, such as Australia, which requires a structural systemic differentiation between executive and judicial powers. But it is important to bear in mind that the key qualities differentiating judicial and executive power are drawn from anterior common law. An inherent executive incapacity to alter the legal position of subjects other than through an authorised exercise of statutory or prerogative power is a principle of common law, rooted in English constitutional history that produced the responsible parliamentary system of government observed in Australian polities.[71] Thus, while this chapter has told a story of Australian doctrine, it highlights constitutional features of executive power that may well be relevant for other jurisdictions, which may also rely on judicial review to safeguard against arbitrariness in executive adjudication.

---

[71] Compare *Plaintiff M68/2015* (n 56) 100-01 [139]–[142] (Gageler J).

9
Missing Evidence? The Duty to Acquire Systemic Data in Public Law

JOE TOMLINSON AND CASSANDRA SOMERS-JOCE*

I. Introduction

The chapters in this book explore the role of facts and evidence in public law adjudication. In this chapter, we examine the relationship between evidence and public law from a different angle: the duties that public law itself places on public bodies to collect systemic data on the operation and impact of their policies and administrative schemes.[1] While this question has received minimal discussion in legal scholarship, it is of immense and growing importance to the practice of government: public officials often determine how far they should proactively inquire as to the impact of public policies or their chosen modes of administration.[2] For instance, if a fixed deadline is established for applications for a particular benefit or status, how far should the public authority take steps to understand the effects of that strict deadline?[3] If a public body decides that the only way to apply for an entitlement should be via an online form, what inquiries need to be made about the effects of that decision? Ultimately, these are decisions about the information public officials need to gather, understand, and analyse in respect of the delivery of public functions, which in turn may generate proof of their effectiveness or tough questions about their appropriateness,[4] or even their legality.[5]

---

*We are grateful to Jed Meers, Dave Cowan, Luke Piper, Natalie Byrom, Anna Powell-Smith, Stergios Aidinlis, Elizabeth O'Loughlin, Simon Halliday, Anne Carter, and Paul Daly for helpful discussions relating to and, in some cases, comments on drafts of this chapter. Any errors remain our own.

[1] The focus of this chapter is English and Welsh administrative law, but similar points of both administrative practice and public law will likely arise in other common law jurisdictions.

[2] For an important recent contribution to these issues in the social welfare context, see J Meers, 'The "Cumulative Impact" Problem in Social Welfare: Some Legal, Policy and Theoretical Solutions' (2022) 44 *Journal of Social Welfare and Family Law* 42.

[3] Such an issue was recently raised in *R (on application of the Joint Council for the Welfare of Immigrants) v Secretary of State for the Home Department* [2021] EWHC 638 (Admin).

[4] In this way, it can advance evidence-based policy-making. We are conscious of the challenges and limitations of this notion in practice but, despite those challenges and limitations, see evidence-based policy-making as critical to the advancement of good government. For an excellent discussion, see P Cairney, *The Politics of Evidence-Based Policy Making* (New York, Palgrave Pivot, 2016).

Such decisions have important implications for the shape of government and the experiences of citizens using public services. Systemic data facilitates understanding of how public administration works in practice. Without systemic data, policymakers are hampered in diagnosing and remedying problems existing in administrative systems. Systemic data can highlight who the users of administrative systems are and can reveal differential outcomes between different groups of users. Without collecting systemic data, the experiences of certain groups can become invisible; this is particularly worrisome in the context of groups with protected characteristics at risk of discrimination. In turn, access to this data allows commentators such as researchers and journalists to scrutinise the systems, drawing attention to systemic issues which in turn contributes to higher levels of accountability.

As public administration becomes increasingly digitalised, systemic data becomes increasingly easy to collect and with much lower costs.[6] Mass data collection no longer requires researchers with clipboards but can be collected and assimilated through administrative infrastructure itself. Yet, this is a domain in which government is often accused of falling short, typically on the basis that a decision was taken not to collect valuable data in the first place.[7]

Against that backdrop, the central question we address in this chapter is simple: what is the public law that regulates decisions by public officials *not* to collect useful data even when such data can be gathered with minimal effort?[8] On the one hand, we show that a 'duty of inquiry' has been an established part of public law since Lord Diplock's judgment in *Secretary of State for Education*

---

[5] Administrative data that is collected is increasingly a feature of public law litigation, see, eg, *R (UNISON) v Lord Chancellor* [2017] UKSC 51. For a discussion, see: Lady Rose, 'A Numbers Game? Statistics in Public Law Cases' (Administrative Law Bar Association Annual Lecture, 5 July 2021). Available at: www.supremecourt.uk/docs/alba-lecture-5-July-2021.pdf, last accessed 4 February 2022.

[6] In this way, this chapter can also be read as part of the necessary project to reassess administrative law in view of the rapidly expanding use of digital technologies within government, see R Williams, 'Rethinking Administrative Law for Algorithmic Decision Making' (2021) 42(2) *Oxford Journal of Legal Studies* 468; J Cobbe, 'Administrative Law and the Machines of Government: Judicial Review of Automated Public-Sector Decision-Making' (2019) 39(4) *Legal Studies* 636; P Daly, J Raso, and J Tomlinson, 'Administrative Law in the Digital World' in C Harlow (ed) *A Research Agenda for Administrative Law* (Cheltenham, Edward Elgar, 2023).

[7] We provide a detailed case study in the final section of this chapter. For another example, see the sustained criticism HM Courts and Tribunals Service has received for failing to collect data as court processes move online. See generally N Byrom, *Digital Justice: HMCTS Data Strategy and Delivering Access to Justice* (The Legal Education Foundation, 2019). Available at: https://research.thelegaleducationfoundation.org/wp-content/uploads/2019/09/DigitalJusticeFINAL.pdf, last accessed 20 April 2023; House of Commons Justice Committee, *Courts and Tribunals reform: Second Report of Session 2019* (HC 190, 2019); House of Commons Public Accounts Committee, *Key Challenges Facing the Ministry of Justice: Fifty-Second Report of Session 2019–21* (HC 1190, 2021).

[8] Questions of data protection law are, of course, relevant to the collection, retention, and management of data. However, while data protection laws may be advanced as a reason to not collect data in certain circumstances, it is a distinct legal framework and its use as a justification to refuse to collect useful data is highly contingent upon context, so we instead focus on the general point of public law in this chapter.

and Science v Tameside Metropolitan Borough Council,[9] and has since developed under the influence of the statutory Public Sector Equality Duty (PSED).[10] On the other hand, despite being routinely used by claimants and applied by the courts for several decades, the duty of inquiry requires broader application, which is yet to be fully realised through judicial review litigation and general practice within official decision-making. In particular, the duty can, and should be, applied at the level of decisions about systemic data collection, rather than solely in relation to individualised administrative decisions. Understanding the duty as including a 'systemic duty of inquiry' is, as we show, in line with existing jurisprudence, as well as the courts' ongoing attempts to articulate a doctrinal architecture capable of responding to systemic failures within public administration (ie, the approach to legal challenges to the foundations of an administrative process, rather than the compliance of a decision-maker's individual decision with that procedure). Overall, we suggest that the established case law in this domain can be viewed as providing a 'duty to acquire systemic data,' which can, and should, be more fully realised in practice.

We make this argument in three parts. First, we set out the established jurisprudence pertaining to the duty of inquiry, both as found in common law and statute. Second, we show how this duty includes principles that can extend to questions of systemic data collection, and how this shift of emphasis fits with a wider trend towards 'systemic' (or 'structural') judicial review. Third, we demonstrate the potential application of the duty in a systemic context by reference to a recent case study in which immigration authorities refused to collect valuable data despite the collection of that data involving minimal cost and effort.

II. The Established Principles of Inquiry in Public Law

The duty of inquiry is a long-recognised part of public law. The duty requires decision-makers to acquaint themselves with the relevant information that they need to make their decision. The starting point when analysing the evolution of the duty of inquiry is the famous decision of the House of Lords in *Tameside*,[11]

---

[9] *Secretary of State for Education and Science v Tameside Metropolitan Borough Council* [1977] AC 1014 (*Tameside*).
[10] Equality Act 2010, s 149(1).
[11] *Tameside* (n 9). The decision was often used in commentary in the years after the judgments to analyse wider trends and issues in administrative law, see, eg C Harlow and R Rawlings, *Law and Administration* (London, Weidenfeld and Nicholson, 1984) 333–34; PP Craig, *Administrative Law* (London, Sweet & Maxwell, 1984) 368; P McAuslan, 'Administrative Law, Collective Consumption and Judicial Policy' (1983) 46 MLR 1, 14–15; P Watchman, 'Palm Tree Justice and the Lord Chancellor's Foot' in P Robson and P Watchman (eds), *Justice, Lord Denning, and the Constitution* (Hanover, Dartmouth Publishing, 1981) 2; JAG Griffith, *The Politics of the Judiciary* (3rd edn, London, Fontana Books, 1985) 135, 37; HWR Wade, *Administrative Law* (4th edn, Oxford, Clarendon Press, 1977) 379–81; DCM Yardley, *Principles of Administrative Law* (London, Butterworth & Co, 1981) 68–71; D Bull, 'Tameside Revisited: Prospectively "Reasonable"; Retrospective "Maladministration"' (1987) 50 *Modern Law Review* 307.

within which Lord Diplock articulated the duty of inquiry which falls upon a decision-maker in the following terms:

> The question for the court is, did the Secretary of State ask himself the right question and take reasonable steps to acquaint himself with the relevant information to enable him to answer it correctly?[12]

Since this important decision, the duty has been expressed in various ways.[13] Justice Fordham, in his classic treatise on judicial review, put the modern principle of the 'duty of sufficient inquiry' in clear terms: '[a] public authority must sufficiently acquaint itself with relevant information, which must fairly be presented and properly addressed'.[14]

The decades following *Tameside* have seen the courts articulating the relevant principles as to how the duty operates, which are now often referred to as the 'Plantagenet' principles.[15] It is now clear that a court should not intervene solely because it considers that further inquiries would have been sensible or desirable. Instead, judicial intervention should take place only if no reasonable authority could have been satisfied based on the inquiries made that it possessed the necessary information. It is for the public body, and not the court, to decide upon the manner and intensity of inquiry to be undertaken.[16] Further, the *Tameside* duty does not include information which comes to light after the decision, unless such information should have been within the knowledge of the decision-maker.[17]

Given the approach that the courts have taken, the duty of inquiry as articulated in *Tameside* can therefore be seen – and usually is seen – as a manifestation of *Wednesbury* review.[18] Despite the reputation of *Wednesbury* claims (ie that they are rarely successful), the common law duty of inquiry has proven to be a routinely used ground of challenge ever since *Tameside*. It has been deployed with some success. In practice, as the Supreme Court has recognised, the application of the *Wednesbury* standard inevitably leads to a variable intensity of review that is

---

[12] *Tameside* (n 9)i 1065.
[13] See, eg, *R (Campaign Against Arms Trade) v Secretary of State for International Trade* [2019] EWCA Civ 1020 [145].
[14] M Fordham, *Judicial Review Handbook* (7th edn, Oxford, Hart Publishing, 2020) 649.
[15] *R (Plantagenet Alliance Ltd) v Secretary of State for Justice* [2014] EWHC 1622 (QB); *R (Balajigari) v Secretary of State for the Home Department* [2019] 1 WLR 4647 CA [70].
[16] *R (Khatun) v Newham London Borough Council* [2005] QB 37 [35].
[17] *R v Secretary of State for the Environment, ex p. Powis* [1981] 1 WLR 584, 597.
[18] *Associated Provincial Picture Houses Ltd v Wednesbury Corporation* [1948] 1 KB 223 (*Wednesbury*). See, eg, *R (Campaign Against Arms Trade) v Secretary of State for International Trade* [2019] EWCA Civ 1020 [58]. On the various faces of *Wednesbury* review, see J Jowell and A Lester, 'Beyond Wednesbury: Substantive Principles of Administrative Law' [1987] *Public Law* 368. However, while the weight of authority treats the duty as a manifestation of *Wednesbury* review, some authorities appear to treat the duty as an aspect of procedural fairness, see, eg, *R (ASK) v Secretary of State for the Home Department* [2019] EWCA Civ 1239 [63]. For a survey of the authorities, see Fordham (n 14) 649–50. Our view is that the doctrinal categorisation of the duty has little practical relevance to the appropriate analysis of the application of the duty.

informed by the context of the decision challenged.[19] The *Tameside* duty has been pleaded successfully across a variety of contexts, including planning,[20] education,[21] the housing of asylum seekers in military barracks,[22] and taxation.[23] Table 9.1 provides a range of examples of cases where a breach of the duty of inquiry has been argued successfully.

Table 9.1 Successful Tameside cases

Case	Facts	Argument made relating to inquiry	Outcome
R (on the application of Dawes) v Birmingham City Council [2021] EWHC 1676 (Admin)	The claimant property owner applied for judicial review of the defendant local authority's decision to make a general vesting declaration in relation to her property under the Compulsory Purchase (Vesting Declarations) Act 1981, s 4.	The claimant's case on the *Tameside* point was that the local authority's actions were a breach of its duty to make reasonable inquiries to ascertain the condition of the property and whether it was in occupation or being marketed for occupation.	It was irrational for the local authority to decide to execute the vesting declaration without having carried out an internal inspection of the property to check its condition, use and occupation, and to require the production of documents on the issue of occupation: '[n]o rational authority could have supposed that the information it had in its possession, or the enquiries it had made, were sufficient for making the decision to exercise its powers of compulsory purchase' [72].

(continued)

---

[19] See, eg, *Kennedy v The Charity Commission* [2014] UKSC 20 [54] (Lord Mance): '[b]oth reasonableness review and proportionality involve considerations of weight and balance, with the intensity of the scrutiny and the weight to be given to any primary decision-maker's view depending on the context.' For a fuller articulation of this position, see PP Craig, 'The Nature of Reasonableness Review' [2013] *Current Legal Problems* 1. See also J Rivers, 'Proportionality and Variable Intensity of Review' (2006) 65(1) *The Cambridge Law Journal* 174.
[20] *R (on the application of Usk Valley Conservation Group) v Brecon Beacons National Park Authority* [2010] 1 WLUK 514.
[21] *Secretary of State for Education and Science v Tameside Metropolitan Borough Council* [1977] AC 1014.
[22] *R (on the application of NB) v Secretary of State for the Home Department* [2021] EWHC 1489 (Admin).
[23] *MH Investments v Cayman Islands Tax Information Authority* [2013] 9 WLUK 285.

Table 9.1 (Continued)

Case	Facts	Argument made relating to inquiry	Outcome
R (Day) v Shropshire Council [2019] EWHC 3539 (Admin)	The claimant sought judicial review of Shropshire Council's decision to grant planning permission for a development of 15 dwellings on land adjoining a recreation ground, which had been sold by the local town council.	The claimant's case on the Tameside point was that the defendant failed to take account of material considerations such as the statutory trust and local and national planning policy on open spaces.	The planning officer failed to take reasonable steps to ascertain the extent of the recreation ground: 'the planning officer failed to take reasonable steps to ascertain the extent of the recreation ground which was created by the Borough Council, following the purchase of the Barker and Capper Lands for that purpose in 1926' [54].
R (CP (Vietnam)) v Secretary of State for the Home Department [2018] EWHC 2122 (Admin)	The claimant brought an application for judicial review challenging the SSHD's failure to properly progress his trafficking claim and the decision to subject him to immigration detention.	The claimant contended that there was a failure to identify and protect him as a victim of trafficking. The defendant instead proceeded to make a negative conclusive grounds decision, yet due to the suspended investigation, they did not have sufficient information to reach this conclusion.	The competent authority could not rationally have concluded that it had sufficient information to reach a 'conclusive grounds' decision in September 2016. It needed to grapple with the inconsistencies between the account given by an arresting officer in March 2016, when indicators of trafficking were noted, and what the police said in an email in September 2016. It ought to have been clear that further information was required, and if inquiries could not be progressed because of the claimant's absence, the investigation ought to have been suspended.

(continued)

Table 9.1 (Continued)

Case	Facts	Argument made relating to inquiry	Outcome
R (B) v Worcestershire County Council [2009] EWHC 2915 (Admin)	The claimants sought judicial review of a decision of Worcestershire County Council to close a day care centre of which they were the service users.	The claimant's case was that the decision to close the centre was *Wednesbury* irrational because the local authority had not yet made the necessary assessment of how many staff would be needed at the other day centres to meet their needs.	It was not apparent from the evidence that any appropriate analysis had been undertaken: 'reasonable steps were not taken to provide the decision-maker with the relevant information to enable the decision-maker to make a rational decision' [95]. Instead, it was clear that the local authority had applied a broad-brush approach.

Alongside the development of the common law jurisprudence, the duty of inquiry has found a new, particularised expression in section 149 of the Equality Act 2010 (PSED).[24] The PSED places a duty on public authorities,[25] and those who exercise public functions,[26] to have due regard to the need to eliminate discrimination,[27] advance equality of opportunity,[28] and foster good relations between those who do and do not share a protected characteristic.[29] The protected characteristics within the Act are age, disability, gender reassignment, marriage and civil partnership, pregnancy and maternity, race, religion or belief, sex, and sexual orientation.[30] Each of the first two limbs of the PSED contained within section 149 requires a public authority to keep their duties under review, and to gather information relevant to its duty so that it can have due regard to the need to eliminate discrimination in the

---

[24] The PSED replaced and expanded a range of existing provisions, including the Race Relations (Amendment) Act 2000 (which amended s 71 of the Race Relations Act 1976) and similar provisions introduced as amendments to the Disability Discrimination Act 1995 and the Sex Discrimination Act 1975. For general commentary on the intersections of public law and equality law, including the PSED, see A Straw, *Discrimination in Public Law* (London, Legal Action Group, 2022).
[25] Equality Act 2010, s 49(1).
[26] ibid s 149(2).
[27] ibid s 149(1)(a).
[28] ibid s 149(1)(b).
[29] ibid s 149(1)(c).
[30] ibid s 4.

discharge of public functions.[31] Through this legislative scheme, both the PSED and the common law duty of inquiry can effectively place a similar duty of inquiry on decision-makers, with the PSED described variously as a 'sensible way of framing the *Tameside* duty'[32] and as 'involv[ing] a duty of inquiry'.[33]

The Courts have now developed extensive jurisprudence pertaining to the PSED.[34] As regards the duty of inquiry, four observations can be made about the principles that can be derived from the case law. First, it is well established that the PSED can involve the imposition of a duty of inquiry. As Elias LJ's oft-quoted judgment in *Hurley & Moore* put it:

> It is also alleged that the PSED in this case involves a duty of inquiry. The submission is that the combination of the principles in *Secretary of State for Education and Science v Tameside Metropolitan Borough Council* [1977] AC 1014 and the duty of due regard under the statute requires public authorities to be properly informed before taking a decision. If the relevant material is not available, there will be a duty to acquire it and this will frequently mean than some further consultation with appropriate groups is required. Ms Mountfield referred to the following passage from the judgment of Aikens LJ in Brown (para [85]):
>
> '… the public authority concerned will, in our view, have to have due regard to the need to take steps to gather relevant information in order that it can properly take steps to take into account disabled persons' disabilities in the context of the particular function under consideration.'
>
> I respectfully agree.[35]

This statement was subsequently adopted in the leading case of *Bracking*,[36] as part of a bundle of 'uncontroversial principles'[37] and has been further affirmed in multiple other judgments.[38] Second, the precise extent of a duty of inquiry that the PSED places on a public authority is informed by the context of a particular

---

[31] ibid s 29(6).
[32] C Knight, 'Automated Decision-Making and Judicial Review' (2020) 25 *Judicial Review* 21, 23.
[33] *R (Ward & Others) v Hillingdon LBC* [2019] EWCA Civ 692 [71].
[34] The leading case remains *Bracking and others v Secretary of State for Work and Pensions* [2013] EWCA Civ 1345. For an overview and analysis of the case law, see A McColgan, 'Litigating the Public Sector Equality Duty: The Story So Far' (2015) 35(3) *Oxford Journal of Legal Studies* 453. See also T Hickman, 'Too Hot, Too Cold or Just Right? The Development of the Public Sector Equality Duties in Administrative Law' [2013] *Public Law* 325.
[35] *R (Hurley & Moore) v Secretary of State for Business, Innovation and Skills* [2012] EWHC 201 (Admin) [89–90].
[36] *Bracking* (n 34) at [26(8)(ii)].
[37] ibid [27].
[38] See, eg, *Hotak v Southwark LBC* [2015] UKSC 30 [73]; *R (Ward) v LB Hillingdon* [2019] EWCA Civ 692 [71]; *Forward v Aldwyck Housing Group Ltd* [2019] EWHC 24 (QB) [40]; *R (Bridges) v Chief Constable of South Wales* [2020] EWCA Civ 1058 [181].

decision or function.[39] Recently, in *R (Rowley) v Minister for the Cabinet Office*, Fordham J explained this aspect of the duty in the following terms:

> The principles concerning compliance with the PSED are contextual in their application ... The extent of the 'regard' which must be had is what is 'appropriate in all the circumstances' and 'weight and extent of the duty are highly fact-sensitive and dependent on individual judgment'... In the present case the following linked themes, regarding the principled application and enforcement of the PSED duty, are of particular significance: (i) importance; (ii) proactivity; and (iii) rigour, together with the recognised virtues of (iv) evidence-based thinking; and (v) legal sufficiency of enquiry.[40]

Third, it is evident that the duty is continuing.[41] Fourth, the duty is non-delegable.

> The Equality and Human Rights Commission also produces Technical Guidance on how to implement the PSED.[42] Chapter 5 sets out the need to engage with 'equality evidence' when discharging the PSED.[43] Elsewhere, the Guidance sets out that decision-makers should 'remain alert to new evidence suggesting that discrimination or other prohibited conduct is, or could be, occurring and take appropriate action to prevent this happening'.[44] Furthermore, the Guidance provides that, under the PSED, public bodies should consider whether they have 'enough information about levels of participation in [its] activities of people with different protected characteristics to enable it to have due regard to encouraging participation'[45] and that ensuring this may involve the collection of data broken down by protected characteristic.[46]

As with the common law duty of inquiry, cases which deal with the PSED span a wide range of contexts across public policy and administration. Table 9.2 provides an overview of a range of successful duty of inquiry cases that have been argued under the PSED.

---

[39] *R (AD) v Hackney LBC* [2019] EWHC 943 (Admin) [83]; *R (Refugee Action) v SSHD* [2014] EWHC 1033 (Admin) [121], [149]–[151]; *R (Law Centres Federation Ltd) v Lord Chancellor* [2018] EWHC 1588 (Admin) [75]–[76].
[40] *R (Rowley) v Minister for the Cabinet Office* [2021] EWHC 2108 (Admin) [40].
[41] *R (Ward) v LB Hillingdon* [2019] EWCA Civ 692 [71]–[74] (Lewison LJ):

> I would not hold that Hillingdon were in breach of the PSED in carrying out the initial equality impact assessment in 2013. At that stage it had not been shown that there was any reason for Hillingdon specifically to have considered non-UK nationals or refugees. But by the time of the 2016 assessment Mr Gullu had made his challenge in court. In the light of that challenge, I consider that Hillingdon ought at least to have considered the position of non-UK nationals. But they did not. I would therefore hold that Mr Gullu has established a breach of the PSED.

R (Unison) v Lord Chancellor [2015] EWCA Civ 935 [121].
[42] The Equality and Human Rights Commission, *Technical Guidance on the Public Sector Equality Duty: England* (February 2021). Available at: www.equalityhumanrights.com/en/publication-download/technical-guidance-public-sector-equality-duty-england, last accessed 20 April 2023.
[43] ibid [5.14]–[5.16]. See also [5.18], [5.21], [5.25], [5.37], and [5.40].
[44] ibid [3.6].
[45] ibid [3.31].
[46] ibid [3.32].

Table 9.2 Successful public sector equality duty inquiry cases

Case	Facts	Argument made relating to inquiry	Outcome
R (Bridges) v Chief Constable of South Wales [2020] EWCA Civ 1058	The claimant brought a judicial review challenging the use of automated facial recognition technology by South Wales Police.	It was argued that South Wales Police breached the PSED as it had not taken reasonable steps to investigate whether the technology had a racial or gender bias, as required by the PSED.	The PSED ground succeeded. Public concern about the relationship between the police and BAME communities had not diminished, and the duty was important to ensure that a public authority did not inadvertently overlook the potential discriminatory impact of a new, seemingly neutral, policy. The police force had never investigated whether AFR had an unacceptable bias on grounds of race or gender. The fact that the technology was being piloted made no difference.
R (Law Centres Federation Ltd) v Lord Chancellor [2018] EWHC 1588 (Admin)	The claimant applied for judicial review of the Lord Chancellor's decision to enlarge the geographic areas for which housing possession court duty scheme contracts were awarded. The scheme enabled those defending possession proceedings to obtain free, emergency legal assistance.	The claimant submitted that the decisions breached the PSED because the defendant had failed properly to acquaint himself with the necessary information on which they should have been based and had instead proceeded on an unfounded assumption that the introduction of larger contracts would improve sustainability. As a result, vulnerable clients would no	The relevant legislation did not require the defendant to make a specific fact-finding about the sustainability or viability of the schemes; the question was whether, having rationally chosen sustainability as a relevant factor, the defendant had obtained sufficient information on that topic to enable him to make a lawful decision that there was a problem which would be solved by moving to bigger scheme areas, and whether he had gone about his inquiries in a manner that was compatible with the public sector equality duty. However, there was no evidence as to why it was

(continued)

Table 9.2 *(Continued)*

Case	Facts	Argument made relating to inquiry	Outcome
		longer have access to 'wraparound' services which local law centres were currently providing but which were not covered by legal aid.	thought that larger HPCD scheme areas would be regarded as more attractive by providers. The defendant's central justification for the proposed changes was based on assumption, conjecture or anecdotal evidence. The decision was one that no reasonable decision-maker could reach on the state of the evidence.
R (on the application of Danning) v Sedgemoor DC [2021] EWHC 1649 (Admin)	The claimant applied for judicial review of a grant of planning permission for a change of use that would see a pub converted to a dwelling.	The claimant's case was that the committee had not asked itself whether the planning decision it was required to make could have any implications in relation to the PSED.	The Planning Committee did not ask itself whether the planning decision that it was required to make could have any implications for the PSED. There is a complete absence of evidence to the contrary. Accordingly, the claimant has established that the Council failed to comply with its duty.
R (on the application of DMA) v Secretary of State for the Home Department [2020] EWHC 3416 (Admin)	The claimants sought judicial review of the Secretary of State's approach to her duty to provide or arrange for the provision of accommodation for destitute failed asylum seekers under the Immigration and Asylum Act 1999 Pt I, s 4(2).	The argument on the PSED was that once the Secretary of State had reached a decision that she had a duty to accommodate under relevant legislation, she fell under a PSED duty to monitor the provision of that accommodation for individuals who had a disability.	The Secretary of State was in breach of the public sector equality duty in failing, once she had reached a decision that she had a duty to accommodate, to monitor the provision of that accommodation to individuals who had a disability.

(continued)

Table 9.2 (Continued)

Case	Facts	Argument made relating to inquiry	Outcome
		She had not had due regard to the need to eliminate discrimination and to advance equality of opportunity between persons who shared the protected characteristic of disability and persons who did not.	

III. The Systemic Dimension of the Duty of Inquiry

The duty of inquiry, both within and outside the statutory framework of the PSED, is now a well-established component of the public law landscape. At common law, the principles are clear. At the same time, it has found new expression in statute through the PSED. However, despite having been routinely used by claimants and applied by the courts for several decades, the duty of inquiry should have much broader application than has yet been fully realised in official and legal practice. The duty can, and should be, applied at the level of systemic decisions, rather than solely in relation to individualised administrative decisions. In particular, where a decision is taken *not* to collect certain relevant systemic data on the operation of a policy or administrative system despite such collection involving a minimal positive obligation on the state – or, to put that another way, where officials decline a convenient opportunity to collect systemic data – then this could constitute a breach of the duty of inquiry. The applicable test of legality for such decisions is the – inevitably context-specific and variable intensity – standard found in *Wednesbury*.[47] In this way, the established jurisprudence stemming from *Tameside* and the PSED can helpfully be viewed as providing a 'minimum duty to acquire systemic data'.

---

[47] *Wednesbury* (n 18). This test has been rephrased is numerous ways (most notably by Lord Diplock in *CCSU v Minister for Civil Service* [1985] AC 374, 410) and there remains some disagreement about the best articulation of it. For an excellent analysis, see Lord Carnwath, 'From Judicial Outrage to Sliding Scales – Where Next for Wednesbury?' (Administrative Law Bar Association Annual Lecture, 12 November 2013). Available at: www.supremecourt.uk/docs/speech-131112-lord-carnwath.pdf, last accessed 4 February 2022.

We should be clear that what we are proposing is not a novel direction for public law; rather, we are arguing that the jurisprudence surrounding the duty of inquiry has been under-utilised and consequently under-developed.[48] We are identifying an important application gap. There is no reason in principle that the duty of inquiry should not have application at a systemic level, and the courts have recognised this by hearing claims based on the duty of inquiry concerning systemic issues. For instance, in the recent landmark Court of Appeal decision in *Bridges*, there was extensive discussion of how the PSED related to the controversial deployment of automated facial recognition by the South Wales police.[49] The Court of Appeal held that public bodies must take positive steps to identify and address risks of algorithmic discrimination:

> In all the circumstances, therefore, we have reached the conclusion that SWP have not done all that they reasonably could to fulfil the PSED. We would hope that, as AFR is a novel and controversial technology, all police forces that intend to use it in the future would wish to satisfy themselves that everything reasonable which could be done had been done in order to make sure that the software used does not have a racial or gender bias.[50]

A particularly clear example of how a system-level application of the duty of inquiry is entirely uncontroversial can been seen in a recent claim by the Joint Council for the Welfare of Immigrants. The claimant argued that the Secretary of State for the Home Department failed to collect sufficient systemic data relevant to the adoption and implementation of a cut-off date for a certain category of immigration applications.[51] The claim was put in both PSED and *Tameside* terms. On the particular facts of the case the claim was refused permission, but the salient feature of the litigation for the purposes of our analysis is that both the Administrative Court and the Secretary of State accepted both that there was a duty of inquiry and that the applicable test was the *Wednesbury* standard.[52] Lieven J concluded:

> I accept that there is a duty of inquiry pursuant to *Tameside*. It seems to me that must be inherent within s.149. But the law is clear that a judicial review can only be brought in respect of an alleged failure to meet the duty of enquiry on Wednesbury rationality grounds. To some degree, I accept that Wednesbury will be context specific, whilst remaining a necessarily high test for a claimant.[53]

---

[48] We provide a case study which shows the under-realisation of this duty in government practice in the final section of this chapter.
[49] *Bridges* (n 38). For further examples, see *R (Flinn Kays) v Secretary of State for Work and Pensions* [2022] EWHC 167 (Admin); *R (Rights: Community: Action) v Secretary of State for Housing, Communities and Local Government* [2020] EWHC 3073 (Admin).
[50] *Bridges* (n 38) [201]. For commentary on this decision and the earlier decision of the Administrative Court, see J Purshouse and L Campbell, 'Automated Facial Recognition and Policing: A Bridge Too Far?' (2022) 42 *Legal Studies* 209; J Maxwell and J Tomlinson, 'Proving Algorithmic Bias in Government Decision-Making' (2020) 20(2) *Oxford University Commonwealth Law Journal* 352.
[51] *R (on application of the Joint Council for the Welfare of Immigrants) v Secretary of State for the Home Department* [2021] EWHC 638 (Admin).
[52] ibid [14].
[53] ibid [21].

The reason that these types of decision are open to review, and they have been treated as such, is straightforward: they are subject to the *Wednesbury* standard in the exact same way that non-systemic, individualised administrative decisions are subject to that standard. If a decision not to collect systemic data (or an omission to even consider it to the same effect), when viewed in its context, is 'a decision so unreasonable that no reasonable authority could have possibly made it', then it, too, will be unlawful.[54] In a way, the duty of inquiry simply provides the language to express that orthodox point.

Furthermore, viewing the duty of inquiry through the prism of a minimum duty to acquire systemic data also accords with the courts' attempts in recent years to articulate a doctrinal architecture in public law for responding to systemic failures within public administration.[55] As a species of judicial review, systemic review is distinct insofar as it challenges the foundations of an administrative process, rather than the compliance of a decision-maker's individual decision with that procedure. For instance, in *The Lord Chancellor v Detention Action*, the fast-track appeals provisions under the Tribunal Procedure Rules 2014 were challenged.[56] The Court of Appeal clarified the test for structural defects (those 'inherent in the system itself'),[57] finding when applying this test that the appeal system was 'structurally unfair and unjust.'[58] Lord Dyson MR set out the principles as follows:

> (i) in considering whether a system is fair, one must look at the full run of cases that go through the system; (ii) a successful challenge to a system on grounds of unfairness must show more than the possibility of aberrant decisions and unfairness in individual cases; (iii) a system will only be unlawful on grounds of unfairness if the unfairness is inherent in the system itself; (iv) the threshold of showing unfairness is a high one; (v) the core question is whether the system has the capacity to react appropriately to ensure fairness (in particular where the challenge is directed to the tightness of time limits, whether there is sufficient flexibility in the system to avoid unfairness); and (vi) whether the irreducible minimum of fairness is respected by the system and therefore lawful is ultimately a matter for the courts. I would enter a note of caution in relation to (iv). I accept that in most contexts the threshold of showing inherent unfairness is a high one. But this should not be taken to dilute the importance of the principle that only the highest standards of fairness will suffice in the context of asylum appeals.[59]

These principles were subsequently endorsed by the Court of Appeal in *IS v Director of Legal Aid Casework*.[60] In the more recent Supreme Court decision of

---

[54] *Wednesbury* (n 18) 230.

[55] F Powell, 'Structural Procedural Review: An Emerging Trend in Public Law' [2017] *Judicial Review* 83. On the wider context of systemic failures in administration, see R Thomas, 'Analysing Systemic Administrative Justice Failures: Explanatory Factors and Prospects for Future Research' (2021) 43(3) *Journal of Social Welfare and Family Law* 339.

[56] *The Lord Chancellor v Detention Action* [2015] EWCA Civ 840. See also *R (Howard League for Penal Reform) v Lord Chancellor* [2017] EWCA Civ 244.

[57] ibid [27].

[58] ibid [45].

[59] ibid [27].

[60] *IS v Director of Legal Aid Casework* [2016] EWCA Civ 464 at [16].

R (on the application of A v Secretary of State for the Home Department), there was an attempt to clarify the precise nature of this line of authorities.[61] The Court sought to stem any suggestion of a new set of free-standing principles of public law. It was critical of a test based on 'unacceptable risk,' seeking to instead steer back towards a test which asks whether the policy in question authorises or approves unlawful conduct by those to whom it is directed.[62] However, the Court still found that Lord Dyson MR's articulation of the principles was correct.[63]

It has also become increasingly recognised in legal scholarship that this form of judicial review may have particular utility in responding to the changing dynamics resulting from the advancement of digital forms of administrations.[64] Carol Harlow and Rick Rawlings, for instance, observe:

> [T]here will be a demand for some creative forms of judicial review litigation ... Increased dependency on decision-making systems framed in terms of digitisation and AI can again be said to place a special premium on wide-ranging external review founded on systemic values. The Detention Action and Howard League cases provide an important clue. We see significant potential in structural procedural review for judicial engagement in this brave new world.[65]

This suggestion was further echoed by Lord Sales, a current UK Supreme Court Justice, in what is quickly becoming a widely cited and influential public lecture on 'Algorithms, Artificial Intelligence and the Law'.[66] In relation to the example of algorithmic systems in the public sector, he stressed the appropriateness of applying conventional public law principles to system-level decisions:

> There should also be scope for legal challenges to be brought regarding the adoption of algorithmic programs, including at the ex ante stage. In fact, this seems to be happening already. This is really no more than an extension of the well-established jurisprudence on challenges to adoption of policies which are unlawful and is in line with recent decisions on unfairness challenges to entire administrative systems.[67]

Reframing established duties of inquiry as a minimum duty to acquire systemic data fits neatly with the move in public law to recognise the system-level application of well-established principles of public law, particularly in digital systems where systemic data is much more likely to be less burdensome to collect.

---

[61] *R (on the application of A v Secretary of State for the Home Department)* [2021] UKSC 37.
[62] *Gillick v West Norfolk and Wisbech Area Health Authority* [1986] AC 112.
[63] *R (on the application of A v Secretary of State for the Home Department)* [2021] UKSC 37 [67]–[68].
[64] For an extended discussion in relation to automated administrative decision-making, see A Chauhan, 'Towards the Systematic Review of Automated Decision-Making Systems' [2021] *Judicial Review* 285. See also J Tomlinson, K Sheridan, and A Harkens, 'Judicial Review Evidence in the Era of the Digital State' [2020] *Public Law* 740.
[65] C Harlow and R Rawlings, 'Proceduralism and Automation: Challenges to the Values of Administrative Law' in E Fisher, J King and A Young (eds), *The Foundations and Future of Public Law* (Oxford, OUP, 2020) 290–91.
[66] Lord Sales, 'Algorithms, Artificial Intelligence and the Law' (2020) 25 *Judicial Review* 46 [43].
[67] ibid, citing *Detention Action* (n 56).

IV. Application of the Minimum Duty to Acquire Systemic Data

We now turn to demonstrate the application of the duty of inquiry at a systemic level, by reference to an official decision pertaining to an administrative system relating to immigration in the UK. Our case study relates to the EU Settlement Scheme, the administrative system established to allow EU citizens to apply to remain in the UK after Brexit.[68] We develop our analysis through this case study for three main reasons. First, to provide a recent example of an important refusal decision by public officials to collect valuable systemic data – despite it requiring little obligation to be placed on the public authority – and set out the nature of the problems that can flow from such decisions. Second, to show how the application of the well-established public law principles set out above can and should wrap around such decisions, including how common reasons given (where any reasons are given) for refusals to collect data ought to factor into the legal analysis. Third, to demonstrate the relevance and importance of equalities data in this context.

The settled status scheme required EU citizens resident in the UK to make applications to remain. Due to the considerable number of people eligible to apply for settled status (at the start of the scheme approximately 3 million applications were expected, but it transpired to be over 5 million), and the need for those applications to be processed over a relatively short period, the Home Office decided to use an end-to-end online process with automation at its centre. In reality, this was probably the only way to deliver the stated underlying policy objective – to register all EU citizens who wished to remain in the UK by a fixed date – without incurring excessive cost.[69]

The online application form for settled status relied on two digital platforms: an app downloadable on a mobile phone or tablet, and an online form on the UK Government's website. Those who fell within the scope of the scheme were required to submit information on both platforms, which evidences the three broad categories required to meet the criteria set out in the relevant Immigration Rules: identity, residence, and suitability.[70] Applicants are then directed to an online form to complete. Once the application was completed, it was processed by an automated system which checked the applicant's data against data held by HM Revenue and Customs and the Department for Work and Pensions (DWP). The administrative infrastructure established to process settled status applications, and pursue the policy goals, was therefore heavily digitalised at all stages.

---

[68] For a detailed analysis of the policy background and general design of the system, as well as the novel issues it raises, see J Tomlinson, 'Justice in Automated Administration' (2020) 40 *Oxford Journal of Legal Studies* 708; J Maxwell and J Tomlinson, *Experiments in Automating Immigration Systems* (Bristol, Bristol University Press, 2022) ch 3.

[69] Home Office, *EU Settlement Scheme: Statement of Intent* (21 June 2018).

[70] Immigration Rules Appendix EU: Citizens and Family Members and Immigration Rules (25 February 2016).

A range of concerns were expressed about how different elements of the policy underlying the settled status scheme and the way the scheme was operationalised may have a range of harmful effects on individuals.[71] Many of the concerns about the policy and the design of the system possessed an equalities dimension, insofar as they were related to the potential differential treatment of people by reference to certain protected characteristics or a combination of protected characteristics.[72] For instance, some were concerned that those who are digitally excluded – a group that intersects with various protected characteristics – may find it more difficult to apply through the online process and may even be less likely to realise that they need to apply in the first place. Others were concerned that the novel use of digital-only proof of immigration status – which is the only proof of settled status resulting from a successful application – would lead to those with settled status being disadvantaged in the job and property rental markets.[73]

Reflecting the reality that the policy and the administrative system would inevitably have to process vulnerable people and complex cases, the Home Office produced a Policy Equality Statement.[74] The overall conclusion by the Home Office presented in that Statement is that there is some indirect indiscrimination built into the scheme but it cannot be deemed unlawful and should be seen as a proportionate means of achieving a legitimate aim, particularly in view of a range of mitigation measures that were being deployed. As part of its supporting analysis, the DWP accepts a range of examples of where the scheme may have adverse equalities impacts. For instance, the EUSS application system is said to be likely to indirectly discriminate against women, as the automated checks for evidence of continuous residence fail to cover certain welfare payments which women are

---

[71] For a full account and analysis of these concerns, see J Tomlinson, 'Justice in Automated Administration' (2020) 40 *Oxford Journal of Legal Studies* 708; Maxwell and Tomlinson *Experiments in Automating Immigration Systems* (n 68) ch 3.

[72] M Sumption and Z Kone, 'Unsettled Status? Which EU Citizens are at Risk of Failing to Secure their Rights after Brexit?' (*Oxford Migration Observatory*, 12 April 2018). Available at: https://migrationobservatory.ox.ac.uk/resources/reports/unsettled-status-which-eu-citizens-are-at-risk-of-failing-to-secure-their-rights-after-brexit/, last accessed 20 April 2023; *Uncertain Futures: the EU Settlement Scheme and Children and Young People's Right to Remain in the UK* (The Children's Legal Centre briefing, March 2019). Available at: www.childrenslegalcentre.com/wp-content/uploads/2019/03/EUSS-briefing_Mar2019_FINAL.pdf, last accessed 20 April 2023; *How the EU Settlement Scheme Affects Women and Girls* (NPC, October 2018). Available at: www.thinknpc.org/wp-content/uploads/2018/10/How-the-EU-settlement-scheme-affects-women-and-girls.pdf, last accessed 20 April 2023; *Not so Straightforward* (Greater Manchester Immigration Aid Unit report, November 2019) https://gmiau.org/not-so-straightforward/, last accessed 20 April 2023; *Brexit, EU Settlement Scheme and the Roma Communities in the UK* (Roma Support Group Report, June 2020). Available at: www.roma-supportgroup.org.uk/uploads/9/3/6/8/93687016/roma_brexit_euss_report_16.06.2020_final.pdf, last accessed 20 April 2023.

[73] For a full analysis of the serious risk of discrimination in respect of this element of the system, see: J Tomlinson, J Maxwell and A Welsh, 'Discrimination in Digital Immigration Status' (2022) 42 *Legal Studies* 315.

[74] Home Office, *Policy Equality Statement: EU, other European Economic Area and Swiss citizens resident in the UK and their family members* (November 2020). Available at: https://assets.publishing.service.gov.uk/government/uploads/system/uploads/attachment_data/file/936478/EUSS_PES_November_2020.pdf, last accessed 4 February 2022.

more likely to receive, such as Child Benefits, making the application process more complicated for women.[75] Given this, the DWP adopted a 'Strategy for handling vulnerability in the Settlement Scheme' which had three components: 'Application management' 'Enforcement response' and 'Use of status'.[76] A central question – both to the success of the policy generally and, more specifically, to the mitigation measures to prevent discriminatory impacts – is who applied, and what was their experience of being processed through the Home Office system? To that end, it appears to be highly valuable to collect data concerning the protected characteristics of those applying to, and being processed through, the scheme. That dataset would allow government and others to look at the equalities dimension of the cohort of people applying and if they appear to be receiving differential treatment within the scheme, most importantly in terms of outcomes.

It is important to underline at this point the relevance of the fact that this was an administrative system with an online application followed by an automated process. The whole system was end-to-end digital. If the Home Office wanted to collect data on protected characteristics, it would not require a person with a clipboard manually recording answers from millions of applicants. It would simply involve adding a few extra boxes on the online form that would, over the course of time, generate an enormous dataset. The principal burden being placed on the public authority in this instance is the maintenance of that dataset which – particularly given the value of data, the size of the population affected by the system, and the fact the Home Office is already maintaining datasets around the same system – is marginal. In terms of the positive obligation placed on the state, in practice this burden would generally be akin to – or perhaps even less than – the obligations imposed on public authorities by the requirement to adhere to orthodox procedural fairness principles. It cannot be said to involve the imposition of a positive obligation that reaches beyond the institutional or constitutional limits of the courts without also calling into question the foundations of modern administrative law itself.

Against that backdrop, it is striking that the Home Office decided only to collect minimal protected characteristics data relating to age, sex, and nationality (insofar as that corresponds to race). In taking this decision, the Home Office actively decided *not* to collect data relating to other important protected characteristics; characteristics such as disability, sexual orientation, gender reassignment, religion and belief and pregnancy and maternity. This data is crucial for an accurate evaluation and assessment of how the EUSS application system works in practice. This data deficit creates blind spots; without an insight into the user-experience of individuals with these protected characteristics, differential treatment such as indirect

---

[75] ibid 71.
[76] D Neal, *A further inspection of the EU Settlement Scheme* (*Independent Chief Inspector of Borders and Immigration*, 13 January 2022) 38. Available at: https://assets.publishing.service.gov.uk/government/uploads/system/uploads/attachment_data/file/1046018/A_further_inspection_of_the_EU_Settlement_Scheme___July_2020_to_March_2021.pdf, last accessed 20 April 2023.

discrimination is far more difficult to detect, and therefore far more difficult to remedy. This was, put simply, an official decision to refuse to collect data that was available with minimal burden on the Home Office and, by taking that course, the department effectively curtailed anyone's capacity (including its own) to undertake a comprehensive system-wide analysis of the equalities impact of the policy and its mode of implementation.

The Independent Chief Inspector of Borders and Immigration criticised this decision-making process and its impact on the possibility of any serious evaluation relating to whether the Home Office's strategy to mitigate discriminatory impacts worked:

> The Home Office eventually published a Policy Equality Statement (PES) for the EUSS in November 2020. Neither the delay nor the PES itself were well received by stakeholders. The PES provides a comprehensive account of the potential impact of the EUSS policy on those with protected characteristics, support mechanisms to mitigate the impact and a commitment to ongoing review. However, in the absence of data capture of applicants' protected characteristics, beyond age, sex and nationality insofar as that corresponds to race, it is difficult to see how the Home Office can demonstrate it has fully evaluated any actual impact or remained alert to unanticipated impacts. Consequently, it cannot be confident that any disadvantages are 'proportionate'.[77]

The decision-making process pertaining to the collection of protected characteristics information from settled status is a clear example of public officials refusing to collect valuable systemic data even though its collection involves minimal burden. As the Chief Inspector observes, that decision has effectively hamstrung a proper equalities analysis of the scheme and therefore increases the risks that people with protected characteristics are being discriminated against in ways that are not visible.

The only remaining question is whether there is any justification for the approach to the systemic collection of protected characteristics data taken by the Home Office.[78] The most detailed articulation, on the public record, of the rationale for this approach was given in response to the Chief Inspector's criticism: that the Home Office has 'sought to limit the data requested from applicants … to that necessary to decide the application, to keep the process simple and streamlined as required by the Citizens' Rights Agreements'.[79] This reflects a common justification

---

[77] ibid 6.

[78] Based on our current understanding of administrative practice in this domain, we believe there are three commonplace justifications that are provided for refusals to collect systemic data, even where such collection involves minimal effort: (1) the burden and costs of dataset maintenance; (2) data protection law; and (3) collection of data creates attrition within a system. We do not have space to provide a full analysis of each of these justifications in turn, but it is important to observe that none of them provide a generally applicable shield for public authorities that refuse to collect data. Whether they are sufficient to discharge a body's public law duties will turn heavily upon the particular factual context.

[79] Home Office, *Response to the ICIBI's report on the EU Settlement Scheme* (13 January 2022) [1.2]. We, however, note this issue has not been tested in litigation and other justifications may have been advanced if it were.

given when officials refuse to collect systemic data. The logic is essentially that government forms should ask for no more information than is necessary so as not to deter people from completing them. Accessible government forms that are easy for citizens to use are, of course, important (if, sadly, not a common reality).[80] However, this reasoning is fundamentally misconceived for at least two reasons. First, it cannot plausibly be suggested, within this context, that a person applying to remain in a country where they are already living will be deterred from doing so by a requirement to tick a few extra boxes on an application form. In its full context, the effect of such a change would not be to render the process of making such an application any less 'simple' or 'streamlined.' Second, the design principle of 'not asking any more questions than strictly necessary to perform the relevant administrative function,' which is usually linked to the *Government Digital Service Standard*, has no basis in law and should certainly not preclude proper consideration of the value of data collection, both generally and in particular in relation to the PSED. In the particular case of the settled status scheme, the Citizens' Rights Agreements provide no added weight in this respect. The reality is, therefore, that, on the proper application of the reasonableness standard in this context, there was no substantive reason for not collecting protected characteristics data in the settled status application process. It is therefore, in our view, a paradigm example of a decision which violates the principles of public law pertaining to the duty of inquiry, as applied at the systemic level, that we have elaborated above.

V. Conclusion

We cannot claim to be proposing some radical new direction for public law in this chapter. Instead, we hope that we have achieved something much more modest: to simply suggest there is an important application gap in practice pertaining to some of the most conventional principles of public law and an increasingly important category of decisions taken by public officials.[81] However, the importance of closing this gap should not be understated in terms of the contribution law can make to good government. Where systemic data on the operation and impact of policies and administrative scheme can be collected with minimal effort, it should be collected. It should be collected so the government, other institutions, and the public can understand the operation of public policy and administration, scrutinise it, make arguments for its betterment, and, if necessary, challenge it. In our view, well-established common law principles of public law, supplemented by the Equality Act 2010, provide a safeguard – in effect, a 'duty to acquire systemic data' –

---

[80] See generally J Meers, 'Forms of Fettering: Application Forms and the Exercise of Discretion in the Welfare State' (2020) 42(2) *Journal of Social Welfare and Family Law* 221.

[81] As stated above, we, of course, accept that further research is required to establish a better understanding of the precise extent and nature of this gap.

against decisions public officials may make that seek to deprive themselves and others of the benefit of such data without reason. It may be hoped such decisions should never occur but, as our case study shows in detail, they do occur, and they cause a range of problems.

Our analysis in this chapter further points to an issue that may be apt for wider consideration relating to legislative reform. Administrative data and decisions relating to its collection will only become more vexed as public administration quickly evolves into a form where the collection of such data is much easier for public authorities. In the same way that large private technology companies have developed 'platform power' through the mass collection of data,[82] government is now occupying the role of a digital platform in many similar ways.[83] The legal conversation in this domain is often geared towards questions of data protection and privacy law, and rightly so. However, public authorities may also seek, intentionally or without thought, to keep themselves and others in the dark by not collecting valuable data even when they are able to do so. The decisions that are made about collecting valuable administrative data that can inform the assessment of the operation of government and facilitate scrutiny and improvement are an equally important component of puzzle. In this chapter, we have drawn upon existing principles that, in our view, can provide a helpful, minimum legal framework for such decisions. We think it ought to be more proactively advanced in governmental and legal practice. But this approach to framing administration decision-making is, of course, not an ideal way of providing the optimum standards around decisions critical to the success or failure of modern administration.[84] We should be aspiring to governance that does more than the bare minimum to maintain legality in this domain. The consideration of a legislative framework that optimises the regulation of public decisions as to whether systematic administrative data is collected may well be a worthwhile project for those in pursuit of better public administration.

---

[82] O Lynskey, 'Regulating "Platform Power"' (2017) LSE Law Society and Economy Working Paper Series 01/2017. Available at: https://papers.ssrn.com/sol3/papers.cfm?abstract_id=2921021, last accessed 20 April 2023; S Zuboff, *The Age of Surveillance Capitalism: The Fight for a Human Future at the New Frontier of Power* (New York, Profile Books, 2019).

[83] T O'Reilly, 'Government as a Platform' (2011) 6(1) *Innovations: Technology, Governance, Globalization* 13.

[84] F Schauer and R Zeckhauser, *The Trouble with Cases*, in DP Kessler (ed), *Regulation versus Litigation: Perspectives from Economics and Law* (Chicago, University of Chicago Press, 2011).

10
The Treatment of Facts in South African Administrative Law

GLENN PENFOLD AND CORA HOEXTER[*]

I. Introduction

As in the common law world more generally, the treatment of factual questions and evidence has received scant attention from South African administrative lawyers. The neglect of this area belies the significance of the topic, as facts and evidence can be crucial to the outcome of administrative law review. However, their role and relevance vary widely. In some cases, the approach is fairly routine: the court simply asks whether the vitiating fact has been proved on a balance of probabilities. A court might, for example, need to decide whether the decision-maker considered submissions received from an interested party, complied with a procedural jurisdictional fact, or acted with an ulterior purpose. In other cases, the correct approach to facts is more difficult. For instance, an assessment as to the existence of a substantive jurisdictional fact[1] can be complex. It is by no means straightforward to assess whether an appointee to a post is 'fit and proper'[2] or that a measure is 'necessary' for a particular statutory purpose.[3]

In this chapter we focus on two of the most interesting and most contested areas of the South African courts' treatment of facts in administrative law review.

---

[*] We thank the editors and the anonymous peer-reviewers for their helpful comments on a previous draft.

[1] Review for non-jurisdictional or 'material' mistake of fact is less likely to throw up tricky factual issues given that this ground applies only to facts that are 'uncontentious and objectively verifiable': *Dumani v Nair* 2013 (2) SA 274 (SCA) [32], with reference to *E v Secretary of State for the Home Department* EWCA Civ 49; [2004] QB 1044 [66].

[2] In *Democratic Alliance v President of the Republic of South Africa* 2013 (1) SA 248 (CC) [14]–[26], the Constitutional Court held that the statutory requirement that the National Director of Public Prosecutions must be 'a fit and proper person' constituted an objective jurisdictional fact in respect of the decision to appoint such person.

[3] See, eg, *Minister of Co-operative Governance and Traditional Affairs v British American Tobacco South Africa (Pty) Ltd* [2022] 3 All SA 332 (SCA) (*BATSA*) [98]–[106] (the state had not shown that a ban on the sale of tobacco was 'necessary' to protect the public or to deal with the destructive effects of the COVID-19 pandemic, and the ban was thus ultra vires).

First, courts are sometimes required to scrutinise the impact of an administrative act – its expected benefits and costs – or the administrator's consideration of that impact. This can involve evidence on matters incapable of empirical proof or in which fact and policy are intertwined. Difficult questions arise in this context as to when courts might insist on factual evidence, when they might rely on intuition or common sense, and as to the deference that the court might owe to the administrator's findings of fact. Secondly, the factual context can be highly relevant to the court's exercise of its discretion to decide upon a just and equitable remedy. In this chapter we consider the relevance of facts when a court is deciding whether invalid administrative action ought to be set aside and whether an order of substitution is justified. While our main aim is to explore the courts' handling of factual questions in South African administrative law, we also offer some suggestions as to how these questions might best be approached in future.

Before moving to these themes, we provide some essential information about administrative law review in South Africa and its general approach to evidence.

II. Administrative Law Review and Evidence

There are two main 'pathways' to administrative law review in modern South African law.[4] The primary pathway is the Promotion of Administrative Justice Act 3 of 2000 (PAJA), which applies to decisions that constitute 'administrative action'. The PAJA aims to give effect to the constitutional rights to just administrative action[5] and, in section 6(2), sets out the grounds for review of administrative action. The second main pathway is legality review. This species of review applies to the exercise of all public power.[6] It was conceived as a mere 'safety net'[7] for those instances where the PAJA does not apply but has, over time, expanded to cover a wide range of administrative law review grounds.

Administrative law review, whether instituted under the PAJA or the principle of legality,[8] is usually brought on application in terms of Rule 53 of the Uniform Rules of Court.[9] This rule requires review proceedings to be instituted by way of

---

[4] See generally C Hoexter and G Penfold, *Administrative Law in South Africa* (Cape Town, 3rd edn, Juta & Co Ltd, 2021) 148–78.
[5] Constitution of the Republic of South Africa, 1996 (Constitution), s 33.
[6] See, eg, *AAA Investments (Pty) Ltd v Micro Finance Regulatory Council* 2007 (1) SA 343 (CC) [29]. cf *President of the Republic of South Africa v Democratic Alliance* 2020 (1) SA 428 (CC) [32]. On the grounds of review encompassed by legality review, see Hoexter and Penfold (n 4) 157–61.
[7] *Minister of Health v New Clicks South Africa (Pty) Ltd* 2006 (2) SA 311 (CC) [97], quoting C Hoexter, '"Administrative Action" in the Courts' [2006] *Acta Juridica* 303, 308.
[8] Some uncertainty remains as to whether Rule 53 applies to the review of *all* exercises of public power: see *President of the RSA v DA* (n 6) [24]–[26], [32].
[9] Government Notice R48 *GG* 999 of 15 January 1965, as amended. Rule 53 is, however, not the exclusive procedure for review proceedings. Review may also be brought in terms of an ordinary application provided for in Rule 6 of the Uniform Rules of Court, or even by way of action proceedings: *Jockey Club v Forbes* 1993 (1) SA 649 (A) 660–62; *Mamadi v Premier of Limpopo Province* [2022] ZACC 26 (6 July 2022) [27]–[33].

notice of motion supported by a founding affidavit 'setting out the grounds and the facts and circumstances upon which [the] applicant relies to have the decision or proceedings set aside or corrected'.[10] It is trite that an applicant must generally make out both its factual and legal case in its founding papers.[11]

Significantly, Rule 53 requires the administrator to produce the record of the proceedings that are the subject of the review application. It also allows the applicant an opportunity to amend its notice of motion and to supplement its founding papers on examination of the record. The record consists of 'the documents, evidence, arguments and other information' before the administrator at the time the decision was made, and includes 'every scrap of paper throwing light, however indirectly, on what the proceedings were, both procedurally and evidentially'.[12] In recent years the Constitutional Court has clarified that the record includes the deliberations of the decision-making body.[13]

Production of the record is a vital mechanism aimed at ensuring that the relevant facts are known to the parties and placed before the court. It ensures that the applicant does not bring the review 'in the dark'.[14] But even before litigation, a prospective applicant may gain a more complete picture of the facts by requesting written reasons for administrative action under the PAJA, section 5 or access to records in terms of the Promotion of Access to Information Act 2 of 2000 (PAIA). Moreover, it is possible for a litigant to ask the court to direct that the rules of discovery apply to the application;[15] but this mechanism is rarely employed.

Unlike action proceedings, applications or motion proceedings are 'not designed to determine probabilities' and thus 'cannot be used to resolve factual issues'.[16] The South African courts thus require special mechanisms to deal with disputes of fact. In the absence of a referral to oral evidence,[17] a device seldom used in review proceedings, our courts rely upon the *Plascon-Evans* rule and its exceptions.[18] In terms of this rule, a final order may be granted in application proceedings if 'those facts averred in the applicant's affidavits which have been admitted by the respondent, together with the facts alleged by the respondent, justify such an order'.[19] The exceptions add that the applicant's version is to be preferred where the respondent's denial of a fact alleged by the applicant does not

---

[10] Uniform Rules of Court, r 53(1) and (2).
[11] See, eg, *Esau v Minister of Co-operative Governance and Traditional Affairs* 2021 (3) SA 593 (SCA) [60].
[12] *Johannesburg City Council v The Administrator, Transvaal (1)* 1970 (2) SA 89 (T) 91G–H.
[13] *Helen Suzman Foundation v Judicial Service Commission* 2018 (4) SA 1 (CC) [22]–[27].
[14] *Jockey Club* (n 9) 660E.
[15] Uniform Rules of Court, r 35(13).
[16] *National Director of Public Prosecutions v Zuma* 2009 (2) SA 277 (SCA) [26].
[17] Uniform Rules of Court, r 6(5)(g). On the use of this rule in the context of r 53 applications, see *Mamadi* (n 9), [41]–[45].
[18] *Plascon-Evans Paints Ltd v Van Riebeeck Paints (Pty) Ltd* 1984 (3) SA 623 (A).
[19] ibid 634E–635D.

raise 'a real, genuine or *bona fide* dispute of fact' or where the respondent's version is so far-fetched or clearly untenable that it can be rejected on the papers.[20]

The next part of this chapter deals with the impact of administrative acts in the light of this background.

III. The Impact of Administrative Acts

Broadly speaking, in review proceedings, the impact of an administrative act is most likely to feature in one of two ways. The more straightforward is where an applicant contends that the administrator failed to consider the likely impact of the act. This ground of review – failing to consider a material, relevant consideration – has a venerable common law pedigree and is now reflected as a review ground both in the PAJA, section 6(2)(e)(iii) and, in modified form, as part of legality review.[21]

The application of this review ground in a particular case is both a factual and a legal matter. While the finding that the administrator failed properly to consider the likely impact requires a factual assessment, the question whether and to what extent the administrator was obliged to consider the likely impact is a legal one. In the context of the substantive review grounds, rationality and reasonableness, the likely impact of a discretionary administrative act will invariably be a relevant consideration. However, the extent to which the administrator was required to assess that impact will vary depending on factors such as the nature of the power, the context in which it is exercised, the information before the administrator, and the text and purpose of the empowering statute.

The second way in which the impact of an administrative act is likely to feature is when the applicant relies on one or both of those substantive grounds. As to rationality, an exercise of public power is open to challenge, by way of both PAJA and legality review, where it is not rationally connected to the purpose for which the power was conferred.[22] This rational connection is absent if the administrative act is not 'reasonably likely' to produce its desired effect.[23] Put differently, rationality requires that 'the means chosen to achieve a particular purpose must reasonably be capable of accomplishing that purpose'.[24] It follows that a court

---

[20] ibid. See also *NDPP v Zuma* (n 16) [26]; *Minister of Social Development v SA Childcare (Pty) Ltd; MEC, Social Development, Eastern Cape v SA Childcare (Pty) Ltd* [2022] ZASCA 119 (29 August 2022) [17]–[20].

[21] *Democratic Alliance v President of the RSA* (n 2) [39].

[22] *Pharmaceutical Manufacturers Association of SA: In re Ex parte President of the Republic of South Africa* 2000 (2) SA 674 (CC) [85]; PAJA s 6(2)(f)(ii)(bb). The remainder of s 6(2)(f)(ii) adds that administrative action may be reviewed if it is not rationally connected to the purpose for which it was taken, the information before the administrator, or the reasons given for it by the administrator.

[23] *Minister of Justice and Constitutional Development v SA Restructuring and Insolvency Practitioners Association* 2018 (5) SA 349 (CC) (*SARIPA*) [58].

[24] ibid [55].

adjudicating a rationality challenge might be called upon to assess the likelihood that the intended beneficial impact will be achieved.

Reasonableness review, which applies only to exercises of public power that qualify as administrative action,[25] potentially involves even more rigorous scrutiny of the action's impact. Administrative action may be challenged on this ground if it is disproportionate[26] or otherwise falls short of the standard of a reasonable administrator.[27] Various factors are relevant in assessing reasonableness, including 'the impact of the decision on the lives and well-being of those affected'.[28] This takes in both sides of the impact coin: the beneficial and adverse impact of the decision. In reasonableness review, then, a court might be asked to consider the action's likely benefits and costs as well as whether the costs are proportionate to the benefits: a cost-benefit analysis of sorts.

We now turn to consider the courts' approach to the impact of administrative acts, starting with the beneficial side of the coin.

A. Beneficial Impact

There is a dearth of case law addressing the approach to be adopted where it is uncertain whether an administrative act will achieve its desired objective. The issue has, however, been canvassed in a number of cases dealing with Bill of Rights challenges. This body of case law presents a useful reference point for our purposes for two reasons. First, the administrative law review grounds of rationality and reasonableness (and sometimes substantive jurisdictional facts)[29] can raise similar issues to those that arise under the Constitution's limitation clause, s 36, including an assessment of proportionality.[30] Secondly, in recognition of the Constitution's supremacy and the fact that any law or conduct inconsistent with the Constitution is invalid,[31] PAJA, section 6(2)(i) stipulates that administrative action may be reviewed on the ground that it is unconstitutional. In this way, a wide range of constitutional violations can become a concern of administrative law.

Section 36(1) of the Constitution provides that the rights in the Bill of Rights may be limited to the extent that the limitation is 'reasonable and justifiable in

---

[25] PAJA, s 6(2)(h). Despite its literal import ('so unreasonable that no reasonable person could have so exercised the power or performed the function'), the Constitutional Court has interpreted s 6(2)(h) to mean simply a decision a reasonable administrator could not have made: *Bato Star Fishing (Pty) Ltd v Minister of Environmental Affairs* 2004 (4) SA 490 (CC) [44].

[26] *Ehrlich v Minister of Correctional Services* 2009 (2) SA 373 (E) [42].

[27] *Bato Star* (n 25), [44]: 'an administrative decision will be reviewable if ... it is one that a reasonable decision-maker could not reach'. See also Hoexter and Penfold (n 4) 479–81.

[28] ibid, *Bato Star* [45].

[29] For instance, legislative requirements that an administrative act must be 'necessary', 'required' or 'appropriate'.

[30] A requirement to assess the proportionality of an administrative act might also, in appropriate cases, flow from the administrative law duty to consider materially relevant considerations.

[31] Constitution, s 2.

an open and democratic society based on human dignity, equality and freedom' taking into account all relevant factors, including 'the relation between the limitation and its purpose' and 'less restrictive means to achieve the purpose'.[32] As Plasket JA noted in *Esau*,[33] these two factors – which form 'the heart of the limitation enquiry' – involve asking 'whether there is a rational connection between the infringements and their purpose; and whether the means chosen were proportionate'. These questions echo those that arise in administrative law.

In a section 36(1) enquiry, the burden of justification rests on the party who asserts that the law or conduct is justified. Importantly, 'to the extent that justification rests on factual and/or policy considerations' that party must place the relevant factual material or policy considerations before the court.[34] Writing on behalf of the Constitutional Court in *Minister of Home Affairs v National Institute for Crime Prevention and the Reintegration of Offenders (NICRO)*,[35] Chaskalson CJ explained the justification analysis as follows:

> This calls for a different enquiry to that conducted when factual disputes have to be resolved. In a justification analysis facts and policy are often intertwined. There may for instance be cases where the concerns to which the legislation is addressed are subjective and not capable of proof as objective facts. A legislative choice is not always subject to courtroom fact-finding and may be based on reasonable inferences unsupported by empirical data. When policy is in issue it may not be possible to prove that a policy directed to a particular concern will be effective. It does not necessarily follow from this, however, that the policy is not reasonable and justifiable. If the concerns are of sufficient importance, the risks associated with them sufficiently high, and there is sufficient connection between means and ends, that may be enough to justify action taken to address them.

After reiterating that where justification 'depends on factual material, the party relying on justification must establish the facts on which the justification depends', Chaskalson CJ observed that in those cases in which justification depends on policy, sufficient information as to the policy should be placed before the court so as to allow an opportunity of rebuttal through 'countervailing factual material or expert opinion'.[36] He added that, while a failure to place this information before the court can be fatal, there may be cases where, despite the absence of this information, a court is able to uphold a justification claim 'based on common sense and judicial knowledge'.[37]

In *NICRO* itself, the court rejected the state's arguments that the disenfranchisement of prisoners was justified. It held that the state had not established the

---

[32] On the general approach to the limitation clause, see *S v Manamela and Another (Director-General of Justice Intervening)* 2000 (3) SA 1 (CC) [32]–[34].
[33] *Esau* (n 11) [139].
[34] *Moise v Greater Germiston Transitional Local Council: Minister of Justice and Constitutional Development Intervening* 2001 (4) SA 491 (CC) [19].
[35] 2005 (3) SA 280 (CC) (*NICRO*) [35].
[36] ibid [36].
[37] ibid.

factual basis for its argument based on lack of resources and the cost of facilitating voting by the affected prisoners.[38] Also, insufficient information had been produced about the policy considerations underpinning the measure, save for general statements such as that the government did not want to be seen to be soft on crime.[39]

The judgment of the highest court in *Teddy Bear Clinic for Abused Children v Minister of Justice and Constitutional Development*[40] is also noteworthy. This case involved a challenge to the criminalisation of consensual sexual conduct between adolescents (aged between 12 and 15) based on various constitutional rights. In support of their challenge, the applicants put up an expert report prepared by a child psychiatrist and a clinical psychologist. The report opined that the prohibitions would be ineffective and harmful as they would have an adverse effect on children's development, foster negative attitudes to sexual relations, increase the risk of unsafe sexual conduct and make children more reluctant to seek guidance from adults.[41] In response, the state did not take issue with the expert report but argued that the prohibitions served two purposes: (i) to deter adolescents from engaging in sexual conduct, thereby reducing the risks of unwanted pregnancies and sexually transmitted diseases; and (ii) to empower parents and guardians to emphasise the risks of early sexual intimacy. The court rejected both arguments. In a unanimous judgment, Khampepe J noted in relation to (i) that, while a court might, in the normal course, be prepared to assume the deterrent effect of a criminal prohibition, the position was different where the applicant had put up expert evidence to the contrary.[42] The state had failed to show that the prohibitions 'can reasonably be expected to control' the risks it identified and the evidence before the court was that the prohibition would not deter early sexual intimacy but would rather drive it underground.[43] Turning to (ii), Khampepe J held that the prohibitions would 'have the opposite of their intended effect' as they would disempower caregivers in dealing with adolescents, particularly given the statutory obligation to report child sex offences.[44] The court concluded that there was no rational link between the prohibitions and their stated purposes.[45]

NICRO and *Teddy Bear Clinic* illustrate that an assessment of the justifiability of a measure might depend on one of two types of evidence: evidence as to factual matters (such as evidence of lack of resources and costs that was not led in *NICRO*) or expert opinion evidence[46] (relied upon in *Teddy Bear Clinic*). Sometimes these

---

[38] ibid [39]–[40], [49].
[39] ibid [41], [44]–[46], [66].
[40] 2014 (2) SA 168 (CC).
[41] ibid [43]–[47], [72]–[73].
[42] ibid [88].
[43] ibid [87], [89].
[44] ibid [91], [92].
[45] ibid [94].
[46] In South African law, expert opinion evidence is admissible where the expert can assist the court in deciding the issue before it by virtue of specialist knowledge, training, skill or experience. See PJ Schwikkard and SE van der Merwe, *Principles of Evidence* (Cape Town, 4th edn, Juta & Co Ltd, 2016)

two types of evidence are intertwined. For example, an economist giving evidence as to the likely impact of a new regulatory measure might ultimately offer his or her expert opinion on an all-things-considered basis. However, this would invariably be based on facts relating to the relevant industry or analogous industries, such as the costs involved in operating within the industry, the level of efficiency or competition in the industry, the extent to which the industry contributes to job creation or the fiscus, and perhaps even the consequences of previous regulatory interventions.

The recent judgment of the Supreme Court of Appeal in *Esau*[47] is especially interesting for our purposes as it dealt with a challenge, on both Bill-of-Rights and administrative law grounds, to regulations that imposed a national lockdown in response to COVID-19. For the most part, the court found that the restrictions were a rational and proportionate response to the pandemic.[48] It rejected the contention that less invasive measures, such as mask-wearing, social distancing and hand-sanitising, would suffice to contain the virus. In doing so, the court relied upon the evidence of Professor Karim, an epidemiologist and chairperson of the Ministerial Advisory Committee on COVID-19. Karim indicated that the promotion of such measures through health messaging would take time and that a lockdown was the most effective and immediate way to regulate the public's behaviour.[49]

However, the court struck down two regulations as unconstitutional as well as irrational and unreasonable under the PAJA,[50] including a curtailment of exercise to specified activities within 5 km of one's home and between the hours of 6.00am and 9.00am. In addition to finding the restrictions on exercise disproportionate,[51] Plasket JA noted that, perversely, the short period increased the risk of transmission by encouraging people to congregate.[52] In making this finding the court apparently relied on common sense and, understandably, did not require expert evidence.

Also of interest is the case law in respect of the tobacco sales ban that was controversially imposed, by regulation, in response to the COVID-19 pandemic. In the first case, *Fair-Trade Independent Tobacco Association v President, RSA*,[53] the applicants rather surprisingly relied only on a rationality challenge. In rejecting this challenge the Gauteng High Court placed emphasis on the medical literature and expert reports and opinions put up by the state as to the link between smoking and

---

99–102. In the context of review applications, a court decides whether these requirements are met at the time of preparing its judgment on the merits, although an application to strike out all or part of the expert's affidavit might mean that the court decides separately on the admissibility of the evidence.

[47] *Esau* (n 11).
[48] ibid [142].
[49] ibid [126].
[50] ibid [147], [152].
[51] ibid [146], [152].
[52] ibid [145].
[53] 2020 (6) SA 513 (GP) (*FITA*).

severe illness from COVID-19, despite the criticism directed at this evidence by the applicant.[54] The court saw its role as determining whether the state's evidence provided 'a sufficient rational basis' for banning tobacco use as a means to curb the spread of the virus and to prevent a strain on the country's healthcare facilities.[55] Its role was not to assess whether that evidence was 'so cogent and conclusive as to establish a substantive or direct link with higher Covid-19-disease progression in smokers when compared with non-smokers', nor to 'undertake an in-depth comparison as to which of the parties' medical-research reports and opinions are better or more cogent than that of the other'.[56]

The reasoning and outcome in *FITA* may be contrasted with the subsequent judgment in *BATSA*,[57] in which the Supreme Court of Appeal upheld a constitutional challenge to the self-same tobacco ban. The court held that the ban limited various rights, including the rights to human dignity, property and freedom of trade, and emphasised the state's duty to establish the facts on which its argument of justification depended.[58] The court concluded that the state had fallen short in this regard. The state had not established that smokers were more likely than non-smokers to develop severe COVID-19 disease (the scientific evidence on this score being inconclusive), and it had failed to establish that stopping smoking for a short period would reduce the risk of severe infection.[59] The rapid growth of the illegal trade in tobacco meant that the ban had also failed to achieve its stated purpose of reducing the incidence of smoking; and finally, the ban was disproportionate in that the harm it caused outweighed its benefits.[60] Schippers JA concluded for a unanimous court that the extent to which the impugned regulation limited fundamental rights was disproportionate, 'particularly given the lack of factual and scientific evidence to support its promulgation'.[61]

It will be apparent that South African courts generally adopt a fairly rigorous approach to the production of evidence when the state seeks to justify limitations of rights based on factual assertions, particularly where the applicant has put up evidence suggesting that the limitation will not achieve its desired purpose or will indeed have the opposite effect.[62] However, the courts recognise that not all governmental purposes are susceptible of 'courtroom fact-finding' and that justifiability may sometimes be established by reasonable inference or common sense.

---

[54] ibid [36]–[40].
[55] ibid [41].
[56] ibid.
[57] *BATSA* (n 3).
[58] ibid [32], [36].
[59] ibid [45]–[55].
[60] ibid [56]–[79].
[61] ibid [78].
[62] See also *Centre for Child Law v Minister of Justice and Constitutional Development* 2009 (6) SA 632 (CC) [54]–[60] (upholding a challenge to the imposition of minimum sentencing for offenders aged 16 and 17). For a surprisingly less rigorous approach in the context of a limitation enquiry, see *British American Tobacco South Africa (Pty) Ltd v Minister of Health* [2012] 3 All SA 593 (SCA) (rejecting a challenge to a tobacco advertising ban).

This approach should apply equally to the judicial assessment of the stated purpose of an administrative act and the relation between that act and its purpose. This is both because there can be no rational connection between means and ends if the act is not 'reasonably likely' to produce its desired effect,[63] and because an act that is unlikely to serve its intended purpose will generally be unreasonable. We say 'generally' to allow for exceptional circumstances where the decision-maker reasonably believes, at the time of making the decision, that the act will serve its purpose, but it subsequently transpires that this is not the case or is not likely to be the case.

It is, however, important to take note of a key difference between the Constitution's limitation enquiry and administrative law review. While in a limitation enquiry the state (or other party relying upon the limitation) bears the burden of justification,[64] in administrative law the applicant bears the onus of establishing a reviewable irregularity.[65] In addition, courts may be required to show greater respect to the administrator's 'findings of fact and policy decisions'[66] in an administrative law review than a Bill of Rights challenge.

That being so, we suggest that in cases in which the applicant asserts that an administrative act (X) is unlikely to achieve its stated purpose (Y), the following approach ought to be adopted: (i) the applicant must put up a plausible basis for contending that X is not reasonably likely to achieve Y, which basis may be based on factual evidence or expert opinion (empirical data, statistical analysis, or expert economic, sociological, psychological or medical evidence) or, where appropriate, on inferential reasoning or common sense; (ii) if the applicant's plausible basis is based on factual evidence or expert opinion, the administrator must produce factual evidence or expert opinion of its own demonstrating either that the applicant's evidence is materially flawed or that X is in fact reasonably likely to result in Y;[67] and (iii) if the applicant's plausible basis is based on inference and common sense, the administrator may counter this through either inferential or common-sense reasoning of its own or by means of factual evidence or expert opinion which shows that X is reasonably likely to result in Y. If material disputes

---

[63] *SARIPA* (n 23) [58].

[64] *S v Makwanyane* 1995 (3) SA 391 (CC) [102]. The court in *NICRO* (n 35) [34] described the burden to justify a limitation as 'an *onus* of a special type'.

[65] See, eg, JR de Ville, *Judicial Review of Administrative Action in South Africa* (Durban, rev edn, LexisNexis Butterworths, 2005) 314–15. See also, in the context of a legality review, *New National Party of South Africa v Government of the Republic of South Africa* 1999 (3) SA 191 (CC) [19]: '[a]n objector who challenges the electoral scheme … bears the onus of establishing the absence of a legitimate government purpose, or the absence of a rational relationship between the measure and that purpose'. *cf* C Plasket, 'The Fundamental Right to Just Administrative Action: Judicial Review of Administrative Action in the Democratic South Africa' (PhD thesis, Rhodes University, 2002) 516–17.

[66] *Bato Star* (n 25) [48].

[67] As the court remarked in the context of the Bill of Rights challenge in *Teddy Bear Clinic* (n 40) [96]:

[W]here one party has put forward cogent expert documentary evidence indicating that the impugned provisions do not pass constitutional muster, the party seeking to uphold the validity of those provisions must advance evidence of a similar nature if he or she is to have any hope of success. Mere statements from the bar will not suffice.

of fact arise in this context, the administrator (as the respondent) would, in the absence of a referral to oral evidence, enjoy the benefit of the *Plascon-Evans* rule.[68] However, this should not attenuate the administrator's duty to make out a cogent case on the facts in response to an assertion, based on plausible evidence, that the administrative act is not likely to achieve its purpose. A 'culture of justification'[69] surely demands no less.

B. Adverse Impact

On the flip side of the impact coin, courts sometimes need to engage with the adverse impact of an administrative act. This occurs most commonly in relation to assertions that the administrator failed to take relevant considerations into account or acted unreasonably.

The approach of the Constitutional Court in *New Clicks*[70] is illuminating. The case dealt with a challenge to various aspects of medicine pricing regulations promulgated by the Minister of Health on the recommendation of a specialist Pricing Committee. The review application included a challenge to the maximum dispensing fee to be charged by pharmacists, which the empowering legislation (Medicines and Related Substances Act 101 of 1965, section 22G(2)(b)) required to be 'appropriate'. Faced with expert evidence submitted by the applicants to the effect that the level of the dispensing fee would put many pharmacies out of business, the court struck down the fee. Although the issue split the court, the judges forming the majority found that the fee was not 'appropriate'[71] or that the Minister and the Pricing Committee had failed to have proper regard to various relevant considerations, including the viability of the pharmacies under the dispensing-fee regime.[72]

In judgments that analysed the evidence and the record in some detail, Chaskalson CJ and Ngcobo J identified several shortcomings in the facts put up by the state.[73] For example, while Chaskalson CJ accepted the state's submission that the imposition of the regulated fee might change the market, as some pharmacies would close and the volumes of the remaining ones would thus increase, he noted the dearth of evidence to show the impact of this on the profitability of pharmacies and on access to medicines, especially in rural areas.[74] Chaskalson CJ went on to say:

> The only direct evidence of the impact of the dispensing fee on the viability of pharmacies is that contained in the written representations made to the Pricing Committee

---

[68] See the discussion of the rule in Part II above.
[69] See generally, E Mureinik, 'A Bridge to Where? Introducing the Interim Bill of Rights' (1994) 10 *South African Journal on Human Rights* 31.
[70] *New Clicks* (n 7).
[71] ibid [404].
[72] ibid [543].
[73] ibid; see, eg, at [342], [364], [378], [391]–[393], [535], [536], [541], [549], [558].
[74] ibid [388].

which form part of the record, and in the expert evidence relied on by the Pharmacies. Although there are criticisms of it, there is a substantial body of evidence which called for an answer by the Pricing Committee and the Minister. This, however, was not forthcoming.

...

'Accountability, responsiveness and openness' on the part of government are foundational values of our Constitution. An allegation has been made by professional organisations representing pharmacists that the dispensing fee will destroy the viability of pharmacies, and impair access to health care. That allegation is supported by a sufficient body of evidence to show that this is a real possibility. In the circumstances the applicants were under an obligation to explain how they satisfied themselves that this would not be the result of the dispensing fee prescribed in the regulations. They were the only persons who could provide this information. They did not, however, do so. Absent such explanation, there is sufficient evidence on record to show that the dispensing fee is not appropriate.[75]

Ngcobo J added that the Pricing Committee and the Minister were required to 'address the need for pharmacies to exist in a meaningful way' and 'be able to demonstrate that they have done so'.[76] He concluded that they had not.[77]

As noted above, in administrative law review proceedings, it is the applicant who bears the onus of establishing a ground of review and who must make out a factual as well as a legal case in its founding papers, and the respondent who has the benefit of the *Plascon-Evans* rule. However, that benefit may be easily lost by the respondent who fails to deny or contradict the applicant's factual averments, or who fails to do so meaningfully. In the context of review for unreasonableness based on adverse impact, the case of *Ehrlich*[78] illustrates this phenomenon well.

The decision being challenged was that of the second respondent, the head of a prison, who had refused the applicant and other medium-category inmates access to a section of the prison where the gymnasium was located. It appeared that several maximum-category convicts had recently been moved to that section, and the head was concerned to segregate prisoners in the different categories. However, the effect of the decision was to terminate a karate development programme that the applicant, a qualified karate instructor, had been facilitating in the gymnasium for about two years. The court concluded that the decision was unreasonable in a number of respects: it undermined statutory imperatives relating to the rehabilitation of prisoners and was discriminatory, irrational, disproportionate and unduly onerous in its effects.[79]

As with other such cases, this conclusion depended largely on facts showing the adverse impact of the decision on 'the lives and well-being of those affected'.[80] What is revealing in this regard is the court's readiness to accept the applicant's factual averments, even if unsubstantiated, where these were not denied or challenged by

---

[75] ibid [402] and [404]; see also [664]–[666] (Sachs J).
[76] ibid [531]; see also [536].
[77] ibid [543], [576].
[78] *Ehrlich* (n 26).
[79] ibid [43]–[44].
[80] *Bato Star* (n 25) [45].

the respondents. Amongst other key facts, Plasket J was willing to accept the applicant's undisputed evidence regarding the status of the karate programme in terms of the relevant departmental policy; the success of the programme and its value to the wellbeing and rehabilitation of prisoners; and its uniqueness as the only market-related skills development programme offered at the prison[81] – matters, one might suppose, more typically within the knowledge of the respondents. Notably, too, the court accepted the applicant's averment that there was no other suitable venue for the karate programme in the prison. Though this was indeed denied by the respondents, who suggested two alternative venues, the court found that insufficient evidence had been tendered regarding the suitability of these possible venues.[82] The court's robust attitude was no doubt encouraged by the reprehensible way in which the respondents had conducted the litigation, making 'efforts to frustrate the applicant at every turn',[83] and by sympathy for an applicant who was not only disadvantaged by incarceration but also unrepresented.

Reticence on the part of the administrator was similarly decisive in *Medirite (Pty) Ltd v South African Pharmacy Council*,[84] a case illustrating the 'fact-driven inquiry' that is typical of judicial review on the grounds of rationality and reasonableness. The case concerned a new rule made by the South African Pharmacy Council to the effect that a pharmacy located within other business premises would have to be permanently enclosed from the other premises by means of a floor-to-ceiling wall or partition. The appellant, which operated over a hundred pharmacies within the premises of a supermarket chain, challenged the rule under the PAJA and was ultimately successful. The Supreme Court of Appeal readily accepted that a box-like enclosure of this type would have severe consequences for affected pharmacies in terms of expense and inconvenience: for example, it would impede the free flow of customers and complicate ventilation and lighting.[85] Yet there was no explanation in the Rule 53 record or in the respondents' papers as to why it regarded the measure to be necessary. Written reasons provided to the appellant by the council (in response to an earlier request under the PAJA) emphasised the importance of clear demarcation of pharmacies and the need to simplify the minimum standards of demarcation – but the existing rules already called for clear demarcation, and the new measure was hardly a simple solution.[86] In the absence of a 'factual foundation that demonstrated any existing mischief that needed to be addressed' by way of such a wall, the court found the decision arbitrary and irrational.[87]

The measure was also held to be unreasonable on the basis that the costs – the expense involved and the adverse consequences for the supermarket business

---

[81] *Ehrlich* (n 26) [18] (status); [20] and [43] (value and success); and [24] (uniqueness). In contrast, the applicant's claim that many medium-category prisoners had been allowed unsupervised access to the section was substantiated: see [35].
[82] ibid [30]–[32].
[83] ibid [26].
[84] [2015] ZASCA 27 (20 March 2015) [6].
[85] ibid.
[86] ibid [11]–[15].
[87] ibid [16].

model – were wholly disproportionate to the benefits sought to be achieved. In this regard, the council had failed to indicate why it felt that a less onerous type of demarcation would not have sufficed and had compounded this error by conceding that it might be open to a less drastic alternative. In short, the council had failed to justify its use of a sledgehammer to crack a nut.[88]

Ultimately, as Leach JA explained, the council was 'obliged to weigh up the effect of its rules on those affected'.[89] This observation sheds light on the nature of the proportionality enquiry in administrative law review and how it may differ from proportionality in a Bill of Rights challenge. In a reasonableness review, proportionality is not concerned with 'pure' proportionality of outcome, as it does not involve a comparison between the likely beneficial and adverse effects of the administrative act in an absolute manner. Rather, the question is whether the administrator weighed those effects appropriately. Thus, the evidence to be led relates primarily to the disproportionality of the administrative act viewed through the lens of the information before the administrator, or the information that the administrator ought to have sourced. In line with this, it is generally impermissible for an applicant for reasonableness review to lead *new* evidence of adverse impact.

Part III of this chapter has explored the crucial role played by facts when a court is assessing the impact of an administrative act, whether that impact is beneficial or adverse. In Part IV, we turn to the relevance of facts and information in the context of remedy.

IV. Facts and Remedy

In judicial review proceedings, the PAJA, section 8(1) empowers a court to make 'any order that is just and equitable'. It goes on to list various remedial possibilities, including the remedy primarily associated with administrative law review: setting aside (quashing). However, whether this or any other remedy presents a just and equitable solution in a particular case can depend critically on facts concerning its likely effects. Then, too, the amount of information available to a court is germane to the exercise of its power in exceptional cases to 'substitute' the decision rather than remit it to the original decision-maker.

A. Setting Aside

It is well established in South African administrative law that setting aside is a discretionary remedy. In recent years the exercise of this discretion has attracted attention in the context of public procurement, where setting aside has sometimes been refused for reasons of practicality, pragmatism and fairness. In a case concerning a

---

[88] ibid [18]–[22].
[89] ibid [21].

tender for the disposal of medical waste, for instance, the court reasoned that setting aside the unlawful award would not only disrupt the provision of an essential service and require further public expenditure but would also have severe consequences for the successful bidder, an innocent party.[90] Conversely, however, a contract for the collection and processing of scrap metal was set aside even where it had only three months left to run.[91] In this instance, relevant facts included the absence of public policy considerations, blameworthy conduct on the part of the winning bidder and the ease with which the work could be taken over by another contractor.

The AllPay matter is an especially dramatic illustration of such factors at work. This *cause célèbre* concerned a massive tender invited by the South African Social Security Agency for the national payment of social welfare grants. The award of a five-year contract to Cash Paymaster Services (CPS) was challenged by an unsuccessful bidder, AllPay, and was ultimately found to have been unlawful.

In *AllPay Consolidated Investment Holdings (Pty) Ltd v Chief Executive Officer, South African Social Security Agency*[92] (the 'merits' judgment) the Constitutional Court declared invalid the award of the tender to CPS in obedience with section 172(1)(a) of the Constitution. However, the court was unwilling to make a final decision on remedy without the benefit of information and argument on issues such as the extent to which the grant payment system would be disrupted if the tender were set aside. Accordingly, the court suspended the declaration of invalidity and directed the parties to furnish information on affidavit, as well as written submissions, on questions such as 'the time and steps necessary, and the costs likely to be incurred, in the initiation and completion of a new tender process for a national social grant payment system'.[93]

A second judgment[94] was devoted to crafting an appropriate remedy in the light of the information provided. The resulting solution effectively minimised the danger of disruption while vindicating the rule of law. It took the form of a declaration of invalidity which the court suspended pending the initiation of a new tender process and an order that, failing a new tender award, the declaration would be further suspended so that the existing five-year contract could run its course.[95]

Where a court exercises its discretion in favour of setting aside, it may also have to consider the possibility of substitution rather than remission to the original decision-maker. As shown by the discussion that follows, facts and information can be highly relevant to this exercise too.

---

[90] *Millennium Waste Management v Chairman, Tender Board: Limpopo Province* 2008 (2) SA 481 (SCA).
[91] *Eskom Holdings Ltd v New Reclamation Group (Pty) Ltd* 2009 (4) SA 628 (SCA).
[92] 2014 (1) SA 604 (CC) [98].
[93] ibid.
[94] *AllPay Consolidated Investment Holdings (Pty) Ltd v Chief Executive Officer, South African Social Security Agency* 2014 (4) SA 179 (CC).
[95] ibid [78].

B. Substitution

At common law, setting aside is usually coupled with remittal to the original decision-maker for re-decision, while substitution of the decision by the court itself is the exception. This is partly explained by the review/appeal distinction and the courts' reluctance to be perceived as usurping administrative powers.[96] However, institutional advantages also play a role. By reason of 'the variety of its composition, by experience, and its access to sources of relevant information and expertise', the administrator is likely to be better equipped than a court to make the decision.[97]

Substitution has traditionally been indicated (i) where the decision is a foregone conclusion; (ii) where further delay would cause the applicant unjustifiable prejudice; (iii) where the original decision-maker has exhibited bias or incompetence; and (iv) where the court is in as good a position as the administrator to make the decision.

Section 8(1)(c)(ii)(aa) of the PAJA is stricter than the common law in that it permits substitution only in 'exceptional cases'. For a number of years, the PAJA test for such cases simply drew on the common law factors. In *Trencon Construction (Pty) Ltd v Industrial Development Corporation of South Africa Ltd*,[98] however, in the context of a construction tender put out by the Industrial Development Corporation (IDC), the Constitutional Court set out to clarify and restructure the PAJA test. It held that while all the common law factors must be considered, the first and fourth weigh more heavily. Indeed, the fourth factor was elevated to a threshold question to the extent that 'there can never be a foregone conclusion unless a court is in as good a position as the administrator'.[99] As Khampepe J acknowledged, the administrator's superior position is largely the product of expertise and information. Accordingly, the court is least likely to match that position at an early stage in the decision-making process, 'where the application of the administrator's expertise is still required and a court does not have the pertinent information before it'.[100]

In this instance, the IDC had disqualified the appellant, the preferred bidder, and had awarded the tender to a competitor. The High Court set aside this action for error of law and took the unusual step of awarding the tender to the appellant. The sole question before the Constitutional Court was whether the High Court had been justified in opting for substitution rather than remission to the IDC. Unlike the Supreme Court of Appeal in the same matter, Khampepe J upheld the substitution order. She was confident that the court was in as good a position as the IDC to award the tender, particularly since the error of law had occurred right at the end of the procurement process. The only step that remained was approval by the IDC's executive committee, so the court had the benefit of all the

---

[96] *National Energy Regulator of South Africa v PG Group (Pty) Ltd* 2020 (1) SA 450 (CC) [90].
[97] *Gauteng Gambling Board v Silverstar Development Ltd* 2005 (4) SA 67 (SCA) [29].
[98] 2015 (5) SA 245 (CC).
[99] ibid [50].
[100] ibid [48].

information and recommendations that would have been before that committee.[101] Khampepe J went on to find that the award to the appellant was a foregone conclusion and it would be unfair to remit the matter to the IDC.[102]

In *Gavrić v Refugee Status Determination Officer*,[103] the same court went considerably further after setting aside the adverse decision of a Refugee Status Determination Officer (RSDO). Here, as the court acknowledged, the applicant's refugee status under the Refugees Act 130 of 1998 was by no means a foregone conclusion.[104] Nevertheless, and notwithstanding the court's relative lack of expertise, the majority forged ahead and decided that status, partly on account of significant delays and partly on the basis that the information at its disposal put the court in a *better* position than the RSDO to make the decision.[105] The court went on to rule that the applicant was not eligible for asylum under the Refugees Act, section 4(1)(b) as there was a reasonable belief that he had committed serious non-political crimes. Most unusually, then, the substitution order went against the applicant. All in all, and as the dissenting judges cogently pointed out,[106] *Gavrić* hardly seemed the ideal case for such an order. The majority seems indeed to have disregarded the sage advice of O'Regan J in *Bato Star* about the dangers of attributing to courts 'superior wisdom in relation to matters entrusted to other branches of government'.[107]

In other cases, the absence of relevant facts has played a crucial role in courts declining to grant substitution even where their frustration with the administration pulled in the opposite direction. In *Intertrade Two (Pty) Ltd v MEC for Roads and Public Works, Eastern Cape*,[108] for example, the court found that the provincial administration had delayed unreasonably in awarding tenders for maintenance and repair work at state hospitals. As a result, the court was tempted to make the award itself. Plasket J pointed out on behalf of a full bench that the applicant had endured 'shameful treatment' at the hands of the administration over a lengthy period and that the administration had displayed 'an alarming degree of ineptitude', gross incompetence and 'a disturbing contempt for the Constitution and for the people of the province'.[109] The resulting delays in the award of the tenders had placed the lives and wellbeing of patients at risk.[110] However, the court reluctantly held that it was not possible for it to award the tenders as it did not have enough information to do so. As Plasket J acknowledged, the court's decision to make such an award would be irrational if it were made without adequate information.[111]

---

[101] ibid [57]–[58].
[102] ibid [59]–[78].
[103] 2019 (1) SA 21 (CC).
[104] ibid [83] and [84]–[115].
[105] ibid [83].
[106] Not least because the majority effectively operated as a court of first and last instance and without the benefit of oral argument. On these and other points, see the judgment of Jafta J (Dlodlo AJ concurring) [122]–[163].
[107] *Bato Star* (n 25) [48].
[108] 2007 (6) SA 442 (Ck).
[109] ibid [5], [43].
[110] ibid [17].
[111] ibid [43].

He went on to remark that 'there are limits on the powers of the court to repair damage that has been caused by a breakdown in the administrative process' and noted the irony that the court might have been able to order substitution had the administration made a better job of the tender process – as the relevant information might then have been before the court.[112]

V. Concluding Remarks

This chapter contributes to an area of South African administrative law that has been rather neglected despite its great practical significance: the courts' treatment of factual questions and evidence in judicial review. We have highlighted the importance of facts and evidence in administrative law review in two contexts. First, establishing certain grounds of review (whether under the PAJA or the legality principle) may require the court to evaluate the likely impact of an administrative act, beneficial or adverse, or the administrator's weighing of its likely effects. Secondly, facts are often relevant to remedy. The court's choice of setting aside or some other remedy may well depend upon information as to the likely effects of that remedy, and the power of substitution in exceptional cases generally depends upon the court's being as well informed factually as the administrator.

While administrative law review never takes place in a factual vacuum, this chapter has shown that the relevance of facts and the way in which they are established can vary considerably, as can the court's attitude to the need for formal evidence. We have proposed an approach to the judicial assessment of the stated purpose of an administrative act and the relation between the act and its purpose. A crucial question that remains is when the courts will insist upon factual evidence or expert opinion substantiating the link between the act and its purpose, when this link may be established by inferential reasoning or common sense, and when a combination of the two will be appropriate. The correct approach will likely depend on the facts of each case. As the Supreme Court of Appeal has noted, whether a decision is rationally related to its purpose is, by its nature, 'a factual enquiry blended with a measure of judgement'.[113]

In the case of remedies, it is important for the courts to adopt and maintain the flexible approach that is implicit in the task of determining just and equitable relief. As we have seen, at times this requires courts to be conscious of not only their lack of institutional competence but also the limitations of the facts that have been placed before them. It may also, in appropriate cases, require the court to call for additional legal submissions and affidavits in order to be able to make an informed decision based on the prevailing facts.

---

[112] ibid [46].
[113] *Minister of Home Affairs v Scalabrini Centre* 2013 (6) SA 421 (SCA) [66].

11
Mistake of Fact as a Ground of Review: Distinct and Defensible

HANNA WILBERG*

I. Introduction

One of the main issues concerning facts in public law adjudication is whether mistakes of fact should give rise to a ground of judicial review. The leading case establishing mistake of fact as a distinct ground of review is still the decision of the England and Wales Court of Appeal in *E v Secretary of State for the Home Department*.[1] The status of the case remains somewhat uncertain in both the United Kingdom (UK) and New Zealand (NZ). It has still not been authoritatively approved by the UK Supreme Court,[2] and some decisions have noted concerns about its scope.[3] For NZ, it was adopted by the Supreme Court in *Ririnui v Landcorp Farming Ltd*,[4] but the treatment there was very brief and quite ambivalent.[5]

At the same time, there has been a much broader move towards greater scrutiny of factual determinations in judicial review, forming part of the various modern expansions of substantive review.[6] It may seem that *E* has been overtaken by these

---

*My thanks go to Ah Song Sunwoo, Jovana Nedeljkov and Yoav Zionov for research assistance, and to the New Zealand Law Foundation for generously funding Yoav's work. Thanks also for helpful comments and discussion to the attendees at the SLS 2019 Annual Conference, University of Central Lancashire, September 2019; a Cambridge Centre for Public Law seminar in September 2019; and the 'Public Law in Three Nations' Symposium, University of Melbourne, December 2015, where I presented versions of this chapter; and to Professor Christopher Forsyth for a helpful e-mail exchange. Any errors and infelicities remain my own.

[1] *E v Secretary of State for the Home Department* [2004] EWCA Civ 49, [2004] QB 1044.
[2] As noted in Christopher Forsyth, 'Error of Fact Revisited: Waiting for the "*Anisminic* Moment"' (2018) 23 JR 1, 8–9. In *IA (Iran) v Secretary of State for the Home Department* [2014] UKSC 6 [54]–[55], the Supreme Court set out the *E* requirements but did not find them satisfied in the case; similarly, see *Rainbow Insurance Co Ltd v Financial Services Commission* [2015] UKPC 15, not citing *E* but effectively finding its requirements not made out.
[3] See, eg, *Shaheen v Secretary of State for the Home Department* [2005] EWCA Civ 1294, [2006] Imm AR 57.
[4] *Ririnui v Landcorp Farming Ltd* [2016] NZSC 62, [2016] 1 NZLR 1056, [54].
[5] For discussion, see H Wilberg, 'Mistakes about Mistake of Fact: The New Zealand Story' (2017) 28 *Public Law Review* 248, Part IV.
[6] See, eg, P Daly, 'Facticity: Judicial Review of Factual Error in Comparative Perspective' in P Cane et al (eds), *The Oxford Handbook of Comparative Administrative Law* (Oxford, OUP, 2020).

broader developments. A separate ground with the strict limits set in *E* may now seem redundant, and perhaps a little quaint.

In this chapter I argue that the ground in *E* should be approved and query whether it is redundant. It should be approved because the limits set in *E* deal with the objections to mistake of fact as a ground. It may not be redundant because it applies in cases that are not clearly covered by the broader move towards greater scrutiny of factual determinations.

Discussion in this chapter is confined to UK and NZ law. I will not engage here with the particular constitutional and statutory contexts that would be relevant to this discussion in other common law jurisdictions.

In the three main parts of this chapter (Parts III to V), I will seek to illuminate the limits of mistake of fact as a ground of review, why it is defensible, and how it remains distinct and useful.

To help define the limits of mistake of law as a ground of review, Part III will focus on the first and especially the second of the requirements established in *E*: the fact must be an existing fact, and must be 'established' in the sense of being 'uncontentious and objectively verifiable'.[7] On my proposed understanding, the second requirement excludes challenges to evaluative determinations of two types: evaluation of the facts in applying a broad or vague legal test, and evaluation of conflicting evidence in arriving at findings of facts.

The attraction of this understanding, as I will argue in Part IV, is that it allows the ground to serve its desired purpose of serving justice and good government, while avoiding three objections to review of factual determinations. The first objection is that, for constitutional reasons, judicial review must not encroach on the merits. In response to this, I will argue that factual determinations are part of the merits only if they involve one of the two types of evaluative determination. The second objection is that judicial review is not a suitable procedure for fact-finding. However, there is no need for a fact-finding procedure if there is no conflicting evidence. Finally, the third objection is that judicial review of factual determinations may unduly compromise finality and may go beyond proportionate dispute resolution. The answer to this objection depends on what other avenues of dispute-resolution are available. However, I will argue that this concern carries less weight where review is used to correct incontrovertible mistakes rather than to re-open contested evaluative factual determinations.

Finally, as I will argue in Part V, the mistake of fact ground on this understanding remains potentially distinct and useful. It is not clearly rendered redundant by the broader expansion of substantive review, including the increased scrutiny of factual determinations. Two features of the ground can be identified as distinct. First, it is available (subject to the materiality test) for a single erroneous factual conclusion or understanding, regardless of whether it renders the outcome unreasonable or disproportionate. Secondly, this ground is available regardless of whether the context calls for more intensive review or a proportionality test.

[7] *E* (n 1) [63], [66].

Before I expand on these arguments, let me set the scene in Part II, by outlining the apparently conflicting normative concerns that are engaged by review of factual determinations.

II. The Apparent Normative Tension

Underlying the debate about whether and to what extent mistake of fact should be a ground for review, there is an apparent tension. On the one hand, there are weighty reasons to quash decisions that are affected by an incontrovertible factual error. A decision-maker who laboured under a material error of fact was never in a position to consider the true merits of a person's case.[8] Justice and fairness for affected individuals therefore calls for a remedy.[9] Furthermore, the rule of law and fidelity to legislative choices are also implicated: a statutory regime will not operate as intended in such a case.[10]

On the other hand, the courts' judicial review jurisdiction must be limited for equally weighty constitutional reasons: judges exercising the supervisory jurisdiction must respect a statutory decision-maker's authority. This is often expressed as distinguishing judicial review from a full appeal on the merits. Where that distinction and that limit are disregarded, courts usurp the role of the statutory decision-maker. In doing so, they fail to respect Parliament's allocation of authority to that decision-maker. The limit and distinction also reflect the limits of the courts' constitutional legitimacy and institutional capacity relative to executive or administrative decision-makers. The latter are democratically accountable, directly or indirectly, and have procedures for public participation. They also have better procedures for exploring the full range of options and better access to expertise and experience to help with judging those options. Two fundamental constitutional principles are thus engaged: parliamentary sovereignty and separation of powers. The limits arising from these considerations have been widely understood as entailing rejection of mistake of fact as a ground of review, because such a ground was seen as going to the merits.[11]

Unless courts are to discard this limit of judicial review, and simply arrogate to themselves full authority to make the decision again, there must always be *some*

---

[8] For a similar point, see C Forsyth and E Dring, 'The Final Frontier: The Emergence of Material Error of Fact as a Ground for Judicial Review' in C Forsyth et al (eds), *Effective Judicial Review: A Cornerstone of Good Governance* (Oxford, OUP, 2010) 259–60.
[9] See S Elias 'Judgery and the Rule of Law' (2015) 14 Otago LR 49, 55, in the context of court decisions: 'Nothing rankles like a mistake of fact.'
[10] E Liu, '"Fairness" for Mistake of Fact: a Mistake in Fact' [2020] PL 428, 440–41.
[11] See, eg, H Woolf et al, *De Smith's Judicial Review* (London, 8th edn, Sweet & Maxwell, 2018) [11-036], [11-051]; PA Joseph, *Constitutional and Administrative Law in New Zealand* (Wellington, 5th edn, Brookers, 2021) 1064; M Kent QC, 'Widening the Scope of Review for Error of Fact' [1999] Judicial Review 239, [2], [15]; *JC Pring v Wanganui District Council* (1999) 5 ELRNZ 464; [1999] NZRMA 519 (CA) [7].

autonomy reserved for the statutory decision-maker. Therefore, it is never an argument for expansion of review that, in the absence of such expansion, people will have to live with decisions which a court considers wrong in some sense: that is a necessary aspect of the power being the statutory decision-maker's power, not the reviewing court's. The question is where to draw the line and how to strike the balance between the decision-maker's autonomous authority and the court's supervisory powers.

III. The Limits: What the Second Requirement Means

My first main question concerns what is meant by mistake of fact as a distinct ground of review. The main issue here is how to understand the limits of the ground as set out in the four requirements of the test in *E*.

First, however, a preliminary point. Mistake of fact as a new and distinct ground of review implies, in my view, review of factual determinations on a substitutionary 'correctness' standard. That must be so, because rationality review of factual determinations has always been available. *Edwards v Bairstow* allowed the courts to intervene where a decision was not tenable in light of the facts found and on a proper understanding of the law.[12] *Re Erebus Royal Commission; Air New Zealand Ltd v Mahon* allowed intervention when there was no probative evidence to support the determination.[13] While those grounds were available only in extreme cases, the threshold for intervention is now lower in contexts that attract heightened scrutiny.[14] The new ground established in *E* adds to this by allowing courts to intervene on a substitutionary 'correctness' standard, but only for strictly limited types of error. I now turn to consider those limits on the ground.

The four requirements established in *E* are as follows:[15]

(1) The mistake must be 'as to an existing fact, including as to the availability of evidence'.
(2) The fact must be 'established' in the sense of being 'uncontentious and objectively verifiable'.
(3) The party relying on the mistake must not be responsible for it.
(4) The mistake must be material, though not decisive.

---

[12] *Edwards (Inspector of Taxes) v Bairstow* [1956] AC 14 (HL) 36.
[13] *Re Erebus Royal Commission; Air New Zealand Ltd v Mahon* [1983] NZLR 662 (PC) 671, 681.
[14] For discussion of how this applies to factual determinations, see Part V below.
[15] *E* (n 1) [63], [66].

I will focus here on the second requirement. New Zealand cases have similarly noted that it is not a mistake to adopt one of two or more reasonably open conclusions in relation to the facts.[16]

In order to avoid the three objections outlined in the introduction, my argument is that the second requirement in *E* must be understood as being designed to avoid challenges to evaluative determinations. Understood this way, the second requirement encompasses two separate aspects. First, the mistake must lie in finding or understanding the facts,[17] rather than in evaluating the facts for the purposes of applying a broad or vague legal test. Alleged mistakes as to the latter are not 'objectively verifiable' in terms of the test in *E*. Secondly, there must be no need to evaluate conflicting evidence in order to find the facts. Otherwise, the alleged mistake is not 'uncontentious'.

In this part, I explain these two aspects of the 'not evaluation' limit and survey the support in the commentary and case law for them.

A. Not Evaluation of Facts for the Purpose of Applying a Broad or Vague Test

The first type of evaluative determination that cannot be challenged as a mistake of fact on my proposed understanding is evaluating the facts for the purposes of applying an evaluative legal test. This is to be distinguished from mistaken findings or understandings of fact, which can be challenged. The latter involve some error in engaging with the evidence: for instance, misunderstanding the evidence or overlooking relevant parts of the evidence. This distinction has also been proposed by Christopher Forsyth and other commentators.[18]

Let me give some examples of mistakes in fact-finding that were held to qualify as a mistake of fact, and rightly so on my understanding. One example is found in *Charter Holdings v Commissioner of Inland Revenue*.[19] The plaintiff

---

[16] See, eg, *New Zealand Fishing Industry Association Inc v Minister of Agriculture and Fisheries* [1988] 1 NZLR 544 (CA), 552 (Cooke P); *Northern Inshore Fisheries Companies Ltd v Minister of Fisheries* (HC, Wellington, CP 235-01, 4 March 2002, Ronald Young J) [49].

[17] My category of finding the facts includes both primary findings and inferences, as long as they are factual inferences drawn from the evidence, as opposed to legal inferences drawn from an evaluation of the facts (for the latter use of the term inference, see, eg, *Benmax v Austin Motor Co Ltd* [1955] AC 370 (HL) 733–34, 736, 737).

[18] Forsyth (n 2) 8–9. See also Forsyth and Dring (n 8) 258 (this test preserves the decision-maker's area of judgment); R Williams, 'When is an Error not an Error? Reform of Jurisdictional Review of Error of Law and Fact' [2007] PL 793, 797–98; Liu (n 10) 443–44. For examples that suggest both of my proposed limits, see M Elliott and JNE Varuhas, *Administrative Law: Text and Materials* (Oxford, OUP, 2016) 76.

[19] *Charter Holdings Ltd v Commissioner of Inland Revenue* [2016] NZCA 499. This case did not cite or adopt *E* (n 1); it relied on older NZ authority instead.

company's director had failed to claim a tax credit for business losses when filling in the relevant tax return form, and his explanation was that he had misunderstood the form. An Inland Revenue officer disbelieved that explanation, and instead concluded that the director must have subsequently invented the losses in question. She took that view because she mistakenly thought that the director had correctly filled in the same form for his personal tax return. In fact, the same incorrect response had been given in that other form. The mistake in this example was due to misapprehending the state of the available evidence.[20]

A further example is found in *R (Haile) v Immigration Appeal Tribunal*.[21] This pre-dated *E* but, as noted in *E*, already effectively applied the mistake of fact ground recognised in that case.[22] The decision-maker determining an asylum claim confused two different organisations. The claimant in his evidence referred to an organisation called EPRP. The decision-maker mistook this as a reference to a different organisation called EPRF. On that basis, he considered the evidence not credible. Had he understood that the reference was to the EPRP, then the evidence would have been perfectly credible. The mistake in this case was due to misunderstanding a part of the evidence.[23]

The same line was also drawn by the Supreme Court in *R (A) v Croydon London Borough Council*,[24] albeit the Court was not relying on the mistake of fact ground. The Court held that evaluative questions of fact, such as whether a child is 'in need', were for the decision-maker. In contrast, factual questions on which there is a right or wrong answer were for the court. Whether a person is a 'child' fell into the latter category, since the term was defined by reference to a set age limit.[25] The Court presented these points as simply matters of statutory interpretation. It did not mention mistake of fact, nor did it consider that recourse to the jurisdictional fact doctrine was needed.[26] However, the distinction and its use to allocate power between the decision-maker and the court directly correspond to the limit on the mistake of fact ground that I am proposing in this part.

This proposed limit is also consistent with both the outcome and the reasoning in *Puhlhofer v Hillingdon LBC*.[27] This case has often been cited for strict deference

---

[20] This was one of several errors alleged in this case, but the only one that clearly meets the *E* requirements. The other errors concerned evaluative questions but may have satisfied the 'no evidence' ground established in *Re Erebus* (n 13).

[21] *R (Haile) v Immigration Appeal Tribunal* [2001] EWCA Civ 663, [2002] INLR 283.

[22] *E* (n 1) [58].

[23] Further examples of mistakes in fact-finding or in understanding the facts include the mistakes that were successfully relied on in *Glover v Secretary of State for the Environment* [1981] JPL 110; *Hollis v Secretary of State for the Environment* (1984) 47 P & CR 351; *R (Ahmed (Naeem)) v Secretary of State for the Home Department* [2004] EWCA Civ 552; *Zhao v Legal Complaints Review Officer* [2012] NZHC 3247, [2013] NZAR 193; *Deliu v Hong and Legal Complaints Review Officer* [2012] NZHC 158, [2012] NZAR 209; *Deliu v Hong* [2015] NZHC 492.

[24] *R (A) v Croydon London Borough Council* [2009] UKSC 8, [2009] 1 WLR 2557.

[25] ibid [26]–[27].

[26] It is difficult to know what to make of this: see, eg, P Craig, *Administrative Law* (London, 9th edn, Sweet & Maxwell, 2021) [17-013]–[17-014].

[27] *Puhlhofer v Hillingdon LBC* [1986] AC 484 (HL).

on questions of fact and hence against mistake of fact as a ground.[28] Yet the factual question at issue would not have qualified as mistake of fact on my proposed understanding. It concerned the application of a vague term that very much called for evaluation of the facts: whether a boarding house qualified as 'accommodation' for the purpose of a statutory duty to house the homeless. Moreover, the much-cited passage calling for strict deference on questions of fact was expressly addressed to this type of evaluative question: where the 'fact involves a broad spectrum ranging from the obvious to the debatable to the just conceivable'.[29]

Finally, the proposed exclusion of this type of evaluative factual question is also consistent with cases such as *R v Monopolies and Mergers Commission ex p South Yorkshire Transport*[30] and *Bryson v Three Foot Six Ltd*.[31] In this line of cases, courts have applied the highly deferential rationality test established in *Edwards v Bairstow*[32] to questions concerning the application of broad or vague legal tests. In *South Yorkshire Transport*, the relevant question was whether a merger had resulted in the business covering a 'substantial' part of the United Kingdom.[33] In *Bryson*, the issue was whether Mr Bryson was an employee rather than an independent contractor.[34] The definition of 'employee' in the Act and in case law took the form of a complex evaluative test, requiring several factors to be weighed. If the alleged mistakes had qualified as mistakes of fact in terms of *E*, that would now entail the court correcting the mistake rather than reviewing for rationality. However, on my proposed understanding, the alleged mistakes did not qualify as mistakes of fact: they concerned the evaluation of the facts for the purposes of applying a broad or vague legal test.[35]

Confusion can arise about this final line of cases, because they concern the difficult line between law and fact.[36] They are authority that while the interpretation of statutory tests is a question of law, the application of those tests can be a question of fact if the test leaves room for judgment in application. But the point here is that questions of fact are not all the same.[37] Where application of a statutory test is

---

[28] See, eg, TH Jones, 'Mistake of Fact in Administrative Law' [1990] PL 507, 518, where the point being made here is briefly acknowledged as a 'complicating factor'.
[29] *Puhlhofer* (n 27) 518.
[30] *R v Monopolies and Mergers Commission ex p South Yorkshire Transport Ltd* [1993] 1 WLR 23 (HL) (*South Yorkshire Transport*).
[31] *Bryson v Three Foot Six Ltd* [2005] 3 NZLR 721 (SC).
[32] *Edwards v Bairstow* (n 12).
[33] *South Yorkshire Transport Ltd* (n 30) 32–33.
[34] *Bryson* (n 31) [3]–[5], [13]. Further examples of this type of factual mistake that does not qualify under *E* include *Vodafone New Zealand Ltd v Telecom New Zealand Ltd* [2011] NZSC 138; *Moyna v Secretary of State for Work and Pensions* [2003] UKHL 44, [2003] 1 WLR 1929.
[35] cf Joseph (n 11), 1063–65, claiming that *Bryson* establishes that review for mistake of fact in New Zealand is restricted to cases where the *Edwards v Bairstow* test is satisfied. I suggest this view should be rejected.
[36] The meaning and application of 'employee' is a classic example of the difficulty in drawing this line between law and fact: Craig (n 26) ch 16.
[37] See ibid [17-002].

classified as a question of fact on the basis that the test leaves room for judgment in application, it is not the type of factual determination that can be challenged by the mistake of fact ground as defined in *E*. A challenge to this type of determination fails to meet the second requirement in *E* on my proposed understanding.

It is worth noting that this proposed distinction between different types of factual determinations has also been invoked in the context of general appeals. It is, of course, axiomatic that the scope of a general appeal is larger than the scope of judicial review. However, issues still arise as to the extent to which an appellate court should substitute its views for that of the first instance court. In that context, it has been said that questions involving evaluation of the facts are 'closely analogous to the exercise of discretion' and should be approached in the same way on appeal.[38]

Evaluation is involved in applying the law whenever the law uses evaluative terms such as 'substantial', or complex evaluative test such as that for 'employee'. That means that not all questions of application are evaluative: there are others that are susceptible of simple right and wrong answers. For instance, we have already seen in *Croydon* that the legislation defined 'child' by reference to a clear-cut age limit. There was therefore no evaluation required to apply this term. Similarly, in *Oggi Advertising Ltd v Auckland City Council*, a bylaw imposed different requirements for registration of billboards depending on the date of construction.[39] Applying that legal test involved no evaluation of the facts.

B. Not Evaluation of Conflicting Evidence

Even where a mistake lies in finding or understanding the facts, it may still fail the second requirement in *E* by failing the other aspect of that requirement: on my proposed understanding, establishing the correct facts must not call for evaluation of conflicting or contested evidence. A similar limit has been proposed by Kent.[40] This limit has also featured in the cases on the mistake of fact ground. However, authority on it is somewhat mixed, as we will see.

One example of a contested factual issue is resolving a conflict between witnesses by assessing their credibility and reliability. The House of Lords has noted generally that such factual disputes cannot readily be resolved in judicial review proceedings.[41] In *VH (Malawi) v Secretary of State for the Home Department*, the

---

[38] *Assicurazioni Generali SpA v Arab Insurance Group Practice Note* [2002] EWCA Civ 1642, [2003] 1 WLR 577 [16]; affirmed in *Datec Electronics Holdings Ltd v United Parcels Service Ltd* [2007] UKHL 23, [2007] 1 WLR 1325 [46]–[47]. See also *Biogen Inc v Medeva plc* [1997] RPC 1 (HL) 45.

[39] *Oggi Advertising Ltd v Auckland City Council* [2005] NZAR 451 (HC).

[40] Kent (n 11): the mistake must be 'manifest' in the sense of not requiring a prolonged or heavily contested inquiry. See also Elliott and Varuhas (n 18) 76 for examples that suggest both of my proposed limits.

[41] *E v Chief Constable of the Royal Ulster Constabulary* [2008] UKHL 66, [2009] 1 AC 536 [31].

Court of Appeal applied this to the mistake of fact ground.[42] A challenge to the weighing of conflicting evidence did not satisfy the second requirement in *E*;[43] review was available only on grounds of *Wednesbury* unreasonableness.[44]

In *Bubb v Wandsworth London Borough Council*, a disputed question of fact had to be determined by reference to a great deal of circumstantial evidence.[45] Again, this could be challenged only on rationality grounds.[46] Yet another example is weighing up conflicting expert evidence or competing scientific opinion. Attempts to invoke versions of the mistake of fact ground in relation to this type of issue have also been rejected.[47]

In contrast, examples of cases where this aspect of the second requirement was met are again provided by *Haile*[48] and *Charter Holdings*.[49] The decision-maker in *Haile* misheard the applicant's reference to EPRP as a reference to a very different organisation called EPRF. There was no conflict in the evidence: the problem lay purely in the decision-maker's attention to that evidence. In *Charter Holdings*, the Inland Revenue officer's belief that the company's director had correctly completed the relevant form on another occasion was due to the officer's incorrect memory of the relevant evidence (the other completed form), which clearly showed the opposite.

In some cases, however, this aspect of the second requirement in *E* has not been observed. This may have been the case in *Oggi*, where the mistake concerned the date on which a billboard had been constructed.[50] Although this met the first aspect of the second requirement in *E* (it concerned finding or understanding the facts), it may not have met the second aspect. The reviewing Court had before it two affidavits that apparently conflicted concerning the date of construction. The Court granted leave to permit cross-examination in an attempt to resolve this conflict.[51] However, if there really was a conflict that could be resolved only by cross-examination, then the second aspect of the established fact requirement was not met:[52] the relevant fact was not established by uncontentious evidence.

---

[42] *VH (Malawi) v Secretary of State for the Home Department* [2009] EWCA Civ 64.
[43] ibid [48].
[44] ibid [27]. For less-explicit instances, see, eg, *Clifford Lamar Ltd v Gyenge* [2011] NZCA 208, [2]–[5]; *Ali v Deportation Review Tribunal* [1997] NZAR 208 (HC), 219.
[45] *Bubb v Wandsworth London Borough Council* [2011] EWCA Civ 1285, [2012] HLR 13.
[46] ibid [32]–[33].
[47] See, eg, *Brook Valley Community Group Inc v Trustees of the Brook Waimarama Sanctuary Trust* [2017] NZHC 1844, [21]; *New Zealand Climate Science Education Trust v National Institute of Water and Atmospheric Research Ltd* [2012] NZHC 2297, [2013] 1 NZLR 75; *Isaac v Minister of Consumer Affairs* [1990] 2 NZLR 606 (HC) 637.
[48] *Haile* (n 21).
[49] *Charter Holdings* (n 19).
[50] *Oggi* (n 39).
[51] ibid [4].
[52] Perhaps in this case, calling for more evidence could have removed the apparent conflict. Neither of the two deponents as to the date of the billboard's construction was the person who applied for registration, while the affidavit by that person was silent on the date of construction question, and indeed was ultimately found to have been 'economical with the truth': ibid [22].

The decision in *Croydon* is notable for insisting that on a question that has right or wrong answers, such as a person's age, the Court should assess conflicting evidence for itself.[53] As already noted, however, the Court was not invoking the mistake of fact ground established in *E*. Rather, this approach relied on what the Court took Parliament to have intended. *Croydon* was distinguished in *Bubb* on that basis.[54] While the Court in *Croydon* treated this point as not dependent on a jurisdictional fact argument,[55] its approach to contested factual issues is exactly the approach that applies when a fact is classified as a jurisdictional fact.[56]

C. Application of the Second Aspect where Mistake Concerns Availability of Evidence

Finally, it is worth clarifying that mistakes of fact in some cases may concern facts or evidence that are quite contentious, yet meet both aspects of the second requirement. According to the first part of the test in *E*, mistakes as to an 'existing fact' may take the form of a mistake as to the availability of evidence on a particular matter.[57] The evidence in question may itself be contentious or call for evaluation, as long as there is no dispute that it was available.[58] For instance, in *R v Criminal Injury Compensation Board ex p A*, the Board deciding a compensation claim concluded there was no evidence to support the claim of sexual violation.[59] The Board was unaware of the existence of a police doctor's report on a medical examination of the claimant, which stated that her findings were consistent with that claim.[60] On the available evidence as a whole, there was still room for disagreement on whether the violation in fact occurred,[61] but it was indisputable that the doctor's report was available and was relevant evidence.[62]

IV. Defending the Ground: Strong Argument in Favour and Avoiding Three Objections

My next question concerns the justification for adopting mistake of fact as a ground. The attraction of the limits I explained in the previous part, aside from

---

[53] *Croydon* (n 24) [27].
[54] *Bubb* (n 46) [18]–[20].
[55] *Croydon* (n 24) [29].
[56] See Craig (n 26) [17-013]–[17-014].
[57] *E* (n 1) itself involved this type of mistake.
[58] This point appears to have been overlooked or misunderstood in *Chalfont v Chiltern District Council* [2014] EWCA Civ 1393 [106].
[59] *R v Criminal Injuries Compensation Board ex p A* [1999] 2 AC 330 (HL).
[60] ibid 343. Although the Lords preferred to decide the case on grounds of natural justice (ibid 345), this was said in *E* (n 1) [63]–[66] to have been a good case for mistake of fact review.
[61] Expressly acknowledged in the *Criminal Injuries Compensation Board* case (n 60) 343, 346.
[62] Elliott and Varuhas (n 18) 76.

being consistent with much of the relevant case law, is that they render the ground readily justified and defensible. On the one hand, the arguments for correcting mistakes apply with full force. On the other hand, this understanding of the ground avoids three objections. These are the constitutional objection to merits review; that judicial review is not a suitable procedure for fact-finding; and that judicial review of factual determinations would unduly compromise finality and would go beyond proportionate dispute resolution.

A. Arguments in Favour of Error Correction Apply with Full Force

As noted earlier, there are weighty arguments in favour of correcting factual errors. Justice demands it, because a decision-maker who laboured under a material error of fact was never in a position to consider the true merits of a person's case.[63] Furthermore, the rule of law and fidelity to legislative choices are also implicated: a statutory regime will not operate as intended in such a case.

We can now see that both these arguments apply with full force where the mistake in question does not involve evaluation in either of the two senses discussed above. Such a mistake is an incontrovertible mistake. The law would indeed be seriously amiss if it did not provide recourse in such cases of incontrovertible mistake, provided the mistake is material and not the claimant's responsibility (the remaining two requirements of the test in *E*).

There is, of course, also an argument for allowing claimants to challenge factual determinations involving evaluation of the facts or of the evidence. However, I will argue next that it is this type of challenge that attracts the objection to merits review, with the consequence that challenges will attract judicial review only on a rationality standard that involves at least a measure of deference.

B. Avoiding the Constitutional Objection to Merits Review

We saw earlier that the constitutional objection to merits review appears to be in tension with the need to correct mistakes. However, I will argue here that this objection, properly understood, does not apply to mistake of fact as a ground of review, provided the ground does not apply to evaluative factual determinations in either of the two senses discussed above. These two limits to the ground can be seen as designed to avoid the objection to merits review.

Flowing from the constitutional objection to merits review, the judicial review jurisdiction is usually said to be confined to considering the legality of decisions

---

[63] See also Forsyth and Dring (n 8) 259–60 for a similar point.

and the fairness of the procedures adopted by a decision-maker.[64] The substantive merits were accordingly long considered not reviewable at all.[65] According to *Edwards v Bairstow*, review on the merits was available only where a decision was so unreasonable as to compel the inference that there must have been an error of law.[66]

That fiction was abandoned by Lord Diplock in *Council of Civil Service Unions v Minister for the Civil Service* in favour of accepting *Wednesbury* unreasonableness[67] or irrationality as a ground in its own right, alongside illegality and procedural unfairness.[68] It is now generally accepted that irrationality involves some judicial evaluation of the substantive merits of a decision-maker's exercise of a discretion or finding of fact.[69] The principle against merits review now takes the form of insisting on a rationality standard of review for this ground. Traditionally, that rationality standard was highly deferential, but the intensity of review now varies.[70] Either way, that standard involves at least a measure of deference, in contrast with the substitutionary 'correctness' standard that applies to questions of legality and procedure.

The question is how this limit on judicial review applies to review of factual determinations. The usual approach is to treat all factual determinations as part of the merits, along with exercises of discretion.[71] On that basis, both fact and discretion are reviewable only on a rationality standard. The distinction between law and fact is thus considered one of the crucial lines that determine the appropriate standard review.[72]

My argument is that the equation of facts with the merits needs to be reconsidered. Not all factual determinations are part of the merits: I argue that only those factual determinations that involve evaluation are part of the substantive merits of a decision. Let me explain.

We need to do some unpacking of the notion of the merits. It helps to bear in mind the function of this notion. That function is to mark out those questions on which a reviewing court must defer to the statutory decision-maker by reviewing

---

[64] *Chief Constable of North Wales Police v Evans* [1982] WLR 1155, 1173, 1174; JC Pring (n 11); *Unison Networks Ltd v Commerce Commission* [2007] NZSC 74, [2008] 1 NZLR 42, [54].

[65] Until *Anisminic v Foreign Compensation Commission* [1969] 2 AC 147 (HL), such complete exclusion of review was the norm for any questions that were considered to fall within the decision-maker's jurisdiction, even questions of law.

[66] *Edwards v Bairstow* (n 12) 36.

[67] *Associated Provincial Picture Houses Ltd v Wednesbury Corporation* [1948] 1 KB 223 (CA).

[68] *Council of Civil Service Unions v Minister for the Civil Service* [1985] 1 AC 374 (HL) 440–41.

[69] See, eg, A Lester and J Jowell, 'Beyond *Wednesbury*: Substantive Principles of Administrative Law' [1987] PL 368, 369–70; P Craig, 'The Nature of Reasonableness Review' [2013] CLP 1, 2, 4–5. See also, eg, *Hu v Immigration and Protection Tribunal* [2017] NZHC 41, [2017] NZAR 508, [23].

[70] *R v Ministry of Defence, ex p Smith* [1996] QB 517 (CA).

[71] See, eg, H Woolf *De Smith's Judicial Review* (n 11) [11-036], [11-051]; Joseph (n 11) 1064; Kent (n 11), [2], [15]; JC Pring (n 11) [7]: '[i]t is well established that in judicial review [proceedings] the Court does not substitute its own factual conclusions for that of the consent authority.'

[72] See, eg, H Woolf *De Smith's Judicial Review* (n 11) [11-036].

only on a rationality standard rather than on a substitutionary 'correctness' standard. To be designated as a merits question, a question should therefore engage one or both of the arguments in favour of deference: deciding it must be part of the authority Parliament allocated to the statutory decision-maker; or something which executive or administrative decision-makers are better qualified to do than reviewing courts, in terms of constitutional legitimacy, institutional capacity or both.

In light of this, the merits are best understood as involving *evaluation* of competing options for the purposes of *choosing* between them. That is the type of question on which courts ought to defer by reviewing only on a rationality standard, not a substitutionary one.[73] This evaluation test certainly fits the paradigm case of a merits question: the exercise of discretion that involves weighing up a range of competing considerations to determine the best outcome in the circumstances.

Applying this evaluation test, the merits do include factual determinations, but only those that involve evaluation. As we have seen, there are two types of evaluative determinations about facts: evaluation of facts for the purpose of applying an evaluative legal test; and evaluation of conflicting evidence for the purpose of finding the facts. In my view, the reason why these are excluded from the mistake of fact ground is that they do indeed concern the merits.

Where, on the other hand, a question concerns identification of an objectively correct answer with no room for evaluation or choice, the reasons for deference are not engaged. The authority that Parliament allocates to statutory decision-makers is the power to evaluate options and choose between them. Respecting that allocation of authority does not entail respect for incontrovertible mistakes. Similarly, the decision-maker's greater legitimacy due to direct or indirect democratic accountability is only relevant where the decision involves choice or evaluation. The same, finally, also goes for the decision-maker's better access to procedures for exploring a range of options and to expertise and experience to help chose between those options: those are relevant where the decision involves evaluation.

Hence there is no objection to review on a substitutionary standard where a question involves no evaluation. That applies to factual determinations that do not involve evaluation of either of the types I have identified.[74] If it is accepted that the mistake of fact ground is confined to such non-evaluative factual determinations, then the objection to merits review does not apply.

---

[73] How review on questions of statutory interpretation fits into this picture is beyond the scope of this chapter. Arguably, questions of statutory interpretation often involve an element of evaluation. Yet the orthodox approach insists that such questions are for the court and thus attract substitutionary review. There is room for debate on whether this orthodox approach ought to be maintained: see, eg, the essays in part B of H Wilberg and M Elliott (eds) *The Scope and Intensity of Substantive Review: Traversing Taggart's Rainbow* (Oxford, Hart Publishing, 2015) 263. But even if it is maintained, we can still take the view that the merits comprise all evaluative questions other than questions of legal interpretation.
[74] See also Forsyth (n 2); Forsyth and Dring (n 8) 258; Williams (n 18) 798; S Nason, *Reconstructing Judicial Review* (Oxford, Hart Publishing, 2016) 156.

This proposed evaluation classification cuts across the familiar law/fact divide, according to which questions of fact call for deference while questions of law must be reviewed on a substitutionary standard. My argument is that evaluation rather than fact is the feature that identifies the merits, and hence the area where deference is called for. Questions of fact are not part of the merits, just like questions of law, as long as they do not involve evaluation.

Some proponents of mistake of fact as a ground of review have taken a different view. Notably, Paul Craig argues that complex factual findings that involve evaluation should be included in the mistake of fact ground.[75] My disagreement with this, however, concerns only the best route, not the right outcome. As already noted, I see the mistake of fact ground as always involving substitution of judgment, just like the illegality and procedural fairness grounds, but I see it as available only for non-contentious pure fact-finding and understanding of the evidence. Craig takes the different route of including challenges to the evaluation of facts in the mistake of fact ground, but then proposing a variable standard of review for that ground. On his proposed approach, the standard in a case involving a challenge to an evaluation of facts will usually be rationality, rather than substitution of judgment, while in cases of simple factual error, the standard will be one of substitution.[76] What matters for avoiding the merits review objection is to avoid review of evaluative determinations on a substitutionary 'correctness' standard.

C. Avoiding the Objection from the Limits of Judicial Review Procedure

The second objection to a mistake of fact ground is specifically concerned with review of factual determinations. This objection can again be avoided by insisting on the second requirement in E, as I will show in this section.

Judicial review has generally been held not to be available for correcting a decision-maker's resolution of disputed questions of fact, because it is not a suitable procedure for that.[77] The reason for this is found in the particular procedures that have traditionally characterised judicial review.[78] In particular, evidence is ordinarily by affidavit, and cross-examination is allowed only by special leave.[79] This is a problem for challenges involving disputed questions of fact because it has always been considered that hearing and seeing witnesses' oral evidence and

---

[75] Craig (n 56) [17-023]. cf Elliott and Varuhas (n 18) 76.
[76] Craig (n 56) [17-030]–[17-034].
[77] M Demetriou and S Houseman, 'Review of Error of Fact – A Brief Guide' [1997] *Judicial Review* 27, 27–28; H Woolf *De Smith's Judicial Review* (n 11) [17-042]; *R v Derbyshire County Council ex parte Noble* [1990] ICR 808 (CA) 813.
[78] *Ex parte Noble* (n 77) 813.
[79] Bubb (n 46) [24]; G Taylor, *Judicial Review: A New Zealand Perspective* (Wellington, 4th edn, LexisNexis NZ, 2018) [10.19], [10.26]–[10.29].

cross-examination is the best basis for assessing their credibility and reliability, in order to resolve factual disputes between them.[80]

The short point for present purposes is that this concern simply does not apply if the challenge to a factual determination does not turn on any disputed question of fact. If it is accepted, as I have argued, that the mistake of fact ground excludes such challenges, then this objection does not apply to mistake of fact as a ground.

D. Avoiding the Finality Objection

The third objection to mistake of fact as a ground flows from the need for finality and proportionate dispute resolution.[81] Disputes should not be endlessly prolonged, and the time and resources devoted to resolution of disputes should not be disproportionate.[82] Re-opening factual determinations is considered problematic for those reasons.

We can see the strength of this consideration by the fact that it features even when courts are hearing general appeals, meaning full appeals on the merits, from lower courts rather than from executive or administrative decision-makers. The constitutional and institutional reasons for the limits on judicial review do not apply in that context. Yet even there, courts do not ordinarily conduct a *de novo* hearing of the evidence, even though a power to rehear the evidence exists.[83] And when they have not done so, they accord appropriate respect to the factual findings of the primary fact-finder who saw and heard the witnesses.[84]

However, the question of proportionality involves balancing the relevant competing values and interests, and finality is merely one of those. Where an incontrovertible mistake has been identified, the need to correct that mistake weighs heavily against the need for finality.

The need for correction would arguably be outweighed only where there are other strong features against it. This might be the case where there has already

---

[80] See, eg, *Cook v Thomas* [2010] EWCA Civ 227; *Assicurazioni Generali SpA* (n 38) [22]; *Benmax* (n 17); *Powell v Streatham Manor Nursing Home* [1935] AC 243 (HL) 255, 256.

[81] See generally *Shaheen* (n 3); *R (SO (Eritrea)) v London Borough of Barking and Dagenham* [2014] EWCA Civ 1486 [23]; *The Ampthill Peerage* [1977] AC 547 (HL) 569.

[82] *R (Cart) v Upper Tribunal (Public Law Project Intervening)* [2011] UKSC 28, [2012] 1 AC 663 [51].

[83] *Ealing London Borough Council v Richardson* [2005] EWCA Civ1798, [2006] C P Rep 19; *Shotover Gorge Jet Boats v Jamieson* [1987] 1 NZLR 437 (CA), 440 (Cooke P).

[84] *Halsbury's Laws of England* (5th edn, 2010) vol 12A [1531]. See also *Powell v Streatham Manor* (n 80) 256; *Robinson v Chief Constable of West Yorkshire Police* [2018] UKSC 4, [2018] AC 736 [82] (Lord Mance), [123] (Lord Hughes). In *Austin, Nichols & Co Inc v Stichting Lodestar* [2007] NZSC 103, [2008] 2 NZLR 141, [3]–[5], the New Zealand Supreme Court adopted a modified position, insisting that an appellate court must come to its own conclusion on the facts. However, it still accepted that a lower court which has heard and seen the witnesses has a special advantage in making credibility findings and an appellate court may judge that it has no basis for rejecting the lower court's reasoning.

been one or more appeals on the merits, and where the appellate body was a specialist tribunal. In such a context, it might perhaps be thought that allowing a generalist court to re-open factual findings, even on the grounds that there has been an incontrovertible mistake, introduces a risk of further mistakes. Similarly, it has been proposed that non-availability of other avenues for correcting the error should be a requirement for the mistake of fact ground.[85] Such other appropriate avenues would include the original decision-maker re-opening his or her own decision.[86]

E. Conclusion on Defensibility

This exploration of the arguments for and against correcting mistakes of fact supports recognition of mistake of fact as a ground of review, provided the ground excludes challenges to the two types of evaluative factual determinations identified in Part III. On the one hand, the arguments in favour of correcting factual errors apply with full force if the ground is limited in this way. On the other hand, two of the usual objections to review of factual determinations do not apply if the ground is limited in this way, while the third objection is much weaker.

V. The Ground is Distinct and Remains Useful

It remains to deal with one objection to mistake of fact as a ground of review that is specific to the strictly limited version that I have so far defended. The broader move towards greater scrutiny of factual determinations in judicial review may cast doubt on the significance of a limited separate ground of review for mistake of fact. In this part I will argue that the limited version of the mistake of fact ground discussed in the previous two parts remains at least potentially distinct and useful.

Let me start by exploring the basis of the objection: what developments might be said to render the mistake of fact ground redundant? Much of the expansion in the scrutiny of factual determinations does not do so, as it involves more intensive scrutiny on questions of evaluation. This is true of the general erosion of the divide between law and fact that is leading to more intensive review of the evaluative factual determinations that were previously shielded from intensive review

---

[85] Kent (n 11).
[86] On the availability of the power to do this, see HWR Wade and C Forsyth, *Administrative Law* (Oxford, 11th edn, OUP, 2014) 191–94; *E* (n 1); *Shaheen* (n 3). In NZ, there is a general power to do so in the Legislation Act 2019, s 46 (NZ).

by that distinction.[87] It is also true of some aspects of the expanded review of factual determinations as part of heightened scrutiny or the proportionality test that apply when rights and other important interests are affected.[88] In that context, courts closely scrutinise the adequacy of the evidence[89] and the cogency of the reasoning based on it.[90] Both are evaluative matters. Given that the mistake of fact ground, on the understanding I have defended, does not apply to evaluative determinations, these aspects of the expanded review of factual determinations do not overlap with the new mistake of fact ground.

There are, however, some points at which these expansions may intersect with the mistake of fact ground. The demand for justification in rights cases has led courts to assert a power to reconsider findings of fact for themselves in deciding whether the proportionality test is met, as well as to consider facts which have arisen since the time of the challenged decision. That includes power to receive evidence, including oral evidence.[91] This could result in the court finding an incontrovertible factual error, which may invalidate a step in the decision-maker's justificatory reasoning. For instance, a factual mistake affecting the assessment of a relevant risk may invalidate the balance struck between the need to guard against that risk and the impact on the right.[92]

Inadequate attention to evidence, or misunderstanding the evidence, is another reasoning flaw that would count as a mistake of fact but can also invalidate a decision on heightened scrutiny or pursuant to the illegality test.[93] The illegality ground of failure to have regard to mandatory relevant considerations has also been pressed into service in this regard: particular factual enquiries have been designated as implied mandatory relevant considerations.[94]

---

[87] See, eg, Daly (n 2) 901. For a much-noted instance of a court explicitly questioning the distinction, see *Jones v First Tier Tribunal* [2013] UKSC 19, [2013] 2 AC 48, [46].

[88] On which, see Varuhas, ch 6 in this book.

[89] See, eg, *Minister of Justice v Kim* [2021] NZSC 57, [2021] 1 NZLR 338; *R (Aguilar Quila) v Secretary of State for the Home Department* [2011] UKSC 45, [2012] 1 AC 621 [47]–[58], [74]–[77]; *Grounded Kiwis Group Inc v Minister of Health* [2022] NZHC 832, [325], [328].

[90] See, eg, *Wolf v Minister of Immigration* [2004] NZAR 414 (HC) [68].

[91] *R (Kiarie) v Secretary of State for the Home Department* [2017] UKSC 42 [46]–[47]; *Pinnock v Manchester City Council* [2011] 2 AC 104, [74].

[92] This is a likely explanation of a NZ case in which mistakes of fact were among the successful grounds of appeal in a challenge relying on the NZ Bill of Rights Act 1990: *Taylor v The Chief Executive of the Department of Corrections* [2015] NZCA 477, [2015] NZAR 1648, [94]–[100].

[93] See, eg, *Wolf* (n 90) [66]–[67]; *KV (Sri Lanka) v Secretary of State for the Home Department* [2019] UKSC 10, [30], [34].

[94] See, eg, *CREEDNZ v Governor-General* [1981] 1 NZLR 172 (CA) 183; *R (National Association of Health Stores) v Secretary of State for Health* [2005] EWCA Civ 154, [58]–[65]; *Quake Outcasts v Minister for Canterbury Earthquake Recovery* [2015] NZSC 27, [2016] 1 NZLR 1. Another instance may perhaps be found in *Cripps v Attorney-General* [2022] NZHC 1532.

There is an arguable overlap even with *Wednesbury* unreasonableness. It could be said that an incontrovertible mistake would surely be struck down as unreasonable even on that highly deferential standard.

The question is whether these overlaps or intersections render the mistake of fact ground redundant. I suggest that these alternative routes for addressing mistakes of facts have at least two relevant limits by comparison with the mistake of fact ground. First, it is not clear that they allow a decision to be invalidated due to a mistake concerning a single relevant fact. Secondly, with the exception of the final point, they are available only in contexts that attract heightened scrutiny or the proportionality test. In light of these limits in the alternative routes, the separate mistake of fact ground remains at least potentially distinct and useful.

A. Available for a Mistake as to a Single Relevant Fact

The first potential limit of the alternative routes is that an incontrovertible mistake concerning one single relevant fact will not always render the resulting decision or outcome unreasonable, even on a heightened scrutiny standard, or disproportionate. Where it does not, the law is uncertain as to whether that decision will be struck down. I will expand on that but let me first set out the contribution of the mistake of fact ground in this situation.

The mistake of fact ground clearly does apply to invalidate decisions that are affected by a mistake concerning one single relevant fact – subject to a materiality test. For instance, in *Haile*,[95] the mistaken understanding represented just one of six reasons for an adverse credibility finding against an asylum claimant. That finding may still have been reasonably open in light of the other five valid reasons, in which case the decision to reject the asylum claim was still reasonable. Indeed, the Court commented that the claimant had 'little ground for optimism' on reconsideration.[96] Yet the Court upheld the challenge on grounds of mistake of fact.[97]

This potency of the mistake of fact ground in relation to mistakes concerning a single relevant fact has also given rise to one of the main concerns about the mistake of fact ground. Why should an error at one perhaps rather trivial step in the reasoning process invalidate the decision? Dealing with this concern is the role of the fourth requirement in *E*: the error must be sufficiently material.

This materiality requirement is especially important in relation to one particular version of mistake of fact: a mistake as to the availability of evidence.[98] For most

---

[95] *Haile* (n 21).
[96] ibid [28].
[97] Other examples include *Charter Holdings* (n 19); *R (March) v Secretary of State for Health* [2010] EWHC 765; *Cabo Verde v Secretary of State for the Home Department* [2004] EWCA Civ 1726.
[98] That is given in *E* as the alternative to a mistake as to an existing fact, the first requirement in *E*. Concerns about allowing review for this type of mistake were raised in *Shaheen* (n 3) [27]–[29].

decisions, there will be a great range of evidence that could potentially be relevant. Some of it will be crucial, but some of it will be of limited significance. Decisions cannot be invalidated whenever a claimant locates some evidence that is potentially relevant. The mistake must be sufficiently material.

On the other hand, however, arguably an incontrovertible mistake should be capable of invalidating a decision without needing to show that it renders the overall decision unreasonable. This is especially important in cases, like *Haile*, where the mistake concerns an existing fact that is relevant to the decision, rather than a mistake about availability of evidence. In that type of case, the materiality test should not be too stringent.

Authority is somewhat divided on the precise terms of the materiality test.[99] *E* simply stated that the mistake must be material but need not be decisive.[100] *Haile* adopted a test that amounts to a presumption of materiality for mistakes as to an existing fact. The mistake invalidated the decision because 'it cannot confidently be said to have made no ultimate difference to the result'.[101] It may be that the test does and should vary both according to the type of mistake and according to the context, such as the importance of what is at stake. We should also note that statute in the UK now provides a further materiality test as a condition for relief.[102]

Let me turn then to consider whether correcting a material mistake concerning a single fact could also be achieved by relevant aspects of the broader expansion of review of factual determinations. As we saw, proportionality or heightened scrutiny often involves detailed scrutiny of all the steps in a decision-maker's reasoning. Like mistake of fact, this can and often does result in errors being identified at individual steps. However, the usual understanding of proportionality or heightened scrutiny is that the ultimate question concerns the rationality or proportionality of the overall decision.

For instance, in *Wolf*, the much-cited New Zealand case on heightened scrutiny, the Court catalogued a number of reasoning flaws before concluding that *the decision* could not survive heightened scrutiny.[103] Similarly in *Taylor*, the Court in upholding a challenge on grounds of freedom of expression as guaranteed by the NZ Bill of Rights Act 1990 also relied on errors of fact.[104] The relationship between these two grounds was not made clear. But one obvious reading is that the factual errors were seen as defeating the proportionality justification for limiting the right.

---

[99] For more demanding materiality tests, *W v Staffordshire County Council* [2006] EWCA Civ 1676, [18]; *Glaxo Group Ltd v Commissioner of Patents* [1991] 3 NZLR 179 (CA) 184.
[100] *E* (n 1) [66].
[101] *Haile* (n 21) [25].
[102] Senior Courts Act 1981 s 31(2A)–(2C).
[103] *Wolf* (n 90) [66]–[72].
[104] *Taylor* (n 92) [46]–[47], [60]–[91].

Having said that, this approach is not authoritatively settled. Courts may well be open to relying on an incontrovertible mistake concerning one single fact to invalidate a decision on heightened scrutiny or when applying the proportionality test. It would likely depend on how searching a standard is applied, and on how material the error was. That assessment may not be significantly different from setting the appropriate materiality test for mistake of fact as a separate ground.

A further objection should be mentioned but can be disposed of. It might be said there is nothing unusual in a ground of review relying on an error at one individual step in the reasoning. For instance, illegality grounds such as irrelevant or mandatory considerations and the right to a hearing concern an individual step in the reasoning. Courts generally insist that such errors invalidate a decision unless satisfied that the error could have made no difference.[105] However, these grounds involve a breach or misunderstanding of some applicable legal test or requirement, whether found in the common law (the right to a hearing) or set out expressly or by implication in statute (irrelevant or mandatory considerations). That is different from the errors that are addressed by the mistake of fact ground. Those often concern a single fact that does not directly answer an applicable legal test or requirement.[106]

For instance, in *Haile*, we can say that credibility was a legal test or requirement that formed part of the overall test for determining asylum claims. The mistake of fact in *Haile* went to credibility, but it was merely one of the considerations that affected the assessment of credibility. In that regard, therefore, mistake of fact does operate at a more granular level than those illegality and procedural propriety grounds.

Having said that, we also saw that as part of the broader expansion, the mandatory relevant considerations ground has sometimes been used to identify particular facts as mandatory to consider.[107] Sometimes those facts do not directly answer an applicable legal test: they are considered mandatory because of their significance in the factual circumstances.[108] This might sometimes offer a route for correcting an incontrovertible mistake as to one single relevant fact. However, it is likely that a mistake on this route needs to be more material than is the case for the mistake of fact ground.

In summary, aspects of the broader expansion of review of factual determinations may at least in some cases be available to invalidate a decision due to an incontrovertible mistake concerning a single fact that does not directly answer an

---

[105] *Secretary for Justice v Simes* [2012] NZCA 459, [2012] NZAR 1044, [64]–[65].
[106] In *E* (n 1) [62], this was why the Court considered that many mistakes of fact could not be challenged on grounds of failure to take account of mandatory considerations.
[107] See, eg, *CREEDNZ* (n 94), *National Health Stores* (n 94).
[108] See, eg, *Quake Outcasts* (n 94).

applicable legal test or requirement. However, this is uncertain, and may only work in some cases.

B. Available without Heightened Scrutiny or Proportionality

The second limit of the alternative routes for addressing incontrovertible mistakes is that those routes are very limited in contexts where heightened scrutiny or proportionality are not available.

The traditional *Wednesbury* unreasonableness ground is even less likely than those newer approaches to invalidate the resulting decision due to a mistake concerning one single relevant fact. The ground is widely understood as concerning the reasonableness of the outcome.[109] An individual mistake would therefore invalidate a decision only if that mistake was sufficiently significant to render the decision as a whole *Wednesbury* unreasonable. For less decisively material mistakes, therefore, reliance on this route would work, if at all, only in contexts where heightened scrutiny is available. In contrast, the mistake of fact ground is available regardless of whether the context calls for more intensive review or for a proportionality test.

On this point, there is room for disagreement whether this limit is a problem. It may be that allowing decisions to be invalidated due to a mistake about a single relevant fact would lead to heightened scrutiny by the back door: it might invite the sort of step-by-step examination of the decision-maker's reasoning that is otherwise only available when the context calls for heightened scrutiny.[110] Still, that concern needs to be weighed against the strong arguments for correcting incontrovertible mistakes.

VI. Conclusion

In this chapter, I have sought to illuminate the limits, defensibility and distinctiveness of mistake of fact as a ground of review. The ground is best understood as limited to factual mistakes that do not involve evaluation of the facts or of conflicting evidence.

---

[109] See, eg, Jones (n 28); Taylor (n 79) [14.39]–[14.40]. See also *Lewis v Wilson & Horton Ltd* [2000] 3 NZLR 546 (CA) [92].

[110] This concern featured in *Wakelin v Read* [2000] OPLR 277 (CA) 13; *Phillpott v Chief Executive of the Department of Labour* HC Wellington CIV-2005-485-713, [36]–[37], [76]; *A v Legal Complaints Review Officer* [2013] NZHC 1100, [34], [37].

On that basis, it is justified by strong concerns about justice and fidelity to legislative choices, and because it avoids or reduces three objections. It avoids objections to merits review and to fact-finding in judicial review proceedings, and the concern about finality carries less weight.

The significance of the ground may be diminished by the broader move towards greater scrutiny of factual determinations in judicial review. However, it may still be a distinct feature of the mistake of fact ground that a sufficiently material incontrovertible mistake concerning a single relevant fact suffices to invalidate a decision. It is not clear that other extensions of scrutiny of factual determinations would always be available to achieve this; and it is unlikely to be available in contexts where heightened scrutiny or proportionality do not apply.

PART III
Facts in Broader Perspective

12

Indigenous Oral History in Canadian Courts: The Law of Fact-finding and the Wrong Mistake

HILARY EVANS CAMERON*

I. Introduction

Canada's treatment of Indigenous people over the past century 'can best be described as "cultural genocide".'[1] The Report of the country's Truth and Reconciliation Commission (TRC) recently laid bare how state and church authorities interned generations of children in residential schools in order to separate them from their families and culture. Many 'were abused, physically and sexually, and they died in the schools in numbers that would not have been tolerated in any school system anywhere in the country, or in the world'.[2] Searchers have since found many hundreds of their unmarked graves. They expect to find thousands more.[3]

In the wake of the TRC Report, more settlers on this territory are belatedly joining Indigenous people in imagining a just future that looks very different from its colonial past and present. For scholars of evidence law, this has meant

---

* The author would like to thank Rahul Saily for his very helpful research assistance.

[1] Truth and Reconciliation Commission of Canada, 'Honouring the Truth, Reconciling for the Future: Summary of the Final Report of the Truth and Reconciliation Commission of Canada' *Government of Canada*. Available at: https://publications.gc.ca/site/eng/9.800288/publication.html, last accessed 24 January 2023.

[2] ibid, Preface, v–vi.

[3] I Mosby and E Millions, 'Canada's Residential Schools Were a Horror' (Scientific American, 1 August 2021). Available at: www.scientificamerican.com/article/canadas-residential-schools-were-a-horror/, last accessed 24 January 2023; K Deer, 'Why it's Difficult to Put a Number on how Many Children Died at Residential Schools' (CBC News, 29 September 2021). Available at: www.cbc.ca/news/indigenous/residential-school-children-deaths-numbers-1.6182456, last accessed 24 January 2023; A McKeen, 'How Many Indigenous Children's Graves Remain to be Found in Canada?' *Toronto Star* (Vancouver, 24 June 2021). Available at: www.thestar.com/news/canada/2021/06/24/how-many-indigenous-childrens-graves-remain-to-be-found-in-canada.html, last accessed 24 January 2023.

examining the role that this law plays in this process.[4] This chapter considers one aspect of this law: how Canadian courts treat Indigenous oral history evidence. It joins the work of legal scholars in other settler states who have made similar investigations.[5]

To establish Aboriginal title or an Aboriginal right under the Canadian Constitution, Indigenous litigants must prove historical facts.[6] A quantity of Indigenous historical knowledge is unwritten, 'passed orally from generation to generation'.[7] The traditional common law approach to fact-finding would reject this evidence in favour of the written records created by settlers.[8] In a series of judgments at the turn of the millennium, the Supreme Court of Canada recognised the resulting injustice: the traditional approach could 'render nugatory' Aboriginal title and rights claims.[9] The Court responded with changes to this law designed to ensure that Indigenous oral history evidence receives 'equal and due treatment' in Canadian courts.[10]

This chapter uses an error burden framework to evaluate these changes. Part I describes this framework. Part II outlines the Supreme Court's approach and argues that its changes to the law of evidence do not and cannot address the injustice that the Court has identified. Part III proposes a further amendment to the law

---

[4] See D Milward, 'Doubting What the Elders Have to Say: A Critical Examination of Canadian Judicial Treatment of Aboriginal Oral History Evidence' (2010) 14 *The International Journal of Evidence and Proof* 287; J Borrows, 'Listening for a Change: The Courts and Oral Tradition' (2001) 39 *Osgoode Hall Law Journal* 1; K Drake, 'Indigenous Oral Traditions in Court: Hearsay or Foreign Law?' in K Drake and B L Gunn (eds), *Renewing Relationships: Indigenous Peoples and Canada* (Saskatoon: Native Law Centre, 2019); V Napoleon, 'Delgamuukw: A Legal Straightjacket for Oral Histories?' (2005) 20 *Canadian Journal of Law and Society* 123; D Isaac, 'Novel Science or Oral History? The Admissibility of Co-Produced Information in Canadian Courts' (2019) 56 *Alberta Law Review* 881; J Peterson, 'Judicial Treatment of Aboriginal Peoples' Oral History Evidence: More Room for Reconciliation' (2019) 42 *Dalhousie Law Journal* 483; A Potamianos, 'The Challenges of Indigenous Oral History Since *Mitchell v. Minister of National Revenue*' (2021) 26 *Appeal* 3.

[5] See, eg, N Mahuika, *Rethinking Oral History and Tradition: An Indigenous Perspective* (New York, OUP, 2019); K Biber, 'Fact-finding, Proof, and Indigenous Knowledge: Teaching Evidence in Australia' (2010) 35 *Alternative Law Journal* 208; H M Babcock, '[This] I Know from My Grandfather: The Battle for Admissibility of Indigenous Oral History as Proof of Tribal Land Claims' (2012–2013) 37 *American Indian Law Review* 19.

[6] For a review of the relevant legal frameworks, see Milward, 'Doubting What the Elders Have to Say' (n 4); Napoleon, 'Delgamuukw' (n 4).

[7] Milward, 'Doubting What the Elders Have to Say' (n 4) 289. See B Miller, *Oral History on Trial: Recognizing Aboriginal Narratives in the Courts* (Vancouver, University of British Columbia Press, 2012); A Ray, *Telling it to the Judge: Taking Native History to Court* (Montréal, McGill-Queen's University Press, 2011). Although this chapter refers to 'oral history', the term used by the Supreme Court and in much of the scholarship, this term may mislead, as some of this evidence should be recognised as law rather than history. See discussion at (n 43).

[8] See C McLeod, 'The Oral Histories of Canada's Northern People, Anglo-Canadian Evidence Law, and Canada's Fiduciary Duty to First Nations: Breaking Down the Barriers of the Past' (1992) 30 *Alberta Law Review* 1276, 1280–83.

[9] *Delgamuukw v British Columbia* [1997] SCJ No 108 [87], citing *Simon v The Queen* [1985] 2 SCR 387; see also *R v Van der Peet* [1996] 2 SCR 507; *Mitchell v Canada (Minister of Revenue)* 2001 SCC 33.

[10] *Mitchell* (n 9) [39].

of fact-finding in Aboriginal title and rights claims to reduce the unfair burden of proof on Indigenous litigants.

II. Error Burdens in the Law of Fact-finding

Questions of fact lie at the heart of many Aboriginal rights and title claims. In any litigation that hinges on questions of fact, a party's *burden of proof* is the measure of how hard they will have to work to win their case. Along with many real-world factors, three intersecting areas of law determine the weight of a party's burden: the substantive doctrine, the law of admissibility and the law of fact-finding.[11]

The law's architects affect the weight of the parties' burdens when they design, and redesign, its substantive elements. The Supreme Court of Canada recently held, for example, that it was unfair to expect plaintiffs in tort claims to prove that they had suffered a 'recognized psychiatric injury' as a condition for claiming damages for mental injury caused by negligence. The Court removed this element from the test to be met, lightening the plaintiffs' burden.[12] Conversely, the Canadian legislature responded to the concern that the accused in sexual assault trials were too easily able to establish mistaken belief in a complainant's consent. It imposed a new factual requirement – this defence will not be available to an accused who 'did not take reasonable steps, in the circumstances known to the accused at the time, to ascertain that the complainant was consenting'[13] – which adds to the burden of an accused attempting to raise this defence.[14]

The body of law that governs the admissibility of evidence likewise affects the weight of a party's burden by determining which evidence they will be able to use to prove their allegations. Here too the law's architects may adapt its requirements to address perceived injustice. In an attempt to combat prevalent 'rape myths' and sexist stereotypes, as well as abusive cross-examination of complainants, the Canadian legislature had at one point restricted categorically an accused's ability to enter evidence of a complainant's sexual history in sexual assault trials. The Supreme Court loosened these restrictions, finding that they lightened the prosecution's burden of proof to an unconstitutional degree.[15]

This chapter considers the third body of law that operates in tandem with the substantive doctrine and the rules of admissibility to determine a party's burden of proof. This is the law that guides decision-makers in deciding whether a fact is

---

[11] Real-world factors affecting the weight of burdens of proof include the party's access to resources, their vulnerability as litigants, and their susceptibility to being misunderstood or wrongly disbelieved. See H Evans Cameron, *Refugee Law's Fact-finding Crisis: Truth, Risk, and the Wrong Mistake* (Cambridge, CUP, 2018) ch 3.
[12] *Saadati v Moorhead*, 2017 SCC 28.
[13] Criminal Code (RSC, 1985, c C-46) s 273.2.
[14] In such cases, while the onus remains on the prosecution, the accused bears the 'persuasive burden' of demonstrating that they took reasonable steps.
[15] *R v Seaboyer; R v Gayme* [1991] 2 SCR 577.

established by the evidence before them. By determining how decision-making doubt should resolve, it allocates a party's *error burden*, the extent to which that party will suffer from the decision-maker's uncertainty.

A. Allocating Error Burdens: Tipping the Scales

Lady Justice's blindfold and balanced scales are misleading. They suggest that legal decision-makers are expected to be neutral. Yet, to reach a conclusion under conditions of uncertainty, a decision-maker can never be neutral. They must answer two questions that force them to pick a side, two questions that determine who will benefit and who will suffer from their doubts: How sure do I have to be? What should I do if I cannot decide whether I am sure enough?

The answers to these questions will determine whether and to what extent an allegation – a *statement* – will pay the price for the decision-maker's uncertainty. These answers therefore reflect an *error preference*, a judgment about the two kinds of potential mistake that hang in the balance. Should the decision-maker err on the side of accepting true statements (and accept a greater proportion of false statements), or should they err on the side of rejecting false statements (and reject a greater proportion of true statements)? Which mistake is worse and by what margin?

If legal decision-makers could decide for themselves case-by-case how they would prefer to err, this would violate the bedrock legal principle that 'like cases should be treated alike'.[16] Instead, to avoid inconsistent and arbitrary decision-making, the law's architects must answer this foundational normative question. They must decide how the scales will tip. In every area of law, the architects' error preference is reflected in how they design the law of fact-finding, in how they use the structures – onus, standards of proof, presumptions – whose sole purpose is to constrain how decision-makers resolve their doubts.

Blackstone's maxim is one of the most famous ideas in the Anglo-American common law: it is 'better that ten guilty persons escape than that one innocent suffer'.[17] The architects of this law through the centuries have preferred by orders of magnitude to err against the prosecution. Judges and juries may treat the accused badly and some accused worse than others.[18] At the level of the legal theory, however, the accused is 'tenderly regarded by the law'.[19] The fact-finding

---

[16] See A Marmor, 'Should Like Cases Be Decided Alike?' (2005) 11 *Legal Theory* 27.

[17] Bl Comm 352, cited in A Volokh, 'n Guilty Men' (1997) 146 *University of Pennsylvania Law Review* 173, 174.

[18] See S Bielen, W Marneffe and N Mocan, 'Racial Bias and In-Group Bias in Virtual Reality Courtrooms' (2021) 64 *Journal of Law and Economics* 269; A Alesina and E La Ferrara, 'A Test of Racial Bias in Capital Sentencing' (2014) 104 *American Economic Review* 3397; M M Rehavi and S B Starr, 'Racial Disparity in Federal Criminal Sentences' (2014) 122 *Journal of Political Economy* 1320.

[19] 'Every safeguard is thrown about him. The requirements of proof are many, and all moral, together with many technical, rules stand between him and any possible punishment': *People v Riley*, 33

balance tips firmly in their favour: the prosecution bears the onus and must prove its allegations against a high standard of proof, resulting in more mistakes overall but fewer at the expense of the accused.[20]

In contrast, to the architects of the civil law in common law jurisdictions, mistakes in favour of the plaintiff or the defendant are 'equally regrettable'.[21] The civil law would remain neutral if it could. Since the scales must tip, however, its architects have preferred, for a host of practical reasons, to err against the moving party. The plaintiff's obligation to prove their claim on a balance of probabilities resolves doubt at their expense, but by the narrowest margin. While not nearly as heavy as the prosecution's, their error burden is nonetheless heavier than the defendant's.[22]

B. Determining Error Preference: The Wrong Mistake

How do the law's architects decide which mistake to prefer and by what margin? Theorists suggest that judgments about error preference in law reflect an assessment of both the magnitude and the likelihood of the potential harms at stake.[23]

(i) Magnitude

In measuring the magnitude of a mistake, traditional legal theory suggests that the law's architects engage in a rational weighing of the *error costs* associated with it. These include the costs to the parties themselves as well as costs to the broader community. A more recent psychologically informed approach suggests, however, that this process is less rational and, in particular, that it responds to the *salience* of the harms under consideration. In law, as elsewhere, salient harms 'punch above their weight,' while less salient ones seem to matter less than they should: they are more easily left 'off screen' and neglected.[24]

(ii) Likelihood

As between errors of equal magnitude, standard economic utility theory suggests that decision-makers will preferentially avoid the one more likely to occur.

NE 2d 872, 875 (Ill 1941), cited in S Baradaran, 'Restoring the Presumption of Innocence' (2011) 72 *Ohio State Law Journal* 723, 724 fn 2.

[20] See E Lillquist, 'Recasting Reasonable Doubt: Decision Theory and the Virtues of Variability' (2002) *UC Davis Law Review* 85; Evans Cameron (n 11) ch 1.

[21] D Hamer, 'The Civil Standard of Proof Uncertainty: Probability, Belief and Justice' (1994) 16 *Sydney Law Review* 506, 509, 513.

[22] For discussion, see Evans Cameron (n 11).

[23] ibid.

[24] ibid 11–14.

This consideration plays only a minor role in law, however, because the law assumes a priori that both kinds of error are equally likely. The notion that decision-makers must presume an equal *base rate* – that at the outset they should assume that all statements have an equal chance of being true or false – is the essence of what it means not to pre-judge.[25] In two kinds of circumstances, however, the law's error preference can be seen responding to concerns about likelihood: when it adjusts to correct for what its architects perceive as a disproportionately high likelihood of either actual or expected error.

The law's architects may feel that, on a given set of facts, certain statements are very likely to be true or false. In such cases, since they think they have a sense of what the actual base rate is, they may prefer to dispense with the law's default. They will design the law to make it correspondingly easier or harder for this statement to be accepted. The Canadian criminal law, for example, presumes from the single fact that a person was sitting in the driver's seat of a car that they were operating it,[26] and presumes from the twin facts that a person's driving was impaired, and that they had driver-impairing drugs in their system, that these drugs were the cause of that impairment.[27] If the architects' assessment of the base rates in these circumstances is correct, by resolving doubt more easily in favour of accepting these conclusions, this kind of intervention will reduce the likelihood of *actual error*. If these statements are very often true, reducing the proportion of rejections will lead to a reduction in the number of mistakes.

As noted above, two kinds of mistake typically hang in the balance in fact-finding: *false rejections* (rejecting a true statement) and *false acceptances* (accepting a false statement). Where the evidence needed to prove a statement is unavailable, however, a decision-maker can only make one kind of error: since they will always reject the statement, a false rejection is the only kind of mistake they can make.

The likelihood of actual error under such circumstances is unknowable. It will depend on the actual base rate of false and true statements. If all such statements are both unprovable and false, the number of false rejections will be zero: all rejections will be accurate. As the number of statements that are unprovable but true increases, so will the number of false rejections. Yet assuming an equal base rate, the proportion of *expected errors* that the decision-maker will make at that statement's expense remains the same: 100 per cent. Despite equal odds of being true, the statement will always pay the full price for the decision-maker's doubts.

---

[25] Decision-makers are expected to approach the evidence 'without any notion of who has the better case': R A Posner, 'An Economic Approach to the Law of Evidence' (1999) 51 *Stanford Law Review* 1477, 1508. See also Evans Cameron (n 11) 8.
[26] Criminal Code (n 13) s 320.35.
[27] ibid s 320.31(6).

Where the party putting forward a statement will typically have insufficient or limited access to the evidence that they would need to prove it, the law may therefore intervene to lighten their load, particularly where the opposing party has better access to relevant information. Posner suggests that a concern about 'the inequality of the parties' resources for gathering and presenting evidence' helps to account for the decision to impose a heavy burden of proof on the prosecution in criminal cases,[28] and examples in civil and administrative law abound.[29] Canadian law recognises, for example, that refugee claimants often lack access to the evidence that would corroborate their claims. The law therefore presumes that they are telling the truth unless the contrary is established.[30] Depending on the actual base rate of false and true statements in these cases, this presumption may reduce or increase the number of mistakes. Its aim, regardless, is to remedy the unfairness of a fatally heavy error burden.

C. Resolving Doubt: The Fact-Finding Obstacle Course

(i) Onuses, Standards of Proof, Presumptions

Three elements of the law of fact-finding combine to set and adjust the parties' error burdens: onuses, standards of proof, and presumptions. To see how these structures work together to resolve doubt, picture an obstacle course: a track with a wall at the end. To be accepted as 'fact,' a statement must make it over the wall. Throughout a legal hearing, the parties will be sending statements down the track. The party with the *onus* to prove a statement is responsible for sending it running. The *standard of proof* determines how high the wall will be.

Imagine that any statement that makes it over the wall is put in a box and marked as 'fact'. The next statements to run can use this box to help them to get over the wall. As the hearing progresses, the running statements will have more and more boxes at their disposal.[31]

> The first statement – 'It was raining' – makes it over the wall. It is now in a box.
>
> The second statement – 'The ground was wet' – will use that first 'fact' box to help it to get over the wall.

---

[28] Posner (n 25), 1505, 1543.
[29] See B L Hay and K E Spier, 'Burdens of Proof in Civil Litigation: An Economic Perspective" (1997) 2 *The Journal of Legal Studies* 413, 426; C R Williams, 'Burdens and Standards in Civil Litigation" (2003) 25 *Sydney Law Review* 165, 179; R K Winter, 'The Jury and the Risk of Non-persuasion' (1971) *Law and Society Review* 335, 336; Al Stein, 'Allocating the Burden of Proof in Sales Litigation: The Law, its Rationale, a New Theory, and its Failure' (1995) 50 *University of Miami Law Review* 335.
[30] *Maldonado v Canada (Minister of Employment and Immigration)* [1980] 2 FC 302 [5]. See discussion in Evans Cameron (n 11) 87–96.
[31] See discussion of the linking of preliminary findings in 'chains' of inferences, also known as 'catenate inferences' or 'inference networks', in Evans Cameron (n 11) ch 8.

A *presumption* hands the running statement a 'fact X' box that it is permitted to use – unless and until the other side successfully runs the statement 'NOT X'. If the statement 'NOT X' makes it over the wall and becomes 'fact NOT X,' the law will take back the 'fact X' box and the runner can no longer use it. Note that the process involved in proving positive and negative statements is identical. The notion that one cannot prove a negative is as wrong in law as it is in logic.[32] The party hoping to prove 'NOT X' will simply pile up the available fact boxes and hope that this negative statement makes it over the wall.

> The first statement – 'It was raining' – is now in a box.
>
> The second statement – 'The ground was under an overhang' – is now in a box.
>
> The third statement – 'The ground was not wet' – will use these two 'fact' boxes to get over the wall.

By deciding which statements have to run, what kind of help they will get, and how high the wall will be, the law's fact-finding structures determine which party will have the harder job. To adjust the balance, the law can switch the runner; it can give or take away presumptions; and it can raise or lower the wall.

(ii) *Confidence, Doubt, Resolution, and Paralysis*

A couple of tweaks to this illustration capture further nuances that clarify the role of confidence, doubt, resolution, and paralysis, and that highlight a function of the onus that will be important for this chapter's analysis.

This obstacle course metaphor implicitly reflects one of the premises of legal epistemology: that decision-makers can observe the truth as it emerges from the evidence. They can uncover, discover, 'find' the facts. A real decision-maker, of course, cannot watch the runner at the wall and simply observe whether they make it over. A real decision-maker has to predict whether the runner will succeed. Imagine, therefore, that the running statement presents its collection of boxes to the decision-maker at the starting line. These boxes will be of various shapes and sizes, and the decision-maker must eyeball them and decide – does the statement have enough to make it over?

As noted above, decision-makers are expected to start this exercise without preconceptions. They are expected to start every analysis in *doubt*. As they begin to work through their impressions, the more likely they think it is that the statement will make it over the wall, the more *confidence* they will have in it. *Resolution* is the point at which the decision-maker feels able to decide: the point at which they believe that they know enough to make the call, one way or the other, despite any lingering uncertainty. *Paralysis* occurs when the decision-maker is unable to decide. When they cannot resolve their doubts, the onus, the law's tiebreaker, steps in.

---

[32] See SD Hales, 'Thinking Tools: You Can Prove a Negative' (2005) 4 *Think* 109.

Ending paralysis is its only job.[33] If, at the end of the day, the decision-maker is on the fence, the party with the onus loses.

Why are some doubts unresolvable? What causes paralysis? The common law's 'characteristic mode of reasoning,' reasoning by inductive inference, focuses decision-making attention on a single running statement.[34] This tends to hide the fact that no statement runs alone. Every time a statement takes a shot at the wall, a second statement is running alongside: its negation. If statement X is trying for the wall, statement NOT X is trying too.[35] When these pairs of statements run together, there are four possible outcomes. The first two lead to resolution. The second two cause paralysis.

In the first condition, the decision-maker is confident in the statement but not the counterstatement.

X makes it over.

NOT X does not.

This poses no problem. Statement X is now 'fact X'. The fact that NOT X was not proven may not even be worth mentioning; it is just the logical corollary.

In the second condition, the reverse, the decision-maker is confident in the counterstatement but not the statement.

X does not make it over.

NOT X does.

This, too, poses no problem for a decision-maker. Since statement X failed, it is not proven. Legally, logically, there may be no need to take the further step and affirm the counterstatement; if the accused is not guilty, there is no need to declare them innocent. But depending on the context, the decision-maker may well, and in the next breath, take the next step: 'In fact, I find NOT X.'

The problem for a decision-maker comes in either of the last two conditions. The decision-maker may not be confident in either statement:

X does not make it over.

NOT X also does not make it over.

Here the decision-maker thinks to themselves: I do not know what to believe. Logically, I must accept one of these statements. But I just cannot see how either is the case. Paralysis here is caused by the *lack of confidence* in both statements.

---

[33] See discussion in Evans Cameron (n 11) 8.
[34] T Anderson, D Schum and W Twining, *Analysis of Evidence (Law in Context)* (2nd edn, Cambridge, CUP, 2005) 80; Evans Cameron (n 11) ch 8.
[35] In an inductive model, the shadow runner is the statement's simple negation. In a model based on abductive inference ('inference to the best explanation'), the shadow runner is the strongest available counter theory. For the real-world consequences of this distinction in legal fact-finding, see Evans Cameron (n 11) ch 8.

On the flip side, the decision-maker may be confident in both statements:

X makes it over.

NOT X also makes it over.

While clearly incompatible with rational reasoning, being capable of 'holding two contradictory beliefs in one's mind simultaneously and accepting both of them' is a noted human ability.[36] Psychologists have suggested that it is, in fact, 'a normal and probably universal feature of the human condition'.[37] Paralysis here is caused, then, by the decision-maker's *confidence* in both statements.

(iii) How the Onus Breaks Ties

This helps to clarify how the onus works. To break a tie, the onus tells the decision-maker to ignore one set of results.

To resolve the first paralysis problem, where the decision-maker is paralysed by a lack of confidence,

X does not make it over.

NOT X also does not make it over.

putting the onus on statement X takes the second set of results off the table. The onus says: if 'X does not make it over' this is all you need to know. Ignore the fact that 'NOT X also does not make it over'. Ignore your lack of confidence in the counterstatement.

To resolve the second paralysis problem, where the decision-maker is paralysed because they are confident in both statements,

X makes it over.

NOT X makes it over.

putting the onus on statement X takes the first set of results off the table. The onus says: if 'NOT X makes it over,' this is all you need to know. Ignore the fact that 'X also makes it over'. If, paradoxically, you believe that the prosecution has proven its case, but you also believe that there is a reasonable doubt about the guilt of the accused, the tie goes to the runner: ignore your confidence in the prosecution's case and find for the accused.

The key point moving into the next part of this chapter is that, in functioning as a tiebreaker, the onus operates by selectively discounting decision-making confidence. This allows a decision-maker to decide without being confident in either

---

[36] G Orwell, *Nineteen Eighty-four* (London, Martin Secker & Warburg, 1949) 270, quoted in H J Irwin, N Dagnall and K Drinkwater, 'Belief Inconsistency in Conspiracy Theorists' (2015) 4 *Comprehensive Psychology* 1.

[37] Irwin, Dagnall and Drinkwater (n 36) 2.

the statement or the counterstatement. It also means that the party that bears the onus can lose despite the decision-maker being confident in their claim. And they can lose despite the decision-maker having no confidence in the suggestion that their claim is false. Understanding the role that confidence plays in legal fact-finding is crucial to recognising how the current law disadvantages Indigenous litigants in Aboriginal land and title claims.

III. The Supreme Court's Approach to Indigenous Oral History Evidence

The Supreme Court of Canada recognised in its judgment in *Delgamuukw* that the burden of proof on Aboriginal title and rights litigants was overly heavy; so heavy, in fact, that it risked rendering their claims 'nugatory'.[38] Oral history evidence may be 'crucial' for establishing the statements that Indigenous litigants must prove to win their claims: for many Indigenous litigants, this evidence is 'the only record of their past'.[39] But since this kind of evidence presents 'challenges', discussed below, it may well be 'consistently and systematically undervalued'.[40]

In response, the Court 'exhorted lower courts to apply the rules of evidence flexibly' when deciding whether to admit this kind of evidence.[41] Since the Court did not modify these rules, however, legal barriers to admissibility remain.[42] Moreover, even if all oral history evidence were categorically admissible, whether and to what extent this would lighten the burden of proof on Indigenous litigants depends on what judges make of that evidence. In deciding whether it supports the Indigenous parties' statements, how do judges understand it?[43] How do they weigh it? What conclusions do they draw from it? How do they resolve their doubts about it?

The Court in *Delgamuukw* rightly noted that how judges approach fact-finding may place 'an impossible burden of proof'' on Indigenous litigants.[44] The Court recognised, as a consequence, that 'the laws of evidence must be adapted' to allow

---

[38] *Delgamuukw* (n 9) [87]; see also *Van der Peet* (n 9) [68].
[39] ibid [84].
[40] ibid [98].
[41] Drake (n 4) 12.
[42] ibid.
[43] While this chapter considers the role of oral history in supporting findings of fact, scholars note that 'Indigenous oral traditions contain not only ancestral knowledge but also the law of Indigenous nations'; they should be understood as law and relied upon for their normative content, to 'inform the legal test to determine title, the benefits that title bestows, or the law that would function in a title area': F Harland, 'Taking the 'Aboriginal Perspective' Seriously: The (Mis)use of Indigenous Law in Tsilhqot'in Nation v British Columbia' (2018) 16/17 *Indigenous Law Journal* 21, 24. See, eg, discussion in Napoleon (n 4); Drake (n 4).
[44] *Delgamuukw* (n 9) [87], [101]; see generally [89]–[101].

oral history evidence not only to be admitted but also to be 'placed on an equal footing with the types of historical evidence that courts are familiar with, which largely consists of historical documents'.[45] Adjudicating such claims fairly will 'demand a unique approach to the treatment of evidence'.[46]

Four years later, however, the same Court in *Mitchell* moved away from this idea of adapting the laws of evidence. While noting that 'it is imperative that the laws of evidence operate to ensure that the aboriginal perspective is "given due weight by the courts"',[47] the Court stressed that oral history evidence should not be 'interpreted or weighed in a manner that fundamentally contravenes the principles of evidence law'.[48] The Court took the opportunity to 'clarify'[49] its earlier invitation to change the law:

> There is a boundary that must not be crossed between a sensitive application and a complete abandonment of the rules of evidence. As Binnie J. observed in the context of treaty rights, '[g]enerous rules of interpretation should not be confused with a vague sense of after-the-fact largesse'.[50]

In particular, to avoid 'a complete abandonment of the rules of evidence', the civil law's traditional fact-finding obstacle course must be maintained:

> Claims must still be established on the basis of persuasive evidence demonstrating their validity on the balance of probabilities.[51]

After *Mitchell*, the notion of putting oral history evidence 'on an equal footing' with documentary evidence lives on, not as an invitation to change the law, but as a normative guiding principle:

> Placing 'due weight' on the aboriginal perspective, or ensuring its supporting evidence an 'equal footing' with more familiar forms of evidence, means precisely what these phrases suggest: equal and due treatment.[52]

This 'equal and due treatment' principle does not address the error-burden problem that the Court has identified. In the context in which it is operating, it cannot change the second-class status of oral history evidence. Even if it could, placing this evidence 'on an equal footing' would still mean that, in a contest between a Crown statement supported by written historical evidence and an Indigenous statement supported by equally persuasive oral history evidence, the Indigenous statement would lose every time.

---

[45] ibid [87].
[46] ibid [82].
[47] *Mitchell* (n 9) [84].
[48] ibid [38].
[49] ibid [47].
[50] ibid [39].
[51] ibid.
[52] ibid [39].

A. 'Equal Footing' Requires Equal Confidence prima facie

As a guiding principle, the Court's words are significant. In *Delgamuukw*'s wake, lower courts have given oral history evidence more considered attention and at times have given it credence when it does not conflict with the written record.[53] But allowing that a mode of evidence can be probative is the threshold requirement for '*meaningful* consideration',[54] not *equal* consideration. To be on an 'equal footing', this evidence would need to stand a fair chance against competing documentary evidence. To avoid pre-judgment, the judge would need to begin the fact-finding exercise assuming an equal base rate of probative value for both modes of evidence. In other words, they would need equivalent confidence in both, all else being equal.[55]

As the Court notes, written records are 'the types of historical evidence that courts are familiar with'.[56] For centuries, Canadian courts have been confident this kind of evidence can get a statement over the wall. In contrast, as the Court also notes, in a Canadian courtroom, '[m]any features of oral histories would count against … their weight as evidence of prior events'.[57] And judges in Canadian courts are overwhelmingly settlers.[58]

It would take robust optimism to believe that judges will have equal confidence in both modes of evidence. On the contrary, likely nothing short of a full-throated endorsement would convince them that oral and written history are prima facie equally probative. The Court has been neither willing nor able to provide such an endorsement.

For a start, it would be unusual. Deciding what weight to give evidence, as the Court notes in *Mitchell*, is 'generally the domain of the trial judge, who is best situated to assess the evidence as it is presented'.[59] While the law of evidence regularly addresses the 'threshold' reliability of categories of evidence for the purpose of determining admissibility, it shies away from commenting on their 'ultimate'

---

[53] See *Tsilhqot'in Nation v British Columbia* [2007] BCJ No 2465 BCCA; *Jim Shot Both Sides v Canada* [2020] 1 FCR 22 (overturned on other grounds: *Canada v Both Sides* [2022] FCJ No 151 FCA). See discussion in Potamianos (n 9).

[54] Mitchell (n 9) [29].

[55] Recall that confidence in a statement is the decision-maker's measure of how likely it is to make it over the wall. Confidence in a statement's supporting evidence, correspondingly, is the decision-maker's measure of how much that evidence increases that likelihood. The more confidence the decision-maker has in the evidence, the more confidence they will have in the statement that it supports. The decision-maker has equal confidence in two modes of evidence if they believe that both can equivalently increase the likelihood of the statements that they support.

[56] *Delgamuukw* (n 9) [86].

[57] ibid.

[58] 'Since 2016, 3 per cent of federal judicial appointments have been Indigenous': O Stefanovich, 'Federal Court Justice Says Judicial Diversity Targets Need 'Aggressive' Timelines' (CBC News, 30 June 2020). Available at: www.cbc.ca/news/politics/stefanovich-diversity-justice-system-1.5625586, last accessed 24 January 2023.

[59] *Mitchell* (n 9) [36].

reliability when it comes to fact-finding.[60] For this reason, the Court refused to 'set out "precise rules" or "absolute principles" governing the interpretation or weighing of evidence in aboriginal claims'.[61]

More fundamentally, there is little indication that the Court itself has equal confidence in the probative value of oral history evidence. The Court does recognise that this evidence has value. It can be 'highly compelling' (but also 'highly dubious').[62] If the trial judge in *Delgamuukw* had properly assessed the oral history evidence, he might have made 'very different' findings of fact (although the judge at the retrial, properly instructed, 'might well share some or all' of his conclusions).[63] In addressing why this evidence has value, the Court stresses repeatedly that it is important because it shares 'the aboriginal perspective'[64] and because it 'may offer evidence of ancestral practices'.[65] The former is, of course, only helpful to the extent that the judge feels that the 'aboriginal perspective' is factually relevant. The latter stops conspicuously short of suggesting that this evidence may be a reliable way to learn about the past more broadly – such as, for example, in deciding who said what to whom.[66]

On the contrary, the Court suggests that this evidence contains a mixture of 'history, legend, politics and moral obligations', some elements of which 'are tangential to the ultimate purpose of the fact-finding process at trial – the determination of the historical truth'.[67] In overturning the lower court's judgment in *Delgamuukw*, the Court does not dispute the judge's finding that the oral histories in that case 'did not accurately convey historical truth' and 'were insufficiently detailed'.[68] The Court rather comments that 'these are features, to a greater or lesser extent, of all oral histories'.[69] What stands out from these judgments is not the Court's confidence in oral history as a mode of evidence, but rather its feeling that there are powerful normative reasons, discussed below, to consider it '[n]otwithstanding the challenges created by [its use] as proof of historical facts'.[70]

B. 'Equal Footing' on the Traditional Civil Law Obstacle Course

Moreover, even if judges could be convinced to have equal confidence in oral history as a mode of evidence, as long as Indigenous parties' statements 'must

---

[60] See discussion in *R v Khelawon* [2006] SCJ No 57 [50]–[55]; *R v Blackman* [2008] SCJ No 38 [56].
[61] *Mitchell* (n 9) [36].
[62] ibid [39].
[63] *Delgamuukw* (n 9) [107]–[108].
[64] ibid [81]–[82], [84], [98].
[65] *Mitchell* (n 9) [32].
[66] See *Benoit v Canada* [2002] 2 CNLR 1 (FC); *Benoit v Canada* [2003] 3 CNLR 20 (FCA).
[67] *Delgamuukw* (n 9) [86].
[68] ibid [98].
[69] ibid [89].
[70] ibid [87].

still be established on the basis of persuasive evidence demonstrating their validity on the balance of probabilities',[71] compelling Aboriginal title and rights claims will fail.

To see this in operation, imagine the simplest version of the relevant proof scenario. The question before the Court is whether an Indigenous people occupied Area A at the time in question. Oral history evidence affirms that they did. Written records make no mention of them. The judge begins with equal confidence in both kinds of evidence prima facie and ultimately finds that they have equal probative value.

If the judge has little confidence in either party's evidence, neither statement will make it over the wall. The onus will then tell the judge to disregard their lack of confidence in the Crown's evidence. The Crown wins the point. Occupation of Area A is not proven, despite the judge's finding that the written records are dubious.

If the judge has sufficient confidence in both parties' evidence, both statements will make it over the wall. The onus will then tell the judge to disregard their confidence in the Indigenous party's statement. The Crown wins the point. Occupation of Area A is not proven, despite the judge's finding that the oral history evidence is just as compelling.

The Court has made a category mistake in trying to address the error burden problem by changing how it treats Indigenous evidence. To address the error burden problem, it must change how it treats Indigenous statements. The Court's decision to maintain the civil law's default fact-finding structures ensures that doubt will resolve against Indigenous parties. That their evidence must overcome a wide confidence gap ensures that this doubt will resolve against them by a wide margin. As generations of critical theorists have observed, 'equal footing' is not much use on a tilted playing field.

IV. The Wrong Mistake

Canadian law should recognise that Aboriginal title and rights claims are a paradigm case where the fact-finding obstacle course should depart from the common law default and resolve doubt in favour of the moving party. The Crown should bear the onus of proving that the facts underlying the claim have not been established. Considering the magnitude and likelihood of the harms that hang in the balance, Canadian law should recognise that rejecting true statements that support these claims is the wrong mistake.

---

[71] *Mitchell* (n 9) [39].

A. Magnitude

From *Van der Peet* on, the potential harms to Canada and to settlers' interests have been front and centre in the courts' discussions of fact-finding error costs in Aboriginal title and rights claims. The Supreme Court cautions that these claims can strain 'the Canadian legal and constitutional structure',[72] especially if treated with too much 'largesse'.[73] Its closing words in *Delgamuukw* suggest an undercurrent of existential settler anxiety: 'Let's face it. We are all here to stay'.[74]

The potential harms to Indigenous parties of errors at their expense have not caught the courts' attention in the same way. Indeed, concerns about the potential harm to Canada are at times so salient that they not so much outweigh, as simply eclipse, the counterbalancing harms. The Federal Court of Appeal, for example, highlighted the 'gravity of the consequences' of accepting an Indigenous party's claim that it was treaty-exempt from paying taxes. Since a mistake in their favour would wrongly deprive Canada of revenue, the trial judge should have been more careful when he decided to accept their evidence. The Court makes no mention of the 'gravity of the consequences' of a mistake of the opposite kind: that the Indigenous litigants will continue to pay money that they do not owe.[75]

The Supreme Court does note, however, that decisions about fact-finding should be made 'in a manner commensurate with ... the promise of reconciliation' contained within the section of the Canadian Constitution that recognises Aboriginal rights.[76] Settlers on this territory are increasingly recognising this promise as essential to our collective future. As the TRC Report notes, however, '[g]etting to the truth was hard, but getting to reconciliation will be harder'.[77] The Canadian government has committed to building a new 'nation-to-nation, government-to-government, and Inuit-Crown relationship' with Indigenous people 'based on recognition of rights, respect, co-operation, and partnership',[78]

---

[72] *Van der Peet* (n 9) [49].

[73] *Mitchell* (n 9) [39].

[74] *Delgamuukw* (n 9) [186]. Some have suggested that underlying these concerns is also the ever-present fear that this kind of evidence can simply be invented: 'The central anxiety that creeps up on all of us then, is, "What if they are making this up?"': A D Etinson, 'Aboriginal Oral History Evidence and Canadian Law' (2008) 6 *Central European Journal of Canadian Studies* 97. For a discussion of the cost to the national ego of the fear of being played for fools, and how this factor can affect error preference in legal fact-finding, see H Evans Cameron, 'The Battle for the Wrong Mistake: Error Preference and Risk Salience in Canadian Refugee Status Decision-making" (2019) 42 *Dalhousie Law Journal* 1.

[75] *Benoit FCA* (n 66) [26].

[76] *Mitchell* (n 9) [29]. 'The existing aboriginal and treaty rights of the aboriginal peoples of Canada are hereby recognized and affirmed': Constitution Act, 1982, Schedule B to the Canada Act 1982, 1982, c. 11 (UK).

[77] TRC Report (n 1) Preface, vi.

[78] Her Majesty the Queen in Right of Canada, as represented by the Minister of Justice and Attorney General of Canada (2018) 'Principles: Respecting the Government of Canada's Relationship with Indigenous Peoples' *Department of Justice Canada*. Available at: www.justice.gc.ca/eng/csj-sjc/principles.pdf, last accessed 24 Jan 2023, 3; see also UN General Assembly, *United Nations Declaration on the Rights of Indigenous Peoples*: resolution/adopted by the General Assembly, 2 October 2007, A/RES/61/295.

but 'the pace of real substantive change remains glacial' and '[r]econciliation has a shelf life. Goodwill doesn't last forever.'[79] Some part of the price that Canada must expect to pay for centuries of oppression will come in the form of fact-finding errors in Aboriginal title and rights claims. Any remaining hope of reconciliation cannot survive a process that reduces these costs by placing 'an impossible burden of proof' on Indigenous litigants – a process that ensures, as Milward rightly notes, that 'Canadian sovereignty is thereby sustained at the expense of Aboriginal interests'.[80]

B. Likelihood

If Canadian courts prefer to uphold the default assumption that both kinds of mistake in civil claims have equally serious consequences, they should nonetheless resolve doubt in favour of Indigenous statements to offset the disproportionately high expected likelihood of errors at their expense.

Unlike Indigenous litigants, the Crown does not need to rely on oral history to prove its statements. It can rely instead on 'the types of historical evidence that courts are familiar with.'[81] Any biases in this evidence will be in its favour. While the Court has held that oral history 'to a greater or lesser extent' does 'not accurately convey historical truth',[82] historians and anthropologists acknowledge that the same is true of the written record: documents prepared by settlers reflect settler perspectives.[83] As Miller notes, in the years since *Mitchell*, in contests between Crown and Indigenous academic experts, 'the courts have commonly preferred the views of the Crown'.[84] Against this backdrop, expecting Indigenous parties to establish that their evidence is not only equally persuasive, but more persuasive, is unjust.

The Court in *Mitchell* suggests that there is a 'boundary' that divides the status quo from lawlessness. On one side is a 'sensitive application' of the current law; on the other, a 'complete abandonment of the rules of evidence'. Between the two, however, there is ample room for adapting the law in a way that does not 'fundamentally contraven[e] the principles of evidence law'.[85] As noted above, one important

---

[79] E Jewell and I Mosby, 'Calls to Action Accountability: A 2021 Status Update on Reconciliation' (Yellowhead Institute, 2021). Available at: https://yellowheadinstitute.org/resources/calls-to-action-accountability-a-2021-status-update-on-reconciliation/, last accessed 24 January 2023.
[80] Milward, 'Doubting What Elders Have to Say' (n 4) 288.
[81] *Delgamuukw* (n 9) [86].
[82] ibid [98].
[83] See Ray (n 7); Miller (n 7); Napoleon (n 6) 135. For a discussion of authorial perspectives in historical sources generally, see WK Storey and M Cowan, *Writing History: A Guide for Canadian Students* (5th edn, Oxford, OUP, 2019) 31–32.
[84] Miller (n 7) 91. See also Milward (n 4) 287; Napoleon (n 4); Potamianos (n 4).
[85] *Mitchell* (n 9) [38].

principle of evidence law is that its fact-finding structures should compensate for the parties' unequal access to probative evidence, where this unequal access will significantly affect the expected likelihood of error. Since lowering the standard of proof beneath the 'balance of probabilities' would cause judges to accept as proven a statement that they think is unlikely to be true, which runs fundamentally counter to the inductive process at the heart of legal reasoning,[86] the law in such cases reverses the onus.[87]

To reject Indigenous statements, judges should be more confident in the Crown's evidence. Indeed, given the wide confidence gap and the Constitutional imperative of reconciliation, they should be significantly more confident. The Crown should be required to show 'clear and convincing evidence' of its claim that the facts underlying an Aboriginal title or right are not established. The Supreme Court has rejected this intermediate standard at common law, admitting only two proof thresholds, the civil 'balance of probabilities' and the criminal 'beyond a reasonable doubt'.[88] Aboriginal rights and title stand outside of the common law, however, and as the Court made clear in *Delgamuukw*, 'the common law rules of evidence should be adapted to take into account the *sui generis* nature of aboriginal rights'.[89] If, in the words of the TRC Report, '[v]irtually all aspects of Canadian society may need to be reconsidered'[90] surely this includes the law's standards of proof.

V. Conclusion

The common law's default fact-finding structures are not ends unto themselves. They are a means to achieve normative outcomes. Courts must be open to modifying them as needed when their effect is normatively misaligned.[91]

In the case of Indigenous oral history evidence, redesigning the law's fact-finding obstacle course would have one practical consequence. Some Canadian judges have expressed alarm at the notion of accepting as fact statements that do not withstand 'scrutiny' when investigated using social scientific methods of inquiry: 'public wrongs cannot be atoned by abandoning scientific standards' in our understanding of the past.[92] If nothing else, reversing the onus allays this

---

[86] For an argument that induction should be abandoned in certain fact-finding contexts in favour of a different mode of inferential reasoning, see Evans Cameron (n 11) ch 8.
[87] See sources in nn 28 to 30.
[88] *FH v McDougall* [2008] 3 SCR 41.
[89] *Delgamuukw* (n 9) [3] [82]; *Mitchell* (n 9) [38].
[90] TRC Report (n 1) Preface, vi.
[91] See, eg, Lillquist (n 20); Evans Cameron (n 11).
[92] *Samson Indian Nation and Band v Canada* [2006] 1 CNLR 100 [454], citing an expert report authored by A von Gernet; *Benoit FCA* (n 66) [11]. See also A von Gernet, 'What My Elders Taught Me: Oral Traditions as Evidence in Aboriginal Litigation' in O Lippert et al (eds), *Beyond the Nass Valley: National Implications of the Supreme Court's Delgamuukw Decision* (Calgary, The Fraser Institute, 2000).

concern. For Indigenous parties to establish a claim, their statements need not be accepted as proven. This is not to suggest that these statements *should not* be accepted as proven, but rather that changing the legal structure removes one philosophical/psychological barrier to accepting Indigenous claims.

Beyond this, it is an open question whether and to what extent the law's fact-finding obstacle course constrains how decision-makers reason.[93] Regardless, as long as judges in Canadian courts are quite confident in the Crown's evidence, requiring the Crown to prove its statements, even on a higher standard of proof, will make no difference to the outcome in the litigation. Adapting the law of fact-finding may do little to support decolonisation. Many more fundamental changes to Canadian laws and legal institutions are needed to take seriously the work of creating a new way of living together on this territory.[94] Adapting is, however, the very least that the law of fact-finding can do.

---

[93] See D J Devine, *Jury Decision Making: The State of the Science* (New York, New York University Press, 2012) ch 2; Lillquist (n 20); the sources referenced in n 18.

[94] See Jewell & Mosby (n 77); Milward (n 4); M McCrossan, 'Advancing Dishonourable Relations: Legal Reasoning, Indigenous Rights, and Strategic Uses of Reconciliation' (2019) 100 *Studies in Political Economy* 9.

13
Political Science in the Courtroom: Potential and Pitfalls

ZIM NWOKORA AND JAYANI NADARAJALINGAM[*]

I. Introduction

There is a long tradition of courts relying on expert evidence. This chapter investigates how evidence from political science has been used by Australian courts, the High Court especially, and how this engagement might be fruitfully deepened. It is motivated by our suspicion that while political science evidence has been used on occasion by the High Court, this engagement has rarely been acknowledged and, moreover, it occurs less than it perhaps should. We think that there are understandable reasons that might explain why insights from political science have so far been peripheral to adjudication, and such concerns are not unique to law's relationship to political science.[1] However, as we will argue, courts can work through these issues in order to make the most of the available expertise while minimising the risks from doing so.

To set the terms of the discussion, we mean by 'political science' the academic study of politics. Its scholars, often referred to as 'political scientists', analyse political phenomena (ie institutions, processes, events and relationships) with specialised empirical methods that include statistical analysis of a large number of cases (ie 'large-n' studies), comparative analysis of a medium number of cases, and single-case (or 'small-n') studies.[2] Very different kinds of knowledge result from application of these methods. Large-n research aims to identify correlations in the relationship between variables, such as 'democracy' and 'economic growth', and

---

[*] For helpful feedback on this chapter, the authors would like to thank Anne Carter, Patrick Emerton, Jeremy Gans, Kateena O'Gorman, Hayley Pitcher, Adrienne Stone, Joe Tomlinson and participants at the 2019 Facts in Public Law Adjudication Workshop, funded by the Academy of the Social Sciences in Australia.

[1] See, eg, for a discussion of courts' engagement with history in the Australian context, T Josev, 'Australian Historians and Historiography in the Courtroom' (2020) 43 *Melbourne University Law Review* 1069.

[2] While normative political theory is often considered to be part of the 'political science' discipline, our arguments in this chapter focus on the empirical side of the discipline.

interconnects with similarly designed work in economics, psychology, and sociology. Small-n research aims to provide a 'thick description' of decision-making, whether in government or in a more informal setting, and it bears close similarities with the inquiries undertaken by anthropologists, historians, qualitative sociologists and geographers.[3] The 'comparative method' has been described as lying between these poles because it seeks to identify patterns that hold across the limited range of contexts under examination.[4] There are vigorous debates among political scientists about the application, merits and limitations of these and other methods, and such methodological debates have been an important driver of the discipline's development. The question that we engage with here, however, is whether the knowledge, or 'facts', emerging from political science scholarship can contribute to adjudication and, if so, how it should be incorporated into the legal process.

At first glance, it might seem sensible for judges and lawyers to steer clear of political science and its intramural debates. Yet, though understandable, this position is misguided in our view. Courts, in general, should engage with political science despite the challenges in doing so; and the Australian courts, in particular, could do so more thoroughly than they have in the past, in ways that could improve the quality of adjudication. We reach this conclusion based on the following claims. The first is that insights from political science research – what might be described as 'political science evidence' – bear on issues of relevance to the courts, including on constitutional questions. The adjudication process will therefore be poorer in the absence of such evidence. While there has been some recognition of this potential for political science to contribute to adjudication, there are also lingering concerns that may explain, at least in part, the weak uptake of political science by courts in Australia (and in many other countries).[5] Among these concerns is the suspicion that political science evidence is not robust enough for courts to rely on, and the fear that moves in this direction may put at risk the judge's delicate role in a liberal democracy. While these are serious issues, the appropriate response to them, in our view, is not to abandon wholesale the effort to incorporate political science into adjudication, but rather to consider what procedures might be used to work through the problems that arise. That way, the evidence that political science can generate is made available to the courts while the risks that follow from this mode of engagement are managed and mitigated as much as possible.

---

[3] See, eg, RAW Rhodes, *Everyday Life in British Government* (Oxford, OUP, 2011); for applications to informal settings, see V Boege et al, 'On Hybrid Political Orders and Emerging States: What is Failing – States in the Global South or Research and Politics in the West?' (2008) 8 *Berghof Handbook Dialogue Series* 15.

[4] A Lijphart, 'Comparative Politics and the Comparative Method' (1971) 65 *The American Political Science Review* 682; D Collier, 'The Comparative Method: Two Decades of Change' in DA Rusto and KP Erickson (eds), *Comparative Political Dynamics: Global Research Perspectives* (New York, Harper Collins, 1991).

[5] See N Petersen, 'Avoiding the Common-Wisdom Fallacy: The Role of Social Science in Constitutional Adjudication' (2013) 11 *International Journal of Constitutional Law* 294.

The remainder of the chapter fleshes out this argument. In Part II, we explain how and why political science knowledge can contribute to adjudication. Part III discusses the challenges of handling such evidence in the legal process, arguing that the best response to these problems is careful thinking about incorporation strategies. Part IV identifies three strategies – judicial notice, statements of agreed facts and remittal to lower courts – that have been used for a variety of purposes by the High Court of Australia (HCA), and which might provide avenues to further incorporate political science evidence into courtroom decision-making. Though there are overlaps between some of the strategies we discuss and those advanced in previous studies of law's relationship to social science, our focus on political science (rather than the social sciences as a whole) and the Australian context (which has not received much attention in this research agenda) results in differences with this previous work.[6] In Part V, we discuss an opportunity for engagement with political science that was missed due to underutilisation of the strategies we identify. The conclusion summarises the chapter's arguments and points to some of the issues it raises that warrant further research.

II. Why Political Science in the Courtroom?

The most basic way that political science evidence can add value in a courtroom context is by expanding and augmenting the factual basis for decision-making. Like other forms of knowledge, political science can be applied to legal problems to improve our understanding of the issues at stake.[7] On the face of it, this might seem like an intuitive argument since courts have long relied on experts from a wide range of fields – including medical doctors, scientists, statisticians, economists and others – to contribute to the body of evidence they draw on.[8] We might therefore expect that a similar argument would apply to political science and its practitioners. Indeed, the case for drawing political science evidence into the legal process might seem particularly compelling given the symbiotic relationship between the subject matter of this discipline and that of constitutional law (in particular, constitutions often establish the structures that political scientists then go on study). As chapter 4 in this collection notes, constitutions 'contain various

---

[6] See, eg, R Dworkin, 'Social Sciences and Constitutional Rights' (1977) 41 *Educational Forum* 271; Josev (n 2); Petersen (n 6).

[7] It should be noted that an important rule of evidence is as follows: 'A witness may not give an opinion on matters calling for the special skill or knowledge of an expert unless the witness is an expert in such matters.' Thus, with the exception of expert witnesses, witnesses 'must state facts, not opinions': JD Heydon, *Cross on Evidence* (Chatswood, LexisNexis Butterworths, 2020) 1089. See also DM Dwyer, *The Judicial Assessment of Expert Evidence* (Cambridge, CUP, 2008).

[8] See, eg, T Golan, 'The History of Scientific Expert Testimony in the English Courtroom' (1999) 12 *Science in Context* 7; RA Posner, 'The Law and Economics of the Expert Witness' (1999) 13 *Journal of Economic Perspectives* 91.

political mandates: that is, ... [they] ... set[] out requirements concerning political events that must occur, and political institutions that must exist'.[9]

In fact, political science features rarely in constitutional adjudication – particularly beyond the context of 'judicial notice' (one of the mechanisms we discuss below) – in Australia.[10] Indeed, this seems to be a wider trend across established democracies.[11] The United States and Canada stand out as exceptions, but even in these countries the integration of political science is a relatively recent development and it has been more limited and less influential than the uptake of evidence from other social science disciplines, especially economics. For sure, there are practical hurdles that have impeded the use of political science by courts, and we discuss several of these barriers in the next section. But we also suspect that the lack of engagement with political science is due to perceptions among judges and lawyers about the nature of political science knowledge. Putting this view bluntly, it is the belief that political science evidence is not comparable to the evidence from the natural and health sciences or from other social sciences, especially economics. This suspicion may be expressed or manifest itself in several ways. One version is the sense that political science evidence is not *technical* in the same way as evidence from other fields. Therefore, its findings, or at least those of relevance to the legal process, are 'common knowledge' of which an intelligent non-specialist should be aware. On the other hand, the political science findings that might be considered as falling beyond 'common knowledge' are of little use to courts because of their topic of focus, or because this work reveals knowledge that is 'political' in the sense that it deals with controversies about fundamental values that are better handled by the elected branches of government than by courts.

Following this argument, there will be little value in 'incorporating' political science evidence into the court process because this is already being done (insofar as it would be beneficial to do so) through sensible decision-making on the basis of common knowledge about political matters. This belief, we argue, needs to be revised. Admittedly, some of what might be regarded as political science evidence will correspond to the intuitions of a sensible person. For instance, it might seem

---

[9] See Emerton and Nadarajalingam, Chapter 4 in this volume.

[10] To provide an indicative, though admittedly crude, assessment of the frequency of political science citations in the Australian legal system, we performed a LexisNexis search of 'political science' mentions in Australian courts since 1 January 1932 (until 15 May 2022). The search yielded only 150 mentions, including 10 from the HCA. Furthermore, many of these mentions were merely descriptions of a witness's academic qualifications (eg a person who holds a bachelor's degree in political science), not references to political science evidence.

[11] Petersen (n 6). Political science has been used by the Canadian courts to inform their decision-making especially on cases involving the Charter of Rights and Freedoms: see, eg, RE Charney, 'Evidence in Charter Cases: Expert Evidence and Proving Purpose' (2004) 16 *National Journal of Constitutional Law* 1; M Da Silva, 'Trial Level References: In Defence of a New Presumption' (2012) 2 *Western Journal of Legal Studies* 4. In the United States, political science evidence has been particularly influential in reapportionment and voting rights cases: see, eg, RL Engstrom and MP McDonald, 'The Political Scientist as Expert Witness' (2011) 44 *PS: Political Science and Politics* 285; L Leigh, 'Political Scientists as Expert Witnesses' (1991) 37 *PS: Political Science and Politics* 771; KR Mayer, 'Is Political Science Relevant? Ask an Expert Witness' (2010) 8 *The Forum* 6.

'intuitive' to expect that restrictions (ie caps) on election campaign spending by political parties can make electoral contests more balanced, an outcome sometimes described as 'levelling the playing field'.[12] But this point can be *grounded* to a greater or lesser extent depending on the quality of evidence supporting it. The plentiful documented evidence, from a variety of contexts, that caps are associated with more competitive elections strongly supports this intuition.[13] Yet, as with many observations of this kind, there are alternative intuitions that lead to a different expectation. For example, some believe that caps do not work to achieve their purported aims because they simply lead to displacement (the campaign funds that have been restricted by the caps in one area find their way into the political system via another opening).[14] The probably greater evidence in favour of the first intuition does not *prove* that the introduction of caps into a jurisdiction will result in its elections becoming more balanced. However, given the state of the scholarship on this question, this seems to be a reasonable starting point from which adjustments might be considered based on the peculiarities on the ground. The intuition would be weakly grounded without such evidence and there would be no compelling reason to accept it ahead of another fairly plausible hypothesis.

In short, political science evidence can bolster our confidence in some intuitions and directly challenge others. Furthermore, because an important goal of such research is to generate counter-intuitive knowledge, political science evidence may sometimes generate new intuitions that were not otherwise available within the legal process. To give an example, let us consider this potential in the context of citizenship cases. Courts are often required to adjudicate complex questions about citizenship, relying on information from state institutions – embassies, foreign ministries, national archives and the like – from countries around the world to determine, for instance, an individual's current citizenship status or to clarify a country's historical citizenship requirements. While a case may turn on information of this kind, there is ample evidence that countries vary significantly in their capacity to generate, organise and supply reliable citizenship data. This point may not be widely recognised in the court system of an advanced industrialised democracy. Yet, the scholarship on state institutions from the subfield of comparative politics provides a potentially useful lens through which to understand such

---

[12] See, eg, *McCloy v New South Wales* (2015) 257 CLR 178.
[13] For evidence supporting this conjecture in the United States, see DM Primo, J Milyo and T Groseclose (2006) 'State Campaign Finance Reforms, Competitiveness and Party Advantage in Gubernatorial Elections' in J Samples (ed), *The Marketplace of Democracy: Electoral Competition and American Politics* (Washington DC, Cato-Brookings, 2006). In Australia, see Z Nwokora et al, 'Political Finance Regulation and Reform in New South Wales: Toward a Fairer System?' (2019) 65 *Australian Journal of Politics & History* 115. In Denmark and the Netherlands, see A-K Koölln, 'Does Party Finance Regulation Create a Level Playing Field' (2016) 15 *Election Law Journal: Rules, Politics, and Policy* 71. In France, see N Broberg, V Pons, C Tricaud, 'The Impact of Campaign Finance Rules on Candidate Selection and Electoral Outcomes: Evidence from France' (2022) *NBER Working Paper Series* 29805.
[14] S Issacharoff and PS Karlan, 'The Hydraulics of Campaign Finance Reform' 77 *Texas Law Review* 1705.

country differences.[15] This research agenda has developed the notion of 'state capacity' to compare countries in terms of the competences of their state institutions, and it may be useful to courts in assessing, for instance, whether it is credible to claim that a piece of documentary evidence is unavailable.

Besides supplying evidence about political phenomena, political science research can also support courtroom decision-making by contributing to the development of the legal concepts at play in a case. Here, the political science unpacking of a concept might help to give the legal concept a rigorous conceptualisation where one had been lacking, or foreground issues neglected by the legal treatment. Consider, as an example, the characterisation of a state of affairs as a 'crisis' situation. Although such a characterisation – especially if undertaken by key political actors – can have significant implications for democratic governance, including departures from the usual mechanisms of executive accountability, the notion of 'crisis' has often been left undefined (or underspecified) by courts. There exist good reasons why courts have taken this approach. As is well known, cabinet documents are privileged thus, in most cases, cannot be led in evidence. Further, there may be issues of justiciability if one party attempts to argue, for instance, that the executive is deliberately constructing a crisis purely to enliven its power. The difficulties with this approach are laid bare by research on crisis politics, however, which highlights the risk of opportunistic manipulation of 'crises' by executives. As pointed out by Steven Levitsky and Daniel Ziblatt, leading scholars of democratic fragility, a characteristic of 'autocratic-minded leaders' is their willingness to 'exploit (or invent) a crisis in order to justify an abuse of power'.[16] In short, the executive's definition of a crisis may be self-serving. If a court were to take account of the implications of such work, the evidentiary and justiciability constraints will remain, but it might also encourage a more critical starting point in the determination of what qualifies as a 'crisis'.

III. Challenges of Political Science Evidence

If, as we have argued, the integration of political science evidence can have real payoffs for the legal process, then why does this happen so rarely? One way to think about the problem is to view the kind of engagement that we are advocating as having certain 'benefits' but also associated 'obstacles' (emanating from 'risks' either to the legal community or to political scientists) that get in the way of closer

---

[15] See, eg, J Migdal, *Strong Societies and Weak States* (Princeton, Princeton University Press, 1988); JC Scott, *Seeing Like a State: How Certain Schemes to Improve the Human Condition have Failed* (New Haven, Yale University Press, 1998).

[16] S Levitsky and D Ziblatt, 'Why Autocrats Love Emergencies: Crises – Real and Imaginary – Loosen Normal Constitutional Constraints' *The New York Times* (New York, 12 January 2019). Available at: www.nytimes.com/2019/01/12/opinion/sunday/trump-national-emergency-wall.html, last accessed 15 March 2022. See also R Brubaker, 'Paradoxes of Populism During the Pandemic' (2021) 164 *Thesis Eleven* 73.

cooperation. In this section, we identify several such obstacles. While some are specific to the law–political science relationship, others are more generic and bear similarities with the challenges that courts face in their engagements with other disciplines.[17] The section also suggests some ways to manage these obstacles to improve the prospects for the effective incorporation of political science evidence into adjudication.

A. Incentives

The engagement we are advocating requires political scientists to share their knowledge with courts either by serving as an expert witness, or by submitting material as requested by one (or multiple) parties to a case. Either way, they will face unusual incentives in this context compared to those they deal with in their regular work as teachers and researchers.[18] In academic debate, political scientists subscribe to the scientific commitments of 'truth' and 'rigour'. Though these are not unproblematic goals, there is broad consensus on them among (empirical) political scientists. Straying from these standards will (generally) attract stiff penalties (including a speedy rejection letter from the editor of one of the journals that, together, serve as the gatekeepers of disciplinary knowledge). The courtroom 'game' is very different to this. It presents the risk that a political scientist who has been hired as an expert witness may 'seek to please' their sponsors by slanting their testimony to support the sponsor's interests. For example, they might downplay the kinds of caveats that would be standard fare for a journal article, giving their courtroom testimony an air of certainty that is unwarranted based on the existing knowledge base.

In our view, the risks here are likely to be manageable through well-designed procedures. As with any expert, the political scientist's professional reputation will serve as a check on what they are prepared to say. When there is a consensus on a question of fact, the scholar whose testimony conflicts with this mainstream position without explanation is likely to suffer from a loss of credibility and will become known for holding biases. We should expect that their evidence will be discounted by a fair legal process and, over time, their attractiveness for expert witness roles will decline while more reliable (ie less-biased) scholars will be more in demand.

Furthermore, as Richard Posner explains in his analysis of economic expert witnesses, a scholar's publication record also puts limits on what they are prepared to say, in ways that can help a court elicit the widely accepted positions among the experts in a field.[19] Since an author's published work will capture their views, expressed within the norms of their discipline, it will be difficult for them to defend

---

[17] See, eg, Josev (n 2).
[18] See, eg, Mayer (n 12); Posner (n 9).
[19] Posner (n 9) 94.

positions that are inconsistent with this work.[20] In fact, Posner argues that, due to the constraining effect of past publications, scholars who are invited to serve as expert witnesses should be expected to have a publication record on the issue about which they are testifying.[21] This seems like a sensible rule in general, though judges might sometimes value practical experience alongside (or more than) a publication record and therefore prefer to rely on evidence from practitioner-scholars or 'pracademics'.[22]

B. Deep Disagreement

While drawing out the political science evidence on a question of fact may not be a big problem when there is scholarly agreement, such a consensus may not exist. Indeed, given the state of the knowledge on many political science topics, deep disagreement on factual questions may be the more common occurrence. In this scenario the most practical approach will be to apply a procedure that enables the competing positions on a debate to be aired, and for a reconciliation at some level of abstraction to be reached. In Part III, we identify a procedure, namely remittal to lower courts, which captures the rationale of this approach as it provides a forum for a (directed) airing of the scholarly debate on a question of fact before the court. The reconciled position that emerges does not need to take a side in the controversy, but rather should aim to describe the range of views of the relevant scholarly community. It will support legal proceedings by helping those involved to identify the points on which there is scholarly agreement, where the experts disagree, and the different plausible positions in those debates. These clarifications can progress the understanding of a complex topic, and reflect the fact that an absence of consensus should not be taken to imply that there is a lack of knowledge about that topic. Ideally, the summary document should be endorsed by the experts who hold competing views, perhaps after some discussion and deliberation. In this sense, it provides a literature review tailored to the needs of the court. Practical questions will arise at this point – including who will compile the report, and what the role of the judge should be in this process – which can be dealt with based on the legal system's traditions and the resources available to the courts and the parties.

C. The Replication Crisis in Political Science

If scholarly disagreements do not make it impossible to feed political science evidence into legal proceedings, a more fundamental challenge is what has been

---

[20] This might sometimes be necessary, eg because of new evidence on a topic.
[21] Posner (n 9) 94.
[22] 'Associate Professor Lokuge not only had the most comprehensive grasp of the academic research, but, by far, the greatest practical, front-line experience in the control of pandemics': *Palmer v State of Western Australia (No 4)* [2020] FCA 1221 [50] (Rangiah J).

described as the discipline's 'crisis' of replication.[23] High-profile instances of studies whose findings could not be replicated, in some cases leading to a retraction of the published article, have stimulated debate about the reliability of political science knowledge. Designing transparent and reliable research has long been a goal for the political science community, but the current debate about replication has been stimulated, in particular, by the increasing use of experimental methods by political scientists from the late 1990s onwards, following many decades in which such methods were regarded as an ideal that was practically impossible for most topics of interest to political scientists.[24] Experimentation in political science takes various forms, but has often involved the random assignment of subjects to control and treatment groups, which can then be compared to assess the effects of an intervention such as a shift of institutional rules or exposure to new information.[25] These methods are particularly useful for demonstrating causal effects. This has made them very relevant for policy but has also increased the incentive to unethically manipulate a research design to generate eye-catching, impactful findings.[26] This risk (and the evidence that some prominent findings cannot be replicated) raises questions about how seriously courts and, indeed, decision-makers in any practical setting, should treat the conclusions of political science research.

An understandable reaction, in light of this debate, would be to simply dismiss whatever the political scientists produce. However, in our view, this would be a counter-productive overreaction. To begin with, as we will explain in Part IV, much of the potential value of this discipline to the legal process comes from conceptual, theoretical and analytical insights: these emerge from the frameworks that political scientists devise to study empirical phenomena and do not depend on precise estimates of empirical effects. Regarding evidence of the latter kind, certainly there is a need, as there is always, for courts to be cautious in interpreting the findings of empirical political science. To assess the quality of such evidence, though, courts should apply procedures that are attentive to the risks of the particular methods (eg experimental, statistical, case studies) that have been used in a study or by a research agenda. Over time, we might expect that 'rules of thumb' will emerge that can help courts to work through the problems that arise: these might include, for instance, subjecting new evidentiary claims, or those based on a single study, to higher thresholds of challenge and substantiation and giving more weight to arguments that have been supported across multiple studies and in meta-analyses of the relevant literature.

---

[23] EM Key, 'How Are We Doing? Data Access and Replication in Political Science' (2016) 49 *PS: Political Science & Politics* 268; DD Laitin and R Reich, 'Trust, Transparency, and Replication in Political Science' (2017) 50 *PS: Political Science & Politics* 172.
[24] See, eg, Collier (n 5).
[25] JN Druckman et al, 'The Growth and Development of Experimental Research in Political Science' (2006) 100 *American Political Science Review* 627.
[26] Laitin and Reich (n 24) 172.

It should be noted that, while there are tasks for the legal system, the problem of evidence verification is primarily one for the political science community to deal with. There have been positive moves in this direction in recent years, including new practices by journals to improve transparency and opportunities for replication.[27] There is also growing awareness of the need to better educate political science students about ethical research designs. One of the frontier issues in this debate about reliability practices concerns the role that the discipline's professional associations should play on such matters. As these associations devise ways to consolidate knowledge and standards, it is important that the range of policymakers to whom political scientists are attuned should include courts and legal practitioners alongside the more commonly targeted groups (ie lawmakers and government bureaucrats).

D. Politicising the Judiciary

Finally, the integration of political science into courtroom processes might raise concerns about the perception of courts and judges. In particular, it might be thought that there is a risk that they will be drawn into contentious values-based debates that many believe are best left to the elected branches – a process sometimes dubbed 'politicisation' – if they consider evidence from the most 'political' of the social sciences. From this standpoint it is no coincidence that in contexts where courts have been more involved in judging fundamental values, they have also been more willing to take on board social science evidence. In the United States, especially since the 1980s, political science evidence has been cited by courts on a diverse range of topics, though most often (and most influentially) in electoral reapportionment and disputes about voting rights, where political scientists have been in demand to clarify the effects of different interventions (eg alternative redistricting plans). More controversially, however, there has also been a view that political (and social) science has been 'weaponised' by politically motivated judges to overturn established precedent.[28] In the more formalistic Australian courts, there are severe limits on the potential for speculative, non-legal sources to be used for this purpose. Yet, we argue that there remains reasonably objective evidence about political phenomena that can be further leveraged within such constraints. By taking account of this evidence, courts will be able to draw on the best available information about political institutions, processes and events while at the same time remaining independent of 'political' disputes about fundamental values and policy priorities.

---

[27] Key (n 24); Laitin and Reich (n 24).
[28] See, eg, P Falk, 'The Prevalence of Social Science in Gay Rights Cases: Synergistic Influences of Historical Context, Justificatory Citation and Dissemination Efforts' (1994) 41 *Wayne Law Review* 1, 5.

IV. Integrating Political Science Evidence

We have argued that courts and the legal process could benefit from drawing on political science evidence in adjudication, despite the challenges in doing so. How should this integration occur, particularly in the Australian context? This section explores three mechanisms – judicial notice, statements on agreed facts, and remittal to lower courts – that the HCA has used for various purposes, including, in a few cases, to consider political science evidence. However, we believe there is scope to use them more, and more effectively, to incorporate political science evidence. It should be noted that our discussion focuses on what is referred to in the literature as *legislative facts* (of which *constitutional facts* are a subset).[29] Legislative facts are questions of fact which '"cannot and do not form issues between parties to be tried" … and which cannot be made to depend on the course of private litigation'.[30] They are typically contrasted against *adjudicative facts* or 'ordinary questions of fact' which, in Gageler's words, 'arise between parties and which are to be tried and determined between parties in accordance with the ordinary rules of evidence'.[31]

A. Judicial Notice

HCA judges, not only in the context of constitutional adjudication but also adjudication more generally, have taken *judicial notice* of the sort of facts that political scientists study. Judicial notice involves the court going beyond strictly legal sources to take account of information that is widely regarded as factual or self-evident. The content of judicial notice material is often described as 'common knowledge' or 'notorious facts'.[32] In the *Communist Party* case, for instance, Dixon J took judicial notice of, among other things, the occurrence of various political events. Described as 'notorious international events' these included '[t]he communist seizure of Czecho-Slovakia, the Brussels Pact of Western Union, the blockade of Berlin and the airlift'.[33] In the same case, Dixon J also took judicial notice of what political scientists would describe as a *causal process* concerning the dynamics of democratic regime termination. In particular, his Honour stated that '[h]istory and

---

[29] On the distinction between 'legislative' and 'adjudicative' facts, see KC Davis, 'An Approach to Problems of Evidence in the Administrative Process' (1942) 55 *Harvard Law Review* 364; KC Davis, 'Judicial Notice' (1955) 55 *Columbia Law Review* 945. For a recent detailed discussion of the distinction, including its relevance in the Australian context, see A Carter, *Proportionality and Facts in Constitutional Adjudication* (Oxford, Hart Publishing, 2021) ch 3. See also S Gageler, 'Facts and Law' (2009) 11 *Newcastle Law Review* 1.
[30] Gageler (n 30), 12–13, quoting *Breen v Sneddon* (1961) 106 CLR 406, 411 (Dixon CJ).
[31] ibid 12.
[32] Heydon (n 8) 199.
[33] *Australian Communist Party v Commonwealth* (1951) 83 CLR 1, 196–97. See also Heydon (n 8) 200–10, 223–24.

not only ancient history, shows that in countries where democratic institutions have been unconstitutionally superseded, it has been done not seldom by those holding the executive power'.[34]

Since the *Communist Party* case, the HCA has regularly taken judicial notice of observations about the evolution of political institutions, in light of changing political and social contexts. In *Lange*, for instance, the court took notice of the following changes in Australia since 1901: '[t]he expansion of the franchise, the increase in literacy, the growth of modern political structures operating at both federal and State levels and the modern development in mass communications, especially the electronic media'.[35] In *Bropho*, the court took notice of how the executive has evolved over the course of the nineteenth and particularly the twentieth centuries. The majority noted that, in Australia, 'the activities of the executive government [now] reach into almost all aspects of commercial, industrial and developmental endeavour'.[36] These are just two of many examples. Importantly, the HCA has also revised, presumably using in part the mechanism of judicial notice, 'past assumptions of historical fact' that were 'shown to have been false'.[37] The most notable of these is the HCA's rejection, in *Mabo*, of the notion that the land that now constitutes Australia was *terra nullius* in 1788.[38] This brings to the fore a key *limitation* of judicial notice, particularly in its application to social and political phenomena: it is constrained by what is considered to be 'common knowledge'. There has always been an acute awareness in First Nations communities (and among those deeply familiar with their experiences) of the fact that governance structures existed in Australia prior to 1788, but the courts could not take notice of this fact until it became 'common knowledge' in the wider community. Other examples could be given of such lags in the updating of (mainstream) 'common knowledge', eg in relation to racism, sexism, and colonisation.

B. Statements of Agreed Facts

The HCA has also taken account of political science evidence, typically in the context of special cases, when the parties file *a statement of agreed facts*.[39] In *Rowe v Electoral Commissioner*[40] and *Pape v Federal Commissioner of Taxation*,[41] for instance, the parties agreed on relevant political material in their respective statements of agreed facts. The filing of a statement of agreed facts in the sense just

---

[34] *Australian Communist Party* (n 34), 187–88.
[35] *Lange v Australia Broadcasting Corporation* (1997) 189 CLR 520, 565.
[36] *Bropho v Western Australia* (1990) 171 CLR 1, 19.
[37] This is Gummow J's explanation of *Mabo (No 2)* in *Wik Peoples v Queensland* (1996) 187 CLR 1, 180. See also Gageler (n 30) 6–7.
[38] See *Mabo v Queensland (No 2)* (1992) 175 CLR 1, 40. Note that in *Mabo (No 2)*, the court also remitted certain findings of fact to the Supreme Court of Queensland: see 115.
[39] See High Court Rules 2004 (Cth), r 27.08.
[40] (2010) 243 CLR 1.
[41] (2009) 238 CLR 1.

described is now common practice in the context of constitutional adjudication when there are complex facts in play.[42] Furthermore, as Gummow, Crennan and Bell JJ state in *Pape*:

> In the determination of the existence of facts said to attract the exercise of the executive power of the Commonwealth, as with other matters of constitutional fact [and presumably legislative facts more generally], the Court may rely on agreed facts.[43]

This mechanism is often an efficient way to incorporate political facts into a case, but it can leave loose ends that manifest, for example, as important but subtle (and at times difficult to detect) disagreements or agreement on 'facts' that it might be useful to subject to further scrutiny.

In *Rowe*, Commonwealth legislation which restricted the time available to enroll to vote in a federal election was challenged. The statement of agreed facts filed by the parties included Annual Reports of the Australian Electoral Commission (AEC) and content from submissions by the AEC to the Joint Standing Committee on Electoral Matters pertaining to the 2010 federal election.[44] The latter included information about the AEC's process of data matching to maintain the electoral roll. These facts might be regarded as fairly straightforward for the legal process to deal with as they were uncontroversial among the parties and the material did not rely on any inferential assumptions. The facts presented played an important role in assisting the HCA in its understanding of the complex processes of voter enrolment and registration.

Pape concerned constitutional law issues arising from the Rudd government's decision to give one-off cash payments to taxpayers in response to the Global Financial Crisis (GFC). As in *Rowe*, the parties agreed on the relevant facts. These included facts about '[t]he existence of certain economic conditions' triggered by the GFC and statements by the Commonwealth Executive Government and several international organisations (the G20, IMF and OECD).[45] The agreed facts had political and economic content and included observations spanning the past, present and future.[46] The court also expressly acknowledged the characterisation of the relevant situation as a 'crisis' as this was not disputed by the parties.[47]

For our purposes, an interesting question is what might have happened if the parties disagreed about whether there was a crisis, or whether the crisis extended to Australia. Hayne and Kiefel JJ note in their dissent that, given the lack of contestation, 'it was not necessary to examine whether it was for this Court to decide what constitutes a "crisis" or an "emergency", or whether it is sufficient that the

---

[42] See Gageler (n 30) 15.
[43] *Pape* (n 42) 88 [229], citing *Thomas v Mowbray* (2007) 233 CLR 307, 517 [629]. See also High Court Rules (2004), particularly r 27.08.5.
[44] See, eg, *Rowe* (n 41) 25 [37].
[45] *Pape* (n 42) 25 [12].
[46] ibid 26–27 [18]–[21], 88 [229]–[230].
[47] ibid 89 [233].

Executive has concluded that circumstances warrant such a description'.[48] They also point out that '[i]f it is for the Court to decide these matters, questions arise about what evidence the Court could act upon other than the opinions of the Executive, and how those opinions could be tested or supported'.[49] Building on our argument in Part II, if the question of whether a crisis existed had been contested and the Court held that it could (independent of the Executive's opinion) reach a judgment on this question, one option available would be to remit the case to a lower court and ask it to ascertain the relevant facts, with the assistance of a political scientist (among other expert witnesses).

C. Remittal to a Lower Court

In contexts where there is contestation amongst parties in relation to the facts, the Court has the option to remit the case to a lower court, asking it to settle the complex facts in contestation. Such remittal is rare, but it has happened. Remittal to a lower court occurred in 2000 in the case of *Airservices Australia v Canadian Airlines International Ltd*,[50] where 'complex questions of fact relevant to constitutional validity were determined by the Federal Court on remitter from the HCA on the basis of expert evidence'.[51] More recently, in the 2020 case of *Palmer*, Clive Palmer challenged Western Australia's border restrictions in the context of COVID-19 and the HCA remitted to the Federal Court the settling of complex questions of fact in epidemiology and public health.[52] The parties (and also the Commonwealth, as intervener) called various expert witnesses and they collectively produced a statement of agreed facts and also identified the questions, of a factual nature, on which they disagreed.[53] The experts were called to give evidence and cross-examined.[54] Despite its obvious benefits, the remittal mechanism is both time consuming and costly. Many of the benefits that it provides could potentially be further incorporated (both formally and informally) by the parties in the lead up to preparing a statement of agreed facts. To the best of our knowledge, the HCA has not remitted cases to hear from political scientists.

V. A Missed Opportunity?

While the mechanisms identified above provide practical, established ways for the Australian courts to engage with political science evidence, they arguably remain underutilised. To make this point, we argue that, in a recent context, in the special

---

[48] ibid 123 [353].
[49] ibid.
[50] (2000) 202 CLR 133.
[51] Gageler (n 30) 15.
[52] *Palmer* (n 23).
[53] ibid [42]–[66].
[54] ibid [8].

case hearing of *Plaintiff M47/2018 v Minister for Home Affairs*, opportunities were missed by the court to take account of political science evidence.[55]

In *Plaintiff M47/2018*, the plaintiff, who had been held in immigration detention for nine years, sought a declaration that his detention was unlawful pursuant to the Migration Act 1958 (Cth) (Migration Act). The plaintiff claimed he was stateless and argued that there was 'in fact, no prospect that he will be removed from Australia to another country'.[56] As a result, the relevant sections of the Migration Act[57] did not authorise his continued detention. The defendants rejected the plaintiff's claim and argued that 'their inability to establish the plaintiff's identity and country of origin is due to the plaintiff's want of cooperation'.[58] The Court, in its reasons, reached the conclusion that:

> Because the plaintiff had contributed to the frustration of lines of enquiry as to his identity and nationality, what might be established about his identity and nationality if he were to assist the Department [of Home Affairs] in its enquiries cannot be known. It certainly cannot be inferred that genuine assistance from the plaintiff would not be helpful.[59]

The Court ultimately held that 'no question arose as to the lawfulness of the plaintiff's detention'.[60]

The issue of modern state capacity, without necessarily contradicting the Court's conclusion that the plaintiff was less than helpful, casts its conclusions in a different and more complex light. The Australian Immigration Department's resources are vast, and its administrative capacity is significant. Given this institutional context, it could be argued that not much should turn on *individual cooperation*. Consider, for instance, the state's capacity in the conduct of criminal investigations where, in most instances, there is a lack of cooperation by the suspects. A capable state institution can normally overcome such intransigence quite easily. From this vantage point, the Court in this case seems to place a great deal – perhaps too much – emphasis on the difference that 'genuine assistance from the plaintiff' would make and too little on the Department's institutional capacity to undertake these sorts of activities *without* an individual's assistance and cooperation.

Furthermore, there was potential in this case for the Court, perhaps prompted by the plaintiff, to consider political science evidence on state naming practices. The plaintiff claimed that he is stateless. Of course, specific facts to do with his identity constitute *adjudicative facts*. However, there are legislative facts that are potentially relevant that are concerned with naming practices in parts of the world

---

[55] (2019) 265 CLR 285.
[56] ibid 290 [4].
[57] Migration Act 1958, ss 189, 196.
[58] *Plaintiff M47/2018* (n 56) 293 [15].
[59] ibid 297 [31]. Note the Department of Home Affairs was previously the Department of Immigration and Border Protection and, before then, the Department of Immigration and Citizenship: 293 [14] fn 19.
[60] ibid 300 [42].

where the state is weak (or largely absent). Modern naming practices are correlated with state capacity because strong states are better able to organise their citizens and enforce their conformity with state-sanctioned identifiers: indeed, this has been an important means by which the state has mobilised its population (especially at times of war). As political scientist James C Scott explains, the 'capacity of state agents to identify an individual … plays an enormous role not only in taxation, but also in conscription, criminal investigations, and so forth'.[61] In the Court's view, the inconsistencies in the plaintiff's statements regarding his name, date of birth and other personal details were either due to deliberate falsehoods or mental illness.[62] Since no evidence was given by the plaintiff in relation to the latter, the Court concluded that the only remaining explanation was the former. Another alternative, however, was that the plaintiff's inconsistent statements were the result of the fact that he did not come from a country with the rigorous naming and identification practices associated with a strong state which may, in turn, have opened up the question of whether he had any formal citizenship. If this possibility had been brought to the Court's attention, remittal to a lower court may have been a plausible next step.

VI. Conclusion

This chapter has argued that political science evidence should be used more extensively to boost the range of facts available to courts. On one level, this may not seem like a particularly novel or counter-intuitive argument since a wide base of expertise features in legal processes. But upon closer inspection, and particularly in Australia (among other countries), very little of this expertise comes from political science and political scientists. As we have shown, factual insights about political phenomena that were germane to matters before Australian courts have not been brought to their attention. On the occasions when some political science evidence has featured in adjudication, there may have been ways to deepen this engagement and thereby expand the evidence base available to the court. Emerging from these observations, then, is our core argument that there is underutilised potential for political science to contribute to adjudication.

Serious challenges will follow from the closer engagement between legal practitioners and political scientists that we advocate. These include the ongoing replication crisis in political science, which has created obstacles to knowledge consolidation and distrust of the discipline's findings. Resolving this problem is a necessary step for political science to have credibility in the courtroom, and doing so is a task for the political science community. At the same time, courts and the

---

[61] JC Scott, 'State simplifications: Nature, Space, and People' (1995) 3 *The Journal of Political Philosophy* 42, 58.
[62] *Plaintiff M47/2018* (n 56) 297 [30].

legal community can take measures to enable the uptake of political science findings into the legal process, by increasing awareness of the kinds of knowledge that political science can produce; by applying procedures to align the incentives of political science expert witnesses with the requirements of fair and efficient adjudication; and by adopting a wider range of strategies to integrate political science evidence into legal proceedings. Each of these steps can be elaborated in ways that go beyond the scope of our discussion, but which might be fruitful lines of inquiry for future research. For instance, the challenge of increasing awareness of political science research and methods, indeed those of social science more generally, is a frontier that raises a whole host of questions. The payoff from working through these problems, however, will be more informed courtroom decision-making on matters with political dimensions. And, in a wider perspective, an extension of the purview of courts as part of the long history of common law evolving the forms of knowledge that it admits as evidence.

14

History and Historical Facts in Constitutional Law

CAITLIN GOSS

I. Introduction

This chapter is an attempt to understand the significant role that historical facts and narratives play in constitutional texts and in constitutional adjudication. Perhaps the most obvious association between history and constitutional law is via the use of historical evidence as to original meaning and content as a way of construing constitutional texts. However, in this chapter I argue that that is only one of the ways in which historical questions arise in relation to the constitution.

Part II explores and categorises the ways in which history is expressly invoked in constitutional texts. Many constitutions appear to refer to history as a way of bolstering their own legitimacy, sometimes rejecting or embracing a past constitutional era. Many references to history in constitutions are preambular and non-justiciable, but some constitutions contain references to history to justify concrete provisions.

Part III identifies a number of ways that history plays a role in the resolution of constitutional disputes. First, courts may be required to apply constitutionally enshrined historical values to contemporary problems, as seen in the South African Constitutional Court case of *Rustenburg Mines v SAEWA*.[1] Secondly, as demonstrated through the discussion of a recent Canadian Supreme Court decision, in *R v Comeau*,[2] courts may investigate the historical linguistic meaning of a constitutional provision, even in jurisdictions that do not adopt an originalist approach. Thirdly, courts may make findings as to the historical origins and development of a doctrine – what Josev has referred to as doctrinal historiography – as part of assessing a matter. Finally, courts may be required to make a determination about an historical matter that is a fact in issue in a dispute.

---

[1] *Rustenburg Platinum Mine v SAEWA obo Bester and Others* [2018] ZACC 13.
[2] 2018 SCC 15.

Part IV considers some of the specific challenges that the invocation and proof of historical matters give rise to in constitutional matters. As other contributions to this collection reveal, there are many complexities in dealing with facts in public law adjudication. However, I attempt to identify some of the peculiar difficulties associated with using and proving historical facts: it can be difficult to know when judges can or should consult historical evidence, and to what standard claims about history should be proved. There are challenges associated with the over-reliance on experts in cases involving historical matters, but there are also challenges for courts attempting to resolve historical matters without recourse to experts. As with other kinds of facts, there is a tendency and risk that courts' findings on historical matters may create factual precedent, which may have a significant impact on future cases.

Part II of this chapter draws upon a broad survey of constitutional texts. In the later parts of the chapter, I discuss in more detail a few recent cases and issues that shed light on some of the challenges that courts face in assessing historical facts. These cases are drawn from South Africa, Canada, the United States of America, and Australia; as countries that are common law jurisdictions or mixed jurisdictions with common law components (South Africa), these countries share some similarities in terms of law, methods of judging and rules of evidence. Rather than attempting to create an exhaustive summary of cases involving historical facts in these jurisdictions, the chapter attempts to highlight a set of common issues and concerns using a few key cases.

Throughout this chapter, I argue that historical facts and narratives often play a significant role in constitutional texts and adjudication. I argue that there are many ways in which history enters constitutional litigation and identify some of these. In arguing that historical claims present specific challenges, I also argue that we cannot separate the more theoretical discussions about what role history should play in constitutional adjudication from the very practical challenges associated with proving historical facts to a satisfactory standard. I argue for caution in making and accepting claims about history in constitutional adjudication, and that greater clarity as to when judges intend to consult history – and to what standard they expect it to be proved – would be desirable.

II. Historical Facts and Narratives are Frequently Cited in Constitutional Texts

There are several ways in which history or historical themes are invoked by drafters of constitutional texts. A full definition of the term 'history', either in general or in the context of constitutional adjudication is well beyond the scope of this chapter. For our purposes, I use the term 'history' to refer to past events, particularly those of public significance. The frequency with which references to history arise in constitutions may at first appear surprising; constitutions are, after all, primarily future-orientated documents, establishing plans for a new constitutional order. However, a search of the Constitute Project's database[3] reveals that references to historical events are common in constitutions and may be found both in preambular sections of constitutions, and in the body of constitutional texts. The tradition of historical description in legal or quasi-constitutional texts has a long history; as Voernamns et al have noted, the Code of Hammurabi, from the eighteenth-century BCE, has a preamble which contains the founding story of the state.[4] In this section I identify a few ways in which history appears in constitutions: as a way of supporting the claim of the new constitution to legitimacy; as a way to directly justify or explain a particular constitutional provision; and in a third, smaller, category, through the constitutional protection or promotion of the teaching of national history.

A. Historical Facts or Narratives are Used to Support Legitimacy Claims in Constitutions

In many cases, constitutions contain references to historical facts or narratives. Constitutional drafters invoking history may be seeking to obtain what Weber describes as legitimacy through 'traditional domination', where the power of the ruler is accepted because of historical reasons, whether that has been continuous, or interrupted.[5] These historical references are interesting in light of the predominance in modern constitutions of what Weber terms the 'rational legal model', in which the legitimacy of a constitution is founded 'on a belief in the legality of enacted rules and the right of those elevated to authority under such rules to issue commands'.[6] These preambular references to history also serve a simple communicative function; in many cases, constitutions contain a summary of the founding of the constitution, or the identity of its drafters, as a way of conveying basic information about the text.[7] From studying these references, it is possible to identify a few key attitudes towards history in constitutional texts. These categories are not absolute, and many constitutions will express some combination of these values, but it is nonetheless helpful to identify certain strains of constitutional historical reference.

First, constitutions may refer to history to *reject* a particular historical period. The legitimacy of the current or emerging constitutional order is premised on the illegitimacy of a previous era. This is common in states emerging from conflict

---

[3] The Constitute Project. Available at: www.constituteproject.org/constitutions?lang=en&q=history&status=in_force&status=is_draft, last accessed 13 May 2022.
[4] W Voermans, M Stremler and P Cliteur, *Constitutional Preambles: A Comparative Analysis* (Cheltenham, Edward Elgar 2017) 6.
[5] M Weber, *Economy and Society: An Outline of Interpretive Sociology*, vol 2 (Berkeley, University of California Press, 1978) 215.
[6] ibid.
[7] See, eg, Constitution of the Republic of Mozambique 2004, Preamble.

or undertaking significant constitutional reform. András Sajó argues that constitutions, rather than being forward looking, 'reflect the fears originating in, and related to, the previous political regime'.[8] The post-invasion Constitution of Iraq (2005) falls into this category, with a clear rejection of the previous period of 'sectarian oppression inflicted by the autocratic clique … recollecting the darkness of the ravage of the holy cities', recollecting that the Iraqi people 'sought hand in hand and shoulder to shoulder to create our new Iraq, the Iraq of the future, free from sectarianism, racism, complex of regional attachment, discrimination, and exclusion'.[9]

The post-apartheid constitutions of South Africa, both the Interim Constitution of 1994 and its successor, the Constitution of 1996, also contain extended language around a rejection of the past. The final Chapter of the Interim Constitution begins:

> This Constitution provides a historic bridge between the past of a deeply divided society characterized by strife, conflict, untold suffering and injustice, and a future founded on the recognition of human rights, democracy and peaceful co-existence and development opportunities for all South Africans, irrespective of color, race, class, belief or sex.[10]

Secondly, other constitutions will hark back to a particular era, seeking to create links to a period viewed by the drafters as constitutionally legitimate. An example of this is the Egyptian Constitution of 2014, which refers to that state's 'great ancestors' in the ancient era. It reads in part:

> In the beginning of history, the dawn of human conscience rose and shone forth in the hearts of our great ancestors, uniting their good intention to build the first central state that regulated and organized the life of Egyptians on the banks of the Nile. It is where they created the most amazing wonders of civilization.[11]

Moreover, the preamble positions the revolution as part of an 'extension of the revolutionary march of Egyptian patriotism', beginning in the twentieth century. The Egyptian Constitution reflects on the role that history plays: 'We believe that we are capable of using the past as an inspiration, stirring up the present, and making our way to the future. We are capable of developing this homeland that develops us'.[12]

In a third category, many constitutions express reformist values in their references to history, containing references to and continuity with particular historical events or traditional values (often indigenous cultural or religious practices), but in the context of a reformist agenda.[13] The constitution of Croatia, enacted in 1993

---

[8] A Sajó, *Limiting Government: An Introduction to Constitutionalism* (Budapest, Central European University Press, 1999) 2.
[9] Constitution of Iraq 2005 (replacing the Transitional Administrative Law 2004).
[10] Interim Constitution of the Republic of South Africa 1993, Postamble/Chapter 16.
[11] Constitutional Declaration (Egypt) 2011, Preamble.
[12] ibid. See also Constitution of the Czech Republic 1993, Preamble.
[13] See discussion on 'refolution' – a combination of reform/revolution in Timothy Garton Ash, cited in J Kis, 'Between Reform and Revolution' (1998) 12 *East European Politics & Societies* 300, 301–2.

following the dissolution of Yugoslavia, specifically identifies the 'continuity of its statehood' and cites a list of historical events in confirmation and elaboration of that statehood including that the state 'shall develop as a sovereign and democratic state in which equality, freedoms and human rights are guaranteed and ensured'.[14]

What do these historical references tell us about constitutional drafters, and texts? It is worth noting that many of these historical references are contained in preambles, which means that in many – though not all – cases they are not directly justiciable.[15] However, they may play a role in constitutional adjudication, by providing courts with an understanding of the constitution and its values.

B. Constitutions Sometimes Use History to Provide Justification for Particular Provisions

Secondly, while constitutional references to history are typically contained in preambles or preliminary constitutional provisions, in some cases history is explicitly invoked to justify particular constitutional provisions. In South Sudan and Uganda, historical events are cited to explain affirmative action policies,[16] while the Rwandan Constitution contains multiple references to the Rwandan genocide, in connection with concrete provisions about welfare, memorial sites, and in justifying the presidential term of seven years.[17] The post-invasion Transitional Administrative Law of Iraq required the government to 'take effective steps to end the vestiges of the oppressive acts of the previous regime', and contained various articles which provided a constitutional basis for the aggressive de-Baathification process that followed the regime change.[18]

C. Constitutions Sometimes Require the Teaching of History

Thirdly, several constitutions mandate the teaching of history, including particular principles that must be taught ('the principles of Bolivarian thought', in Venezuela), or the requirement that history be taught by nationals of that state (El Salvador; Honduras).[19] In this way the constitutional text creates and ensures the continuation of certain state-sanctioned historical narratives or understandings.

---

[14] Constitution of Croatia 1993.
[15] As Voermans et al note, in France the preamble to the French Constitution has been declared 'an integral part of the constitution and [has been] used directly to review the constitutionality of legislation'. In contrast, for example, the US Supreme Court 'has never used the preamble as a parameter for constitutional review': Voermans et al (n 4) 4.
[16] Constitution of South Sudan, art 139(1)(i); Constitution of Uganda 1995, art 32(1).
[17] Constitution of Rwanda 2003, art 172.
[18] Law of Administration for the State of Iraq for the Transitional Period 2004 (Iraqi National Council): Preamble, arts 6, 48A, 58, 59A.
[19] Constitution of Venezuela 1999, art 107; Constitution of El Salvador 1983, art 60; Constitution of Honduras 1982.

In this section I have attempted to provide an overview of the ways in which history is *explicitly* evoked in constitutional texts, and to provide some brief reflections on why these historical references are included in documents that are fundamentally forward-looking.

III. History in Constitutional Adjudication

In the previous section I considered the ways in which history is imported into constitutional texts. In this section, I identify several ways that historical facts and narratives come to be adjudicated upon in courts. These categories are not exhaustive, but this preliminary categorisation represents an attempt to think through the many and varied ways in which history may arise in constitutional disputes.

A. Courts Apply Historical Values Embodied in Constitutional Texts to Interpret Constitutional or Legislative Texts

Here I discuss cases that involve the application of historical facts or values discussed in Section I to concrete disputes.

In interpreting what is a deeply historically informed constitutional text, the Constitutional Court of South Africa has on a number of occasions had to consider the historical context of the rights and values contained in the Constitution. In the early case of *Makwanyane*, for example, the Court declared that the death penalty was unconstitutional, and in so doing, considered and rejected the state's apartheid history.[20]

However even in more mundane matters, like the 2018 case of *Rustenburg Platinum Mine v the South African Equity Workers Association*,[21] constitutionally enshrined historical values have played a determinative role in the adjudication of disputes.

In *Rustenburg*, the Constitutional Court considered an unfair dismissal claim in light of the legacy of apartheid and racial discrimination. The employee, Mr Bester, had referred to a fellow colleague as a 'swart man' (or 'black man') in the context of a dispute over a parking space, and the question arose as to whether his use of this language was derogatory and racist, so as to justify his dismissal. Bester's claim came before a Conciliation Commissioner, who held that the dismissal had been unfair, on the grounds that:

> I really do not see how such a phrase (referring to a physical attribute in order to identify a … person) could be classified as a racial remark. It would be similar to the situation

---

[20] *S v Makwanyane and Another* [1995] ZACC 3.
[21] ibid.

where someone comes into [our] offices not knowing my name and then asking for me by stating the 'wit man' who … parked next to the entrance gate. I will not take any offence to this.[22]

The decision went through several appeals before it was heard by the Constitutional Court. All parties agreed that the correct test for whether Bester's statement constituted derogatory language was an objective one, ie whether 'in the opinion of a reasonable person possessed of all facts, Mr Bester's use of the word[s] "swart man" in this context was derogatory and racist'.[23]

The Constitutional Court acknowledged that it was the first time it had had cause to consider whether 'an apparently neutral race descriptor may be regarded as racially abusive or insulting'.[24] The Court granted leave to appeal on the basis that the Court is 'obliged, as a Custodian of the Constitution, to ensure that the values of non-racialism, human dignity and equality are upheld and in doing so it has a responsibility to deliberately work towards the eradication of racism'.[25]

The Court held that the decision below that the words were 'presumptively neutral':

[F]ails to recognise the impact of the legacy of apartheid and racial segregation that has left us with a racially charged present. This approach holds the danger that the dominant, racist view of the past – of what is neutral, normal and acceptable – might be used as the starting point in the objective enquiry without recognising that the root of this view skews such enquiry. It cannot be correct to ignore the reality of our past of institutionally entrenched racism and begin an enquiry into whether or not a statement is racist and derogatory from a presumption that the context is neutral …

…

The past may have institutionalised and legitimised racism but our Constitution constitutes a 'radical and decisive break from that part of the past which is unacceptable'. Our Constitution rightly acknowledges that our past is one of deep societal divisions … [and they] have not disappeared overnight.[26]

This case demonstrates the potential importance of historical context in constitutional adjudication. The historical context here made an ordinary labour dispute a matter for the Constitutional Court; it determined the interpretation of the words and the outcome of the case; and this case is but one of many cases in which the Constitutional Court has applied and reinscribed the historical values first included in the Interim Constitution of South Africa into the nation's ongoing constitutional jurisprudence.[27]

---

[22] ibid [11], quoting *SAEWA obo Bester v Rustenburg Platinum Mine*, unreported arbitration award of the CCMA, Case No NWRB1692-13 (19 December 2013).
[23] ibid [20], quoting *SA Equity Workers Association o.b.o Bester v Rustenburg Platinum Mine* [2017] ZALAC 23 [16].
[24] ibid [36].
[25] ibid [37].
[26] ibid [48], [52].
[27] See, eg, *City of Tshwane Metropolitan Municipality v Afriforum and Another* [2016] ZACC 19.

Another category of case arises when an historical fact or value is a legislatively or constitutionally *protected* fact. The French Conseil Constitutionnel and the European Court of Human Rights have considered challenges to laws prohibiting the denial of historical events, in connection with the Armenian genocide.[28] In such cases, the Court's role may not involve an assessment of historical facts, but it will involve an analysis of whether historical facts contained in the relevant law have been denied in the given case, and how to balance these against other constitutional values, such as freedom of speech. In this sense, such cases share some similarities with the cases such as *Rustenburg*.

B. Historical Evidence May be Used as an Interpretative Tool

A more common use of history in constitutional adjudication is the use of historical facts as an interpretative tool, or as a means of resolving indeterminacy in a constitutional text. In her scholarly work on the topic, *Constitutions, Courts, and History: Historical Narratives in Constitutional Interpretation*, Renata Uitz examines the role that history plays as an interpretative technique in constitutional decision-making. While Uitz does not argue for discarding 'historical narratives … from the intellectual toolkit of the constitutional interpreter', she argues that the 'most serious peril of historical narratives is not that they perpetuate indeterminacy in constitutional reasoning, but that this potential of theirs is not accounted for' and that this is so in any school of interpretation that invokes history, not just originalist accounts.[29]

This point is illustrated in the decision of the Supreme Court of Canada in *Comeau*. The case illustrates the potential hazards of relying on historical evidence to resolve constitutional indeterminacy, as well as demonstrating the challenges associated with proving historical claims about constitutional texts. This example is enlightening given that history is not *determinative* in Canadian constitutional jurisprudence; rather, it merely forms part of the context for the interpretation of the Constitution Act 1867 (Canadian Constitution). Yet, as will be seen, historical arguments formed the basis of the trial judge's decision, and one of the bases for overturning that decision on appeal to the Supreme Court of Canada. Moreover, the case demonstrates the capacity for reasonable historians – and jurists – to disagree with one another about historical evidence.

The case concerned a Mr Comeau, a resident of New Brunswick, who drove across the provincial border to Quebec to purchase alcohol, in order to avoid the

---

[28] *Perinçek v. Switzerland* ECHR (2015), (Application no 27510/08); see generally U Belavusau, 'Hate Speech', *Max Planck Encyclopedia of Comparative Constitutional Law* (OUP, 2017). Available at: https://papers.ssrn.com/sol3/papers.cfm?abstract_id=3022531, last accessed 1 June 2018.

[29] R Uitz, *Constitutions, Courts and History* (Budapest, Central European Press, 2005) 307.

higher prices in New Brunswick caused by the Liquor Control Act.[30] That Act establishes a provincial Corporation as an approved liquor vendor, and it prohibits holding liquor above a certain quantity obtained from non-Corporation sources. Mr Comeau was fined for holding a relevant quantity of liquor purchased from a non-Corporation vendor, and contested the fine on the basis that the prohibition in the Liquor Control Act is in violation of the Canadian Constitution, section 121.[31] That section states:

> All Articles of the Growth, Produce, or Manufacture of any one of the Provinces shall, form and after the Union, be admitted free into each of the other Provinces.

The central question was, therefore, whether the restrictions imposed by the Liquor Control Act violate the 'admitted free' principle established in section 121. The trial judge found that 'admitted free' amounted to a guarantee of free trade, and that accordingly, the Liquor Control Act was unconstitutional. The Supreme Court reversed this decision, holding – in line with long-established precedent – that the 'admitted free' clause was not a guarantee of untrammelled free trade, but rather a prohibition on customs and tariffs charges between provinces.

It is instructive to analyse the judgment at first instance in greater depth. The trial judge begins by establishing the usual canons of Canadian constitutional jurisprudence: the Constitution requires a 'flexible interpretation',[32] in line with the 'living tree' metaphor which has been 'applied by the Supreme Court of Canada in many cases'.[33] Constitutional language, as the trial judge observes, must still be 'placed in its proper linguistic, philosophical and historical contexts'.[34] The views of the founders thus retain some significance as a 'starting point', but inevitably become 'less and less relevant with the passage of time'.[35]

The trial judge concludes that the leading authority on the interpretation of section 121 (the *Gold Seal* decision[36]), which casts the section as a prohibition on 'customs duties' or 'charges' rather than a broad inter-provincial free trade guarantee, is incorrect. The judge's decision to reject this 95-year-old precedent was founded largely on the expert testimony of a historian, Dr Smith. The trial judge referred to Dr Smith's credentials as 'unimpeachable', accepting the historian's testimony 'without hesitation'.[37] The trial judge rejected the ruling Supreme Court case *Gold Seal*, noting that it is 'decidedly not what was intended by the Fathers of Confederation'.[38] An examination of the judge's reception of the expert's historical evidence reveals several problems.

---

[30] RSNB 1973, s 134(b).
[31] *Comeau* (n 2) [117]–[128].
[32] *R v Comeau* 2016 NBPC 3 [42], citing *Edwards v A-G. Canada* [1930] AC 124.
[33] ibid [42].
[34] ibid [45].
[35] ibid [46].
[36] *Gold Seal Ltd v Alberta (Attorney General)* [1921] SCJ No 43.
[37] *R v Comeau* 2016 NBPC 3 [52].
[38] ibid.

First, at times, the views of the founders are described as though they are clearly knowable, and monolithic. The judge writes that:

> The positive benefits of free trade and the negative effects of trade impediments ... were well known to the Fathers of Confederation and to the politicians in Great Britain during the events leading up to Confederation. Both shared the philosophy that the creation of a true common market ... would be beneficial.[39]

Secondly, there is a lack of clarity as to whether various statements about history derive from evidence of the expert witness, the judge's own knowledge and reading, or some other source. This makes it difficult to assess the historical findings.

Thirdly, the precise scope of the expert's expertise is not defined, and seems to be wide ranging, extending across history, linguistic understandings, economics and law. These matters include the reasons for the economic success of the British colonies and an analysis of the opinions of 'most Americans' with the assertion that '[p]eople associated Britain with fair trade'.[40]

Fourth, experts in the case give evidence on matters of legal interpretation.[41] For example, the trial judge approves of the written evidence of a political scientist to the effect that 'a very robust interpretation of section 121 would operate against the division of powers ... My guess is that you can't have one provision of the Constitution interpreted in a way to obliterate another provision of the Constitution.'[42] This passage is cited not to query the validity of this particular argument – indeed, a similar finding was made by the Supreme Court – but to point out the unusual nature of a political scientist purporting to answer the very question of law that the judge was required to resolve.[43]

On appeal to the Supreme Court, a unanimous bench overturned the trial judge's decision, on several grounds. First, the Court found that *even if* the expert's testimony had established a new interpretation of historical facts, this would not meet the narrow parameters established in *Bedford* for deviating from vertical stare decisis.[44] In contrast to, for example, new evidence about medical matters, questions about historical meaning are questions of interpretation, and do not 'fundamentally shift the parameters of legal debate'.[45]

---

[39] ibid [74].
[40] ibid [89].
[41] ibid [68], [150].
[42] ibid [157]. The expert was described as 'a political scientist' who had 'never published any articles on section 122 of the Constitution ... nor of its historical or political context', but who has *commented* on Supreme Court of Canada decisions. Note the statement was admitted with the consent of both parties.
[43] See J Chin, 'R v Comeau: Who decides history?' (*Truth in Evidence*, 11 June 2018). Available at: www.jasonmchin.com/jason-chin-evidence-blog/2018/6/11/r-v-comeau-who-decides-history-ja9km, last accessed 21 February 2023.
[44] *Canada (Attorney General) v Bedford* 2013 SCC 72 [125] [choose one], cited in *Comeau* (n 2) [17], see generally [17]–[35].
[45] *Comeau* (n 2) [37].

The appellant's success on this ground of appeal was sufficient to overturn the decision, but the Supreme Court went on to consider and reject the historical arguments accepted below. The Court accepts that 'admitted free' is an 'ambiguous' phrase but concludes that there was 'only limited support for the view that [it meant] an absolute guarantee of trade free of *all* barriers',[46] and rejected the trial judge's finding on the interpretation of section 121.[47]

Why focus on a decision of a provincial court, emphatically overturned by the Supreme Court? I do not suggest that the finding of the trial judge is categorically wrong; indeed, several lawyers have criticised the Supreme Court's interpretation and use of history, and its approach to stare decisis.[48] Although the issue may now be closed, judicially, the historical debate remains open. However, the case demonstrates many of the problems that arise when using historical evidence to resolve interpretative indeterminacy. Indeed, even in the Supreme Court, the sources of the Court's historical findings and reasoning are not cited at times; it is difficult for the reader to analyse the basis for the court's conclusions.

C. Legal and Doctrinal History

Just as courts sometimes need to determine the historical meaning of a constitutional text, they may sometimes need to make determinations as to the history of a given doctrine, for example to determine whether a given common law right predated or informed a constitutional provision. In Australia, the High Court has held that the common law privilege against self-incrimination is not a constitutional right.[49] In considering the privilege, judges have often reflected on the origins of the privilege, noting that '[i]t is generally recognised that [the privilege] emerged as a reaction against procedures of the Courts of Star Chamber and High Commission, and in particular their use of the … inquisitorial oath', whereby a 'person might be examined' compulsorily, and 'himself provide the accusation to be made against him'.[50] As Chief Justice Brennan said in *Swaffield*, against 'this historical background, it can be seen why the courts have spoken in terms of

---

[46] ibid [67].
[47] ibid [79], citing Reference re Securities Act, 2011 SCC 66 [7].
[48] A Honickman, 'Comeau is a Casualty of Confused Doctrine' (*Advocates for the Rule of Law*, 24 April 2018). Available at: www.ruleoflaw.ca/comeau-is-a-casualty-of-confused-doctrine/, last accessed 13 May 2022; E Macfarlane, 'In its 'Free-the-Beer' Ruling, the Supreme Court Reveals its Contradictions' (Maclean's 18 April 2018). Available at: www.macleans.ca/opinion/in-its-free-the-beer-ruling-the-supreme-court-reveals-its-contradictions, last accessed 13 May 2022.
[49] *Sorby v The Commonwealth* (1983) 152 CLR 281, 297 (Gibbs CJ); 308 (Mason, Wilson and Dawson JJ), 311 (Murphy J), 313 (Brennan J).
[50] *Environment Protection Authority v Caltex Refining Co Pty Ltd* (1993) 178 CLR 477, 526 (Deane, Dawson and Gaudron JJ).

compulsion to speak'.[51] Tanya Josev observes that in such cases it is common for judges to refer to secondary legal sources, and that the:

> [U]se of doctrinal historiography is a practice internal to law, and the authors of those secondary sources, as historians with legal training, engage in a study which operates within the parameters of law as a discipline ... References to doctrinal historiography by Australian courts ... is not new or novel.[52]

D. Historical Matters are Facts in Issue

In other constitutional or public law cases, the facts in issue – the contested matters that must be resolved to resolve the case – include historical matters. In these cases, historical matters must be formally proved as part of the case. These cases often arise where issues of native title or indigenous land rights are dependent upon the determination of facts at a given time, and where these interact with constitutional questions.[53]

The landmark native title decision of the High Court of Australia in *Mabo (No 2)* involved a detailed consideration of various historical matters, including an analysis of the practices of the indigenous people, territorial boundaries, and the system of self-government that existed prior to the arrival of the British.[54] Tanya Josev has provided an excellent analysis of the way in which history has played a role in Australia's Federal Courts, finding that over a ten-year period, only 29 judgments referred to a historian as an expert witness, of which 27 cases involved a native title claim.[55]

Of course, historical determinations are not limited to constitutional cases. Ilan Wurman reflects on Stephen Sachs' observation that '*Nemo dat* might require us to figure out whether A or B owned Blackacre long ago' and notes that 'no one argues that lawyers shouldn't do history in those contexts ...'.[56] In such cases, historical questions are unavoidable, and they are vitally important to the proper resolution of disputes. As such, the proper proof of these questions becomes even more significant. In this chapter I do not argue that such historical matters can or should be avoided. Rather, I aim to identify the challenges in using historical arguments, and to consider the issues that may arise in proving historical claims.

---

[51] *R v Swaffield* (1998) 192 CLR 159, 201[90], quoting *Caltex Refining* (n 50) 526.

[52] T Josev, 'Australian Historians and Historiography in the Courtroom' (2020) 43 *Melbourne University Law Review* 1069, 1084–85.

[53] SE Gray, 'Indigenous Space and the Landscape of Settlement: A Historian as Expert Witness' (2015) 37 *The Public Historian: A Journal of Public History* 54, 56.

[54] *Mabo v Queensland (No 2)* (1992) 175 CLR 1.

[55] Josev (n 52) 1078–79. For more on this theme, see A Carter, 'The Definition and Discovery of Facts in Native Title: The Historian's Contribution' (2008) 36 *Federal Law Review* 301.

[56] See I Wurman, *A Debt Against the Living: An Introduction to Originalism* (Cambridge, CUP, 2017) 102.

IV. The Challenge of Proving Historical Facts

The focus of this chapter so far has been on the role that history plays in constitutional texts and interpretation, rather than how historical claims in constitutional cases might be proved before the courts. In cases such as those described in IIA, where the constitution explicitly adopts certain historical values, there may be no need to prove any historical matter. In cases such as those involving the use of history as an interpretative technique or in proving adjudicative facts, courts will need to make determinations about historical claims. In this section I consider, briefly, some of the challenges that arise in proving historical matters, in the context of the common law tradition of evidence law.

A. Constitutional Facts: It is Often Unclear When Historical Matters Will be Considered, and to What Standard They Should be Proved

Some historical questions to be determined will amount to *constitutional* facts, while others will be *adjudicative* facts. Constitutional facts are a sub-type of a larger designation, *legislative* or '"lawmaking facts" [that are] resorted to in order to determine what a law should be, or how it is to be applied'.[57] Conversely, adjudicative facts are those that are 'in issue or relevant to a fact at a trial', such as a factual question in a native title case about whether a given group occupied land at a certain time.[58]

It may sometimes be difficult to tell whether a fact is a legislative/constitutional or an adjudicative fact, or to divorce questions that are of a mixed type. Dyson Heydon, a former Justice of the High Court of Australia, provides the example of *Brown v Board of Education*, which involved evidence that could have been used either to prove a factual claim, or as part of the reinterpretation of the Constitution.[59] Heydon has argued that dangers may arise when courts make findings as to constitutional facts, because constitutional facts about construction of the text are 'often not proved by recourse to the conventional rules of evidence' that are used for adjudicative facts.[60] As seen in *Comeau*, significant findings about historical facts may be made without a great deal of clarity as

---

[57] JD Heydon, 'Constitutional Facts' (2012) 23 *Upholding the Australian Constitution: Proceedings of the Twenty-second Conference of the Samuel Griffith Society* 85, 88. Available at: http://classic.austlii.edu.au/au/journals/SGSocUphAUCon/2011/11.html, last accessed 22 February 2023.
[58] Heydon (n 57).
[59] (1954) 347 US 483. Heydon (n 57). On the blurriness in some instances between legislative and adjudicative facts, see S Gageler, 'Fact and Law' (2008–2009) 11 *Newcastle Law Review* 1, 2.
[60] Heydon (n 57) 86.

to the method or standard of proof. Moreover, in such cases there is often a lack clarity or consistency around when history should be considered at all. The rationale for when historical evidence is consulted is not always clear. It can be hard to avoid the concern that historical data may be 'cherry-picked' when it is helpful and avoided when it is not, like 'looking over a crowd and picking out your friends'.[61]

B. The Role of Experts and the Nature of Historical Expertise

In cases that necessitate findings as to historical facts, the question arises as to how those facts are to be proven. In an ordinary case, litigants must prove facts in a case through a combination of oral testimony and documentary evidence, as well as expert evidence where a given matter requires special knowledge or expertise to understand it. In cases involving disputes about historical matters, oral evidence from someone with direct knowledge of the events in question will often not be available. Documents may be available but may require expert interpretation to identify or understand them. In this section I consider some of the challenges associated with relying on expert evidence on historical matters.

In common law jurisdictions, experts are an unusual kind of witness. Unlike ordinary witnesses, they are permitted to: offer opinions, not just observations; speak about things that they have not personally observed; and rely on out-of-court statements even in jurisdictions where the rule against hearsay applies. Expert testimony has the potential to carry great weight with the finder of fact. Where expert witnesses provide testimony therefore, careful attention should be paid to the qualifications of the witness, and the witness's evidence should be limited in scope to their actual area of expertise.

Further, judges should be careful about abdicating judicial decision-making entirely to an expert, by accepting wholesale an expert's opinion about the correct interpretation of a constitutional provision. In some jurisdictions, for example in Canada, this will violate traditional common law rules of evidence, such as the requirement that the expertise of the expert go beyond the common knowledge of the tribunal, and that experts should avoid purporting to answer the very question that is the subject of a dispute, particularly where that amounts to testifying as to the existence of a legal standard.[62] Otherwise, the witness may find themselves in the position of 'ceas[ing] to function as an historian, and instead t[ake] up the practice of law without a licence'.[63]

---

[61] Remark attributed to Judge H Leventhal, cited by PM Wald, 'Some Observations on the Use of Legislative History in the 1981 Supreme Court Term' (1983) 68 *Iowa Law Review* 195, 214.
[62] See *R v Mohan* [1994] 2 SCR 9 [40].
[63] DJ Rothman, 'Serving Clio and Client: The Historian as Expert Witness' (2003) 77 *Bulletin of the History of Medicine* 25, 29, citing AH Kelly, 'When the Supreme Court Ordered Desegregation' *US News & World Report* (5 February 1962) 88.

David J Rothman, a historian who has served as an expert witness in US constitutional cases, wrote:

> To enter the courtroom is to do many things, but it is not to do history. The essential attributes that we treasure most about historical inquiry have to be left outside the door. The scope of analysis is narrowed, the imagination is constrained, and the curiosity, curtailed.[64]

A full consideration of these concerns is beyond the scope of this chapter, but reference to new practices in a number of jurisdictions, such as requiring experts offering conflicting advice to meet and assess the areas of agreement and disagreement in their testimony may prove fruitful, for example.

Helen Irving has stated that 'if judges are to use historical accounts to reach their legal conclusions, they should do so carefully and circumspectly. They should say why they have chosen particular historians over others and on what basis … But even scrupulous judges should not allow historians to settle the law'.[65] As Lord President Cooper said in the context of a dispute involving an expert scientific witness, '[th]e parties have invoked the decision of a judicial tribunal, and not an oracular pronouncement by an expert'.[66]

C. Other Challenges Associated with Making Historical Findings

In contrast to the cases discussed in Part IIIB, in which experts are consulted, in some instances, lawyers and judges may rely on their own understanding of history, without consulting expert witnesses. In many common law jurisdictions, including the United Kingdom, Canada, and Australia, a court may rely 'on its own historical knowledge and may examine history texts to enable it to take judicial notice of the facts of ancient and modern history'.[67] Less formally, lawyers and judges may make or consider historically informed arguments on a range of topics, as for example when considering issues related to the historical meaning of a constitutional provision, or matters of 'doctrinal historiography'.

One challenge that may arise is that of historical expertise and skill. As Bradley Selway QC has observed, 'one of the conceits of the legal profession [is] that its members are necessarily good historians'.[68] As Selway notes, '[e]xperience shows

---

[64] ibid 44.
[65] H Irving, 'Outsourcing the Law: History and the Disciplinary Limits of Constitutional Reasoning' (2015) 84 *Fordham Law Review* 957, 965.
[66] *Davie v Magistrates of Edinburgh* 1953 SC 34, 40.
[67] SN Lederman, AW Bryant and MK. Fuerst, *Sopinka, Lederman & Bryant: The Law of Evidence in Canada* (Ontario, 4th edn, LexisNexis Canada, 2014) 1325; C Tapper, *Cross & Tapper on Evidence* (Oxford, 12th edn, OUP, 2010) 78; *Australian Communist Party v Commonwealth* (1951) 83 CLR 1; JD Heydon, *Cross on Evidence* (Chatswood, 10th edn, LexisNexis Butterworths, 2015) 172.
[68] B Selway, 'The Use of History and Other Facts in the Reasoning of the High Court of Australia' [2001] 20(2) *University of Tasmania Law Review* 129.

that this is not true even of all historians. There is no obvious reason why it should be true of lawyers'.[69]

Indeed, many scholars writing in this area have criticised the tendency of lawyers to generate shoddy 'law-office history' and derided the ability or competence of judges to interpret and make findings within the discipline of history. As Josev argues, a judge's role in making historical findings is 'circumscribed by time constraints and by limited access to wider resources'.[70] Moreover, without assistance from an historian sufficiently qualified and expert in a given time period and subject matter, there is great potential for errors relating to the problem of insufficient historical perspective or background knowledge, as discussed in IIID.

Another option for using historical facts in adjudication is through agreed facts submitted by parties. This process is likely to be efficient and practical for the parties as it allows for undisputed matters to be dispensed with and resolved expeditiously and inexpensively. However, such agreed facts may or may not be reached as the result of a rigorous process of historical investigation. One difficulty is the potential for the historical findings of a court, based or informed by the agreed facts in a given case, to become accepted or influential 'factual precedent' that may go on to affect other cases.

D. The Problem of Historical Perspective

While the focus of this chapter has been on the explicit and deliberate – often contested – use of history in constitutional interpretation, historically based claims arise and may be determinative in subtle and uncontested ways. In his article 'The Irrelevance of Blackstone: Rethinking the Eighteenth-Century Importance of the Commentaries', Minot relies on original historical research to argue that – contrary to the position assumed in judgments of the Supreme Court of the United States – Blackstone's *Commentaries* was not the 'preeminent authority on English law for the founding generation' of lawyers who drafted the American Constitution.[71]

Minot argues that Blackstone has been treated as 'a quasi-mythical being', cited by judges in highly contentious cases, such as *Roe v Wade*,[72] and *Citizens United*[73] and, since its resurgence from 1990, in some 8 per cent of all Supreme Court cases.[74] Minot submits that the 'unchallenged historical consensus that the *Commentaries* were the most widely read law book in late eighteenth-century America' is based on untested assumptions about the availability and influence of Blackstone, whose work was first published in England in 1765, and then in

---

[69] ibid.
[70] Josev (n 52) 1072.
[71] MJ Minot, 'Note: The Irrelevance of Blackstone: Rethinking the Eighteenth-Century Importance of the Commentaries' (2018) 104 *Virginia Law Review* 1360, 1361.
[72] *Roe v Wade* (1975) 410 US (113) 135 (Blackmun J).
[73] *Citizens United v Fed Election Commission* (2010) 558 US 310, 388 (Scalia J).
[74] Minot (n 71), 1360, 1361.

America in 1772.[75] Minot's piece establishes that although some copies of the *Commentaries* were published in America prior to independence, the dominant sources for contemporary lawyers were still Coke, Bacon, and colonial statute books. As Charles R McKirdy argued in a 1976 article, '[b]y far, the most studied law book in colonial America was … Coke upon Littleton'.[76] Minot argues that it was not until the 'first full century after ratification' that Blackstone had his 'golden age in the colonies'.[77] Minot's research relies on reading lists for law students and the students' 'commonplace books' to establish that Blackstone was far from dominant in the minds of the founders at the time of the drafting of the Constitution.[78]

Further, one of the reasons that the *Commentaries* attained such significance after the founding generation (or 'in the early republic') is that they represented a significant advance or change in thinking about the common law.[79] Blackstone's work simplified, categorised and theorised the common law as a coherent whole, highlighting underlying principles and themes, in contrast to its more chaotic and piecemeal presentation prior to Blackstone. This advance in thinking accounts for the success of the *Commentaries* in transforming the common law and our understandings of it; looking back on the state of the common law in the late eighteenth century, it is perhaps natural to think of a great writer of that era as representative of it. The recent decision of the Court in *Dobbs* refers to Blackstone's work, noting that he was 'writing near the time of the adoption of our Constitution' that 'even a pre-quickening abortion was "unlawful"'.[80] According to Minot, Blackstone's *Commentaries* would go on to transform and dominate the early American understanding of the common law, but they could not be said to represent the general understanding of the founding generation.

Minot's article underlines the difficulty, expertise, research and effort required to obtain accurate historical evidence, or even to realise that there is something that might need to be reviewed in the first place.

E. The Potential for Findings to Create Factual or Historical Precedents is Significant

The need for caution when accepting historical evidence is heightened by the possibility of factual or historical findings in a given case to hold influence beyond the case itself. Allison Orr Larsen discusses the 'tendency of lower courts to over-rely

---

[75] ibid 1362.
[76] CR McKirdy, 'The Lawyer as Apprentice: Legal Education in Eighteenth Century Massachusetts' (1976) 28(2) *Journal of Legal Education* 131.
[77] Minot (n 71) 1367.
[78] ibid.
[79] ibid 1363.
[80] *Dobbs v Jackson Women's Health Organization* (2022) 597 US ___ 2022). Note that other authors, including Coke, are discussed in the judgment.

on Supreme Court opinions and to apply generalized statements of fact from old cases to new ones'.[81] This kind of *historical* factual precedent:

> [I]s evident when courts invoke what the [US] Supreme Court has said about history without re-examining the relevant historical account ... For instance, the Supreme Court's explanation in *Hans v Louisiana* of the origin of the Eleventh Amendment has sparked tremendous debate ... as to its accuracy. Some historians suggest that the Hans Court strategically selected statements from the Framers to justify its historical account, ignoring original evidence to support the opposite constitutional understanding. Right or wrong, however, the Supreme Court's history on the Eleventh Amendment is the only historical account on the subject that matters now because it is the one that binds lower courts for questions of state sovereign immunity.[82]

Of course, there are risks of inaccuracy with any type of evidence. What seems distinct about historical argumentation, however, is that there is arguably a tendency amongst lawyers to see the historical domain as part of the legal domain, and thus, something on which they are capable of forming an expert opinion with minimal assistance. The possibility for the creation of 'factual precedent', or the tendency for a particular formulation of history to affect the kinds of litigation that are subsequently brought is particularly important when it is considered that major constitutional cases are relatively rare, so their interpretations of history may be long lasting.

V. Conclusions

In this chapter, I have argued that drafters of constitutional texts invoke historical narratives to justify the legitimacy of the current regime and to communicate its values. I explored the various ways that historical facts or narratives may be relevant to the resolution of a constitutional law dispute: history may play a significant or determinative role in a variety of ways, not just in cases revolving around the original intent of drafters. In the final section, I reflected upon the many challenges that arise for using and proving historical facts in constitutional cases and argued that these challenges create a need for caution on the part of courts. Finally, I argue that rather than viewing the debates about the use of history in constitutional adjudication in the abstract, these debates must be informed by a realistic understanding of the difficulties of proving historical matters to a satisfactory standard.

---

[81] AO Larsen, 'Factual Precedents' (2013) 162 *University of Pennsylvania Law Review* 59, 62.
[82] ibid 90–91.

15

Defactualisation of Justice

SHIRI KREBS

I. Introduction

[This is a] petition against an administrative detention order. We heard the parties' representatives and reviewed the confidential materials. It shows, as required, that the petitioner is a Hamas operative and has connections to this organisation's operatives. He is suspected of involvement in a security-related activity, to a level that can jeopardise the security of the area. Without legal reason to intervene, the petition is dismissed.[1]

These lines are the full decision of the Israeli highest judicial authority – the Israeli Supreme Court, sitting as High Court of Justice (the Court) – in a proceeding challenging the legality of a preventive detention order issued by the Israeli Military Commander in the West bank against Rafat Salem Mahmad, a Palestinian residing in the occupied Palestinian territories under Israeli military rule. Despite the severity of the measure – a preventive detention designed to prevent the detainee from committing a crime in the future (as opposed to an arrest for a criminal act that was already committed) – the Court dismissed the petition in five lines, that contained very little detail. In fact, the decision says more in the facts it is silent about than in the little information it provides. First, it tells us nothing about the detainee: How old is he, where is he from, does he have family, what language does he speak? In the assembly line of the judicial review of preventive detentions, Mahmad's individual characteristics are insignificant. Second, the decision says nothing about the issue at hand: how long is the preventive detention period that is summarily approved? How long has Mahmad been detained already, based on previous detention orders? Where is he being held? What is the severity of an already draconic infringement of his liberty? Third, the decision justifies the detention based on the finding that 'the petitioner is a Hamas operative and has connections to this organisation's operatives' and that he is 'suspected of involvement in security activity, to a level that can jeopardise the security of the area'.[2] However, the decision is silent about any concrete facts and details relating to these broad allegations: what are Mahmad's alleged *connections* to Hamas? What

---

[1] *Rafat Salem Mahmad v Military Judge* HCJ 7097/21 [2021].
[2] ibid.

type of *activity* is he suspected of? What is his alleged *involvement* in that activity? Fourth, the decision is silent about the type, strength and quality of the evidence that served as the basis to implicate Mahmad in terror activity. While the decision mentions that the justices reviewed the 'confidential material',[3] it remains silent about the type of information that is included in the intelligence file that was shared with the justices, including unclassified information such as how many sources were included, or how updated the relevant information is.

This decision is not unique; it is rather a template used, with minor changes, in hundreds of other, similar cases involving preventive detention orders against Palestinians, issued by the Israeli military authorities in the occupied Palestinian territories.[4] In a previous empirical study analysing the decisions of the Israeli Supreme Court in preventive detention cases from 2000 to 2010 I found that only 5 per cent of the hundreds of preventive detention cases examined resulted in somewhat reasoned and detailed judgments.[5] Building on these (and other) empirical findings, this chapter focuses on the Court's fact-finding practices in preventive detention cases. In particular, I argue that the Court's decision in *Mahmad* represents a legal storytelling technique that centres on security narratives and 'otherness' to justify the erasure of individual and humane characteristics of detained persons. This phenomenon, which I term 'defactualisation of justice', also stands for deindividuation and dehumanisation of 'others' in counterterrorism cases more broadly.

This chapter uses the example of the Israeli Supreme Court decisions in preventive detention cases to analyse the role of facts in this legal process, to identify ontological and epistemological constraints, as well as cognitive and systemic biases limiting the fact-finding process, and to develop a critique of fact-finding practices in the adjudication of preventive counterterrorism cases. The chapter begins, in section II, with an analysis of the ontological and epistemological constraints on fact-finding in legal adjudication. It continues, in section III, exploring concrete constraints on the generation of facts in the judicial review process of preventive detention cases, using the Israeli Supreme Court as a case study. Based on this analysis, section IV develops a critique of the Court's fact-finding practices, termed 'defactualisation of justice'.

II. Facts in Adjudication

Facts are the building blocks of legal storytelling and a core part of the practice of adjudication.[6] To apply the law to specific circumstances, judges are required to

---

[3] ibid.
[4] For a comprehensive qualitative and quantitative analysis of the decisions of the Israeli Supreme Court in administrative detention cases from 2000–2010, see: S Krebs, 'Lifting the Veil of Secrecy: Judicial Review of Administrative Detentions in the Israeli Supreme Court' (2012) 45(3) *Vanderbilt Journal of Transnational Law* 639.
[5] ibid 676.
[6] M Damaska, 'Truth in Adjudication' (1997) 49 *Hastings Law Journal* 289, 301; L Laudan, *Truth, Error, and Criminal Law: An Essay in Legal Epistemology* (Cambridge, CUP 2006) 1.

carefully evaluate and analyse information, generating a particular record of 'legal history', vindicated through legal decisions and documents. Two of the working assumptions of the practice of adjudication are that accuracy in fact-finding constitutes a precondition for just decisions,[7] and that fact-finding is a neutral practice, aimed at ascertaining an objective 'truth'.[8] Despite its appeal, this characterisation is misleading, as legal actors (including judges) construct history in a particular way, mediated by legal conventions and social constructs, as well as by ontological and epistemological legal rules. For this reason, facts in adjudication tell a contingent story, often excluding the voices of those who are not a part of the dominant narrative.[9] At the same time, the historical record constructed by legal actors and institutions claims a level of authoritativeness over other forms of histories and social narratives.[10]

A. Legal Ontology and Fact-finding

Ontologically, the language of the law tells people's stories and anchors social narratives through particular legal terms and categories.[11] When legal labels are used to classify groups of people or to categorise events and behaviours, complex social structures and ambiguous situations are inevitably simplified to fit a particular legal category.[12] Some legal labels require clear-cut categorisation of facts into pre-determined bins: guilty or innocent, combatant or civilian, terrorist or not. Grey areas or ambiguities are reinterpreted and redefined to fit with one of the pre-existing legal categories. This process of interpreting facts to fit pre-existing legal categories creates a tension between the brute facts and their legal representation, thus losing information that could have otherwise been meaningful, or even tell a different story altogether.[13]

Moreover, the application of legal terms in itself constructs reality in a specific and contingent manner, creating a tension between the legal meaning of a particular term and its social, ethical, and political meanings.[14] Terms such as

---

[7] Damaska (n 6) 292.

[8] KL Scheppele, 'Just the Facts, Ma'am: Sexualized Violence, Evidentiary Habits, and the Revision of Truth' (1992) 37 *New York Law School Law Review* 123.

[9] L Sarmas, 'Storytelling and the Law: A Case Study of Louth v Diprose' (1994) 19 *Melbourne University Law Review* 701, 703.

[10] A Sarat and TR Kearns (eds), *History, Memory, and the Law* (Ann Arbor, University of Michigan Press 2009) 3.

[11] A Bianchi and M Hirsch, 'International Law's Invisible Frames: Introductory Insights' in A Bianchi and M Hirsch (eds), *International Law's Invisible Frames* (Oxford, OUP, 2021) 13.

[12] Y Shany, 'Binary Law Meets Complex Reality: The Occupation of Gaza Debate' (2008) 41 *Israel Law Review* 68, 69.

[13] Sherwin explores, more generally, the clash between the law's demand for truth and justice and the modem mind's demand for closure and certainty, leading lawyers and adjudication processes to simplify reality, by leaving the 'messy things' out: RK Sherwin, 'Law Frames: Historical Truth and Narrative Necessity in a Criminal Case' (1994) 47 *Stanford Law Review* 39, 40–41.

[14] MS Moore, 'Legal Reality: A Naturalist Approach to Legal Ontology' (2002) 21 *Law and Philosophy* 619, 632; JM Balkin, 'The Proliferation of Legal Truth' (2003) 26 *Harvard Journal of Law and Public Policy* 5, 7.

'terrorist', 'torture' or even 'responsibility' have specific meanings as legal terms, and potentially other meanings outside the law, within broader political or social discourses. When we adopt a legal discourse to interpret reality and determine the truth, our findings relate to the legal reality or legal truth, which may be very different from the moral, ethical, or political interpretation or construction of reality.[15] For example, a legal finding that a government employee is not responsible for torturing a detainee depends on the legal definition and interpretation of both 'torture' and 'responsibility'. However, were a moral interpretation to be applied, our findings concerning the existence of, or responsibility for, torture may be different from our findings following a legal interpretation of these terms.

B. Legal Epistemology and Fact-finding

Legal fact-finding processes determine questions of fact based on legal conventions, procedures and rules of evidence. These rules are utilised to determine which facts can be considered, the required level of certainty for each factual finding, and what can be considered 'true' in the eyes of the law. Epistemological legal rules craft the stories and narratives developed by legal institutions through both a selective approach to facts or details that are included in the narrative and by organising facts by their legal value (assessing their weight and admissibility).

First, epistemological legal rules carve the boundaries of the story itself, by limiting the universe of facts that are included in the legal account of 'what happened'. Only facts which are specifically relevant to establishing legal truth – such as causes of death or intent of the perpetrator – are included. Other facts – for example, relating to the roots of the broader social conflict or context, social processes of dehumanisation, or acts committed outside the temporal or geographical jurisdiction of the adjudicating institution – are excluded. The result is that a story that is told in answering a legal question or via a legal process portrays only a segment of the events, the part that is legally relevant to answer a legal question.

Second, legal epistemology further restructures the story by determining the weight, reliability, sufficiency, and admissibility of the relevant facts. Legal rules determine the value and strength of the information collected, preferring some facts over others. While many of these rules are designed to promote an accurate account of events, they nonetheless make a deliberate choice concerning how to construct reality. Moreover, some rules of evidence or procedure depart from the goal of ascertaining the truth, and favour other purposes, such as protecting national security or police sources. Concrete legal rules, such as the state secrets doctrine

---

[15] Balkin (n 14).

and matters of state or security privileges, further limit fact-finding processes.[16] Either way, law requires us to determine 'what happened' while ignoring (or discounting) some facts that describe or are related to the events in question.

The ontological and epistemological constraints on legal fact-finding processes cannot be thoroughly addressed within the scope of this chapter. Rather, this brief and general introduction is used to demonstrate the contingent nature of legal fact-finding generally, as well as to set the stage for the more nuanced discussion of challenges relating specifically to legal fact-finding processes in the context of counterterrorism cases and, in particular, in the judicial review of preventive detentions of suspected terrorists.

III. Judicial Review of Preventive Detentions

In the last two decades, counterterrorism measures have been characterised by a move from punitive to preventive measures.[17] At the international level, the legislative efforts led by the United Nations Security Council focused on pre-emptive responses to terrorism: from the duty to disrupt transnational terror networks by various means, including by imposing assets freezes and travel bans on individuals and entities associated with terror organisations, to the criminalisation of a variety of preparatory actions, vaguely linked to terrorism.[18] At the national level, many countries introduced new policies and laws embracing preventive measures, including preventive detentions and blacklisting suspected terrorists. In Australia, for example, this era of prevention included creating a legal architecture for preventive detention and control orders, as well as for the criminalisation of preparatory acts and associations.[19] In the UK, methods such as 'proscription, detention without trial, control orders, port controls, data mining and the forfeiture of assets' were introduced as a part of a prevention and disruption strategy, designed to control the threat of terrorism.[20]

---

[16] D Barak-Erez and M Waxman, 'Secret Evidence and the Due Process of Terrorist Detentions' (2009) 48 *Columbia Journal of Transnational Law* 3, 5; SH Cleveland, 'Hamdi Meets Youngstown: Justice Jackson's Wartime Security Jurisprudence and the Detention of 'Enemy Combatants'' (2005) 68 *Alabama Law Review* 1127, 1132–34.

[17] A Vedaschi and KL Scheppele (eds), *9/11 and the Rise of Global Anti-Terrorism Law: How the UN Security Council Rules the World* (Cambridge, CUP 2021); T Tulich, 'A View Inside the Preventive State: Reflections on a Decade of Anti-Terror Law' (2012) 21(1) *Griffith Law Review* 209.

[18] L Ginsborg, 'Moving Toward the Criminalization of "Pre-crime": The UN Security Council's Recent Legislative Action on Counterterrorism' in A Vedaschi and KL Scheppele (eds), *9/11 and the Rise of Global Anti-Terrorism Law: How the UN Security Council Rules the World* (Cambridge, CUP 2021); M de Goede, 'Blacklisting and the ban: Contesting targeted sanctions in Europe' (2011) 42 *Security Dialogue* 499.

[19] M Andrejevic, L Dencik, and E Treré, 'From Pre-Emption to Slowness: Assessing the Contrasting Temporalities of Data-Driven Predictive Policing' (2020) 22(9) *New Media & Society* 1528; Tulich (n 17).

[20] C Walker, 'Intelligence and Anti-Terrorism Legislation in the United Kingdom' (2005) 44 *Crime, Law and Social Change* 387.

These measures generally permit states to preventively limit individuals' liberty based on an anticipated future risk or harm. As core terms (including what constitutes a 'terrorism act') have not been properly defined by the United Nations Security Council, states have been largely left to craft their own definitions and fact-finding processes,[21] resulting in a growing friction between the emerging global counterterrorism law, and both human rights law (HRL) and international humanitarian law (IHL).[22] These pre-emptive counterterrorism measures have been criticised for their lack of appropriate due diligence processes and for infringing on individuals' rights.[23] In particular, preventive counterterrorism measures – both at the international and national levels – have been criticised for their opaque evidentiary standards.[24]

In this chapter I focus on a particular preventive measure – preventive detention – which has become a dominant counterterrorism measure in a variety of jurisdictions in the last two decades.[25] Preventive detention is a legal mechanism that allows state authorities to deprive individuals of their liberty in order to prevent them from committing future crimes or atrocities. Typically, a preventive detention order against an individual is based on confidential intelligence information provided by undisclosed sources, and collected, secretly, by state security agencies. Detention orders must be justified by concrete factual circumstances, resting, mainly, on the quality and reliability of this secret evidence, particularly concerning the severity of the security threat, the activities attributed to the suspected individual, and the possibility to curb the threat using alternative, less-harmful, means. Therefore, the legality of a concrete preventive detention order is heavily dependent upon the quality, breadth and reliability of the intelligence

---

[21] FN Aoláin, 'The Ever-Expanding Legislative Supremacy of the Security Council in Counterterrorism' in A Vedaschi and KL Scheppele (eds), *9/11 and the Rise of Global Anti-Terrorism Law* (Cambridge, CUP, 2021).

[22] B Saul, 'Minorities and Counterterrorism Law' (2018) 15(1) *European Yearbook of Minority Issues Online* 1.

[23] D Hovell, 'Due Process in the United Nations' (2016) 110 *American Journal of International Law* 9.

[24] For criticisms of the evidentiary standards applied at the international level, see: L Ginsborg and M Scheinin, 'You Can't Always Get What You Want: The Kadi II Conundrum and the Security Council 1267 Terrorist Sanctions Regime' (2011) 8(1) *Essex Human Rights Review* 7; G Sullivan and M De Goede, 'Between Law and the Exception: The UN 1267 Ombudsperson as a Hybrid Model of Legal Expertise' (2013) 26 *Leiden Journal of International Law* 833. For criticisms of the evidentiary standards applied at the national level, see: K Roach, 'The Eroding Distinction Between Intelligence and Evidence in Terrorism Investigations' in A Lynch, N McGarrity and G Williams (eds), *Counterterrorism and Beyond: The Culture of Law and Justice after 9/11* (New York, Routledge, 2012); K Roach and C Forcese, 'The Need to Justify and Limit Procedural Innovation in National Security Litigation' (2018) 68(3) *University of Toronto Law Journal* 526.

[25] K Anderson, 'U.S. Counterterrorism Policy and Superpower Compliance with International Human Rights Norms' (2007) 30 *Fordham International Law Journal* 455, 474–81; J Hocking, 'Counter-Terrorism and the Criminalisation of Politics: Australia's New Security Powers of Detention, Proscription and Control' (2003) 49 *Australian Journal of Politics and History* 355; D McGoldrick, 'Security Detention – United Kingdom Practice' (2009) 40 *Case Western Reserve Journal of International Law* 509. For an analysis of preventive detentions in international law and in armed conflict situations, see AS Deeks, *Preventive Detention in Armed Conflict* (2009) 40 *Case Western Reserve Journal of International Law* 403.

on which it is based. How well that information is documented, how closely that information is scrutinised and by whom, are key factors in any assessment of this preventive deprivation of liberty.

Since preventive detention is a mechanism operated and controlled by the executive or military authorities, the question of oversight or judicial review becomes critical. Without an effective review process, individuals may lose their freedom, potentially indefinitely (depending on the concrete legislation), based on secret intelligence information they cannot directly challenge. As was emphasised by the Israeli Supreme Court in the *Mar'ab* case, '[j]udicial review is the line of defense for liberty, and it must be preserved beyond all else'.[26] Similarly, the Supreme Court of the United States emphasised in the *Boumediene* case that 'few exercises of judicial power are as legitimate or as necessary as the responsibility to hear challenges to the authority of the Executive to imprison a person'.[27]

To deal with the problem posed by schemes of secrecy and confidentiality, different countries have developed distinct models of judicial review of preventive detention cases: In Israel, the justices of the Supreme Court have developed a unique 'judicial management' model, while the UK, Canada, and to some extent, the United States, adopted a 'special advocate' model.[28] The Judicial management model rests on ex parte proceedings, in which the judges play a cardinal role in executing an independent, inquisitorial scrutiny of the intelligence information presented to support detention.[29] This model entrusts the justices with the responsibility of being the 'detainee's mouth' during the ex parte part of the hearing, acting, at the same time, as both an inquisitorial judge and a de facto defence lawyer for the detainee.[30] While this model has been generally praised as providing a strong, effective, and robust judicial review of preventive detention cases,[31] empirical examination cast doubt on the proclaimed ability of the justices to effectively represent the detainee's interests during the ex parte proceeding and challenge the information included in the secret evidence file.[32]

As a side note, it should be clarified that Israel employs three distinct preventive detention regimes, which are applied based on the status of the detainees as Israeli citizens, Palestinians from the West Bank, or foreigners which fall under the definition of 'unlawful combatants'. These detention regimes vary both in the

---

[26] *Marab v IDF Commander in the West Bank* HCJ 3239/02 57(2) PD 349, para 26 [2002] (quoting *El-Amla v IDF Commander in Judea & Samaria* HCJ 2320/98 52(3) PD 346, 350 [1998]).
[27] *Boumediene v Bush*, 553 US 723 (2008).
[28] Barak-Erez and Waxman (n 16) 18–24; MT Duffy and Rene Provosi, 'Constitutional Canaries and the Elusive Quest to Legitimize Security Detentions in Canada' (2009) 40 *Case Western Reserve Journal of International Law* 531, 541–43; D McGhee, 'Deportation, Detention & Torture by Proxy: Foreign National Terror Suspects in the UK' (2008) 29 *Liverpool Law Review* 99, 105.
[29] Barak-Erez and Waxman (n 16) 21–22.
[30] Krebs 'Lifting the Veil of Secrecy' (n 4) 653.
[31] SJ Schulhofer, 'Checks and Balances in Wartime: American, British and Israeli Experiences' (2004) 102 *Michigan Law Review* 1906, 1931.
[32] In the study referred to above, this author demonstrated that despite robust and well-advertised legal reasoning, the Court has systematically refrained from invalidating preventive detention orders or intervening in concrete cases: Krebs 'Lifting the Veil of Secrecy' (n 4) 695.

maximum length of detention orders they permit and the authorities that issue and review the detention orders.[33] As the most frequently utilised among the three regimes is the Preventive Detentions Order No 1591 (Order) that applies to Palestinians in the West Bank, I will briefly describe the review process under the Order. The first judicial review of a preventive detention order occurs at the military court. The military court's decision may then be appealed to the Military Court of Appeals.[34] Although the decision of the Military Court of Appeals was designed as the last instance of review, a practice has developed over the years of submitting habeas corpus petitions to the Israeli Supreme Court, sitting as High Court of Justice, to review the decisions of the Military Court of Appeals. It is in this context that the judicial management model was developed – at the Israeli Supreme Court – to review detention orders issued by the military commander in the West Bank as a court of first instance (and not as another formal appeal process).

In contrast to the judicial management model, which is based on active judicial engagement with the secret evidence during ex parte proceedings, the special advocate model relies on 'special advocates', approved by state security authorities, who represent the detainee's interests with respect to the secret evidence. The special advocates are permitted to confront that evidence in closed proceedings, but they are prohibited from discussing this evidence with their client.[35] The special advocate therefore communicates with the detainee before seeing the evidence, but not once she has been exposed to the secret evidence.[36]

Comparing and contrasting these judicial review models and their strengths and weaknesses, it has been argued that the special advocate model enhances participation, while the judicial management model enhances accuracy and can better regulate the detention system across many cases.[37] However, empirical examination, as well as interviews with judges, lawyers, and detainees, cast doubt on both these assumptions.[38]

The UK Parliamentary Joint Committee on Human Rights heard oral evidence from four special advocates. Based on their testimonies, the Joint Committee concluded, in its sixteenth Report on Counter-Terrorism Policy, that proceedings involving special advocates fail to afford a 'substantial measure of procedural justice'.[39] In particular, the Joint Committee identified three core problems with the special advocate model: the limited disclosure of information to the detained individual, the lack of communication between the special advocate and the

---

[33] For a detailed description of each of these regimes, see: Krebs 'Lifting the Veil of Secrecy' (n 4).
[34] Military Order Regarding Preventive Detention (Judea and Samaria) (No 1591), 5767-2007 (Israel), art 1(a).
[35] Barak-Erez and Waxman (n 16) 27–31.
[36] ibid.
[37] Barak-Erez and Waxman (n 16) 36–46.
[38] S Krebs, 'The Secret Keepers: Judges, Security Detentions, and Secret Evidence' in L Lazarus, C McCrudden and N Bowles (eds), *Reasoning Rights: Comparative Judicial Engagement* (Oxford, Hart Publishing, 2014), 197.
[39] House of Lords and House of Commons Joint Committee on Human Rights, *Counter-Terrorism Policy and Human Rights* (Nineteenth Report, 16 July 2007) 51.

person they represent (once they had seen the confidential material), and the low standard of proof.[40] The first two of these problems suggest that meaningful participation of the detained individual is not a strength of this model.

Similarly, interviews with (retired) judges of the Israeli Supreme Court, as well as defence lawyers and state attorneys representing the detainees and the state in these proceedings, suggest that the judicial management model does not enhance accuracy. The Justices revealed how difficult it is for them to challenge the secret evidence or disagree with the security agents' interpretation of it, emphasising that they do not have any tools to examine the accuracy, reliability and sufficiency of the intelligence:

> The judges cannot differ with the security agency's story. How can I? I don't have the defence lawyer jumping to say 'it never happened', 'this is not true'. My ethos, as a judge, is that I have two parties. Of course, I can think by myself, but I need tools, which are missing … for the most part I have very limited tools.[41]

Defence lawyers and state attorneys expressed a similar view. One state attorney described the judicial review process as 'handicapped', while another confessed that '[i]n some cases even I felt that it was too easy'.[42] A defence lawyer further explained why the judicial management model promotes inaccuracy through its weak an ineffective fact-finding process:

> There is no judicial discretion here, since the Justices do not know the facts … [I]n one of the cases in which I served as defence lawyer, it took the security agency two years to tell him [the detainee] what the allegations against him were. Then, when I asked my client about it, it turned out that it was a murder case that happened near his house, in which he had no involvement whatsoever. When I brought this to Court and asked the security agency representatives about it – I could tell that the Justices knew nothing about it. I could see their surprise. It then took two more detention orders until he was finally released.[43]

In summary, both the judicial management model and the special advocate model for judicial review of preventive detentions provide very limited fact-finding tools and cannot overcome the inherent weakness of this handicapped judicial review process. In particular, judicial review models for preventive detention cases lack effective fact-finding mechanisms, generating a process that reproduces unchallenged and unchecked intelligence information with a legal stamp of judicial decisions and authoritative legal records, legitimising prolonged deprivation of individual liberty. The next section focuses specifically on judicial fact-finding in this context, identifying three challenges that limit any model of judicial review of preventive detentions, and linking these challenges with the more general problems of legal ontology and epistemology discussed in section 2 above.

---

[40] ibid 49–55.
[41] Krebs, 'The Secret Keepers' (n 38) 199.
[42] ibid 200.
[43] ibid 199.

IV. The Limits of Judicial Fact-finding in Preventive Detention Cases

As explained above, the ontology and epistemology of legal fact-finding processes generate a particular and situated history of people, processes, and events. Ontological and epistemological legal rules and conventions craft the stories and narratives constructed by legal institutions, through both a selective approach to the facts that are included in the narrative, as well as by organising the included facts by their legal value. Preventive detention cases provide ample examples of the contingent – and limited – view of reality that is generated and affirmed through the judicial review process. Specifically, judicial fact-finding in preventive detention cases is affected by three distinct problems – secrecy, prediction and bias – creating an unbridgeable gap between the complex reality and the legal records that purport to represent it.

A. Secrecy

Legal fact-finding in the adjudication of counterterrorism cases generally, and preventive detention specifically, is meaningfully constrained by concrete legal rules, such as the state secrets doctrine and security privileges, which, by definition, limit the available facts included in the fact-finding process.[44] Specific counterterrorism legislation mandates deviation from the normal rules of evidence, creating ex parte proceedings and lowering the required burden of proof. The reliance on secret evidence and ex parte proceedings means that courts have limited capacity to challenge (or even question) the factual framework presented by the security authorities.[45]

As preventive detentions are designed to prevent future harm, they rely heavily on intelligence information, which is largely confidential and is not revealed to the detainee.[46] Relying on secret evidence inherently challenges fact-finding processes, as it dictates a security narrative that cannot be contested or modified by the detainee, who is unaware of the content – or the sources – of the intelligence against them. The accuracy, reliability and completeness of the intelligence information is not scrutinised by effective cross-examination and the credibility of the sources cannot be questioned or challenged.

Restrictive legal procedures such as ex parte and *in camera* proceedings further constrain legal fact-finding processes in preventive detention cases.[47] Despite the centrality of the open justice principle (requiring that legal proceedings should be

---

[44] Barak-Erez and Waxman (n 16) 5.
[45] Krebs 'Lifting the Veil of Secrecy' (n 4).
[46] Barak-Erez and Waxman (n 16) 5.
[47] ibid 21; H Stewart, 'Is Indefinite Detention of Terrorist Suspects Really Constitutional?' (2005) 54 *University of New Brunswick Law Journal* 235, 245.

open to the public),[48] preventive detention cases are often held *in camera*, namely, behind closed doors. Closed-door proceedings pose a significant danger of unfair and discriminatory decisions.[49] Additionally, due to the secrecy and confidentiality of the intelligence information, such proceedings are typically held ex parte, without the presence of the detainee or their representative. The dynamics that are developed in such closed proceedings lead to several significant implications on the construction of facts: first, the secret evidence creates a special courtroom dynamic which makes deference to the security authorities more likely.[50] Second, excluding the detainee from the legal process that reviews the justification of their detention leads to de-individuation of the decision and makes it easier to construct a factual narrative that erases their unique qualities and characteristics.

B. Prediction

Preventive detention orders are based on prediction. Unlike descriptions of past events, predictions of future occurrences pose challenges to fact-finding processes, as they inherently involve a level of uncertainty.[51] While deciding whether a preventive detention order is legally justified, judges must make predictions about the likelihood that a future risk will eventuate, calculating probabilities about the future. This problem of predicting future risks is, of course, not unique to preventive detentions alone, but rather to any legal context that involves predictive risk assessments, including in constitutional fact-finding.[52] In addition to the uncertainty in making predictions about the future, core facts relating to preventive detentions involve subjective judgments, such as the level of dangerousness posed by the detainee or the reliability of the intelligence.[53]

---

[48] E Cunliffe, 'Open Justice: Concepts and Judicial Approaches' (2012) 40 *Federal Law Review* 385.

[49] N McGarrity and E Santow, 'Anti-Terrorism Laws: Balancing National Security and a Fair Hearing' in V Ramraj et al (eds), *Global Anti-Terrorism Law and Policy* (Cambridge, CUP, 2005).

[50] More generally, courts tend to defer to the executive or security agencies' discretion in matters of national security. This means that even if they had the tools to question the intelligence information presented to them, judges were still likely to accept the security agencies' factual framework and any inferences drawn from it.

[51] For more general discussion of these challenges, see Damaska (n 6) 299.

[52] For example, in considering the inherent uncertainty in various types of constitutional facts, Faigman argues that 'in constitutional fact-finding, the prospect of error ... should be a key element in the development of rules of procedure' [this quote does not exist in this book]: DL Faigman, 'Fact-Finding in Constitutional Cases' in Z Baosheng, TY Man and J Lin (eds), *A Dialogue Between Law and History: Proceedings of the Second International Conference on Facts and Evidence* (Singapore, Springer, 2021).

[53] Faigman has argued that the principal reason for the US Supreme Court's inconsistent use of science is that it continues to approach factual questions as a matter of normative legal judgment rather than as a separate inquiry aimed at information gathering, stating '[t]he Court "interprets" facts, it does not "find" them': DL Faigman, 'Normative Constitutional Fact-Finding: Exploring the Empirical Component of Constitutional Interpretation' (1991) 139(3) *University of Pennsylvania Law Review* 541, 544–45, 549.

Despite this inherent challenge, the various legal regimes governing preventive detentions have not developed fact-finding tools that are sensitive to the predictive and subjective qualities of intelligence information. In a legal tradition that strives for simplification of proof processes – the search for a unified approach toward evidence and proof – judges treat intelligence information similarly to any other brute (or physical) fact. The failure of preventive detention review processes to differentiate between brute facts, facts relying on inferences from formal data, value judgements, and predictions, leads to blindness toward the unique empirical challenges each type of facts entails.[54] As legal practitioners and judges are trained to perform legal tasks and interpretations (rather than a forensic fact-finding exercise), they are primed to focus on what they are uniquely qualified to do: making normative evaluations and interpreting the law.[55] This normative focus comes at the expense of the fact-finding process, creating a risk of mistreatment of facts or even defactualisation (relying on factual assumptions and unchecked factual allegations).

Moreover, the predictive nature of the factual framework means that detainees have very limited tools with which to prove their innocence: how can a person materially prove that that they will not commit an offence or be otherwise involved in terrorist activity in the future? Detentions that are a part of a criminal proceeding relate to past offences and events that already materialised. In such a setting, a defendant *can* (at least theoretically) prove their innocence as to that offence. However, preventive detentions rely on intelligence information suggestive of future dangerousness that is not necessarily linked to any concrete past event or activity (though is sometimes based on past activities or existing networks), and thus a detainee cannot positively prove that the future threat attributed to them would not have materialised.

C. Bias

A particular judicial bias in favour of detention may further jeopardise a court's ability to effectively review preventive detention cases, given the differential risks of false positives and false negatives.[56] A 'false negative' in this context refers to a court's incorrect decision to release from detention a dangerous individual (who may later commit the anticipated harm). A 'false positive' in this context refers to a court's incorrect decision to approve the preventive detention of an

---

[54] MD Risinger, 'Searching for Truth in the American Law of Evidence and Proof' (2013) 47 *Georgia Law Review* 801. See also: MS Moore, 'The Plain Truth about Legal Truth' (2003) 26 *Harvard Journal of Law and Public Policy* 23, 24–26 (distinguishing between propositions of fact, general law, interpretation, value, and logic).

[55] Faigman 'Normative Constitutional Fact-Finding' (n 53) 547.

[56] Van Harten elaborates on three different weaknesses in this regard: the judge is precluded from hearing additional information that the individual could have supplied had he known the Executive's claims; courts are uniquely reliant on the Executive to be fair and forthcoming about confidential information; and the dynamic or atmosphere of closed proceedings may condition a judge to favor

innocent individual (who will not commit any harm if released from detention). The problem is that incorrect court decisions in preventive detention cases are only revealed when a judge makes a false negative error and the anticipated risk materialises.[57] In contrast, false positive errors – incorrect decisions to preventively detain individuals – remain unknown and cannot typically be exposed because of the predictive nature of the predicted harm. This means, that the risk (to the judicial authority) associated with a false negative error is high, while the risk (to the judicial authority) associated with a false positive error is very low, creating a bias in favour of detention.

The result of these challenges is a dynamic 'law fulfilling prophecy':[58] intelligence information implicating a detainee in an anticipated harm is accepted by the judges as evidence of the future risk the detainee poses. This information is accepted both because the judges lack effective tools to question the reliability or sufficiency of the intelligence and due to courts general deference to security authorities in matters of national security. Because the intelligence implicates the detainee in an anticipated behaviour (rather than a past event), the detainee has few avenues in which to challenge the implicating information (as they are unable to provide an alibi or to call an eyewitness to shed light on a future event). Finally, the false positive bias quashes any remaining hesitations in favour of detention. And so, the prophecy (or prediction) that an individual will cause harm in the future is fulfilled through the court's decision, finding that the detainee poses a security threat and giving effect and legal authority to unchallenged intelligence information.

The next section will apply these challenges in the Israeli context, demonstrating these fact-finding weaknesses through concrete cases and shedding light on the outcomes of this flawed process: de-individuation and defactualisation of the judicial review process.

V. Defactualisation of Justice

In September 2022, the time of writing these lines, the number of Palestinians held in preventive detentions by Israeli authorities reached a 14-year record of 784. Eleven of the detainees are Israeli citizens (none of them Jewish) while the remaining 712 are residents of the occupied Palestinian territories.[59] Analysing

---

unduly the security interest over priorities of accuracy and fairness: G van Harten, 'Weaknesses of Adjudication in the Face of Secret Evidence' (2009) 13 *International Journal of Evidence and Proof* 1, 1.

[57] R Kitai-Sangero, 'The Limits of Preventive Detention' (2009) 40 *McGeorge Law Review* 903, 909.

[58] S Krebs, 'The Invisible Frames Affecting Wartime Investigations: Legal Epistemology, Metaphors, and Cognitive Biases' in A Bianchi and M Hirsch (eds), *International Law's Invisible Frames* (Oxford, OUP, 2021).

[59] H Shezaf, 'Number of Prisoners Held Without Trial in Israeli Jails Hits Highest Peak Since 2008' *Haaretz*. Available at: www.haaretz.com/israel-news/2022-08-22/ty-article/.premium/number-of-prisoners-held-without-trial-in-israeli-jails-hits-highest-peak-since-2008/00000182-c053-d60d-a9b6-cfd7a79a0000, last accessed 22 August 2022.

the entire volume of preventive detention decisions issued by the Israeli Supreme Court in the previous year – 55 decisions throughout 2021 – I found that in all of these cases the Court decided to uphold the preventive detention orders.[60] Moreover, of these 55 cases, only four (less than 8%) ended with somewhat detailed decisions, ranging from 3 to 13 pages. Of the remaining 51 cases, 31 ended with very brief judgments (1–2 pages) while 20 were concluded with the same template of 1–3 lines. All 55 cases were decided following a judicial management process, with secret evidence presented to the Court in an ex parte proceeding. In none of the cases did the Court express any hesitancy regarding the sufficiency, credibility or completeness of the information; in all of the cases the Court reaffirmed the security narrative.[61] In the subsections below I analyse the text of two decisions – a brief template and one that is more detailed – to demonstrate how the epistemological limitations detailed lead to de-individuation and defactualisation of the preventive detention process in concrete cases. The defactualisation and deindividuation of the fact-finding process further account for dehumanisation of the detained individuals, which, in turn, strengthen the security narrative and the justification of the detention order.

Returning to the detention decision that opened this chapter – a four-line template lacking any individual characteristics or details – this section explores the de-individuation that such templates entail:

> [This is] a petition against an administrative detention order. We heard the parties' representatives and reviewed the confidential materials. It shows, as required, that the petitioner is a Hamas operative and has connections to this organisation's operatives. He is suspected of involvement in a security-related activity to a level that can jeopardise the security of the area. Without legal reason to intervene, the petition is dismissed.[62]

These few lines – repeated with minor changes in about 20 other decisions in 2021 alone – include very few facts. These facts convey that according to some secret evidence from an unidentified source, the petitioner is a member of Hamas and is suspected of some sort of involvement in an unspecified security activity. The decision reduces the detained individual – Rafat Salem Mahmad – to nothing more than a security hazard. He doesn't have a life, a family, a community; we don't know what his occupation is, where he lives, or how many children he has. To the Court, he is identical in any meaningful way to the twenty other individuals whose detention was approved using the same template. None of them can be distinguished from the others; stripped of any personal characteristics, even the way they jeopardise the security of the area is not distinctive; they are all simply 'involved' in some sort of 'security activity'.

---

[60] As reflected on the Israeli Supreme Court database: https://supreme.court.gov.il/Pages/fullsearch.aspx.

[61] These data result from an analysis of all the preventive detention judgments given by the Court during 2021 and collated through its public database.

[62] *Mahmad* (n 1).

In this assembly line of suspected terrorists, there is no room for human beings. The only individuals who matter – those with faces – are the state attorneys and intelligence agents, presenting confidential materials to the justices in a closed hearing without the presence of the detainee or their lawyer. The special dynamics and trust relations that are engendered through this one-sided process help erase the detainee not only from the hearing, but also from the narrative. Indeed, more than anything, both the template decisions and those that are more detailed and reasoned, reflect a security narrative that overrides any individualisation of the review process, erasing any facts and details that do not engage directly with the intelligence.

The second example demonstrating the defactualisation and de-individuation of the judicial review process is the more detailed decision given in the *Aberah* case.[63] In this case, the Court upheld a detention order against Jaber Mamduch Aberah despite the identification of several severe procedural flaws, including the unjustified refusal of the security authorities to provide Aberah with unclassified information about the factual basis for his detention. The preventive detention order against Aberah was first reviewed by the military court. During the hearing, Aberah's lawyer attempted to refute the secret evidence by asking the military prosecutor questions about its content, including the reason for the arrest and the type of activity of which he was suspected. The prosecutor refused to answer any of the factual questions and laconically stated that any factual information would be presented to the court during the ex parte hearing. As expected, after that hearing, the military court affirmed the detention order. Aberah submitted an appeal against this decision to the Military Court of Appeals. The Military Court of Appeals stressed that the military prosecutor was under a duty to answer questions about the factual information to the maximum extent possible without endangering sources and exposing confidential information. Moreover, after examining the secret evidence in an ex parte proceeding, and while finding the State's *interpretation* of the intelligence information 'correct and appropriate', the Military Court of Appeals noted that the finding that Aberah posed a security threat required a 'certain interpretation' of the intelligence information. Nonetheless, the Military Court of Appeals upheld the Military Court's decision (and the detention order), concluding that the intelligence information against Aberah was reliable and up to date.

As a last resort, Aberah submitted a petition to the Israeli Supreme Court, sitting as the High Court of Justice. The nine-page decision was given by Justice Shoham, who was appointed to the Supreme Court shortly before deciding this case and who had previously served on the Military Court of Appeals. In his decision, Justice Shoham reiterated that the Military Court, as well as the military prosecution, is under 'increased duties' to carefully inspect the intelligence information and to offer the defence any possible information, providing that it will

---

[63] *Aberah v The Military Commander in the West Bank* HCJ 317/13 [2013].

not harm state security. He further emphasised the Court's active role during the ex parte hearing, serving as the 'detainee's mouth' and the importance of effective and meaningful fact-finding process. After considering the secret evidence during the ex parte hearing, Justice Shoham found that there was no reason to deprive Aberah from basic information about the allegations against him, or to abstain from answering the defence counsel's questions, since there was no concern that answering these questions would harm state security in any way. He further concluded that neither the military prosecution nor the Military Court fulfilled their duty to serve as the 'detainee's mouth' during the review process.[64] As a result, the Court suggested that the military prosecutor should be well briefed by the intelligence agents and be prepared to answer the defence counsel's questions in a sincere and genuine effort to provide the defence with meaningful information.

The Court's strong language about the crucial role of meaningful fact-finding in the preventive detention process and the duty of the security authorities to provide the detainee with meaningful information about the facts that form the basis for the detention order stand in stark contradiction with the Court's concrete decision concerning Aberah himself. Instead of releasing Aberah as a result of the substantial flaws in the fact-finding process, which deprived him from a meaningful defence, or returning the case to be re-heard by the Military Court (this time providing Aberah and his counsel with the required information to develop a proper defence), the Court decided to dismiss the petition and uphold the detention order. While stressing the significance of holding a meaningful and effective fact-finding process, in which the detainee can add relevant information or challenge concrete evidence, the Court signalled that this fact-finding process is ultimately inconsequential. Moreover, after examining the intelligence information (ex parte), and without allowing Aberah an opportunity to develop a response to the unclassified part of this information, the Supreme Court noted that the intelligence information is clear and requires no 'interpretation' (disagreeing on this point with the Military Court of Appeals).

This decision emphasises the main weakness of the judicial management model: a limited and ineffective fact-finding process that can only repeat and reiterate the security narrative, while rejecting any outlet or method to challenge this narrative. Essentially, the Court discounted the mere possibility that the limited factual framework presented to it may be enhanced, or that missing facts can potentially influence the review process. It may well be that Aberah posed a grave risk to Israel's security to a level that justified prolonged preventive detention under Israeli law; or that the Court's fact-finding process produced an accurate account in this case. But the Court's approach in Aberah means that we shall never know.

---

[64] ibid.

VI. Conclusion

The chapter demonstrated how concrete epistemological legal processes and rules are used to restrict and redact fact-finding processes, whether through rules of evidence and schemes of secrecy, the institutionalisation of prediction, or the false positive judicial bias that highlights risk and favours detention. The combination of security crisis, secret evidence and preventive measures poses unique challenges to effective fact-finding in the judicial review of preventive detention cases. In Israel, a quasi-inquisitorial judicial management model has emerged to confront these challenges and to provide strong guarantees against arbitrary and unjustified detentions. However, despite confident and robust rhetoric concerning the importance of the review process and the centrality of fact-finding processes within this review, the Court's decisions demonstrate very little sensitivity to meaningful fact-finding and adopt the security narrative even at the face of significant procedural and substantive flaws. The gap between the rhetoric of a few reasoned decisions (emphasising the fact-finding duties of the prosecutors and the court) and the actual practice of the Court (systematically upholding detention orders with very little regard to the individual characteristics of each case), suggests that the normative determinations are no more than lip-service, designed to sustain the Court's ethos as protector of individual liberties.

The epistemological challenges to legal fact-finding discussed above suggest that this strong normative rhetoric hides significant factual gaps that are being routinely closed or covered by applying security narratives. Instead of putting themselves in the detainee's shoes (or serving as their mouth), as the Court's ethos suggests, the justices focus on what they feel confident doing: making abstract normative determinations (for example, highlighting the prosecutor's disclosure duties), while leaving the fate of concrete individuals in the metaphorical and literal hands of the security authorities.

Ultimately, the decisions of the Supreme Court, and its unequivocal acceptance of the intelligence information – after a seemingly robust fact-finding process – transform unchallenged and suggestive intelligence information into authoritative legal facts that are stamped with the Court's seal of approval. The irrelevance of facts – or defactualisation – which stands for deindividuation and dehumanisation of 'others' in counterterrorism cases more broadly, explains why some detainees resort to hunger strikes to reclaim their identity and legacy. It is also a sharp reminder that prolonged preventive detentions are inhumane and unjust and should be renounced by any country that values justice, rule of law principles, and human rights.

INDEX

Administrative decisions
  greater reliance on expert evidence 15
  greater scrutiny of factual matters 14–15
  impact of administrative acts in South African law
    adverse impact 193–6
    beneficial impact 187–93
    substantive grounds for review 186–7
  judicial reluctance to interfere 13
  more detailed records of decisions 15
  new focus on intensity of review 15
  practical and principled difficulties 27–8
  problems of appeal/review distinction 15–16
  recent practical and principled difficulties 15
  scrutiny of 'jurisdictional' facts 14

Administrative law
  Australian approach to judicial review of executive action
    entrenched measure of review 145–6
    inadequacy of default legal norms 146–7
    some scope for review of executive fact-finding 147
  duty of public bodies to collect systemic data
    central question 162–3
    ease of collection 162
    established jurisprudence pertaining to the duty of inquiry 163–72
    extension of duty of enquiry to systemic data collection 172–5
    importance 161–2
    importance of closing legal gap 180–1
    potential application of duty of inquiry in a systemic context 176–80
  'fact work'
    court oversight of 'fact work' 131–40
    two types of 'fact work' 128–31
    underlying difficulties with law/fact distinction 141–2
  impact of human rights
    changes introduced by HRA 100–4
    common law review claims distinguished 104–6

    hangover of the standard account 111–13
    limits of evidence within proportionality analysis 113–15
    renewed interest in 'augmented' legality principle 118–22
    ripple effects on substantive review 116–18
  mistake of fact as ground for review
    apparent tension underlying the debate 203–4
    avoiding the finality objection 215–16
    avoiding the objection from the limits of judicial review procedure 214–15
    defensibility arguments summarised 216
    four requirements established in E 204–5
    implied substitutionary 'correctness' standard 204
    inapplicability of constitutional objection to merits review 211–14
    mistake as to single relevant fact 218–21
    'not evaluation' limit imposed by E 205–8
    no evaluation of conflicting evidence 208–10
    objections to distinctiveness and usefulness of ground 216–18
    weighty arguments in favour of correcting factual errors 211
    where heightened scrutiny or proportionality are not available 221
    where mistake concerns availability of evidence 210
  overview of key questions 3–5
  South Africa's treatment of facts 184–5
    just and equitable remedies 196–200
    'pathways' to administrative law review 184–6
  standard treatment of facts and evidence in English law
    civil procedure distinguished 89
    cross-examination of witnesses rarely permitted 90
    limitations on new evidence 89–90

one significant driver of change 98–9
procedural reforms in 1970s 88–9
rationales – duty of candour 96–8
rationales – judicial review as a supervisory jurisdiction 91–4
rationales – pragmatic concerns 95–6
Appeal/review distinction 15–16, 27, 198
Australia
approach to judicial review of executive action
entrenched measure of review 145–6
inadequacy of default legal norms 146–7
some scope for review of executive fact-finding 147
construal of citizenship attending Papua New Guinea's independence
central question 72–4
determinative question – was Mr Lee an immigrant 76–8
facts of case 67–9
indifference and dismissiveness of Australian government 82–3
interpretation of Constitution 75–6
legal issues involving two processes of national independence 70–2
relationship between immigrant status and nationality 78–82
executive incapacity as constitutional rationale for ultra vires
inherent incapacity premise 153–4
materiality marker for legality 156–7
traditional principle of parliamentary supremacy 153–4
judicial review of legislation on federalism grounds 11, 16
relationship between courts and parliaments
application of the proportionality test 30–3
Australian position on the spectrum 37
benefits of clear criteria 40
courts as ultimate arbiters 47
danger of hampering parliamentary engagement 40–1
need for criteria to assess parliamentary engagement 38–9
proposals for structured proportionality testing 42–6
questions of parliamentary privilege 41–2
spectrum of inter-institutional relations 34–7
role of facts about social and institutional arrangements

appropriate use of facts in context of implied freedom of political communication 62–4
inappropriate use of facts in context of implied freedom of political communication 64–5
mind-independence of institutions and events 57–9
need for an appropriate form of reasoning 59–62
significance of institutional mandates 51–3, 53–7
various roles that facts can play 51–3
role of historical evidence in constitutional adjudication 274
standard of reasonableness applied to executive fact-finding
law since 2010 150–3
law to 2010 148–50
use of political science evidence
concerns about the politicising of the judiciary 254
development of legal concepts 250
discipline's 'crisis' of replication 252–4
expanding and augmenting the factual basis for decision-making 247–8
generation of new intuitions 249–50
importance and relevance 246
incentives to overcome underlying obstacles 251–2
integration through judicial notice 255–6
integration through statements of agreed facts 256–8
missed opportunity 258–60
need for practical approach to deep disagreements 252
overcoming challenges to greater use 260–1
'political science' defined 245–6
remittal of contested facts to lower court 258
underlying objections 248–9

'Brandeis briefs' 18

Canada
facts as constitutional causes of action
assisted suicide 24–5
binding effect of *stare decisis* 26
centrality of fundamental rights 23
challenge to sex work laws 23–4
difficulties of providing reliable and direct evidence 25

distinctively Canadian phenomenon   23
inherent limitations   26–7
power in the hands of first-instance
  judges   25–6
practical and principled
  difficulties   27–8
factual assessments in public law
  proceedings   11–12
judicial review of legislation on federalism
  grounds   11, 16–17
oral history of indigenous peoples
  allocation of a party's error
    burden   228–9
  determining which mistake to prefer
    and by what margin   229–31
  establishment of Aboriginal title or
    rights   226
  historical cultural genocide   225
  hopes for a just future   225–6
  need for a new approach   239–42
  need for more fundamental changes   242–3
  role of confidence, doubt, resolution,
    and paralysis   232–5
  role of onuses, standards of proof, and
    presumptions   231–2
  Supreme Court approach to
    evidence   235–9
role of historical evidence in constitutional
  adjudication   270–3
systemic challenges to the legality of
  regulatory regimes   20, 21–2
use of 'Brandeis briefs'   18
use of political science evidence   248
Causes of action *see* **Constitutional
  causes of action**
Citizenship
construal of arrangements attending Papua
  New Guinea's independence
  central question   72–4
  determinative question – was Mr Lee an
    immigrant   76–8
  facts of case   67–9
  indifference and dismissiveness of
    Australian government   82–3
  interpretation of Constitution   75–6
  legal issues involving two processes of
    national independence   70–2
  relationship between immigrant status
    and nationality   76–8
importance of rigorous naming and
  identification practices   260
Israeli preventive detention
  regimes   287, 293

role of political science evidence   249
systemic challenges to the legality of
  regulatory regimes   21–2
Constitutional adjudication
see also **Judicial review**
construal of citizenship attending Papua
  New Guinea's independence
  central question   72–4
  determinative question – was Mr Lee
    an immigrant   76–8
  facts of case   67–9
  indifference and dismissiveness of
    Australian government   82–3
  interpretation of Constitution   75–6
  legal issues involving two processes of
    national independence   70–2
  relationship between immigrant status
    and nationality   78–82
facts as constitutional causes of action
  assisted suicide   24–5
  binding effect of *stare decisis*   26
  centrality of fundamental rights   23
  challenge to sex work laws   23–4
  difficulties of providing reliable and
    direct evidence   25
  distinctively Canadian phenomenon   23
  inherent limitations   26–7
  power in the hands of first-instance
    judges   25–6
  practical and principled difficulties   27–8
judicial review of administrative action
  greater reliance on expert evidence   15
  greater scrutiny of factual matters   14–15
  judicial reluctance to interfere   13
  more detailed records of decisions   15
  new focus on intensity of review   15
  practical and principled difficulties   27–8
  problems of appeal/review
    distinction   15–16
  recent practical and principled
    difficulties   15
  scrutiny of 'jurisdictional' facts   14
judicial review of legislation
  compliance with fundamental rights   17
  difficulties of providing reliable and direct
    evidence   17–18
  feature of federal systems   16–17
  judicial notice   18
  mechanisms of restraint   19
  non-justiciability   18–19
  practical and principled difficulties   27–8
  proportionality review as 'semiprocedural
    judicial review'   18

overview of key questions 2–3
political science evidence 8
relationship between courts and parliaments
   application of the proportionality test 30–3
   Australian position on the spectrum 37
   benefits of clear criteria 40
   courts as ultimate arbiters 47
   danger of hampering parliamentary engagement 40–1
   need for criteria to assess parliamentary engagement 38–9
   proposals for structured proportionality testing 42–6
   questions of parliamentary privilege 41–2
   spectrum of inter-institutional relations 34–7
rise of facts in different adjudicative contexts
   importance 7–8
role of facts about social and institutional arrangements
   appropriate use of facts applied to free political communication 62–4
   inappropriate use of facts applied to free political communication 64–5
   mind-independence of institutions and events 57–9
   need for an appropriate form of reasoning 59–62
   significance of institutional mandates 51–3, 53–7
   various and many roles that facts can play 51–3
role of historical facts
   alternatives to use of experts 277–8
   application of historical values to interpret constitutional or legislative texts 268–70
   dangers inherent in expert evidence 276–7
   determinations as to the history of a given doctrine 273–4
   difficulties of fact classification 275–6
   difficulties of obtaining accurate historical evidence 278–9
   inclusion in constitutional texts 264–5
   overview of key questions 263–5
   resolution of facts in issue 274
   significance of findings which create precedents 279–80
   support for legitimacy through 'traditional domination' 265–7
   teaching of history as constitutional mandate 267–8
   use of historical facts as an interpretative tool 270–3
   use to justify particular constitutional provisions 267
South Africa
   adverse impact of administrative acts 193–6
   beneficial impact of administrative acts 187–93
   systemic challenges to the legality of regulatory regimes
      difficulties of providing reliable and direct evidence 20
      identification of source of the violation 20
      importance of demonstrating a causal link 21–2
      liberal contemporary approach 20
      limitations to scope of challenge 21
      practical and principled difficulties 27–8
      underlying challenges 19
   use of political science evidence 248

Constitutional causes of action
   assisted suicide 24–5
   binding effect of *stare decisis* 26
   centrality of fundamental rights 23
   challenge to sex work laws 23–4
   difficulties of providing reliable and direct evidence 25
   distinctively Canadian phenomenon 23
   inherent limitations 26–7
   power in the hands of first-instance judges 25–6
   practical and principled difficulties 27–8

Cross-examination of witnesses
   impact of human rights on administrative law adjudication
      changes introduce by HRA 100–2
      hangover of the standard account 113
   standard treatment of facts and evidence in English law 100–4

Deference
   judicial review of legislation 19
   limitations on constitutional freedoms
      application of proportionality test 30–3
      spectrum of inter-institutional relations 34–7

Duty of candour
  judicial review of administrative action   14–15
  standard treatment of facts and evidence in English law   96–8

Duty of inquiry
  established jurisprudence pertaining to the duty of inquiry
    PSED (Equality Act 2010)   167–9
    successful public sector equality duty inquiry cases   170–2
    successful *Tameside* cases   165–7
    Tameside as starting point   163–7
  established part of public law   162–3
  extension to systemic data collection
    in accord with doctrinal architecture   174–5
    'minimum duty to acquire systemic data'   172
    Wednesbury standard as applicable test   173–4
  importance of closing legal gap   180–1
  potential application in a systemic context
    Eu Settlement Scheme as case study   176–9
    rationale for approach   179–80

Evidence
see also **Facts**
  admission of fresh evidence
    determination of proper procedure   93–4
    expert evidence   94
    factual questions about jurisdiction   93
    proof of bias or misconduct   94
    to show what material was before the decision-maker   93
  constitutional adjudication in South Africa
    adverse impact of administrative acts   193–4
    beneficial impact of administrative acts   191–2
  difficulties of providing reliable and direct evidence
    facts as constitutional causes of action   25
    judicial review of administrative action   13
    judicial review of legislation   17–18
    systemic challenges to the legality of regulatory regimes   20
  duty of public bodies to collect systemic data
    central question   162–3
    ease of collection   162
    established jurisprudence pertaining to the duty of inquiry   163–72
    extension of duty of enquiry to systemic data collection   172–5
    importance   161–2
    importance of closing legal gap   180–1
    potential application of duty of inquiry in a systemic context   176–80
  historical evidence *see* **Historical evidence**
  impact of human rights on administrative law adjudication
    changes introduce by HRA   100–4
    common law review claims distinguished   104–6
    hangover of the standard account   111–13
    limits of evidence within proportionality analysis   113–15
    particular features of human rights claims   107–10
    renewed interest in 'augmented' legality principle   118–22
    ripple effects on substantive review   116–18
  Israeli preventive detention regimes
    challenges faced by predictions of future occurrences   291–2
    crucial role of meaningful fact-finding   296
    restriction and redaction of fact-finding processes   297
    risk of judicial bias   292–3
    secrecy   290–1
  mistake of fact as ground for review
    not evaluation of conflicting evidence   208–10
    requirements established in *E*   205
    where mistake concerns availability of evidence   210
  political science evidence *see* **Political science evidence**
  social science evidence *see* **Social science evidence**
  standard treatment of facts and evidence in English law
    civil procedure distinguished   89
    cross-examination of witnesses rarely permitted   90
    limitations on new evidence   89–90
    one significant driver of change   98–9
    procedural reforms in 1970s   88–9
    rationales – duty of candour   96–8

rationales – judicial review as a supervisory jurisdiction   91–4
rationales – pragmatic concerns   95–6

Executive adjudication
Australian approach to judicial review of executive action
  entrenched measure of review   145–6
  inadequacy of default legal norms   146–7
  some scope for review of executive fact-finding   147
importance of Australian experience in other jurisdictions   157–9
incapacity as constitutional rationale for ultra vires
  inherent incapacity premise   154–6
  materiality marker for legality   156–7
  traditional principle of parliamentary supremacy   153–4
standard of reasonableness applied to executive fact-finding
  Australian law since 2010   150–3
  Australian law to 2010   148–50
systemic challenges to the legality of regulatory regimes
  difficulties of providing reliable and direct evidence   20
  identification of source of the violation   20
  importance of demonstrating a causal link   21–2
  liberal contemporary approach   20
  limitations to scope of challenge   21
  practical and principled difficulties   27–8
  underlying challenges   19

Expert evidence
facts as constitutional causes of action   23–4
impact of human rights on administrative law adjudication
  changes introduce by HRA   103–4
  hangover of the standard account   111–13
judicial review of legislation   17–18
political science evidence in Australia
  concerns about the politicising of the judiciary   254
  development of legal concepts   250
  discipline's 'crisis' of replication   252–4
  expanding and augmenting the factual basis for decision-making   247–8
  generation of new intuitions   249–50
  importance and relevance   246
  incentives to overcome underlying obstacles   251–2
  integration through judicial notice   255–6
  integration through statements of agreed facts   256–8
  missed opportunity   258–60
  need for practical approach to deep disagreements   252
  overcoming challenges to greater use   260–1
  'political science' defined   245–6
  remittal of contested facts to lower court   258
  underlying objections   248–9
proportionality of legislation   18
reasonableness or proportionality of administrative action   15
role of historical evidence in constitutional adjudication
  alternatives to use of experts   277–8
  application of historical values to interpret constitutional or legislative texts   268–70
  dangers inherent in expert evidence   276–7
  determinations as to the history of a given doctrine   273–4
  difficulties of fact classification   275–6
  difficulties of obtaining accurate historical evidence   278–9
  inclusion in constitutional texts   264–5
  overview of key questions   263–5
  resolution of facts in issue   274
  significance of findings which create precedents   279–80
  support for legitimacy through 'traditional domination'   265–7
  teaching of history as constitutional mandate   267–8
  use of historical facts as an interpretative tool   270–3
  use to justify particular constitutional provisions   267
social science evidence
  challenge to Canada's sex work laws   23–4
  judicial review of administrative action   13
  proportionality reviews   18
  structured case management approach   112–14
standard treatment of facts and evidence in English law
  admission of fresh evidence   94
  pragmatic concerns   96

Index

'Fact work'
court oversight of 'fact work'
    judicial fact assembly 135–7
    review of fact assembly 132–5
    review of fact deployment 137–40
    underlying principles and
        difficulties 131–2
two types of 'fact work' 128–31

Facts *see also* **Mistake of fact**
about social and institutional arrangements
    affecting constitutional adjudication
    appropriate use of facts applied to free
        political communication 62–4
    inappropriate use of facts applied to free
        political communication 64–5
    mind-independence of institutions and
        events 57–9
    need for an appropriate form of
        reasoning 59–62
    significance of institutional
        mandates 51–3, 53–7
    various and many roles that facts can
        play 51–3
central questions 1–2
as constitutional causes of action
    assisted suicide 24–5
    binding effect of *stare decisis* 26
    centrality of fundamental rights 23
    challenge to sex work laws 23–4
    difficulties of providing reliable and
        direct evidence 25
    distinctively Canadian phenomenon 23
    inherent limitations 26–7
    power in the hands of first-instance
        judges 25–6
    practical and principled difficulties 27–8
duty of public bodies to collect
    systemic data
    central question 162–3
    ease of collection 162
    established jurisprudence pertaining to the
        duty of inquiry 163–72
    extension of duty of enquiry to systemic
        data collection 172–5
    importance 161–2
    importance of closing legal gap 180–1
    potential application of duty of inquiry in
        a systemic context 176–80
    impact of human rights on administrative
        law adjudication
    changes introduce by HRA 100–4
    common law review claims
        distinguished 104–6

hangover of the standard
    account 111–13
limits of evidence within proportionality
    analysis 113–15
particular features of human rights
    claims 107–10
renewed interest in 'augmented' legality
    principle 118–22
ripple effects on substantive
    review 116–18
increasing significance 1
Israeli preventive detention regimes
    importance 282–3
    role of legal epistemology 284–5
    role of legal ontology 283–4
standard treatment of facts and
    evidence in English law
    civil procedure distinguished 89
    cross-examination of witnesses rarely
        permitted 90
    limitations on new evidence 89–90
    one significant driver of change 98–9
    procedural reforms in 1970s 88–9
    rationales – duty of candour 96–8
    rationales – judicial review as a supervi-
        sory jurisdiction 91–4
    rationales – pragmatic concerns 95–6
use by administrative
    decision-makers 126–8

Fairness *see* **Procedural fairness**

Fundamental rights
facts as constitutional
    causes of action 23
judicial review of legislation
    mechanisms of restraint 19
    proportionality test 17
    systemic challenges to the legality of
        regulatory regimes 20

**Governmental fact-finding and
    deliberations**
see also **Executive adjudication**
construal of citizenship attending Papua
    New Guinea's independence
    central question 73–4
    indifference and dismissiveness of
        Australian government 82–3
'duty of candour' 14–15
impact of human rights on administrative
    law adjudication 108
importance for factual
    determination 7–8
judicial review of legislation 17

obligations to interpret and apply
  constitution 38
rationales for standard treatment of facts and
  evidence in English judicial review
  duty of candour 96–8
  judicial review as a supervisory
    jurisdiction 91–4
  significance of institutional mandates 56

Hidden nature of facts and evidence
  recurring theme 7
Historical evidence
  importance 8
  interpretation of PNG's Constitution
    74–9, 82
  oral history of Canada's indigenous peoples
    allocation of a party's error
      burden 228–9
    determining which mistake to prefer and
      by what margin 229–31
    error burdens in the law of
      fact-finding 227–8
    need for a new approach 239–42
    need for more fundamental
      changes 242–3
    role of confidence, doubt, resolution, and
      paralysis 232–5
    role of onuses, standards of proof, and
      presumptions 231–2
    Supreme Court approach to
      evidence 235–9
  role in constitutional adjudication
    alternatives to use of experts 277–8
    application of historical values to
      interpret constitutional or
      legislative texts 268–70
    dangers inherent in expert
      evidence 276–7
    determinations as to the history of a given
      doctrine 273–4
    difficulties of fact classification 275–6
    difficulties of obtaining accurate historical
      evidence 278–9
    inclusion in constitutional texts 264–5
    overview of key questions 263–5
    resolution of facts in issue 274
    significance of findings which create
      precedents 279–80
    support for legitimacy through 'traditional
      domination' 265–7
    teaching of history as constitutional
      mandate 267–8

  use of historical facts as an interpretative
    tool 270–3
  use to justify particular constitutional
    provisions 267
Human rights
  greater scrutiny of factual matters in
    UK 14–15
  impact on administrative law adjudication
    changes introduce by HRA 100–4
    common law review claims
      distinguished 104–6
    hangover of the standard account 111–13
    limits of evidence within proportionality
      analysis 113–15
    renewed interest in 'augmented' legality
      principle 118–22
    ripple effects on substantive review 116–18
  Israeli preventive detention regimes
    effect of prolonged preventive
      detentions 297
    friction with emerging global
      counterterrorism law 286
  relationship between courts and parliaments
    application of proportionality test 33
    spectrum of inter-institutional
      relations 35–6
    systemic challenges to the legality of
      regulatory regimes 21–2
    use of special advocates 288–9

Illegality *see* **Legality principle**
Indigenous oral history of Canada
  determining which mistake to prefer
    and by what margin
    likelihood 229–31
    magnitude 229
  error burdens in the law of
    fact-finding 227–8
  establishment of Aboriginal title or
    rights 226
  historical cultural genocide 225
  need for a new approach
    Crown should bear onus of proof 239
    likelihood 241–2
    magnitude 240–1
  need for more fundamental changes 242–3
  obstacles to fact-finding
    role of confidence, doubt, resolution, and
      paralysis 232–5
    role of onuses, standards of proof, and
      presumptions 231–2
  Supreme Court approach to evidence

Court's category mistake in addressing
     error burden problem   238–9
  flexible application of burden of
     proof   235–6
  threshold requirement of 'meaningful
     consideration'   237–8
Indigenous peoples of Canada
  allocation of a party's
     error burden   228–9
Institutional mandates
  appropriate use of facts applied to free
     political communication   62–4
  inappropriate use of facts applied to free
     political communication   62–4
  mind-independence of institutions and
     events   57–9
  need for an appropriate form of
     reasoning   59–62
  significance   53–7
  various and many roles that facts can
     play   51–3
Irrationality see **Rationality**
Israeli preventive detention regimes
  de-individuation of court decisions
     case of *Aberah*   295–6
     crucial role of meaningful
        fact-finding   296
     no room for human beings   295
     statistics   293–4
  facts in adjudication
     importance   282–3
     role of legal epistemology   284–5
     role of legal ontology   283–4
  judicial review
     focus on pre-emptive counterterrorism
        measures   285–7
     importance of oversight   287
     judicial management
        model   287–9
     models to deal with secrecy and
        confidentiality   287
     three distinct regimes   287–8
     use of special advocates   288–9
  limits of judicial fact-finding
     challenges faced by predictions of future
        occurrences   291–2
     risk of judicial bias   292–3
     secrecy   290–1
     restriction and redaction of fact-finding
        processes   297
  template of a typical court
     decision   281–2

Judicial notice
  developments in the role of executive
     governments   64
  facts of ancient and modern history   277
  free elections   63
  historical evidence in constitutional
     adjudication   277
  political science evidence   248, 255–6
  proportionality of legislation   18
  relationship between courts and
     parliaments   43
Judicial review
  see also **Administrative law;
     Constitutional adjudication**
  of administrative action
     difficulties of providing reliable and direct
        evidence   13
     greater reliance on expert evidence   15
     greater scrutiny of factual matters   14–15
     judicial reluctance to interfere   13
     more detailed records of decisions   15
     new focus on intensity of review   15
     practical and principled difficulties   27–8
     problems of appeal/review
        distinction   15–16
     proportionality review as 'semiprocedural
        judicial review'   18
     recent practical and principled
        difficulties   15
     scrutiny of 'jurisdictional' facts   14
  Australian approach to review of executive
     action
     entrenched measure of review   145–6
     inadequacy of default legal norms   146–7
     some scope for review of executive
        fact-finding   147
  benefits of multi-disciplinary approach
     importance   8
  of 'fact work'
     court oversight of 'fact work'   131–40
     two types of 'fact work'   128–31
  interdependence of different component
     parts   87
  Israeli preventive detention regimes
     focus on pre-emptive counterterrorism
        measures   285–7
     importance of oversight   287
     judicial management model   287–9
     models to deal with secrecy and
        confidentiality   287
     three distinct regimes   287–8
     use of special advocates   288–9

of legislation
  compliance with fundamental rights   17
  difficulties of providing reliable and direct evidence   17–18
  feature of federal systems   16–17
  judicial notice   18
  mechanisms of restraint   19
  non-justiciability   18–19
  practical and principled difficulties   27–8
standard treatment of facts and evidence in English law
  civil procedure distinguished   89
  cross-examination of witnesses rarely permitted   90
  limitations on new evidence   89–90
  one significant driver of change   98–9
  procedural reforms in 1970s   88–9
  rationales – duty of candour   96–8
  rationales – judicial review as a supervisory jurisdiction   91–4
  rationales – pragmatic concerns   95–6
systemic challenges to the legality of regulatory regimes
  difficulties of providing reliable and direct evidence   20
  identification of source of the violation   20
  importance of demonstrating a causal link   21–2
  liberal contemporary approach   20
  limitations to scope of challenge   21
  practical and principled difficulties   27–8
  underlying challenges   19

Jurisdiction
  admission of fresh evidence   93
  scrutiny of 'jurisdictional' facts   14
  standard applied to executive fact-finding
    Australian law since 2010   153
    Australian law to 2010   149

Law/fact distinction
  positive and a negative elements   140–1
  recurring theme   7
  underlying difficulties with judicial review   141–2
  use in various contexts   141
  utility   128

Legality principle
  executive incapacity as constitutional rationale for ultra vires   156–7
  'fact work'
    judicial fact assembly   135–7
    review of fact assembly   132–5
    review of fact deployment   137–40

factual assessments of administrative action   15
impact of human rights on administrative law adjudication   104, 107, 118–22
judicial review as a supervisory jurisdiction   91–2
mistake of fact as ground for review   211–12
'pathway' to administrative law review in South Africa   184–5
standard treatment of facts and evidence in English law   88
systemic challenges to regulatory regimes   27

Legislation
'fact work'
  judicial fact assembly   135–7
  review of fact assembly   132–5
  review of fact deployment   137–40
  two types of 'fact work'   128–31
impact of human rights on administrative law adjudication   108–9
judicial review of legislation
  compliance with fundamental rights   17
  difficulties of providing reliable and direct evidence   17–18
  feature of federal systems   16–17
  judicial notice   18
  mechanisms of restraint   19
  non-justiciability   18–19
  practical and principled difficulties   27–8
  proportionality review as 'semiprocedural judicial review'   18
role of historical evidence in constitutional adjudication   268–9
significance of institutional mandates   55
systemic challenges to the legality of regulatory regimes
  difficulties of providing reliable and direct evidence   20
  identification of source of the violation   20
  importance of demonstrating a causal link   21–2
  liberal contemporary approach   20
  limitations to scope of challenge   21
  practical and principled difficulties   27–8
  underlying challenges   19
use of facts by administrative decision-makers   126–8

Mandates *see* **Institutional mandates**
***Merton* principles**
  failure to meet the required standard   147

Index   309

Mistake of fact
  court oversight of 'fact work' 131–2
  as a ground of review
    apparent tension underlying the
      debate 203–4
    avoiding the finality objection 215–16
    avoiding the objection from the limits of
      judicial review procedure 214–15
    defensibility arguments summarised 216
    four requirements established in E 204–5
    implied substitutionary 'correctness'
      standard 204
    inapplicability of constitutional objection
      to merits review 211–14
    mistake as to single relevant fact 218–21
    'not evaluation' limit imposed
      by E 205–8
    no evaluation of conflicting
      evidence 208–10
    objections to distinctiveness and useful-
      ness of ground 216–18
    weighty arguments in favour of correcting
      factual errors 211
    where heightened scrutiny or proportion-
      ality are not available 221
  interconnection between substance and
    process 99
  oral history of Canada's indigenous peoples
    allocation of a party's error
      burden 228–9
    determining which mistake to prefer and
      by what margin 229–31
    error burdens in the law of
      fact-finding 227–8
    need for a new approach 239–42
    need for more fundamental
      changes 242–3
    role of confidence, doubt, resolution, and
      paralysis 232–5
    role of onuses, standards of proof, and
      presumptions 231–2
    Supreme Court approach to
      evidence 235–9
  review of fact deployment 138–40
  underlying difficulties with law/fact
    distinction 141–2
Mistakes of law
  court oversight of 'fact work' 131
  standard applied to executive fact-finding
    Australian law since 2010 151
    Australian law to 2010 148
  underlying difficulties with law/fact
    distinction 141–2

**Multi-disciplinary approaches to fact and
  evidence** *see* **Historical evidence;
  Political science evidence; Social
  science evidence**

New Zealand
  mistake of fact as ground for review 201,
    205, 219
Non-justiciability
  adjudication of individual rights or
    liabilities 143
  judicial review of administrative action 14
  judicial review of legislation 18–19
  references to history in constitutions 263

Papua New Guinea
  denial of Australian citizenship
    central question 72–4
    determinative question – was Mr Lee an
      immigrant 76–8
    facts of case 67–9
    indifference and dismissiveness of
      Australian government 82–3
    interpretation of Constitution 75–6
    legal issues involving two processes of
      national independence 70–2
    relationship between immigrant status and
      nationality 78–82
Parliamentary privilege
  human rights claims 109
  judicial review of legislation 18
  relationship between courts and
    parliaments 41–2
Parliaments
  rationales for standard treatment of facts
    and evidence in English judicial
    review 91–2
  relationship between courts and parliaments
    application of the proportionality
      test 30–3
    Australian position on the spectrum 37
    benefits of clear criteria 40
    courts as ultimate arbiters 47
    danger of hampering parliamentary
      engagement 40–1
    need for criteria to assess parliamentary
      engagement 38–9
    proposals for structured proportionality
      testing 42–6
    questions of parliamentary privilege 41–2
    spectrum of inter-institutional
      relations 34–7
    significance of institutional mandates 53, 55

Policies *see* **Governmental fact-finding and deliberations**
Political mandates *see* **Institutional mandates**
Political science evidence
  see also **Social science evidence**
  importance 8
  institutional mandates 58
  use in Australian courts
    concerns about the politicising of the judiciary 254
    development of legal concepts 250
    discipline's 'crisis' of replication 252–4
    expanding and augmenting the factual basis for decision-making 247–8
    generation of new intuitions 249–50
    importance and relevance 246
    incentives to overcome underlying obstacles 251–2
    integration through judicial notice 255–6
    integration through statements of agreed facts 256–8
    missed opportunity 258–60
    need for practical approach to deep disagreements 252
    overcoming challenges to greater use 260–1
    'political science' defined 245–6
    remittal of contested facts to lower court 258
    underlying objections 248–9
Precedent
  'admitted free' clause 271
  criteria to assess parliamentary engagement 38
  facts as constitutional causes of action 24–7
  full meaning and implications of an institutional mandate 65
  immigration power precedents 78
  judicial fact assembly 135–7
  legislation 141
  new interpretation of historical facts 272–3
  politicising of judiciary 254
  potential for findings to create factual or historical precedents 279–80
Procedural fairness
  impact of human rights on administrative law adjudication 104
  Israeli preventive detention regimes 295
  judicial review as a supervisory jurisdiction 91
  mistake of fact as ground for review 211–12

Proportionality
  impact of human rights on administrative law adjudication
    common law review claims distinguished 105
    limits of evidence within proportionality analysis 113–15
    particular features of human rights claims 107–8
  judicial review of administrative action 15
  judicial review of legislation
    compliance with fundamental rights 17
    judicial notice 18
    'semiprocedural judicial review' 18
  mistake of fact as ground for review 221
  relationship between courts and parliaments
    application of the proportionality test 30–3
    Australian position on the spectrum 37
    benefits of clear criteria 40
    courts as ultimate arbiters 47
    danger of hampering parliamentary engagement 40–1
    need for criteria to assess parliamentary engagement 38–9
    proposals for structured proportionality testing 42–6
    questions of parliamentary privilege 41–2
    spectrum of inter-institutional relations 34–7
Public sector equality duty 167–72

Rationality
  factual assessments of administrative action 15
  impact of administrative acts in South African law 195–6
  impact of human rights on administrative law adjudication 104–5, 107
  institutional mandates 54
  judicial review of legislation 17–18
  mistake of fact as ground for review 213
  review of administrative acts in South Africa 186–7
Reasonableness
  duty of inquiry
    established jurisprudence pertaining to the duty of inquiry 164–5
    extension to systemic data collection 173–4
    executive incapacity as constitutional rationale for ultra vires

inherent incapacity premise 153-4
materiality marker for legality 156-7
traditional principle of parliamentary
   supremacy 153-4
factual assessments of administrative
   action 14-15
impact of administrative acts in South
   African law 193-6, 195-6
impact of human rights on administrative
   law adjudication 107, 117-18
judicial review as a supervisory
   jurisdiction 91
judicial review of legislation 17
proportionality on a spectrum of inter-institutional relations 34, 36-8
review of administrative acts in South
   Africa 187
standard applied to executive fact-finding
   Australian law since 2010 150-3
   Australian law to 2010 148-50

Reasoned decisions
duty to acquire systemic data 181
executive decision-makers 158
factual bases of the decision 92
greater scrutiny of factual matters 14-15
legislative decision-making 39
Merton principles 134

Records
duty of public bodies to collect
   systemic data
   central question 162-3
   ease of collection 162
   established jurisprudence pertaining to the
      duty of inquiry 163-72
   extension of duty of enquiry to systemic
      data collection 172-5
   importance 161-2
   importance of closing legal gap 180-1
   potential application of duty of inquiry in
      a systemic context 176-80
of proceedings
   need for more detailed
      record-keeping 15
   South Africa's rules 185-6

Remedies
judicial review of administrative
   action 14
mistake of fact as ground for review 203
South Africa's treatment of facts
   setting aside 196-7
   statutory powers 196
   substitution 198-200

Restraint *see* **Deference**

Setting aside
Australian law since 2010 151
Australian law to 2010 148
South Africa's treatment of facts 184-5,
   196-7, 199-200

Social science evidence
see also **Political science evidence**
challenge to Canada's sex work laws 23-4
judicial review of administrative action 13
proportionality reviews 18
structured case management
   approach 112-14

South Africa
impact of administrative acts
   adverse impact 193-6
   beneficial impact 187-93
   substantive grounds for review 186-7
just and equitable remedies
   setting aside 196-7
   statutory powers 196
   substitution 198-200
'pathways' to administrative law
   review 184-6
role of historical evidence in constitutional
   adjudication
   application of historical values to
      interpret constitutional or
      legislative texts 268-9
   support for legitimacy through 'traditional
      domination' 265-7

**Spectrum of inter-institutional
   relations** 34-7

Stare decisis *see* **Precedent**

Substitution
mistake of fact as ground for review 204,
   212-14
South Africa's treatment of facts 198-200

Systemic data
duty of public bodies to collect
   systemic data
   central question 162-3
   ease of collection 162
   established jurisprudence pertaining to the
      duty of inquiry 163-72
   extension of duty of enquiry to systemic
      data collection 172-5
   importance 161-2
   importance of closing legal gap 180-1
   potential application of duty of inquiry in
      a systemic context 176-80

Ultra vires principle
Australian approach to review of executive action 145
executive incapacity as constitutional rationale for ultra vires
inherent incapacity premise 153–4
materiality marker for legality 156–7
traditional principle of parliamentary supremacy 153–4

importance of Australian experience in other jurisdictions 157–8
'Unacceptable risk' test 21
United States
institutional mandates 56
refugee claims 21–2
Unreasonableness see **Reasonableness**

Wednesbury **unreasonableness** *see* **Reasonableness** *see* **Irrationality**

Milton Keynes UK
Ingram Content Group UK Ltd.
UKHW051254260624
444777UK00006B/56